*Investing at a Discount:
$aving on Commissions,
Management Fees,
and Costs*

Investing at a Discount: $aving on Commissions, Management Fees, and Costs

Mark Coler

New York Institute of Finance
New York • London • Toronto • Sydney • Tokyo • Singapore

Library of Congress Cataloging-in-Publication Data

Coler, Mark D.
    Investing at a discount : saving on commissions, management fees, and costs / Mark Coler.
        p.   cm
    Includes index.
    ISBN 0-13-503467-1
    1. Discount brokers—United States—Directories. 2. Mutual funds—United States—Directories. I. Title.
HG4907.C654 1990
332.6'78—dc20   90-39199
                                                                                     CIP

This publication is designed to provide accurate and authoritative information in regard to the subject matter covered. It is sold with the understanding that the publisher is not engaged in rendering legal, accounting, or other professional service. If legal advice or other expert assistance is required, the services of a competent professional person should be sought.

From a Declaration of Principles
Jointly Adopted by
a Committee of the American Bar Association
and a Committee of Publishers and Associations

© 1990 by NYIF Corp.
A Division of Simon & Schuster, Inc.
A Paramount Communications Company

All rights reserved. No part of this book may be reproduced in any form or by any means without permission in writing from the publisher.

Printed in the United States of America

10 9 8 7 6 5 4 3 2 1

Contents

Preface   xi

PART ONE—DISCOUNT BROKERAGE

1. Investing at a Discount: Questions and Answers   3
    Discount Brokerage   3
    Mutual Funds   11

2. A Discount Brokerage Primer   13
    History   13
    Costs   14
    Safety   15
    Order Execution   18
    Services   19
    Where Discounters Differ   21
    The Real Difference   22

3. Investment Advice for the Independent Investor   23
    Publications at a 20% Discount   23
    Newsletters—Special Introductory Offers and
        Discounts   24

	Other Publications	26
	Associations	26
	Television	26
	Other Sources of Advice	27
4.	**Choosing a Broker**	**29**
	Discounter or Full-Service?	29
	Choosing a Discounter	32
5.	**Enormous Savings with a Discount Broker**	**41**
	Stocks	41
	Specific Transactions	44
	Options	49
	Bonds	51
	You Don't Only Save on Commissions	52
6.	**Finding the Right Broker in the Discount Brokerage Directory**	**55**
	Scope	55
	Features	56
	Deep Discounter Designation	60

PART TWO—MUTUAL FUNDS

7.	**The New American Way to Invest**	**65**
	A Mutual Fund Primer	66
8.	**How to Select Mutual Funds . . . and When to Avoid Them**	**73**
	Quality	74
	The Discounters of the Mutual Fund Industry	75
	The Cost of Couch Potato Investing—Is the United States Overfunded?	79

Contents   vii

9. Stock Funds   **81**

   Peter Lynch, Where Are You?   82
   The Stock Fund Directory—Outstanding No-Load
      Funds   83
   Index Funds   84
   Better Than an Index Fund?   85

10. Bond Funds   **91**

   Selecting a Bond Fund   91
   The Illusion of Performance   92
   What Really Counts   93
   The Best of the Bond Funds   93
   One State Funds   94
   High-Yield Funds   95
   Unit Investment Trusts (UITs)   96
   Do You Really Need a Government Bond Fund?   97
   Corporate Bond Funds   98

11. Money Market Funds   **101**

   Earning a Higher Yield   102
   Price Wars   104
   Risk   105
   The Convenience Factor   106
   Treasury Bills   106
   Foreign Money Funds   106

12. International Funds   **107**

   Investment Alternatives to Mutual Funds   109
   Closed-End Funds   110
   Foreign Currency Funds   111
   The Global Portfolio   112

13. Closed-End Funds   **113**

   Don't Buy a New Closed-End Fund   114
   When a Discount May Not Be a Discount   115
   When the Discount is Right   116

PART THREE—OTHER INVESTMENTS AND INVESTMENT VEHICLES

14. Self-Directed IRAs — 121

How Self-Directed IRAs Can Achieve Savings — 122
Maximizing Savings — 123
Tips on Picking an IRA Broker — 124
Active Investors — 125

15. Treasury Bills and Bonds — 129

An Investment Comparison: Treasury Bills vs.
  Money Funds — 130
Who Should Not Use Treasury Bills — 131
Using the Treasury Direct Account — 131
The Reinvestment Option — 133
Other Notes and Bonds — 133
Timing — 134
Resale — 134
Buying Bills and Notes Through a Broker — 134
Government Notes and Bonds — 135
Savings Bonds — 135
Federal Reserve Offices — 137

16. The Futures Market — 143

Discount Futures Brokers — 144
Several Caveats for Stock Investors
  Interested in Futures — 146
The Least Expensive Way in the World to Trade
  Stocks—If You Can Handle It — 148
The Intoxicating Effect of the Futures Market — 150
Saving Money and Protecting Capital
  with Futures — 150

17. Limited Partnerships — 153

The Not-So-Random Walk — 154
Weed Out the Bad Apples — 156

Contents ix

	The Secondary Market	158
	The Do-It-Yourself Discount	160
18.	**Precious Metals, Discount Coins, and Other Purported Discounts**	**165**
	Discounts vs. Bargains	166
	Collectibles	167
19.	**Shareholder Discounts and Privileges**	**169**
	Annual Meeting Goodies	170
	Product and Service Discounts	170
	Dividend Reinvestment Plans	171
	Voluntary Investment Plans—The Ultimate Discount	172

APPENDICES

A.	**The Discount Brokerage Directory**		**175**
	Chapter 1.	The Discount Brokers	177
	Chapter 2.	The Bank Brokers	271
B.	**Everything You Ever Wanted to Know About Discount Brokerage . . . and More**		**343**
	Chapter 1.	To Switch or Not to Switch	345
	Chapter 2.	The Emergence of the Discount Broker	355
	Chapter 3.	Making It On Your Own	363
	Chapter 4.	Essential Mechanics	369
	Chapter 5.	Evaluating Brokerage Firm Features	374
	Chapter 6.	The Art of Dealing with a Discounter	381
	Chapter 7.	Features and Services	389
	Chapter 8.	Frills	402
	Chapter 9.	SIPC Protection	413
C.	**The Discount Futures Broker Directory**		**425**
	Chapter 1.	The Futures Brokers	426

D.	**The Discount Publications Directory**		**437**
	Chapter 1.	Books	439
	Chapter 2.	Mercer Discount Surveys	451
	Chapter 3.	Newsletters	455
E.	**The Mutual Funds Directory**		**479**
	Chapter 1.	Stock Funds	480
	Chapter 2.	Bond Funds	503
	Chapter 3.	Money Market Funds	520
	Chapter 4.	International Funds	532
	Chapter 5.	Other Closed-End Funds	546

Index 559

Preface

This book will not tell you how to turn $10,000 into $1 million—or even guarantee how to double your investment in a year. It is certainly *not* the only investment guide that you'll ever need. But it may well be the only guide you'll ever need to investing at a discount. You hold in your hands the ultimate guide to investing at a discount in the 1990s in the fields of:

Stocks	Mutual Funds
Bonds	Money Market Funds
IRAs	Treasury Bonds
Limited Partnerships	Commodities/Futures
Precious Metals	Shareholder Discounts

With this book, you can easily save hundreds—or thousands—of dollars in investment costs this year—and every year thereafter. My method involves no secret formula; just proprietary information developed over the past seven years that tells you how to take advantage of the investor's revolution that technology and deregulation have wrought in the past decade.

Some of these proprietary findings have been previously disclosed in the *Mercer Surveys* that have been cited and recommended by *Business Week, Changing Times, Fortune, Money,* and many of the other leading financial publications in the United States. I've discussed some of these findings as a guest on Louis Rukeyser's "Wall $treet Week" and other television and radio programs. But until now, a comprehensive book has never been made available to the public.

Investing at a Discount tells you precisely *how* to achieve maximum savings and, most importantly, names names. The directories in the appendices provide the names, addresses, and phone numbers that will turn theory into reality—nearly 400 brokers, mutual funds, and other investment services or sources that will save you money on your chosen investments. The following list highlights just some of what you can expect to learn:

DISCOUNT BROKERS

- How you can cut your commissions from $225 to $25 on a single trade—see Chapter 5, Enormous Savings with a Discount Broker.
- How to consistently save 70 to 90% on your stock commissions—see Chapter 5.
- How much you can expect to save annually—see Chapter 5.
- Who are the deep discounters that offer the greatest savings? Which bank brokers charge least—see "Commission Structure" in Appendix A, The Discount Brokerage Directory.
- How the best know discounters' costs compare with those of others—see Chapter 4, Choosing a Broker.
- Which discounters offer the widest range of products and services, including free newsletters, reports, and quote services—see Chapter 6, Finding the Right Broker . . . and Appendix A, The Discount Brokerage Directory.
- How to decide whether you're suited for discount investing and which of the four types of discounters is most suitable for your needs—see Chapter 4.

Preface   xiii

- How you can buy $100,000 stock without paying a dime commission—see Chapter 19, Shareholder Discounts and Privileges.
- Where a full-service broker could cost less than a discounter—see "Bonds" in Chapter 5.
- How the right discounter can turn a loss into a 14% profit—see "Options" in Chapter 5.

BORROWING

- How you can save up to 50% in interest costs with the right discounter—see "You Don't Only Save on Commissions" in Chapter 5.

MUTUAL FUNDS

- What simple cost-saving rule could have moved your mutual fund from the bottom to the top quarter during the 1980s—see "The Discounters of the Mutual Fund Industry" in Chapter 8, How to Select Mutual Funds . . . and When to Avoid Them.
- Which very popular type of mutual fund should be avoided by most investors—see Chapter 10, Bond Funds.

STOCKS

- What the lowest cost mutual fund in the country with an excellent record is—see Chapter 9, Stock Funds.
- Which top-performing stock mutual funds are available with low sales costs or no sales costs—see Appendix E, The Mutual Funds Directory.
- When a discount is not a discount—see Chapter 13, Closed-End Funds.
- What the least expensive bond and money market funds are—see Chapter 10, Bond Funds and Chapter 11, Money Market Funds, and the bond fund and money market fund directories in Appendix E.

MONEY MARKET FUNDS

- How to pick up another 1/2% per year on your money market fund—see Chapter 11.
- What top grade investment has lower risk, higher yield and the same liquidity as a money fund—see Chapter 15, Treasury Bills and Bonds.

IRAs

- A few simple rules that will let you earn $10,000 more on your IRA over the next decade—see Chapter 14, Self-Directed IRAs.

TREASURY BONDS AND BILLS

- Buying them without paying commission—see Chapter 15.

FUTURES

- Which futures brokers will allow you to trade at a discount—see Chapter 16, The Futures Market and Appendix C, The Discount Commodity Brokers' Directory.

SHAREHOLDER DISCOUNTS

- How shareholders can save up to 75% on certain travel, entertainment, and holiday gift costs—see Chapter 19.

PRECIOUS METALS

- Which discounters sell precious metals with discounted commissions—see Chapter 18, Precious Metals, Discount Coins, and Other Purported Discounts.

Preface

SPECIAL DISCOUNTS

- How can you get introductory offers, free samples, or special discounts on some of the best financial books and best-known newsletters?

The answer to this last question can be found in Appendix D, The Discount Publications Directory. A special deal for the readers of this book has been arranged—over 100 books and newsletters are available at a special discount to you as a reader of *Investing at a Discount: $avings on Commissions, Management Fees, and Costs*. Appendix D outlines the method for ordering and other pertinent information about these useful publications.

Part One

Discount Brokerage

CHAPTER 1

Investing at a Discount: Questions and Answers

There is usually a long and a short answer to every question. This chapter has the short answers; the rest of the book will offer the more detailed explanations.

DISCOUNT BROKERAGE

How does a discounter differ from a regular broker?

Basically, it's much cheaper and you pick your own stocks unassisted or unmolested, as the case may be, by your broker.

Aren't there any other significant differences?

Not really. Years ago there were some. Then again a cup of coffee used to cost a nickel. Both have changed.

How much can I save with a discounter?

A great deal. You can save close to $200 on some $10,000 trades—up to 90% of the full commission rate.

How can they keep costs so low?

Have you ever seen a discount broker with a plush office? Or received a blind call from one of their sales representatives with a hot tip as you sat down to dinner? The answer is "no" and you never will. There are three reasons that their costs are low: (1) low overhead, (2) no research staff, and (3) no sales commissions.

Will I save the same amount with any discounter?

No. You must use the right one for your trading pattern.

Are the best known discounters among the least expensive?

No. They are generally among the more expensive.

Then why do so many people use them?

They often offer a known reputation and a wider range of products, services, and conveniences than the least expensive discounters. They may also have conveniently located offices.

How do I find the right discounter?

You read this book.

Aren't discounters really for people who want bare-bones stock trades?

Here are some of the products and services that today's not-so-bare-bones discounters offer:

    Stocks

    Bonds

    Options

    IRAs (Individual retirement accounts)

    Market, limit, or other orders

    $500,000 SIPC (Securities Investor Protection Corporation) insurance

Investing at a Discount: Questions and Answers   5

Prompt execution and verbal and written confirmation of every trade
A monthly statement
Safekeeping or delivery of securities
Interest on deposits
Toll-free numbers
Municipal bonds
Unit Investment Trusts
GNMAs (Ginnie Maes)
Treasury bonds and bills
Limited partnerships
Futures
New issues
Integrated cash management accounts (CMAs) with checking/brokerage combined
Investment newsletters—quarterly, monthly, or weekly
Research reports
Access to daily reports
24-hour order and quote service
Separate quote lines
24-hour computerized services that automatically give you quotes on your portfolio over the phone
Enhanced monthly statements with securities values, dividend yields, and so on
Home computer order entry and portfolio review
VIP services for active customers
Keoghs and other retirement plans
Precious metals brokerage at a discount
Research libraries available to the public
Daily news on stocks reported over the wire

(For further information see Chapter 6, Finding the Right Broker in the Discount Brokerage Directory, and Appendix A, The Discount Brokerage Directory.)

Isn't the absence of personal investment advice a major drawback?

It could be a real loss if you have a good broker. However, as one financial adviser told me in all seriousness a few years ago, "The biggest risk in dealing with a registered representative at a full-service firm is that they will offer their advice."

If my current broker has been making money for me and keeping up with the market averages, should I switch to save money?

Follow the old adage: "If it isn't broken, don't fix it." Stick with this broker.

I've decided that I want to actively trade. Should I use a discounter or full-service broker?

If you want to make money, use a discounter. Long-term investors can afford the luxury of full-service brokers; traders cannot.

I receive personalized financial planning assistance from my broker. Can I get this from a discounter?

No. But you have to realize that there is a conflict of interest inherent in financial planning with a broker who will be compensated if you elect to buy the products he or she recommends.

A few years ago I offered the following answer to this question: "No, but remember your broker wants a sale; you want a plan. Financial planning with the average broker is rather like meal planning with a shark."

Since then, I've mellowed. The conflict of interest is probably no greater with a broker than with any sales representative or professional recommending a course of action that will cost you (and make him or her) money. The advice may be good; just don't forget the conflict.

How many investors use discounters?

No one really knows, but the best estimates suggest that 20% of the retail trades go through discounters. Institutions don't use discounters nearly as much because they are able to negotiate discount rates from full-service brokers.

Investing at a Discount: Questions and Answers 7

Are savings similar on all trades?

Not at all. Savings are significant on virtually all transactions, but greater on larger trades or higher priced stocks.

Do discount brokers offer discounts on mutual funds?

No. Many discount brokers don't offer mutual funds. Some offer a wide range of low cost "no-load" mutual funds, but they charge a servicing fee. So you would actually pay less by going direct to the fund sponsor, however, it is more convenient to use the discounter.

Is your account safe with a discounter?

Yes. Virtually all discounters are guaranteed by SIPC—a quasi-governmental body which insures your account for up to $500,000.

What happens if a brokerage firm holding my money fails?

SIPC pays.

What if I buy a stock which goes bankrupt?

You pay.

Should everyone use discounters?

No.

Who should use discounters?

Knowledgeable investors who can make their own investment decisions.

In what cases will discounters not save very much?

Primarily when the trade size is small and your full-service broker has a low minimum transaction cost. Discounters generally have a $25 to $35 minimum transaction cost, even if the trade is very small.

Will I get as good a price for my stock when I buy or sell through a discount broker?

Yes. Stock exchange regulations specify that all orders be handled in a specified price-and-time priority. It does not matter who places them. The stock doesn't know what commissions you're paying, and the buyer doesn't care.

Can I trade options and bonds, too, with discount brokers?

Yes. You can trade whatever you would trade with any other broker.

You don't get something for nothing. Honestly, won't I get at least a slightly poorer execution in exchange for a lower commission?

Not in my experience with over a dozen brokers. But don't take my word for it. The *Wall Street Journal* did a survey of investors who use both discount and full-commission firms. Half thought there was no difference. Of those who did, most thought speed of execution and accuracy were *better* with a discount firm.

Can I work with a discounter like a regular broker?

Pretty much. However, if you currently rely on your broker or brokerage firm for advice, you will have to find other sources, since they don't normally offer investment advice.

Are discounters basically better for everything?

No. If you buy a dog with a discounter, it will still be a dog when you sell it. But the care and feeding cost less.

If I need investment advice, where can I get it?

There are many potential sources. A number of the better known publications are listed in Appendix D, The Discount Publications Directory.

Does it really matter which discount firm I use?

It matters a great deal. The price and service variations among discount firms are far greater than among full-commission firms. Some discount firms charge 10 times as much as others for some

Investing at a Discount: Questions and Answers

transactions, and higher cost doesn't necessarily mean better service.

How can I decide which firm to use?

You can get their brochures or review the *Mercer Discount Brokerage Commission Survey* for comparisons. (See publications information in Appendix D.)

Will discount brokers provide safekeeping services at no cost?

Yes, most will.

What about margin-borrowing facilities?

Yes, in some cases at substantially lower costs than most full-commission firms. At these rates, it is normally cheaper to borrow on margin from a discount broker than it is to borrow from a bank.

Will I receive interest on funds?

Most discounters pay interest on your funds.

Can I establish IRA accounts, buy municipal bonds, and enjoy other types of services provided by regular brokers?

Yes, in most cases.

What other types of services do they provide?

There is a great range. Some provide integrated cash management accounts, similar to Merrill Lynch's CMA account. Others offer advisory services of varying degree—from back-up research on individual stocks to detailed monthly reports or research like full-commission firms.

How can I find out which discount brokerage firms offer these services

See Appendix A, The Discount Brokerage Directory.

Is this a comprehensive list of firms?

It includes virtually every firm in the country that could be identified as a discount brokerage firm. I know of no more comprehensive list.

Do I have to live in a big city or on the coast to use these firms?

No. They are located throughout the country. Many of them also have toll-free 800 numbers so that you can open and use an account anywhere without charge.

How many discount brokers are there?

About 80 independents as this book goes to press, plus innumerable banks.

How large are discount brokers?

They range in size from small shops with only a few people to Charles Schwab and Co., with more than 1 million clients.

Do they provide confirmations and monthly statements?

Yes. They include all the information normally contained in a stock-brokerage statement.

How does a discount broker execute a transaction?

In the same way as any other broker. Some execute through their own floor brokers. Most discount brokers, like many other brokers, execute and clear their exchange transactions through a specialized type of broker known as a clearinghouse.

Will I be assigned an account representative?

That depends upon which discount broker you use. Some assign specific account representatives. Others assign the first free account executive to handle your order. You can usually get to deal with a particular person, however, if you prefer.

Is it difficult to open an account?

Giving money to banks, brokers, or bookies is never a problem. Discount brokers are no exception. They are delighted to help, and it's very simple. Usually it takes a few days. But sometimes you can call up and invest the same day.

Investing at a Discount: Questions and Answers

How do I tell my current broker that I am switching?

You don't have to. You simply ask your new broker, for example, the discount broker, for a transfer form. You fill it out and return it and he or she does the rest. It takes a few weeks. It shouldn't be, but it's a fact of life that it is harder to take assets out of a financial institution than to put them in.

MUTUAL FUNDS

Are mutual funds the wave of the future?

They have become enormously popular and can be very valuable, but are often oversold and overused.

But aren't mutual funds without sales fees, the so-called no-load funds, cheaper than stocks?

No. This is a common misconception. The reality is that an investor can easily save over $10,000 over 10 years on a $50,000 investment by investing directly in stocks (see "The Cost of Couch Potato Investing" in Chapter 8, How to Select Mutual Funds . . . and When to Avoid Them).

Don't all mutual funds charge roughly the same?

No. The expense differences are significant.

But don't mutual funds provide diversification?

Yes, but you don't always need it. Isn't one U.S. Government bond safer than a diversified portfolio of 100 corporate bonds?

Do money market mutual funds offer the highest safe yield?

You can often buy U.S. guaranteed Treasury bills that are free from state and local taxes and yield *more* than money funds (which by the way, are not risk-free)(see Chapter 11, Money Market Funds, and Chapter 15, Treasury Bills and Bonds).

How do you get the best consistently high yield on money funds?

Buy those with the lowest expense ratios (see Appendix E, The Mutual Funds Directory), watch out for money fund price wars, and don't be lured by funds that artificially pump up yields (see Chapters 11 and 15).

Just one final question. Why doesn't everyone use discounters?

Many don't know about them.

Inactive investors don't care.

Very small investors won't save much.

Very rich ones don't care.

Some full-service brokers are well worth their cost.

Some people shouldn't.

Others won't bother.

More and more do.

CHAPTER 2

A Discount Brokerage Primer

This is a short course in discount brokerage. It is not-for-credit, but it isn't not-for-profit. Once you understand the basics, you will be prepared for the later discussion of how to cut your commissions up to 90%.

HISTORY

Until May 1975, the stock exchanges fixed the commission rates for all members. If you wanted to trade on the New York Stock Exchange (NYSE), it didn't matter which firm you used. Every firm charged the same commission as they had for nearly 200 years. The Exchange was the country's oldest legal monopoly.

In the 1960s, the institutions began to erode the monopoly by skirting the exchanges and trading in the over-the-counter "third" market. In response, the exchanges allowed lower rates for institutional-size trades. But individual investors were left out in the cold. They had to pay the rates fixed by the exchanges.

The member firms were prohibited from undercutting the fixed commission schedule.

That changed in May 1975. After protracted discussion, the SEC (Securities and Exchange Commission) ruled that the exchanges could no longer require their members to adhere to fixed commission rates. Thus every member could decide how much to charge. "May Day," as it came to be known, arrived less with a bang than a whimper. Most brokers kept on charging the same rates. But a few entrepreneurial souls and far-sighted companies saw an opportunity. They set up firms that offered few of the frills of the traditional brokerage firm, but had one undeniable advantage. They charged much less.

Discount brokerage did not really catch on during the first few years. Old ways die hard. Investors were suspicious. Full-service brokers knocked the competition. The stock market was doing poorly anyhow. Why change?

August 1982 marked the beginning of the great bull market of the 1980s, taking off like a Saturn rocket and drawing hundreds of thousands of investors back into the market in its wake. The discount brokerage firms had learned to market themselves better in the interim. They added frills, shed their downscale image, and began attracting clients. The final aura of respectability was conferred on discount brokerage in 1984, when literally thousands of banks began offering discount brokerage services to the public. A 1984 survey I conducted found that over 3000 banks were offering discount brokerage in one form or another to their clients.

Discount brokerage continued to grow at a less torrid pace throughout the 1980s. Buyouts reduced the number of firms as it did the number of full-service firms, but by the end of the 1980s, there remained over 80 significant independent discounters servicing the public and innumerable banks. There are no precise figures, but estimates are that discounters currently account for 20% of the retail trade.

COSTS

The Cost Structure: How They Keep Costs So Low

Investors who are new to discount brokerage wonder how they can charge a fraction of the cost of a full-service broker. Can anything so cheap really be good? If you are looking for good execution of routine orders without investment advice, a good discounter will carry out this job as well as anyone else. Many studies show this; so does my personal experience.

Discounters can keep their costs down because they don't bear three costs which full-service firms carry:

Sales Rep's Commission. The typical broker will receive 30 to 40% of the commission with a full-service firm. That is his or her compensation for the time spent in servicing the account. By contrast, discount brokers use salaried personnel who are generally lower paid and can handle a much higher volume of orders because order-taking is their main function.

Research Advice. Full-service firms will provide detailed research reports which you can discuss with your broker. While some of the higher priced discount brokers will offer newsletters with investment ideas or suggestions, this is the exception. Where it is provided, the information is not nearly as detailed as a full-service broker offers.

Overhead. If you visit their offices, you will find full-service firms on the main floor; discounters, on the second. Or the eighth. They pay less rent and their offices are not plush. They are more thinly staffed and, except in the largest firms, there's no middle management. These savings find their way to the investor.

Commission Variations Among Discount Brokers

While full-service firms all charge basically the same rates for stocks, there are significant commission variations among discounters. These have become more pronounced over the past few years. For example, the best-known nationally advertised discount brokerage firms typically charge twice as much as the least expensive ones. Part of that cost is in the national advertising; part lies in the fact that they offer a wider range of products and services than the lower cost firms.

SAFETY

The Same Regulatory Structure

While many investors think that discount brokers are a different type of brokerage firm from a full-service firm, the only significant difference is in the marketing. From a regulatory perspective, the discount broker is *identical* to a full-service broker. The SEC and other regulatory agencies recognize no distinctions. Both firms are subject to the same regulatory requirements, capital requirements, and reporting requirements.

SIPC: The Safety Net

While government regulations are often seen as onerous, there is one government regulation that has significantly contributed to the growth of the discount brokerage industry. It has created a safety net which assures that your securities investments in a small discount brokerage firm are as safe as your investment in the largest full-service firm.

The safety net is the Securities Investor Protection Corporation. This quasi-governmental organization is funded by a levy on stock sales and provides $500,000 insurance on every account, with the insurance on cash in the account limited to $100,000. If you have two accounts with two brokers, each is covered for $500,000. (See Appendix B for further information.)

SIPC insures against fraud and financial failures; it does not insure against market risk. If you buy a stock through your broker and he or she goes bankrupt or departs for Brazil, SIPC pays. If your broker recommends a stock and it declines in value; you pay.

Any firm registered with the SEC is required to belong to SIPC. That includes virtually every broker. The exceptions would be firms dealing exclusively in intra-state business or firms that exclusively sell and hold mutual fund shares.

Registered firms display the SIPC label at their office or on their literature. I have never heard of a situation where a firm falsely claimed to belong to SIPC. However, if you are opening up an account with a new firm and want to check them out, you can write to SIPC's membership office to confirm (Securities Investor Protection Corporation, 900 17th St. NW, Washington, DC 20006).

I spoke with a representative of SIPC to find out whether there are any common situations where an investor might think they were covered by the $500,000 securities/$100,000 cash coverage, but were in fact not covered. One situation came to light.

A Discount Brokerage Primer

If funds are left in a brokerage account for other than investment purposes, they are not insured by SIPC. The primary example of this is money left in the account for an extended period to draw interest. As this rule is currently interpreted, if the funds are left on deposit for three months, SIPC insurance definitely covers your funds. From three months to a year, you're probably okay, but there are no guarantees. Beyond a year, you're asking for trouble. However, if the funds are placed in a separate money market fund, with the shares held by the brokerage firm, this is considered a security, and all securities within the $500,000 limit are insured.

The wealthy investor or institutions should be aware that SIPC contends that repurchase agreements (REPOs) are not covered. SIPC litigated this issue once and lost, but their view remains unchanged. The wealthy investor would also do well to remember the $100,000 cash limit. If you sell 3000 shares of IBM at $100, and your broker fails while you're considering your next move, you could be out of pocket $200,000 ($300,000 proceeds less the $100,000 insured limit).

If your account exceeds $500,000, you may want to consider a brokerage firm that offers additional insurance protection. A number of discounters offer excess insurance policies written by major insurance companies which cover losses in excess of $500,000 for an account. The names, brokers, and the size of the policies they offer are listed in Appendix A.

Brokerage firm liquidations are rare. Among the 12,000 firms registered with the SEC, SIPC has only liquidated an average of 7 firms per year during the 1980s. That is roughly one in 2000 firms. This group has included both full-service firms and discounters. There is no particular pattern to firms that fail. As a practical matter, a liquidation normally means that a new voice will answer the phone when you call—an existing firm that has agreed to assume the accounts of the former broker. Most of the time, you would not know that a liquidation had occurred unless you read about it in the newspaper. Most liquidations and transfers occur quickly. However, in an extreme case, if the firms' accounts were in exceptionally bad condition, it could take as long as three months for investors to gain access to their accounts.

If all your assets were in the account being liquidated, and you wanted to sell stocks during the liquidation period, you would not be able to do so. However, you could limit the damage by selling stocks short or buying put options where available. If you're a long-term investor, however, you may not care, as long as you don't need the cash. The government will guarantee eventual delivery of your stock.

ORDER EXECUTION

One of the concerns that has kept investors away from discounters is the belief that they get preferable order execution—better prices for the shares they buy or sell—from full-service firms. Full-service firms don't go out of their way to dispel this belief, and along with some discounters, they frequently tout their ability to get the best prices through their outstanding floor traders on the floors of the stock exchanges.

Some firms cite their large number of floor traders; others discuss how they are strategically deployed on the exchange floor for maximum coverage; others merely claim that they offer outstanding execution, or show pictures of their hard-working traders, straining to get you the last 1/8 of a point.

Yes, good floor traders are important for trade execution. They can make a big difference—if you have a 100,000 share order, maybe even 10,000 shares. But it's doubtful that most of these traders have seen a 300-share order pass through their hands in years. As far as the retail investor is concerned, floor traders, like paper ticker tape, are strictly of historical interest.

The "lady" who handles virtually all your trade on the New York Stock Exchange is called DOT. She also helps out on the American Stock Exchange. The over-the-counter markets have their own counterparts.

DOT is a computer. In 1983, she could handle trades up to about 1000 shares on the floor of the exchange. But in computer terms, 1983 is prehistoric. By 1990, she could handle any market order up to 30,999 shares and limit orders up to 99,999 shares.

In some ways, DOT is very fast. She has been tested to handle up to 600 million shares in a day (the volume on the

A Discount Brokerage Primer

heaviest day in stock market history) and is working toward an 800 million day. Her average execution time per trade is 30 seconds—down from 2 minutes in 1983.

In other ways, like many computers, DOT is a bit slow. She can't tell a discounter from a full-service broker. She doesn't know whether you paid $200 or $25 for the trade. She just takes the trade in the order it was entered and executes it. DOT is an equal opportunity computer.

Virtually everyone uses DOT for retail orders. Whether you enter your order through the most expensive full-service broker or the least expensive discounter, the odds are overwhelming that your order will be handled by DOT on the New York or American Stock Exchanges, or similar equal opportunity computers on the over-the-counter markets.

SERVICES

When it comes to basic services, discounters provide the same services that you have come to expect from a full-commission broker.

Core Services

The terms "bare-bones" and "discounters" used to be synonymous. This is no longer true. Here is a list of core services and products that you can expect from nearly all discounters:

Stocks

Bonds

Options

IRAs

Market, limit, or other orders

$500,000 SIPC insurance

Prompt execution and verbal and written confirmation of every trade

A monthly statement

Safekeeping or delivery of securities

Interest on deposits
Toll-free numbers

Other Possible Services

Other products and services that you will find with some, but not all, discounters include:

Mutual funds
Municipal bonds
Unit Investment Trusts
GNMAs
Treasury bonds and bills
Limited partnerships
Futures
New issues
Integrated cash management accounts with checking/brokerage combined
Investment newsletters
Research reports
Access to daily reports
24-hour order and quote service
Separate quote lines
24-hour computerized services that automatically give you quotes on your portfolio over the phone
Enhanced monthly statements with securities values, dividend yields, etc.
Home computer order entry and portfolio review
VIP services for active customers
Keoghs and other retirement plans
Precious metals brokerage at a discount
Research libraries available to the public
News reported over the wire

A Discount Brokerage Primer

We will discuss some of these in greater detail in Chapter 6, Finding the Right Broker . . . , in connection with Appendix A, The Discount Brokerage Directory.

WHERE DISCOUNTERS DIFFER

So far, I've dealt primarily with the similarities between discounters and full-service brokers. Let's talk about where they differ.

- You receive no unsolicited calls. If you receive an unsolicited call from someone claiming to be a stock discounter broker, be suspicious. Their narrow profit margins don't permit much sales compensation. The caller is probably not a real discounter. (Commodity discounters are a different breed; they call. I discuss why in Chapter 16, The Futures Market.)
- For the lowest cost discounters, the range of investment products is generally narrower.
- You will receive comparable order execution but less personal service. A good discounter will take your orders and requests as competently and politely as a full-service broker, but they will have little time for small talk, and no time to handle small favors that a good full-service broker might do, such as helping you with accounting questions at tax time.

While all firms, to my knowledge, provide annual reports on stocks you own, policies differ on disseminating Standard & Poor's reports or similar information on request. Appendix A tells you what types of additional information each firm offers.

If you would like further detail on these subjects, refer to the section in Appendix A titled Getting Your Frills with a No Frills Broker.

THE REAL DIFFERENCE

"The rich are different from you and I," said F. Scott Fitzgerald. "Yes," Ernest Hemingway is reported to have answered, "they have more money."

As you may have started to realize, a discount brokerage house is fundamentally the same as a full-service broker. Most of the differences are insignificant. There is, however, one fundamental difference. Discounters, with rare exceptions, do not offer personalized investment advice. The potential sources of such advice are the subject of the next chapter.

CHAPTER 3

Investment Advice for the Independent Investor

When you decide to trade with a discounter, you have joined the ranks of the independent investor. A few independents have the time and sophistication to analyze stocks without *any* outside advice at all. They pore through annual reports and quarterly statements, dissecting the numbers and querying company personnel on the results.

These ultra-independents are a rare breed. Most of us prefer a little help from books, financial publications, newsletters, television programs, investment advisers, or brothers-in-law. These sources can be quite inexpensive, especially if the advice is good. With this in mind, I successfully arranged to purchase some of the best-known books and newsletters at a discount and offer them to you at a reduced rate as a service to the readers of this book.

PUBLICATIONS AT A 20% DISCOUNT

Appendix D, The Discount Publications Directory, identifies some of what I consider the better investment books in print.

They cover stocks, bonds, mutual funds, and a range of other investments. These publications range from newly published books covering specialized areas of interests to classics with broad scope and enduring appeal. They provide the type of basics that an investor must master—whether you're trying to grind out an extra percentage or two on a conservative portfolio or beat the market with high flying growth stocks.

The books are described in detail in Appendix D, along with the method for ordering them. They are available to readers of this book at a **20% discount**.

NEWSLETTERS—SPECIAL INTRODUCTORY OFFERS AND DISCOUNTS

One of the most popular means for securing investment advice is through newsletters. They can be weeklies or monthlies. Some are short-term, technically oriented letters that have telephone hotlines available, while others offer a long-term perspective for investors who prefer to hold stocks for years. While many investors probably don't follow all the newsletters' recommendations, they certainly use them as a source of ideas, to supplement their own. Or you can use a newsletter as a comprehensive adviser, like a full-service broker or mutual fund.

For investors who want to invest the minimum amount of time, most newsletters offer a monitored portfolio. They tell you what to buy, what to sell, and when to do it. If the editor is good, newsletters can be a useful and inexpensive form of investment advice. For example, if your portfolio value is roughly $20,000 or higher, it can be less expensive to use a newsletter and a good discounter than a mutual fund or full-service broker.

Newsletters vary significantly in quality. Since anyone can write a newsletter, the field attracts a wide range of talents. Some newsletter writers are brilliant; others are primarily showmen or, frankly, crackpots. Some of the newsletters in

Investment Advice for the Independent Investor

Appendix D have been cited for their outstanding track record. Others have not qualified for such honors. But all of them (with two exceptions[1]) are rated by *The Hulbert Financial Digest*, which was started by Mark Hulbert in the early 1980s to bring some semblance of law and order to the unruly ranks of newsletter advertising. Previously, any publisher's claim would go pretty much unchallenged; then Hulbert's *Digest* began to follow their claims and publish the results. Some publishers didn't agree with the findings, but Hulbert has developed a reputation for accuracy and integrity which has now made him the arbiter of newsletter claims.

This brings to newsletters an important advantage which mutual funds offer but full-service brokers lack: accountability. Mutual funds have track records which can be precisely measured, whereas full-service brokers' records are often unmeasurable; each client's record may vary. With the advent of *The Hulbert Financial Digest*, newsletters' results can now be measured with some degree of accuracy. The fact that these newsletters are rated by the *Digest* means that they have several common traits which make them candidates for inclusion in this book: Their track record can be ascertained, they are reasonably well known, and their recommendations are sufficiently concrete so you are able to tell what they mean. Hulbert omits from coverage any newsletters whose Delphic pronouncements are too vague to follow.

The Newsletter Directory in Appendix D includes some of the best-known newsletters in the country. All of their publishers have agreed to offer introductory offers and/ or special discounts to buyers of this book. The size of the discounts vary, but in some cases, exceed 50% of the regular subscription price. Detailed information about each of them is included in the Newsletter section of Appendix D.

---

[1] The two newsletters in the Directory which are not covered by Hulbert are two of Mercer's new publications: *The Global Portfolio* and *Investing at a Discount, the Newsletter*. The former is primarily for individual investors who want to participate in foreign markets through stocks, bonds, or mutual funds. The latter, as the title suggests, is a bimonthly which keeps investors current on the type of topics covered in this book.

OTHER PUBLICATIONS

There are a number of excellent financial periodicals with which many investors are already familiar. They include:

The AAII Journal (American Association of Individual Investors)
Barron's
Business Week
Changing Times
Financial World
Forbes
Investor's Daily
Money
The New York Times
The Wall Street Journal

These often provide excellent recommendations by knowledgeable experts as well as basic statistical data and good news reports on individual companies.

ASSOCIATIONS

Various clubs and organizations with varying degrees of sophistication exist to service the independent investor. One of the best is the American Association of Individual Investors. Their $49 per year membership includes invitations to many useful lectures and a subscription to their outstanding publication—*The AAII Journal.* You can write to this organization at 625 N. Michigan Avenue, Chicago, Illinois 60611, or call (312) 280-0170.

TELEVISION

Traditional investors may consider television an unlikely source for serious investment advice. But the reality is that investment as entertainment is big business. Television programs are able to attract some of the top money managers for interviews—people you would normally not get to see without the promise of at least $5 million to manage.

If you thrive on inside tips, stick to whispers from your broker. With several million people watching the same show,

Investment Advice for the Independent Investor 27

you certainly do not have the inside track. Nor is it likely that these recommendations are being announced for the first time on television; for all we know both the guest and their top clients may have loaded up on their recommendations well in advance of the show. But you can still get some very good and profitable advice even if the "tips" are shared with 5 million viewers. Some of the best programs available include:

On **CNN**, Stuart Varney's "Business Day" provides good comprehensive business coverage.

FNN has news and interviews with analysts and newsletter writers throughout the day. This financial network also has excellent in-depth analysis by technical analyst John Bollinger and monetary analysis by Ed Hart and several worthwhile programs in the evening including "Moneytalk" and "Profit Motive," hosted by an outstanding investor, Jim Rogers.

Finally, on **PBS**, Louis Rukeyser's "Wall $treet Week" is the oldest and most widely followed stock-oriented program in the country. Rukeyser's trenchant and witty commentary and the consistently high quality of the guests and panelists account for the show's continued popularity. "Adam Smith's Money World" provides excellent in-depth coverage of larger issues, while the nightly "Business Report" provides good business news in an enjoyable format.

OTHER SOURCES OF ADVICE

There are close to 20,000 registered investment advisers who will manage portfolios (usually larger ones) for fees that typically run 1 to 1 1/2% of the portfolio's value annually, depending upon the size of the portfolio. The advantage of this arrangement is that these investment advisers do not have the same conflict of interest as a broker. They are paid a flat fee, so there is no temptation to increase their income by increasing your trading.

Recognizing that some investors may be uncomfortable with the conflict of interest inherent in the brokers' role, some full-service firms have started to offer a system of payment based on service to their clients. You don't pay a commission, but rather a flat percentage of the assets each year. Some discount brokers have also begun to experiment with referring clients to independent firms that offer similar arrangements.

Whatever the merits of these arrangements, from a cost standpoint they are really variants of full-service brokerage or mutual funds. If you are prepared to pay 1 to 1 1/2% per year for advice, you could also deal with a typical mutual fund, or a patient full-service broker who does not churn your account. It's just a question of whom you want to pay to manage your money.

The comparative costs of mutual funds, full-service brokers, and discounters are discussed at length in Chapter 7.

CHAPTER 4

Choosing a Broker

Selecting a broker lies somewhere on the scale of importance between picking a mate and picking a coat. It's less expensive than the former, more expensive than the latter, and in some instances, will outlast both. So it's worth taking time to think about the decision.

At this point you may feel that you already know enough about discount brokerage to decide whether or not it is suited for you. But if you haven't yet decided, this chapter will first offer a few questions and observations to help you in that decision.

The second part of the chapter provides information which will help people decide which type of discounter to use. Discounters are divided into four groups; each type has its respective advantages and disadvantages.

DISCOUNTER OR FULL-SERVICE?

The Importance of Patience

In my experience, full-service brokers come in two categories—very good and very bad. They seldom fall in between. And this is one of the problems in generalizing about full-service brokers.

As one financial adviser with a Big Eight accounting firm told me some years back, "The biggest risk in dealing with a registered representative at a full-service firm is that they will offer their advice." That's the risk of a bad broker.

On the other hand, in addition to several discounters, I use two full-service brokers. Both of them are excellent, patient investors who develop their own investment ideas and offer good advice—which is well worth the additional commission costs.

A key word here is "patient." In order to make sense, a good full-service broker not only has to be smart, but patient as well. Since full-service brokers charge only when they trade, the cost is not prohibitive if you trade infrequently. Since the average cost to buy and sell a stock with a full-service broker is about 4.6% on a $10,000 transaction, it works out to about 1.5% per year if you hold three years. That's much higher than a discounter, but no more than a mutual fund.

On the other hand, it is very difficult, if not impossible, to make money consistently with a full-service broker if you actively trade your account. If you turn over your portfolio four times per year, you're giving away over 18% annually. That exceeds the average annual return on the Dow Jones, S&P 500, or average mutual fund during the 1980s—one of the most profitable decades. The conclusion is inescapable; traders must use discounters.

Apart from the cost factor, there are other considerations affecting whether to use a discounter or full-service broker. Discount brokers are not for everyone. Some investors would do better with full-service brokers. Others will do better to use mutual funds. But an increasing number of investors are taking advantage of the great savings that the right discounter offers.

Here are some questions and observations that will help you to decide whether you're suited for a discounter.

Do you have a full-service broker that is currently doing a good job?

You find your broker pleasant, with a record over time that comes close to matching the widely followed Dow Jones, S&P 500, or other indexes. It's not necessary for him or her to beat or even match the indexes. Coming close means that your broker is

Choosing a Broker

doing as well as most mutual funds. Unless you have a hankering to trade on your own, my advice would be to stick with this broker. A bird in the hand is worth two in the bush.

Are you new to investing and want to learn?

Discounters won't help. You can use a discounter and a newsletter or other financial publications, but you may do better in the early stages to work with a congenial full-service broker with a reputable firm. Write the higher commissions off to an educational experience.

Will you sleep at night if you're watching your own portfolio?

Discount brokerage means making your own decisions. You may use a newsletter or other source for advice, but the decision in the end will be yours. If you're not comfortable with this fact, use a full-service broker or a mutual fund.

Do you secretly find stock investing fun?

Gambling is one of America's fastest growing industries. Billions of dollars are spent each year on lotteries, at casinos, and at off-track betting. People will travel long distances to participate in activities where the odds are statistically overwhelming that they will lose money. Why? It's fun.

Suppose you could go to a casino where the odds were stacked in your favor instead of the house's? You can. Stocks are a form of low-risk gambling which can afford the same enjoyment, and the odds over time are statistically overwhelming that you will make money. It can also be educational and challenging. For those who like crossword puzzles or any kind of intellectual challenge, the stock market offers it all.

If you enjoy stock investing, you're a good candidate for a discount broker. And the pay is not bad for a hobby. (It certainly beats your pay for crossword puzzles!) You're just paying yourself instead of a broker or mutual fund manager.

However, if you find it tedious and nerve wracking, forget it. Unless you have a large portfolio or anticipate much higher than average returns, the return per hour invested will not be great. You are better suited for a mutual fund or full-service broker.

Are you an active trader?

If you are actively trading your portfolio with a full-service broker and making money, you're a perfect candidate for a discounter. As a matter of fact, if you're turning over your portfolio a couple of times per year and not making much money, you're an equally good candidate. With a discounter, you could be making money, as discussed earlier.

An unfair question?

People who conduct surveys know that you can influence the answer by the way you write the question. To prompt the undecided investor to decide whether to switch to a discounter, we phrased the issue as one of choosing either a discounter *or* a full-service broker.

In reality, many people use both. They use full-service brokers for their investment ideas; they use discounters for their own, or for short-term trading. In the end, you may decide to use both. I did.

CHOOSING A DISCOUNTER

There is actually more variation among discounters than among full-service brokers. While some discounters' range of products is limited to stocks, bonds, options, and associated services, others offer a wide range of products and services quite comparable to a full-service broker, plus a few that full-service firms don't offer. Once again, everything but investment advice.

When it comes to commissions, the range of variation among discounters is vastly greater than among full-service firms. Full-service firms impose very similar commission charges; the well-known national firms' commission charges typically fall within a few percentage points of each other.

Discounters are very different from each other in two ways: Their average charges vary tremendously and the commission

Choosing a Broker 33

charge for each trade varies greatly. A firm with an average commission charge might nevertheless offer a very low charge for certain trades, such as stocks under $10 or ordered in excess of 500 shares. For this reason we are reluctant to overemphasize average commission charges.

A firm with an unappealing average commission charge might nonetheless be very competitive for your particular trading pattern. That is why every trade must be analyzed individually, and why Mercer publishes surveys which compare individual commission charges rather than averages.

Nevertheless, when you are selecting among different types of discounters, it's important to look at averages. They provide a useful guide to the costs you're likely to pay for different types of discounters. At Mercer, we divide discounters into four categories: The Deep Discounters, The Big Three, The Bank Brokers, and The Regional Discounters.

Chapter 5 will examine commission costs in greater detail but as a rule of thumb, Figure 4.1 shows four types of discounters and full-service brokers, and what you can expect to pay, based on a basket of 20 stock trades, averaging $8975 per trade.

The four categories of discounters compared are:

1. The average of the 30 least expensive discounters (The Deep Discounters)
2. A typical discounter

Figure 4.1. Comparison of $9000 Trade Average Commissions

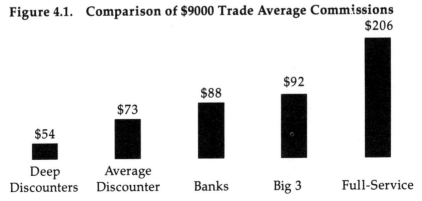

Source: *Mercer 1989 Discount Brokerage Stock Commission Survey*

3. The bank brokers
4. The Big Three (Schwab, Fidelity, and Quick and Reilly)

We don't track the regionals as a distinct group for commission purposes, but they probably average near the rate for a typical discounter.

As a general rule of thumb, if your average trade is near $10,000, you might think of discount costs on stock trades in this way:

- The cost for the least expensive brokers averages about 1/2% or $50 per trade.
- The Big Three and the typical bank broker average closer to 1% or $100 per trade.
- A full-service broker exceeds 2% or $200+ per trade.

The Deep Discounters

This is a term used in the industry to describe the lowest cost firms. I have in turn defined these as the 30 lowest cost firms for either lower value trades (approximately $6300) or high value trades (approximately $13,500). If the firm's average cost for the basket of individual size trades covered by the *Mercer 1989 Discount Brokerage Commission Survey* is among the 30 lowest in the industry on either category, they are included in the Directory in Appendix A. In total, 37 brokers made this list.

The list could have been averaged to reduce the list to the 30 firms whose average commissions for both type trades were lowest, but that would have eliminated some firms that are very attractive. For example, some firms charging as little as 2 or 3 cents per share, half institutional rates or less, would not have made the cut because they have a relatively high minimum. Yet they are among the best if your commission cost crosses their $50 to $75 minimum threshold. It's another indication of how discounters specialize in certain types of trades.

The deep discounters are a varied lot. Some are small, one office firms. Others are large companies with offices in several cities or states. While a few do offer quite a variety of products, most have a narrower range of products and services than the other discounters. That is part of the reason that they can charge such low commission rates. While you will find all the essential stock and option services among the deep discounters, they generally will not offer services such as check writing, municipal bonds, limited partnerships, investment newsletters, or free stock quote lines (although you can always call their office for a quote).

If you are an active trader, the case for using a deep discounter is compelling. You simply can't afford to pay a national broker twice as much for every trade. Even if you only trade once a week, if your average transaction averages about $9000, you will save about $2000 per year using a typical deep discounter instead of a national one. Since many traders use deep discounters, you may be pleasantly surprised with the speed and accuracy of their execution. What they do, they do very well.

The Big Three

If the number of clients is used as the measure, three firms clearly dominate the discount brokerage industry—Charles Schwab, Quick and Reilly, and Fidelity Brokerage. They serve well over 2 million of the roughly 3 million plus Americans that are estimated to use discount brokers.

On average, they charge nearly twice as much as the least expensive discounters, yet they have managed to attract and keep most of the cost-conscious investors who use discounters. Since discount investors are a relatively sophisticated group, their appeal is not just sizzle; they have developed a formula that makes the knowledgeable investor willing to pay more. One reason is that the typical investor who uses the Big Three probably only trades four or five times per year, and therefore may be willing to forego a few hundred dollars in savings for features they value. A more active investor may be forced to be more cost-conscious. Yet over two million investors are willing to pay a premium to use these firms. Their appeal is threefold:

1. They offer major savings versus full-service firms. Their commissions are typically less than half of a full-service firm's.
2. Many investors feel more confident in placing their money with a large, reputable, national firm. Their

office may be nearby and they offer an intangible—a sense of security—for which many investors are willing to pay a premium.
3. They often offer a wider range of products, and their extensive advertising has made them better-known to the smaller investor than their less well capitalized deep discount brethren.

The Big Three have much in common, yet each has their own distinctive personality.

Starting with a single office in San Francisco in 1975, Charles Schwab built his firm into the largest discounter in the country with over 100 offices in 1990 and over 1.3 million customers. In 1983 he sold his firm to Bank of America and bought it back a few years later in a leveraged buyout. It has since prospered under his independent management.

Schwab offers the broadest product line and has been the most active in introducing products to discount brokerage clients that were previously found only with full-service firms. Among others, they offer hundreds of no-load mutual funds that can be purchased for a service fee, a sophisticated computer hookup which allows accessing and analyzing the portfolio, an integrated checking and brokerage system similar to Merrill Lynch's CMA, and a variety of information sources that can be accessed through the computer or telephone.

Starting out at the same time as Schwab, Leslie Quick and his sons have built their operation from a single shop into a nationwide brokerage firm with offices in every state and nearly a half million customers. While no one is certain whether Quick and Reilly outranks the privately held Fidelity in terms of the number of discount brokerage customers, my belief is that they are ranked second among the Big Three.

Quick and Reilly offers a somewhat lower commission schedule, a fair range of products, and an emphasis on the personal touch. Each investor is assigned to a personal account executive, which is not normally the case with most discount brokerage firms, Schwab, or Fidelity.

Fidelity Brokerage is the brokerage arm of the Fidelity family of mutual funds—the largest no-load and low-load mutual fund family in the country with over $100 billion in investors' funds under management among its 145 (at last count) funds. Among the Big Three, it is the only firm that was already quite substantial when deregulation paved the way for discount brokerage in 1975.

In its orientation, range of products, and emphasis on computer delivery systems, it is closer to Schwab than Quick and Reilly. It offers integrated checking and the convenience of easy transfer between its brokerage arm and mutual funds. Recently, Fidelity introduced a deep discount brokerage schedule for clients trading approximately 50 times per year. It is unclear at present whether this is a test or will become a permanent part of their brokerage operation.

The Bank Brokers

Until Bank of America's decision to buy Schwab in 1983, most banks felt they were precluded from entering the brokerage area by the Glass-Steagall Act, a depression era law which prohibited banks from engaging in commercial activities and investment banking at the same time. But when Bank of America decided to challenge the law, they breached the dike, and a wave of banks washed in. By the end of 1984, over 3000 banks were estimated to be in the discount brokerage business.

The Schwab purchase was upheld by the courts, but for many banks, it was a Pyrrhic victory. They found that discount brokerage was not the gold mine they had expected. Like Bank of America, many ultimately left the business, however, some found it to be profitable and others found that their clients liked the service and have retained it for them. While there are fewer banks offering discount brokerage today, consolidations have also thinned the ranks of independents, so there may still be 30 times as many bank discount brokers as independent discount brokers.

However, this overstates the significance of bank brokers in the brokerage market; most of the trading volume goes through independents. Many small banks offer discount brokerage in only the most nominal way. Banks are involved in discount brokerage in varying degrees. Many of the smaller ones are really offering someone else's service with their name on the door, or more accurately, on the statement. You will call a number provided through the bank, and receive a statement with the bank's name on it, but the trade execution and bookkeeping is provided by a third party. Fidelity is probably the dominant firm providing third-party brokerage services to banks. Other banks, however, are more directly involved the operation. They have quote machines and people on premises who will take your order directly and act very much as an independent broker. They may place trades through a third party, but so do most independent brokers. A well-run bank broker can be as efficient as any independent.

Whatever their degree of involvement in the process, most bank brokers offer certain advantages unique to banks: automatic movement of funds on request between your brokerage account and your bank account, the ability to deliver securities to a local office, and the security of knowing that your money is held by a bank. Notwithstanding the S&L (Savings and Loan) problems, in most people's minds, a bank still stands for security.

Still, the bank discounters are an important part of the discount brokerage community, and easily the most diverse group. It is not only their sheer numbers which contribute to the diversity, but also the range of services and commissions. Some banks offer very minimal services and products: A few don't even offer option trading or margin borrowing—products which are available from every independent. On the other hand, others offer a wide range of products, including precious metals and other products not normally available through independents. You will see this diversity as you look at the investment products that different banks offer when you review the section on bank brokers in the Discount Brokerage Directory in Appendix A.

The bank discount brokers are not to be confused with the traditional bank trust departments through which you can purchase or sell shares. These departments traditionally charge full-service commission rates. If you're opening an account with a bank, be sure that their literature indicates a discount brokerage-type account. Don't be concerned if it *doesn't* say it offers discount brokerage as long as they advertise the service as discount brokerage. Many banks still think it is out of character for a bank to offer discount brokerage, so they call it bank brokerage. All of

Choosing a Broker

the banks listed in Appendix A offer discount brokerage, but due to space constraints, the listings are limited to the major banks. Your local bank may very well offer discount brokerage—even if it's not listed.

When it comes to commission charges, banks are the most diverse of all discounters. While the average bank commission charged in the *Mercer Survey* was very close to the average of the Big Three, there were banks that averaged below the typical deep discounter. These are identified in the Discount Brokerage Directory and will be discussed in greater detail in the next chapter.

Regional Discounters

This is our catch-all term for firms which do not fall into the other categories. They may be one-office local firms or have multiple offices throughout several regions—really national in scope—even if they are not the size of one of the Big Three.

They're not deep discounters, but they survive in a business where the number of firms has been declining. This means they must be filling some type of niche. They may offer a more personal touch. Many may offer some type of research report or investment newsletter with stock recommendations. Others offer more features and services than a typical firm. They must be doing something right because they keep the customer coming in the door in a very competitive business.

Their commission charges cover a wide spectrum. They range from firms that didn't quite make the deep discount list to others whose rates exceed those charged by the banks and Big Three. You can ascertain where they fall in this spectrum by requesting their commission schedules and comparing them with the average charges for different types of brokers. This is the subject of the next chapter.

CHAPTER 5

Enormous Savings with a Discount Broker

Now that you know what discount brokerage is all about, and you have information about the different types of discounters, you are ready to learn about the bottom line. You don't go to a discounter for the plush carpets or sage advice. You go to *save money*. How much can you save and how do you do it?

STOCKS

The amount of savings will depend upon a number of factors, including the size of the transaction, the price and number of shares, the type of discounter you use, and of course, the number of times you trade.

Once these factors are determined, your savings can be predicted quite accurately using the findings of the *Mercer 1989 Stock Commission Survey* which analyzes about 5000 stock commission charges by some 175 independent and bank discount brokers. Using a 20-trade sample from the *1989 Survey*, trades which range in size from $1000 transactions (1000 shares at a $1) to $22,500 (300 shares at $75) and average just under $9000 per trade, the following can be stated:

Average Costs

- If you used the least expensive broker for each trade, your cost would average $32 per trade, .36% of the value of the transaction.
- A full-service broker on average would charge $206 per trade, or 2.3% of the value of the transaction.
- Therefore, your savings would average $174 per trade, a savings of *84%*.

In practice, you're not likely to save that much, because there is no single broker that is least expensive for all trades. Therefore, unless you are prepared to open a number of accounts, your average cost would be higher, but not much higher.

If you used a typical broker selected from the list of deep discounters in the Discount Brokerage Directory, you would pay about $54 per trade. If you analyzed their trades, or used the *Mercer Stock Survey* to pick a broker tailored to your trading pattern, you could probably bring the cost with a single broker closer to $45 per trade—roughly an 80% discount. Using a second broker selected because its pricing schedule complements your first broker (what we have termed "complementary pairing"), you could probably shave another $5 from your trade cost.

If you elect to use a bank broker or one of the Big Three, your cost will be closer to $90 per share, significantly higher than the deep discounters, but still a hefty 57% savings over full commission rates—over $100 per trade.

Figure 5.1 provides a graphic illustration of what has been discussed. The bar titled *lowest cost per trade* represents the cost if you used the lowest cost broker for each of the trades in the *Mercer 1989 Stock Commission Survey*.

All other bars represent the cost if you use one of the 10 lowest cost brokers, one of the 20 lowest cost, one of the 30

Figure 5.1. Commission Comparisons

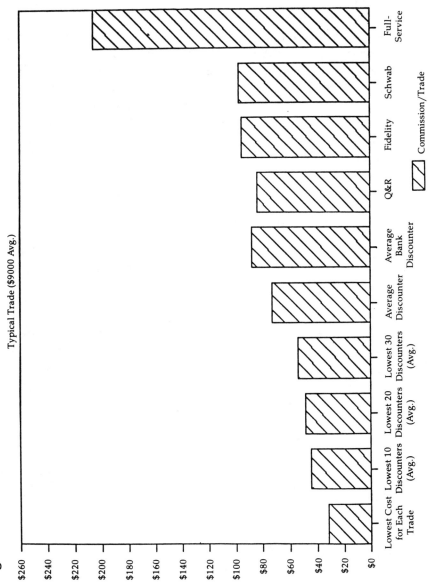

lowest (the average for our deep discounters), a typical discounter, one of the Big Three, a bank, or a full-service broker.

If you trade 10 times per year, and your average trade is near $9000, you can save *$1740 per year.* If you use one of the Big Three or a typical bank, your savings will be *over $1000 per year.*

Figure 5.2, titled Annual Commission Savings, shows what savings could be achieved annually by investors using discounters instead of full-service brokers. It shows the savings for investors trading anywhere from 5 to 50 times per year using different types of discounters. By using the lowest cost discounter for each trade, an investor trading 50 times annually could save $8700 for the year. Even using an average deep discounter, this same trader could save $7600 annually.

SPECIFIC TRANSACTIONS

Averages are useful for illustrative purposes, but people don't trade averages; they trade stocks. The following examples illustrate the type of savings you will find for different specific stock trades:

- If you select the least expensive discounter, you can expect a discount from the commissions charged by full-service brokers of 70% to over 90%. The actual dollar savings will depend upon the specific transaction. Here are some specific examples.

    1000 SHARES AT $5
    Typical full-service broker: $210
    Least expensive discounter: $45
    Savings (percentage):   79%
    SAVINGS: $165

    1000 SHARES AT $10
    Typical full-service broker: $285
    Least expensive discounter: $60
    Savings (percentage):   77%
    SAVINGS: $225

Figure 5.2. Annual Commission Savings

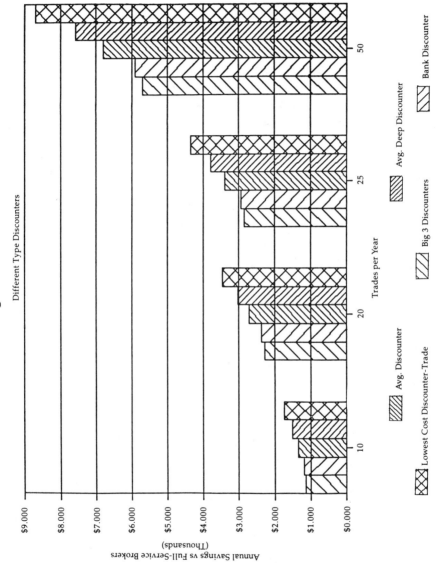

200 SHARES AT $20
Typical full-service broker: $110
Least expensive discounter: $25
Savings (percentage): 69%
SAVINGS: $85

300 SHARES AT $30
Typical full-service broker: $200
Least expensive discounter: $25
Savings (percentage): 88%
SAVINGS: $175

300 SHARES AT $40
Typical full-service broker: $245
Least expensive discounter: $25
Savings (percentage): 90%
SAVINGS: $220

100 SHARES AT $50
Typical full-service broker: $105
Least expensive discounter: $23
Savings (percentage) 78%
SAVINGS: $82

300 SHARES AT $75
Typical full-service broker: $310
Least expensive discounter: $25
Savings (percentage): 92%
SAVINGS: $275

100 SHARES AT $100
Typical full-service broker: $105
Least expensive discounter: $23
Savings (percentage): 78%
SAVINGS: $82

A Few Other Observations about Discounters

There are a few other points worth noting that are not necessarily apparent from these statistics:

Discounters' commissions vary enormously. The average discounter's commissions averaged 2.1 times to be the least expensive for our 25-trade test group and got as high as 3.27 times the least expensive. Even within the deep discounter group, some will charge nearly twice as much as others. Apart from differences among different discounters, savings are also affected by two other factors:

- Savings are greater for higher value transactions.
- Savings are greater for higher priced stocks.

Sharebroker and valuebroker discounters tend to fall into two groups. These are: those who charge on the basis of the value of the transaction and those who charge strictly on the basis of the number of shares. We call the former "valuebrokers" and the latter "sharebrokers." When you're selecting within a category, the valuebrokers will tend to be less expensive for lower price shares and the sharebrokers for higher priced shares (since they charge a flat amount per share).

There is no single, least expensive discounter for all trades. We found 8 different firms who were least expensive for our 25 benchmark transactions.

Complementary pairing. Since some brokers offer the best price for low-priced shares, and others for high-priced shares, you can reduce your cost by using two brokers. Another profitable form of pairing is to select one broker for options and another for stocks. Or in some cases, brokers are very low cost, but have relatively high minimums. You use them for high value transactions and select another for smaller purchases. We call this matching "complementary pairing." It can significantly reduce costs further for certain investors.

A word of caution: Anyone can call themselves a discounter. Some firms offered only a modest 20 to 30% discount, and in a few isolated cases actually charged more than full-commission brokers for some trades. The averages obscure the existence of these high-priced firms.

Commission Costs—The Gap Keeps Growing

Mercer conducted the first *Discount Brokerage Survey* in 1983 in connection with the publication of *70% Off: The Investor's Guide to Discount Brokerage* (New York: Facts on File).

The commission sampled in the *1983 Survey* included 16 trades, ranging from 500 shares at $10 to 200 shares at $100. The smallest value transaction was $3000—100 shares at $30. The largest was $20,000—200 shares at $100. The average value of the 16 transactions was $9594.

Comparing the commissions in the *1983 Survey* with the *1989 Survey.*, we found:

Full-service brokers	+20.83%
20th least expensive discounter:	+ 6.31%
10th least expensive discounter:	+ 2.4 %
Least expensive discounter:	− 1.01%

The full-service brokers charges increased about 21%, roughly the rate of inflation, while the least expensive discounters actually charge slightly less for the trade on average in 1989 than they did in 1983. Other discounters fell in between. One fact is clear: The gap has been increasing.

A major reason for this increase lies in the difference between the way that discounters and full-service firms run. As noted, discounters are computer-driven operations; they have benefited from the continuing increases in productivity in the computer industry which has driven prices down while increasing capacity.

By contrast in the full-service industry, much of the cost is in salaries and overhead. Unlike computers, sales representatives' salaries and landlord's bills have not come down in price; they've gone up. So full-service firms' costs have risen.

It would not be surprising if the gap increased at an even greater rate in the 1990s. Recent pronouncements by full-service firms suggest that they will be increasing their rates even more sharply than usual to help deal with the flood of red ink which has swamped Wall Street. A few discounters have increased rates, but there does not appear to be a wave of increases in the foreseeable future.

OPTIONS

If you view buying an option as the equivalent of buying a ticket in the state lottery, then it doesn't matter much which broker you use. You're not investing much; it's just a flyer. However, if you systematically trade options, you really should be using a discounter; if you trade them actively, you should be using a deep discounter. If there was ever an investor who *should* be using a deep discounter, it's the options trader, who gets hit with higher commissions two ways.

First, the turnover is higher. You can hold a stock for a decade or a century; options' lives are measured in days or months. This means high turnover. If you want to remain fully invested in options for a year, with an average maturity of 2 months, you need to buy those options 6 times and sell them 2 times. That's a 600% turnover. Furthermore, because the value of the typical options transaction is smaller than the typical stock transaction, the commissions tend to be higher as a percentage of principal. This means the costs are higher, so the savings are greater as a proportion of capital.

Based on the *Mercer 1989 Options Commissions Survey*, I found that the lowest deep discounter averaged $36 per trade for our basket of options trades averaging $3300 per trade. The typical full-service broker averaged $156 per trade. The details are set forth in Table 5.1.

Assuming a 400% turnover rate, which is less than the example given above and certainly not high for an options trader, the savings using the lowest cost discounter versus a full-service broker is $480 per year [($156 − $36) × 4] for each $3300 invested.

These numbers speak for themselves. This means a discounter costs 4.4% per year; a full-service broker, 18.9% per year. If you feel that you can give away 14.5% per year and still make money, you are either a genius or grossly overestimate the potential returns in the market. While the firms that are lowest cost for stocks will not necessarily rank in the same order for other instruments such as options, there is sufficient correlation that the general reader should find the deep discount list in the Directory in Appendix A to be helpful. The active options trader

Table 5.1. Commission Comparison—Options Full-Service vs. Least Expensive Discounter

Price per Option	$ 10	$ 20	$ 10	$ 5	$ 5	$ 2	$ 2	$ 2	$ 1	$ 1	Average	Pct of Transaction Value
Number of Contracts	5	1	3	10	5	10	25	5	25	50		
Value of Trade	$5000	$2000	$3000	$5000	$2500	$2000	$5000	$1000	$2500	$5000	$3300	
Least Expensive	$ 30	$ 20	$ 24	$ 40	$ 25	$ 30	$ 60	$ 20	$ 50	$ 62	$ 36	1.09%
Typical Full-Service	$ 140	$ 60	$ 100	$ 190	$ 110	$ 140	$ 270	$ 80	$ 230	$ 240	$ 156	4.73%
Savings	79%	67%	76%	79%	77%	79%	78%	75%	78%	74%	76%	

Source: *Mercer 1989 Discount Brokerage Survey—Options*

may want to refer to the *Mercer Options Survey*. (See Appendix D, The Discount Publications Directory.)

BONDS

The sad truth is that discounters won't save the typical investor much when buying bonds. In some cases, they might even be more expensive than a full-service broker. A major reason is that full-service brokers' charges for bonds have always been very moderate. The standard charge for bonds was historically $5 per bond, subject to whatever the firms' minimum charge per trade may be—typically $25 to $50.

Since most bonds are issued in $1000 denominations, $5 commission for a $1000 face value bond is only a .5% commission. That compares with the 2 to 2.5% rate that full-service brokers typically charge for stocks. Therefore, bond commission rates with full-service brokers are 80% lower than stock commission rates.

The *Mercer 1989 Bonds and Bills Survey* (see Appendix D) found that for a 5-bond trade, discounters typically charge $25 to $50. For a 10-bond trade, they typically charge $34 to $75. Savings can become insignificant for large trades—as low as $80 for a 50-bond trade (less than $2 per bond). But few investors will buy $50,000 of a single corporate bond. (Treasury bonds are a different story, and discussed in a later chapter.)

If you're buying an existing bond, the spread between the bid and the asked price may be a larger cost factor than commissions. A higher percentage of bonds than stocks trades off the exchanges, and for many bonds, the market is thinner. If you're trying to keep your costs down, don't place a market order. Ask for the "bid" and "asked" quotation. If the spread between them is wide, take your time in buying. Leave your order in the middle somewhere until you get a reasonable execution.

For that limited number of investors who do trade bonds frequently and in size, it is worth shopping. If you're buying 20 bonds, the lowest discounters will charge less than half the highest. If you're buying 50, the range is 4 to 1.

Those firms identified as deep discounters in the Directory include some with very good rates for bonds. However, some firms which don't qualify as deep discounters for stock trading may have quite competitive rates as well. If you trade both stocks and bonds, it's a good case for complementary pairing as described previously. Pick one firm for bonds; another, for stocks.

YOU DON'T ONLY SAVE ON COMMISSIONS

Stock commissions are not the only way to save through a discounter. Some discounters offer what may be the lowest cost loans available anywhere to the average individual—margin.

Margin developed a bad name in the 1929 market, and it has never quite shaken it. At that time you could borrow whatever the brokerage firm would lend. If the firm decided to let you put 10 cents down on the dollar, then you could buy $10,000 of stock with only $1000 down. They lent you the rest on margin. The problem came when the market crashed. When your $10,000 stock dropped 10%, you didn't just lost 10%; you lost 100% of your investment. If you were lucky. If you were unlucky, they didn't close out your account fast enough, it dropped another 10%, and you lost twice your investment.

The experience of losing 200% of your investment in two days tends to leave an impression; in this case, it did so on an entire generation which lasted for decades. The effects can still be felt today.

Since that time, margin lending has been regulated. The amount that you can borrow on margin will vary from time to time and depends upon the security that you purchase. Typically, an investor must put up at least half of the cost of the security.

Let's assume that you've decided to treat your family to a very special vacation in Europe this summer and need $15,000 to finance it. You have several credit cards, a good credit record with your local bank, and you own marginable stocks with a market value of $50,000 which you don't want to sell. (Some stocks are not marginable—primarily over-the-counter stocks and low priced stocks.) Where do you go for a loan?

If you use installment payments on your credit card to pay for the trip, it's going to cost approximately 18%—a little more or less depending on which card you use. If you go to the bank, you're likely to pay 2 to 4% over the prime lending rate for an unsecured loan, even with a good credit record. And there might be some additional points or closing costs.

What about your broker? If you look at the Discount Brokerage Directory, you will see a number of brokers that will lend you money near or below "broker's call rates." What does this mean? Broker's call is the rate at which brokers can typically borrow money. It is published in all the business newspapers, and is nearly always below the prime rate. The prime rate is supposed to be the rate at which banks will lend to their prime customers, but it is not. Their best corporate customers can borrow for less. For that reason, some banks now call it their reference rate rather than prime rate. But the prime rate persists, and like broker's call, it is listed in the newspaper.

Let's do some comparisons. As of the time of writing, here's how your alternative loan costs would look. (They will change as interest rates change, but these numbers are typical of normal spreads.)

Credit card: 18%
Bank unsecured loan at 3% over prime: 13%
Loan from discounter lending at brokers' call: 9.25%

With the discounter, there are no closing points or application fees. There are no credit checks and no loan applications to fill out, or bankers to meet.

The only thing you need to borrow money this way is to have marginable securities in a margin account. Establishing the account is just a matter of filling out a form. The margin account does permit the firm to include your securities among its assets, much the same as when you put your money in a bank. But they are held in a margin account in your name, are insured by SIPC, and can be removed from the margin account whenever you pay off the margin loan.

Although margin rates are terrific, this practice should not be overdone. If you margin to the hilt, take out the full 50%, you will receive a "margin call" soon if the value of your stocks drop. If you can't meet that call very fast—within days—the firm can and *will* sell your securities to raise the necessary cash.

This fate can be readily averted. Don't margin to the hilt. Borrow 25% instead of 50%. Then you will not face a margin call unless the value of the securities in your name falls by more than 25%. Since margin rules can get a bit complicated, and may vary from firm to firm, its a good idea to speak with the firm's margin department before taking out a loan.

If your collateral and loan are substantial, the savings will be substantial as well. On a $100,000 loan, you could save $4000 annually, compared to a bank loan. Enough to even reconsider your grandfather's warning to avoid margin borrowing at all cost.

CHAPTER 6

Finding the Right Broker in the Discount Brokerage Directory

Now that you know the theory, the time has come to turn it into practice. If you want to enter the doors of the right discount brokerage office, the Discount Brokerage Directory holds the key.

The complete Directory can be found in Appendix A. It is excerpted from the 1990 version of the *Mercer Discount Financial Directory* (see Appendix D, Discount Publications Directory). But since appendices often go unread, and this one contains such valuable information, this chapter provides a brief summary of what the Discount Brokerage Directory contains and how to use it.

SCOPE

As far as I know, the Directory includes every major independent discount broker that has been in business in recent years. Although new firms spring up each year, and some smaller ones may not be listed, the *Mercer Directory* is generally considered *the* definitive directory on this subject.

When it comes to banks, the Directory is less comprehensive because there are so many banks offering some form of discount brokerage. Hopefully, most of the banks that are significantly involved in the business are included. But you may know of a local bank that offers discount brokerage which is not listed. Its exclusion does not imply that it doesn't deserve to be listed; if you think it's worthwhile, contact Mercer and it will be included in future directories.

FEATURES

Typically, 17 key features are covered for independents; a few less for banks. The following list outlines and explains what is covered.

Name and Address

The address listed is that of the principal office. Banks normally offer brokerage information throughout their branch system, although trading and detailed questions may be referred to a central branch. Therefore, if you recognize your bank's name, but the location listed is not your branch, the odds are very good that you can use your branch.

Interstate bank holding companies vary in policy. If you recognize the name of your bank in the index, but it is in a different state, you should call and check. They probably offer discount brokerage in your state.

Telephone Numbers

The local number and the 800 number are listed.

One of the refreshing aspects of dealing with a discount broker is that they are very open with their information. They will gladly provide you with their commission schedules, no questions asked.

You will find this a pleasant change from the usual response if you have ever asked a typical full-service broker what commissions they charge. Their responses run the gamut from hemming and hawing, to acting offended—as if you had asked

Finding the Right Broker in the Discount Brokerage Directory

to see their personal income tax or undertake some elaborate research project.

Don't be too hard on your local broker. It seems to be the policy throughout much of the full-service brokerage industry to keep their commission rates under wraps. While their computers are all programmed in accordance with their commission schedules, they generally do not permit their brokers to release the schedule to the public. Sometimes, their local brokers don't even have a copy.

Your broker can get you the rate on a case-by-case basis, but it's awkward to ask for the cost every time you trade. After a while, you stop asking, which is precisely what the system is designed to make you do.

By contrast, you will find discounters to be a breath of fresh air. They don't get offended if you ask about the terms and conditions of the relationship. They don't make you ask about the cost every time you trade; their commission schedules tell you exactly how much each trade costs.

Other Office Locations

This provides an indication of the firm's scope, but as noted, especially in the case of banks, it's not designed to be comprehensive.

Insurance Protection

All firms should provide the standard $500,000 insurance offered by the SIPC. Some provide excess insurance, extending the SIPC coverage to several million. This doesn't make much difference unless your account's value exceeds $500,000, but it could be interpreted as suggesting a degree of confidence by the excess insurance carrier in the firm. Where supplemental coverage is provided, the amount of that coverage is listed.

Order Handling

There are two basic methods used to service customers. One is to assign a specific account executive to each account; the other is to use a team system. This section tells you which system each firm uses and whether that firm uses registered representatives exclusively to take orders.

There is no reason to believe that one system works better than the other, but if you like dealing with the same person every time, you may prefer an account executive system.

Clearinghouse

This section identifies the clearinghouse used. A well-known clearinghouse may be reassuring to some investors because this is often the firm that handles or holds your securities in their account, rather than the brokers themselves.

Firm's Exchange Membership

Membership on the New York Stock Exchange or other exchanges are listed. NASD (National Association of Securities Dealers) membership, which tends to be standard, is not listed. This does not imply better trades, but could indicate a better capitalized firm.

Special Account Requirements

This section notes out-of-the-ordinary account requirements of two types: (1) initial account requirements, such as cash required to be in the account before making a trade, and (2) ongoing account requirements. Options may be subject to account limitations more restrictive than those noted here.

Commission Structure

If the designation "DD" appears, this indicates that the firm is designated as a deep discounter. This means that the broker has been identified as one of the 30 independent brokers (or 40 bank brokers) with the lowest average cost for either Mercer's sample of trades averaging approximately $6000 (LO) or $13,000 (HI). If the firm appears on both lists, then both are listed, for example, DD (HI, LO). If your objective is to find the lowest commission costs, you would look for a deep discounter with a HI or LO—depending on which transaction size corresponds most closely to your own. However, don't forget that there are significant differences among the deep discounters both in their average pricing and in how well their pricing matches your trading pattern.

Also indicated is the type of cost system. Mercer has coined the terms for the two types of commission structures used: Those who charge on the basis of the value of the transaction are termed "valuebrokers" and those who charge strictly according to the number of shares traded are termed "sharebrokers."

Margin Interest Costs

The method and level of the charges is described.

As noted in Chapter 5, these charges are worth noting and comparing with your current loan rates. The odds are good that they are much lower. You will also note that different discounters offer a considerable variety of rates.

Interest Paid on Cash Balances

The rate of interest being paid, the method, and the minimum balance necessary for the client to receive it are noted.

Sometimes, the firm uses a rather undefined internal system which results in something related to, but usually below, money market rates. I don't attempt to spell this out. The easiest way to understand the bottom line is often not to ask for an explanation, but to ask for the rate they are currently paying and compare it with market rates.

Additional Charges

Delivery charges, limit order surcharges, and other possible fees are outlined.

Date Firm Established

The date when the firm was founded is given. (It may have begun to offer discount brokerage services later.)

States Where Licensed to Do Business

This category is subject to frequent change and does not necessarily preclude occasional stray accounts in other states.

Investment Products

This section identifies investment products offered by the firm. If you prefer a firm that offers a broader line of products and services, pay particular attention to the last three items in the Directory. The high product service options will stand out here.

Services

Publications or other services provided to assist the investor in making investment decisions are noted.

Notes

Unusual features of the firm are noted here.

These last two categories are constantly expanding. Each edition of the Directory seems to list new features and services.

DEEP DISCOUNTER DESIGNATION

As noted, DD appears next to those brokers that have been identified as among the nation's least expensive for each of two categories: (1) lower value transactions ($6350), and (2) higher value transaction ($13,500). Separate rankings are provided for banks and independent brokers. To be more precise in arriving at the least expensive, 30 brokers were identified that had the lowest average commissions for: (1) 14 separate stock transactions averaging $6350, and (2) 12 separate stock transactions averaging $13,458.

If we reached the 30th broker and the next one had the identical price, that firm was included as well. It didn't make much difference for the independents, but the pricing of some of the banks is so similar that we ended up with 40 banks in the "top 30" using this rule. In the case of banks, a separate geographic listing of the least expensive banks is also provided. (This is not necessary for the brokers, since most of them will take accounts from investors in any part of the country.)

To reiterate some of the conclusions of Chapter 5: If you're looking for the least expensive brokers, the independent brokers' average commission is considerably lower than banks, and the deep discounters are the lowest of the independents.

For example, when averaging the lower values and the higher ones, I found that the average commission cost for independent brokers was $53 for a transaction averaging just under $10,000. By contrast, the average bank commission charge for a similar transaction was $80. Expressed in percentage terms, the average of these independent charges was about .5%; the

Finding the Right Broker in the Discount Brokerage Directory 61

average bank, about .8%. This compares with over 2% for the full-commission brokers. However, there is considerable variation even within this low-cost group. Average bank commissions over 20 trades ranged from $47 to $92 and independent broker commissions ranged from $34 to $72.

Even where average cost for the benchmark trades is similar, there are significant variations among these firms. For example, some are better for high-priced trades; some, for low. If you are an active trader, you should compare their commission schedules with the trades you plan to make before entering a trade. For this reason, it is critical to examine these commission schedules in detail. If you'd rather not take the time to compare the commission schedules, you may be interested in the *Mercer Surveys* (see Appendix D, The Discount Publications Directory).

Before opening an account, it's important to review all the information provided with the account application. Like any directory, this one will become outdated over time. Or firms may have made changes just after our latest update. Or we may have just made a mistake.

Major changes are not likely for most brokers. Firms seldom change their commission schedules overnight, or radically alter their product line. So you can use the Directory to research your choice with confidence, but reserve your final decision until you've reviewed the firm's latest brochure.

Part Two
Mutual Funds

CHAPTER 7

The New American Way to Invest

The mutual fund has been on the American investment stage since the 1920s, but it didn't get a feature-length role until the 1980s. Then it all came together; its fortunes exploded. The mutual fund became the star of American investment.

Its rise mirrors the career of Peter Lynch, the legendary manager of the Fidelity Magellan fund—which made its investors 25 times their money over roughly a 15-year period and outperformed all the competition by a huge margin. When Lynch started managing the fund for Fidelity in the mid-1970s, this preeminent fund group offered a handful of funds and had $4 billion under management. When Lynch retired in 1990 at the age of 46, Fidelity offered 145 separate funds with over $104 billion under management.

Fidelity's story is the story of the mutual fund industry. From modest beginnings, the mutual fund industry grew to over 3000 funds by 1990, with approximately $1 trillion under management—rivaling the entire U.S. banking system and growing much faster.

This enormous growth has derived primarily from growth in the U.S. economy, appreciation in the value of assets, and switching of funds from bank accounts into mutual funds. But to a modest degree, it has come at the expense of direct purchase of equities. While the actual value of stocks and bonds held directly by the U.S. public has increased in the past decade, the percentage of household assets held in stocks has declined from about 25 to 20%.

Clearly, Americans increasingly prefer to pay a middleman to manage their money. The popularity of mutual funds is so great, and their advantages so apparent, that the value of this development is seldom questioned. Is the mutual fund the great equalizer of twentieth century investment, putting the world's top money managers at the disposal of the average investor, or have we simply become a nation of "couch potato" investors? Are mutual funds the junk food of the American investment scene? They are convenient. They are easy to use. They are not high priced. And they come nicely packaged. But is a consistent diet of mutual funds good for your financial health?

For many people, especially the smaller investor, mutual funds are a good way to invest. But many investors are using the wrong mutual fund and some should not be using certain mutual funds at all. They would do better to invest directly.

There is no simple formula that can provide a quick answer to the question of which fund to use or when to avoid mutual funds. That is why this and the next six chapters are dedicated to finding the best fund for different investments and helping you decide when to avoid funds altogether. The serious investor may also wish to consult Appendix D, The Discount Publications Directory, to find out the names of more publications on this topic.

A MUTUAL FUND PRIMER

The Merits of Mutual Funds

A trillion dollar industry doesn't spring up in two decades without some clear advantages.

1. *Diversification* is the first law of investment. The mutual fund lets the small investor reduce his or her risk level. With as little as a few hundred dollars, you can buy into a diversified portfolio of stocks, bonds, money market instruments, and other securities, at home or abroad.
2. *Convenience* sells. The fund lets you write checks, provides your year-end tax forms, and in most cases, offers you the freedom to switch from one type of investment to another, just by making a telephone call.
3. *Professional management* is available. This saves the investor time and presumably buys first-class managers, since legions of investors banded together into a mutual fund creates a pool of hundreds of millions or billions of dollars—enough to attract top talent.
4. *A track record* that you can verify.
5. *Costs* can be reasonable for some uses, if you know which funds to use and how to identify them.

This chapter will review the various types of mutual funds, outline their function and development, and conclude with a discussion of how to identify those with the best performance records. This will establish the basis for the discussion of cost savings in the following chapters.

Basic Fund Types and a Hybrid Structure

While there are some 3000 funds, with the number seeming to swell daily, there are only two basic organization structures. They are known as the open-end and closed-end funds. There is also a hybrid known as the Unit Investment Trust which will be discussed later.

The distinction between the open and closed fund is more than academic; it has significant implications for the pricing action and profit potential of your investment. At times, you will find it advantageous to switch between an open- and closed-end fund to take advantage of their different characteristics.

The Open-End Mutual Fund. If you hear someone talk about a mutual fund, they are generally referring to an open-end fund. It is open-end because the number of shares is *not* fixed. When people buy shares, the number outstanding increases; when they sell shares, it decreases.

When the fund is formed, its management invests the proceeds in the equities, bonds, or investments designated in the charter and described in the prospectus (the legal document which every fund is required by law to provide to a prospective investor before he or she purchases shares). The value of your shares, known as the net asset value, is equal to the percentage of the fund's shares you own, multiplied by the value of the fund. Management performs that calculation every night (no longer a great chore since computers) to prepare the price you see quoted in the mutual funds section of your newspaper each day.

The fund's stock does not trade in the open market, but the fund's sponsor stands ready to buy or sell your shares at the end of the day at the price computed that day. This means you have complete liquidity and a known method of determining price.

The Closed-End Fund. Most investors are familiar with the open-end mutual fund, which is easily the dominant form of fund with 90% of the market, but the closed-end fund has found newly won popularity. Since 1989, the number of closed-end funds has increased from 49 to over 210, and the assets under management from $6.8 billion to $52 billion—nearly a 700% increase!

Whereas the mutual fund sponsor makes the market for an open-end fund, the price for a closed-end fund is set by the market itself. The fund is initially launched through an Initial Public Offering, like any stock, and thereafter trades in the stock market like any other stock.

You buy or sell shares in a closed-end fund in the same way that you buy or sell shares of IBM: You call your broker. The price at which you buy or sell is determined in the same way as IBM's: by the marketplace. When more people want to sell than buy, the price drops; when more want to buy than sell, the price rises. Since the supply of shares is fixed, the prevailing sentiment will tend to drive the price of shares to a premium or a discount to the value of the underlying assets.

The following example illustrates the difference between closed- and open-end funds. With an open-end fund, if one share represents one-millionth of the number of shares outstanding, and the value of the fund's portfolio is $10 million that day, then each share will be worth $10 ($10 million/1 million).

In the case of a closed-end fund, the market sets the price. The market's price will bear some relationship to the underlying value of the fund, but it will vary. Closed-end bond fund prices generally tend to stay closer to net asset value than stocks because the price is supported by their yield. If they trade at too great a discount, their yield would rise above the yield offered by bonds of comparable risk and buyers would come in, driving the price up and the yield down. If the price rose too high, the opposite would occur.

Stock funds, however, are not so tightly tethered to reality. In early 1990, the premiums on funds which invested exclusively in the stocks of certain foreign countries swelled with speculative fever, briefly approaching 100% for some funds. This meant that people were paying $2 for every $1 of stock in the fund, even though you could buy these stocks on the open market in these countries for $1. What really happened was that investors suddenly developed an interest in certain foreign markets, and there were not enough shares of these funds available at the time this surge of interest developed, causing the prices to surge. These price swings create pitfalls for the unwary and opportunities for the astute investor, which will be discussed in Chapter 13.

Unit Investment Trusts. The Unit Investment Trust (UIT) can be described as a half-open fund with absentee ownership. After the initial offering is organized, you generally can sell, but not buy, shares. The managers don't actively manage the fund, just poke their heads in every once in a while to make sure the house is in order. Minimum management is the distinctive feature of a UIT and its principal advantage. Since management is minimal, the same is true of management costs and commissions, since little trading takes place.

Until recently, UITs have been used exclusively as a vehicle to purchase bonds. A portfolio of bonds is identified and purchased at the time the UIT is organized. Unless a drastically adverse event occurs which results in a downgrade of the issuer's credit, the bonds are held to maturity. The UIT has a fixed life (e.g., 20 years) and is dissolved at the end of that period.

This low-cost approach makes good sense for high-quality fixed income securities. You know at the outset what yield to expect for the life of the trust, and you will receive the highest yield possible since the management fees and transactions are minimal.

The Types of Investments

Reportedly, there are limited partnerships which buy bubble gum cards. The mutual fund industry has not yet reached that point, but it's closing the gap. Like the old Howard Johnson ice cream stores, they found that having 28 flavors was not enough to beat the competition. So the number of funds keep expanding.

The vast majority of the over 3000 funds currently available are variations on three basic themes—stocks, bonds, and money funds. Within each of these groups there are many subspecialties, domestic or international stock funds, taxable or nontaxable bond funds, and money funds.

Stock Funds During the 1980s. At the end of 1980s, there were over 1000 stock funds in existence with almost $250 billion in aggregate assets. For an industry to reach that size, it must be doing something right. What stock funds were able to do in the 1980s was make money for their investors: A $10,000 investment in a typical equity mutual fund in 1980 was worth about $40,000 at the end of the decade. The 1980s was truly a decade for equities. Stock funds outperformed bonds and money markets by a substantial margin. While the amount of appreciation was exceptional, the superior performance of stock funds is consistent with the longer term trend.

Several studies have shown that stocks outperform fixed income and money markets over the long-term. The key word is "long-term." You might have had difficulty in persuading investors of the value of equities after the 500-point decline in the 1987 crash. And occasionally, equities turn in a bad decade—the mid-1960s to mid-1970s was a bad decade; the 1980s, a great one.

The top performing funds were the *global* and *international* funds. Both types of funds invest in foreign stocks, but international funds invest almost exclusively in foreign stocks, while globals may have large U.S. holdings as well. The globals were up some 430%; the internationals, a whopping 480%. A $10,000 investment in an average international fund was worth $58,000 10 years later!

The 1980s saw surprisingly similar performances among domestic funds, considering their diverse objectives and strategies. These are categorized in the prospectus which every investor must receive before investing as: growth, aggressive growth, capital appreciation, growth income, equity income, and balanced (or similar terms).

Whatever they might be called, most general categories fell within 10% of each other over the decade, showing appreciation from roughly 320 to 350%. One exception, the small company growth funds, appreciated somewhat less than 300%—still quite close considering the differences.

Bond Funds. Unlike a stock fund, a bond fund offers investors a fairly good idea of what yield to expect if the bonds are held to maturity. In the late 1980s, with inflation below 8% and bonds near 10%, investors could earn substantial real returns on their money after inflation. In this climate, bond funds found favor. By the end of the decade, assets in open- and closed-end bond funds were nearly $300 billion. Over 600 taxable bond funds offer a variety of maturities (short-term to longer-term), risk levels (U.S. Government to junk bonds), and domestic or international issues.

For the investor in a high tax bracket, there are a variety of general purpose municipal bond funds as well as a large number that restrict themselves to issuers in a single state, thereby offering residents of that state the opportunity to receive income which is free from federal, state, or local government taxes.

Money Funds. Money funds are the modern-day equivalent of putting your cash in the bank. They offer convenience similar to a bank account, checking privileges, and, typically, a higher yield than your local bank account. They are essentially higher-interest banking by mail.

Over longer periods of time, money funds, like bank accounts, have underperformed both fixed-income (bond) funds and stock (equity) funds. In the 1980s, the difference was quite substantial. You would have ended the decade with roughly twice as much profit if in 1980 you had invested in a stock fund instead of a money fund. However, in the previous decade you might have done better in a money fund—with a lot less risk.

Money funds look good when other investments look bad. In a period of persistently rising inflation, such as the 1970s, stocks underperform, bonds fall, and money funds shine. Despite the relatively narrow range of yield on their investments, some money funds offer returns which are $1/2$ to 1% higher than comparable money funds. Finding these funds, identifying the associated risks, and other aspects of money funds will be discussed in Chapter 11.

CHAPTER 8

How to Select Mutual Funds... and When to Avoid Them

There are three rules for investing in mutual funds:

1. The cost of couch potato investing is high. Don't use mutual funds needlessly.
2. When you do buy funds, strike a balance between cost and performance.
3. Always buy from the discounters of the mutual fund industry.

Chapters 8 through 13 will discuss how mutual funds fit into investments in the following areas: stocks, bonds and Unit Investment Trusts, money market funds, international funds, and closed-end funds. In each case, I will: (1) describe my method for selecting funds, (2) provide a list of funds that meet my criterion, and (3) discuss when you should not use mutual funds for these type of investments.

Before taking a look at these five different categories of investments, it's worth noting that there are several broad generalizations about mutual funds and their costs that cut across category lines.

QUALITY

In looking for the lowest cost discount broker, one could look exclusively at the commission rate and ignore the product. Whether you buy IBM shares from a discounter or full-service broker, you are still getting IBM. As long as the broker's execution and reporting is satisfactory, management is not an issue. A $100 savings is a $100 savings. There's no quality issue.

Mutual funds are different. You don't want to pay $100 less per year and buy into a mutual fund whose performance is at the bottom of the pack. Where quality management can be identified and is meaningful, it's worth paying the difference. The best measure of quality is past performance. But as every prospectus tells you, past performance is no guarantee of future performance. And many funds have gone on to prove that fact, to their investors' dismay.

So, where does management really make a difference? As the following chapters will explain, in some cases money managers make less difference to investment results than you would imagine—or than they would have you to believe. If the management doesn't make much difference, why pay too much for it? If you have a tonsillectomy, you don't need to hire a brain surgeon.

Appendix E, The Mutual Funds Directory, identifies and provides essential information about stock funds, bond funds, money market funds, international funds, and closed-end funds which offer an appropriate balance between expenses and performance.

How and where the balance is struck between cost and performance will be explored in subsequent chapters. It varies for each type of investment. But there is one conclusion that cuts across all investment lines—always buy funds from the discounters of the mutual fund industry.

As a fan of discount brokerage firms, I regret to report that there is no truth to rumors that discount brokerage firms offer discount mutual funds. They do not. Most don't offer any. Those which do offer them, such as the Big Three, generally provide them as a convenience to clients for a small service fee.

If you want the lowest price, go straight to the discounters of the industry—the no-load and low-load fund sponsors whose ads appear in the financial papers but whose sales representatives never call. That's because they don't pay their sales reps.

THE DISCOUNTERS OF THE MUTUAL FUND INDUSTRY

If you were offered two identical investments, would you elect to pay $10,000 or $10,928 for the same investment? It is an enduring tribute to the persuasive power of the American salesman that, until recently, most investors who bought mutual funds paid $10,928.

Many of these investors probably did not know that they had a choice. The so-called load funds, those sold with a sales fee (load), are sold by commissioned brokers, sales reps, insurance agents, and others who make solicited or unsolicited sales calls. Accordingly, you're not likely to receive the following call.

> *Mr. Jones, How are you today? How is the Misses? I'm calling to let you know about the Zilch fund. It has a great record. Investors are pouring in. The fund manager was just written up in the* New York Times.
>
> *But, Mr. Jones, in the spirit of not merely full but total disclosure, I must point out that there are a dozen other funds that all have equally good records, and you can save $928 by buying from them directly instead of writing your check to me.*

Unfortunately, total disclosure telephone sales representatives would have a rather short career, perhaps even shorter than total disclosure politicians. A sales rep with integrity will not lie and will not sell a product unless he or she believes it is good for the customer. But the rep is not expected to point out that he or she sells a good product, but someone else sells that same product for less. Finding the alternatives is the investor's job. It is still a caveat emptor world.

The competition is the no-load fund—the "discounter" of the mutual fund industry. This fund is sold through advertisements, word-of-mouth, and, occasionally, direct mailings. The investor buys into the fund by sending a check directly to the fund sponsor, bypassing the sales rep. No-load funds really are discounters. Whereas the typical load fund will charge up to 8.5% commission up front, the no-load fund charges nothing. It's a zero-cost discounter.

That is not to say that there are no expenses. No-load fund sponsors and managers also have to make a living. They do this in the same way as load fund managers—by charging a management fee and expenses, which is discussed later. But they do not charge any sales fee.

The case for using a no-load fund is even stronger than the case for using a discount broker. If you have a good, full-service broker, you pay more, but you will get good investment advice and personalized service. This can save you time, make you money, and make your life a little more pleasant. Investors with such a broker may consider the added commission money well spent.

In the case of a load fund, you receive nothing in return. Once the fund is sold, the sales rep has nothing further to do with its management. Nor should you assume the sales fee is going to buy better management. The sales fee does not go to the manager; it goes to the broker. The manager never sees it. Studies confirm that the sales load has no impact on management. No-load and load funds tend to turn in similar performances over time. There's simply no evidence that you're getting more by paying more.

The classic 8.5% sales load can amount to a tidy sum over time. Imagine that you have invested $10,000 in a load stock fund and $10,000 in a no-load stock fund at the beginning of the 1980s. (Assume that $850 was the fee for the load fund, and the $850 you "saved" by choosing a no-load was applied toward your investment.) If your investments earned a 16% annual return during this prosperous period, that sales fee would have cost you *over $4000* by the end of the decade. That is because a no-load fund would have invested that $850, and with compounding, its value mounts. Your load fund would have done quite well—appreciated to over $40,000, but the no-load would have appreciated to over $44,000.

In the "roaring eighties," you certainly would have had no argument with the sales rep who sold you a good load fund. You still made a lot of money. But $4000 on a $10,000 investment is not peanuts, and even in the 1980s, that 8.5% difference was statistically significant. As previously noted, most categories of equity funds turned in surprisingly similar performances during the decade. They fell within 10% of each other, showing appreciation from roughly 320 to 350%.

What was not noted is that these performance ratings do not take the sales fee into account. If the fee was considered, the average no-load fund in any but the lowest category would have matched an average load fund in the top category, and a no-load fund in any other category would have beaten it. All that was statistically necessary to secure a place in the top quartile in the 1980s was to buy a no-load fund in any one of these major categories (except small company growth). (I use the term statistically necessary because there's always a chance of a lemon in any group.)

Comparisons in the financial press frequently blur the performance distinction between load and no-load funds by ignoring the sales load in reporting results. They show the appreciation of a dollar after it has entered the fund, but ignore the front-end load—the fact that up to $850 of the $10,000 investment in a load fund never made it in the fund's door. It went to pay the ticket of admission. Rest assured that this is simply the methodology that the press uses to compute fund performance, not a conspiracy to hide fund costs. No-load funds can be readily distinguished from load funds in the mutual funds section of most publications. Most papers with financial sections show both the offering price and the net asset value of each of the mutual funds they list. If the net asset value and the offering price are the same, you know that it is a no-load fund. Alternatively they may list "NL" in one of the columns to indicate this fact.

In recent years, fund sponsors have learned how to repackage fees so that they do not all show up in the morning papers. A

Figure 8.1. Sample Fee Table from a Mutual Fund Prospectus

	International Equity Fund	Global Income Fund
Shareholder Transaction Expenses		
Sales Load imposed on purchases	None	None
Sales Load imposed on reinvested dividends	None	None
Redemption Fees	None	None
Exchange Fee	$5	$5
Annual Fund Operating Expenses (as a percentage of average net assets)		
Management Fees (after waiver in the case of the Global Income Fund	1.00%	0.00%
12b-1 Fees	0.15%	0.20%
Other Expenses	0.85%	1.99%
Total Fund Operating Expenses	2.00%	2.19%

Example:

You would pay the following expenses on a $1000 investment, assuming (1) 5% gross annual return, and (2) redemption at the end of each time period:

	International Equity Fund	Global Income Fund
1 year	$ 21	$ 23
3 years	66	72
5 years	116	127
10 years	264	289

THESE EXAMPLES SHOULD NOT BE CONSIDERED A REPRESENTATION OF FUTURE EXPENSES WHICH MAY BE MORE OR LESS THAN THOSE SHOWN.

favorite device is the so-called 12b-1 fee, named after the SEC regulation which authorized its imposition. This is a deferred sales fee—a commission on the installment plan. It takes the form of an annual charge, for example, .5% per year. This fee is paid to the fund sponsor, not the manager of the fund. It looks quite harmless, which is how it is intended to look, and typically is coupled with a somewhat lower front-end fee, for example, 5% instead of the once customary 8.5%. This allows the sales rep to cite the lower front-end fee, and mumble when it comes to discussing expenses.

If you are a long-term investor, however, this combination can end up costing more than the traditional 8.5% up-front fee.

Over 10 years, the 5% up-front and .5% annual fees would total 10%; after 15 years, 12.5%. In this case, any time after about the seventh or eighth year (allowing for the interest lost on money taken up front), the investor would have done better with the 8.5% up-front fee.

Until recently, another favorite fee in the modern sponsor's repertoire was the redemption or exit fee. But the SEC recently banned the imposition of exit fees on new funds; it showed the exit fee to the exit. The SEC has been quite successful in getting fund sponsors to clearly label their costs and expenses. All the major fees and expenses are clearly disclosed in the prospectus. Figure 8.1 is a sample from a mutual fund prospectus.

One cost which is not disclosed in the prospectus is the commission paid by the fund for brokerage commissions. For stock funds, the fee typically runs an additional .1 to .3% annually, depending on the turnover of the fund.[1] The exact numbers are available upon request from the fund.

THE COST OF COUCH POTATO INVESTING—
IS THE UNITED STATES OVERFUNDED?

Are we becoming a nation of couch potato investors hooked on junk food investments, overpaying, and taking risks for the convenience of having other people do our homework for us? In short, are we a nation that has too much in mutual funds? Are we overfunded?

Based upon the evidence of the past two decades, the odds are good that you will pay 10 to 20% of the return on your stock fund appreciation to the mutual fund company that manages your money. When you buy a mutual fund, you are hiring a middleman. That middleman will take title to your securities, make your investment decisions, determine your tax consequences, and charge a fee. As middlemen go, that fee is not high. Including commission, on average it ranges from roughly .8% for money funds to over 1.5% for stock funds. But this fee has a larger impact on your return than you might expect.

---
[1] Source: Renburg, W. (1989). Mutual funds and brokerage commissions. *AAII Journal*, 11(1), p. 11.

In the 1980s, that 1.5% for a stock fund reduced your return from stock investments by about 10%. On a one-time basis, it may be nothing to get too excited about, but it does mount up. If you invested $50,000 in a mutual fund, the fund appreciated at 15% per year for 10 years, that 1.5% fee reduced your appreciation over the 10-year period by almost $15,000! Buying, holding, and selling through a discounter with an average turnover would have cost only $3000. That's what a "little" 1.5% fee costs when imposed and annually compounded for a decade on an appreciating asset.

In the 1970s, that 1.5% fee would have looked a lot steeper. The average appreciation of equity funds during that period was less than 5%. If the 1990s turn in the same performance as the 1970s, over 20% of your appreciation could go to the middleman. That is steep in anyone's book. Moreover, expenses have been rising. A study by the Vanguard Group of funds indicated that expenses, on average, increased from .97 to 1.11% during the 1980s, with equity funds increasing by 36%, from between .99% and 1.35%. This does not include commissions paid by the funds on their trades.

What is equally disturbing is that these expenses increased during a period when expenses should have been declining. As mutual funds get larger, economies of scale *should* drive expenses lower. Some of the increase may be due to a rise in the level of services to shareholders, as some fund spokesmen claim, but much is undoubtedly due to funds simply paying themselves higher fees—not an altogether surprising phenomenon in a booming industry.

Whatever the reason, the probability that you will pay 10 to 20% of your appreciation to a mutual fund company is something to weigh against the frequent advantages of mutual funds.

CHAPTER 9

Stock Funds

Nowhere are the advantages and disadvantages of mutual funds better illustrated than in equity mutual funds—stock funds. The 1980s was a splendid decade for stock mutual funds. The sales were never higher; the returns to investors were seldom greater. Yet a disinterested observer could not help but notice that for each of the last seven years of the decade, the professional managers trailed the unmanaged Dow Jones Industrial and S&P 500 indices.

The average mutual fund investor ended the decade happy. A $50,000 investment in a typical equity mutual fund at the beginning of 1980 was worth over $200,000 by the end of the decade (if you invested in a no-load fund.) That return was far in excess of what bonds or bank accounts would have earned. Yet had that same investor placed that same $50,000 to buy the 30 stocks which comprise the Dow Jones Industrial Average, the portfolio would have been worth approximately $265,000 by the end of the decade, less 1.5 to 2% to cover the commissions for the initial purchase.

Professional managers offer various reasons to explain this performance. One frequent rebuttal is that the Dow is too narrow a basket of stocks. But even if the 500 stocks that comprise the S&P 500 Index were used instead of the 30-stock Dow Jones Industrial Average, the total would still have been greater than $250,000—some 25% greater than the average fund. And these fund averages assume you paid *no* sales fee. If you paid an 8% fee, the total of $200,000 quoted previously would be closer to $175,000.

Much of the discrepancy is due to fees. If mutual fund fees average 1.5% per year, over the course of a decade, you will hand over 15% of the portfolio's average value to the fund management. But even excluding fees, managers have generally underperformed the averages. There are some funds with outstanding records, but, as a group, professional managers during the 1980s did not prove that they were worth their cost.

A mutual fund certainly provides diversification, but with the cost of modern discount brokers so low, an investor with $50,000 can easily diversify. With the right discounter, purchasing 30 stocks for even a $50,000 portfolio need not cost more than 1.5 to 2% ($800 to $1000). That's not much more than you pay a typical mutual fund initially—assuming you buy a no-load fund. After that the stocks are free; the fund keeps charging.

If professional managers' results don't justify their costs, and an investor with a $50,000 portfolio can easily and inexpensively diversify, what are we left with? Free checking accounts and a vehicle that is valuable for the investor with a $10,000 portfolio? Is that all that a $300 billion industry comes down to in the end? Is it possible that the emperor is not wearing any clothes?

PETER LYNCH, WHERE ARE YOU?

Until now, our discussion has been based on the average mutual fund. By restricting yourself to investing in those funds whose past performance exceeded the averages, your fund's future performances may exceed the averages. Chapter 1, Stock Funds, in Appendix E, The Mutual Funds Directory, lists some of the best-performing no-load funds of the last five years. We can all

Stock Funds

hope to hitch our wagons to a fund whose wagonmaster is the next Peter Lynch.

There are other features that some investors will find well worth the fund's cost. (They are discussed at the end of this chapter.) But the hard statistics are sobering. It is far from clear that the mutual fund with its professional management is the ideal investment vehicle it is so often portrayed to be.

THE STOCK FUND DIRECTORY—
OUTSTANDING NO-LOAD FUNDS

The chapter on stock funds in Appendix E lists many of the best-performing no-load and low-load funds over the past five years. Within the category of these low-cost funds, I emphasized performance, because exceptional management *can* make a difference. The Peter Lynches have shown us this.

In some cases, the difference they make is substantial. Lynch averaged over 10% per year above the averages during extended periods. In areas such as bonds and money funds, even the superstars can't hope to add much more than 2%.

With the exception of the index funds, which will be discussed later, the variation in annual expenses among mutual funds is not sufficiently large for expenses to be placed ahead of performance. If the funds' performance is outstanding, and its expenses lie within a normal range of variation—which I define as 1 to 2% annually for a domestic equity fund—it is included in the Directory (Appendix E).

For this reason low-load funds are included on the list. I define a fund as low load if its sales fees—including up-front expenses, back-end expenses, and deferred annual fees (12b-1) —are less than 3% over a 5-year period. A purist would omit low-load funds. But in a number of cases, sponsors which generally offer no-load funds will impose a low load on their best-performing funds. In particular, a long-term investor, should not rule out a stock fund with a good performance for a cost that, amortized over 5 years, would not exceed .6% per year.

The justification for including funds with outstanding records, but some sales load and somewhat higher than average annual expenses, could also be viewed from a different perspective. If you're buying a mutual fund, you are buying in the hope of superior performance. Once you have eliminated most of the cost by avoiding load funds, it's worth paying a bit more for the realistic possibility of exceptional performance.

The Directory then provides essential information about many of the best performing no-load and low-load funds in the United States during the 1985–1990 period. I debated whether to use five years or ten years as the selection period, but settled on five, as it reflects the more current performance.

INDEX FUNDS

While there is no principal emphasis on costs in the Directory, one fund is so low cost that it bears mention: the index fund. It can be described as the mutual fund for discounter purists.

For individual investors, it's likely to remain this way. Even no-load fund sponsors have little incentive to sell this fund because its management fee is so low that they make little profit. Recently, its expense ratio was approximately .25%— approximately $1/6$ of the typical 1.5% annual cost of a stock mutual fund.

Nor does the fund have much sex appeal. It merely tries to approximate the S&P 500 Index, buying the stocks in the index or equivalents. You can't beat the averages with an index fund because you *are* the average. This approach to investing has little appeal to individuals, yet it is the hottest trend among many institutions. They are well aware of the disappointing performance numbers for professional managers. An increasing number of institutions have decided that low costs often increase investment returns more than professional management and have turned to index funds.

During the 1980s, the index fund outperformed about 75% of the mutual funds by matching the S&P 500. If you want a mutual fund, but don't want to pay the expense, this is a logical choice.

The dominant index fund of the 1980s was offered by the Vanguard group, the country's largest pure no-load funds family. Others have tried to launch index funds and have fallen by the wayside. In early 1990, two other industry giants, Fidelity and

Stock Funds

Dreyfus, began offering index funds. Whether their efforts will succeed remains to be seen.

BETTER THAN AN INDEX FUND?

What is the least expensive way to invest? It is not a new fund. It is not a product of computers or the investor revolution. It is certainly not something that you will find in the financial columns of your newspapers. It is not news.

The least expensive method of investment extant is a patient investor with a brokerage account. The annual cost of turnover for two types of discounters, a full-service broker, and a mutual fund (without switch charges), is illustrated by Figure 9.1.

The mother of a friend is nearing retirement age. She does not claim to know much about finance. She does not pore over annual reports or newsletters. But she does know when she thinks a company makes a good product. And she is patient. Very patient.

She bought one stock in the early 1950s. It split many times, so she now owns several thousand shares and her adjusted purchase cost is about 25 cents per share. The company's name is Browning Ferris. Somewhere along the way management decided that waste disposal might be a good business. The last time I checked, the stock's price was $37 per share. That means that its current value is *140 times* her original investment. Not only does this appreciation exceed any mutual fund during the period, but she paid no fees other than the commission 30 years ago. If you hold stocks for 30 years, it hardly matters whether you use a full service or discounter. But it does matter whether it is a broker or a mutual fund.

The more patient the investor, the greater the value of direct purchase. Brokers charge nothing; mutual funds charge every month. Over 30 years the amount that you pay a mutual fund will very likely exceed your initial investment.

That may sound improbable, but it is true. The following example illustrates this.

If the stock did not appreciate at all during the 30 years, you would still pay 1.5%/year × 30 years, which equals 45%. Approximately half of your original investment would go to the mutual fund.

Figure 9.1. The Cost of Turnover

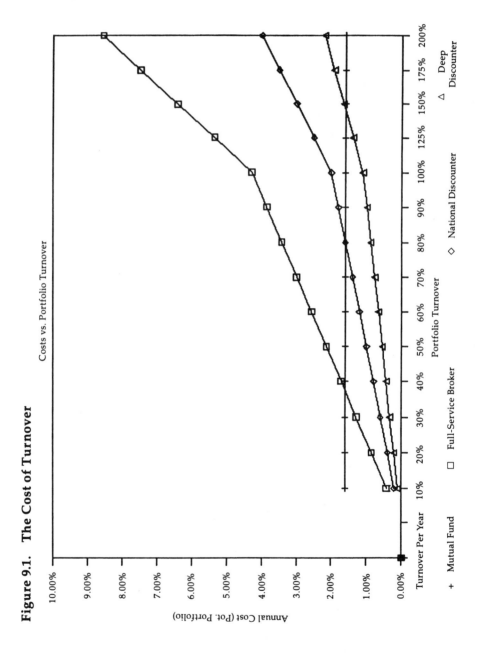

Stock Funds

It doesn't require such legendary patience to make mutual funds worth avoiding. Even if your average holding period for a stock is five years, there are significant savings in staying away from a mutual fund. Table 9.1 shows why.

Table 9.1. Mutual Fund Cost for $100,000 Investment Over 5 Years

1.5% fee on fund that is appreciating 15% per year.

Year	Annual Fee
Year 1	$ 1500
Year 2	$ 1725
Year 3	$ 1984
Year 4	$ 2281
Year 5	$ 2623
TOTAL	$10,113[1]

Assumptions

Deep Discount Broker—one purchase and one sale of all stocks in portfolio at .5% per transaction.

Initial purchase of $100,000 shares at .5% = $500

Sale of $200,000 (value after 5 years with 15% annual appreciation) = $1000

Total cost: $1500

Savings vs. mutual fund: $8500

Big Three Discounters

Initial purchase of $100,000 shares at 1% = $1000

Sale of $200,000 (value after 5 years with 15% annual appreciation) = $2000

Total cost: $3000

Savings vs. mutual fund: $7000

Full-Service Firm at 2.3% per transaction

Initial purchase of $100,000 shares at 2.3% = $2300

Sale of $200,000 (value after 5 years with 15% annual appreciation) = $4600

Total cost: $6900

Savings vs. mutual fund: $3100

---

[1] Total cost is actually significantly understated since it excludes appreciation or interest on the savings. For example, the $1500 cost in Year 1 if reinvested in a fund with 15% annual appreciation, would have exceeded $2500 by Year 5.

Tax Advantages

Direct ownership also offers tax advantages. These are harder to quantify, since they vary in each situation, but they are quite real. My friend's mother never paid a dime of taxes in 30 years. Most mutual funds take profits regularly, which means you will pay taxes regularly, even if you don't sell any shares. Even if you like to take profits regularly, when you own your own stocks, you decide when to take profits. If income is higher this year, you can decide to defer them.

Also of value to some investors is the fact that you can take delivery of the stock; there is no middleman holding your shares. While I know of no instance in which a major mutual fund went insolvent through bad management or fraud, and the likelihood seems remote, there is no theoretical reason why it could not happen. In that event, SIPC would not insure your losses since it does not insure mutual funds. (This is to be distinguished from the case where a broker holding the mutual fund for your account becomes insolvent, not the mutual fund itself. In this case, SIPC would insure that you received the mutual fund shares.)

Who Then Will Benefit from Mutual Funds?

I don't mean to suggest that mutual funds don't serve a valuable purpose for many investors. The following lists some who can benefit from them.

1. Inexperienced investors who do not have the time nor the inclination to learn.
2. Investors with portfolios under $20,000 who are interested in a diversified portfolio of stocks, but are not interested in stock management.
3. Large investors who understand the statistics, are not interested in direct investing, and will feel better paying for professional management.
4. Investors who like to trade in and out of the market actively. A fund without a sales fee may very well be cheaper than a discounter.

5. Many investors who are interested in international issues and high-yield bonds. (These will be discussed in a later chapter.)
6. Investors who pick funds that can outperform the averages. The Mutual Funds Directory will help with these choices.

CHAPTER 10

Bond Funds

In the case of stock funds, it is appropriate to pay a bit more for better past performance; in the case of bond funds, it is not. The Bond Fund Directory in Appendix E includes useful information about bond funds that meet one criteria—their expense ratios are low.

SELECTING A BOND FUND

No Peter Lynches in the Bond Industry

I don't believe in paying more for the track record in a bond fund because bond fund managers generally cannot beat the market with sufficient consistency or by a large enough amount (if they can beat it at all) to justify paying the difference. In support of this view is a recent study by the *Hulbert Financial Digest*.[1] Among 18 newsletters making bond recommendations studied by the *Digest* during a recent period, only one managed to beat

---
[1] Source: *Hulbert Financial Digest*. (February 1990).

the market. It isn't just the newsletter writers who aren't having luck beating the bond market. "The bond markets are even more efficient than the stock markets," says George Ball, chairman of Prudential Bache, "so it's all the more difficult for any one person to out perform the market."

Peter Lynch reportedly averaged over 200 trips per year to meet company management during the period that he compiled his spectacular track record with the Magellan fund. Presumably this gave him an edge over his less energetic counterparts in the stock fund industry.

In the bond fund sector, there are no companies to meet. There are just a lot of people guessing about the direction of one variable—interest rates. There is no inside edge and there are no Peter Lynches in the bond industry.

THE ILLUSION OF PERFORMANCE

In reading the press, it may seem that some bond funds are performing much better than others. This is really an illusion, which generally falls into one of the following two categories.

The Maturity Illusion

You read in the newspapers that Fund X led the bond funds in performance. It appreciated 10% while the average bond fund was up only 5%. This suggests Fund X has impressive management, but in reality it often only means that this fund has either very long term or very short term average maturity bonds.

When interest rates go down, zero-coupon bonds show up on the top of the list. They have the longest duration—roughly equivalent to the longest maturity—which means they will benefit most from an interest rate decline. Conversely, if interest rates rise, the zero-coupon funds will appear on the bottom of the performance comparisons, while the funds with the shortest duration will appear on top.

The Yield Illusion

Even worse than selecting bonds on the basis of their recent performance is picking funds with the highest yield. Even within the circumscribed charter of high-quality bond funds,

Bond Funds

there are ways to pump up yields. A manager can buy low-quality bonds or inflate yields through tricks of the trade; for example, some bond funds sold "calls"—granting the buyer of the calls the right to purchase their bonds at a specific price. The premium earned on sales of these calls swelled their income and made the current yield look very good. Then interest rates dropped, bond prices rose, and the fund incurred losses in covering the calls which reduced its income. With the benefit of hindsight, investors found out that their total return over the period would have been higher if they had stayed with a regular bond fund instead of reaching out for the highest yield.

WHAT REALLY COUNTS

The single factor which will most affect your return on a bond fund is neither the management nor the expense ratio: It's *when* you buy the shares in the fund.

If you bought a bond fund when rates were low, you saw its price plummet as rates rose and new higher yielding bonds drove down the price of the older, lower yielding bonds. If you bought in the early 1980s when Treasury bonds were yielding 15%, your bond fund did quite well, due to a high rate of return and the fact that the value of your bonds appreciated as interest rates went down.

Unfortunately, without a crystal ball, you can't count on buying low and selling high; it is beyond your control. But the one factor you *can* control is expenses. If the expenses are lower, the yield will be higher.

THE BEST OF THE BOND FUNDS

The Bond Fund Directory in Appendix E includes corporate and government, taxable and nontaxable, and long- and short-term bonds that meet the following criteria.

- Their annual expense ratio has typically been below .7%, which places them in the lowest quartile among the funds we follow for expenses.

Table 10.1. 1987 Median Expense Ratios for No-Loads

Assets in Millions	Stock Funds	Bond Funds
$500+	.70%	.68%
$250–$500	.94	.75
$100–$250	1.00	.80
$ 50–$100	1.10	.86
$ 25–$50	1.29	.86
$ 10–$25	1.45	.99
$ 10 and less	1.63	.85
Overall	1.16	.80

Source: Jacobs, S. (1989). *The No-Load Fund Investor.* New York: Dow Jones Irwin.

- The net asset value of the fund exceeds generally $100 million. In the case of most mutual funds, the expenses decrease as the amount of assets under management increases. Table 10.1 indicates the relationship between expenses and fund size during the period indicated.

Bond funds with assets under $100 million generally are not included in this book because of my concern that such funds may be able to keep their expenses low only for as long as the sponsor is absorbing expenses during the buildup period. The sponsor could change its mind and expenses would escalate. They are included in the *Discount Mutual Fund Survey* published by Mercer (see Appendix D) because a periodical is able to track such expenses on a more current basis to see if they have been increased by the sponsor.

The decision whether to invest in a taxable or nontaxable bond fund is mainly a matter of your tax bracket. If you're in a high tax bracket or a high tax state, then you may want to consider municipal bonds.

ONE STATE FUNDS

Omitted from this Directory are One State funds. These are municipal bond funds that invest exclusively in securities issued by

Bond Funds

governmental entities within a single state. The advantage of these funds is that the interest is free from federal, state, and local tax to residents of that state. In high-tax states, this can be a considerable advantage. If you are in a high-tax state these funds are worth considering. They are easy to obtain as well. Simply select a few fund sponsors from the Directory which offer general municipal bond funds with low expenses. (These same sponsors will offer One State bond funds.) Call and ask them for a bond fund for your state. If you live in a populous, high-tax state, the odds are good that you will find one.

HIGH-YIELD FUNDS

Also omitted from the Directory are high-yield funds as their sponsors call them; or "junk bond funds," as they are more commonly known. Among all the income-oriented mutual funds, it is in high-yield funds where performance should matter most since they are closest to equities. Each issue can be carefully scrutinized, analyzed for cash flow coverage, cyclicality, debt ratios, and so on. Over time, some skilled managers should outperform others by a significant amount. Then high-yield funds could begin to be treated like equity: look for no-load funds with good performances and without excessive expenses.

However, the problem with rating the performance of junk bond funds is now becoming apparent. Until recently, we have seen their results only during good times. High-yield funds were born in the early and mid-1980s, when leveraged buyouts and junk-financed takeovers created a high level of marketable debt. During the late 1980s, the riskier the fund, the higher the yield, the better the performance.

Now the chickens have come home to roost. Many of yesterday's stars are today's dogs. Those funds that topped the list during the boom cycle with high yields are stacked up at the bottom of the list as actual and threatened bankruptcies sink the value of their holdings. It has become clear that it will be impossible to judge which funds have performed best over the cycle until the current wave of bankruptcies subsides.

Given the wild volatility of these funds, I am reluctant to suggest expenses alone as the basis for selecting funds, so they have been omitted from the Bond Fund Directory. However, some are included in the Closed-End Fund Directory if you would like further information.

UNIT INVESTMENT TRUSTS (UITs)

UITs are listed with bonds since most UITs are, in effect, bond funds. They are not listed in a directory because unlike open- or closed-end bond funds, existing UITs are generally not available for purchase. They are sold to investors when initially issued but are not available thereafter for resale. If an investor wants to sell his or her interest, it is generally sold straight back to the sponsor who will purchase the interest at or about the market value of the underlying securities.

Brokerage firms have recently launched UITs for equities. The concept has been greeted with something less than critical acclaim. A "Bronx cheer" would be a more accurate description. A portfolio of securities is purchased at the time the UIT is organized with the aim of dissolving the UIT and distributing the profits in five to ten years. Most critics have challenged the concept. They believe that such inactive management is inconsistent with good equities management.

As I see it, that is not the real problem with equity UITs. If a fixed basket of stocks, like the Dow Jones Industrials, can outperform the active fund managers in many years, why can't other selected portfolios of stocks do the same? The real problem with the equity is that overzealous sales representatives have been switching their clients from one UIT to another, increasing their transaction costs astronomically by imposing frequent up-front costs, thereby eliminating its major advantage of keeping costs low.

If a sales rep or mailing solicits your participation in a UIT, and you want to decide whether to participate, the cost side is easy to analyze.

1. Jot down the sales fee for the UIT.
2. List the annual management fee.

Bond Funds

3. Multiply the management fee by the number of years until the trust dissolves, or the number of years that you expect to hold your interest.
4. Get the latest prospectus for the best comparable mutual fund.
5. Check the expenses section. It will show you the comparable figures for 1, 3, 5, and 10 years.
6. You probably should mark up higher front-end costs a bit to allow for the discounted value of money, but following these five steps will give you a fairly good approximation.

That covers the cost side. If the UIT comes out ahead, you should still ask yourself one final question: Will I really hold the UIT as long as I have estimated? If you know that you're the type to buy and change your mind, you'd probably do better with an open-end mutual fund. Most UITs have sales charges; no-load funds don't. If you change your mind early, you won't be penalized by the sales fee.

DO YOU REALLY NEED A GOVERNMENT BOND FUND?

A Good Way to Kick the Couch Potato Habit

If you are trying to kick the couch potato investing habit, I suggest you start with one of the most popular mutual/closed-end funds of recent years—government bond funds. These have sold very well for the last few years because sales reps can stress the advantages: high and known yield and the safety of the U.S. government behind the bond. It all sounds very good, and it sells.

But if you read the fine print, you will typically find that you are paying about 10% of the yield to the fund manager. In addition, if you bought from a sales rep, you paid his or her commission. But consider this: Two of the main reasons that people are willing to pass on 10% of their yield to a mutual fund manager is to have the convenience of professional management and the chance to diversify.

Why do you need professional management? What can a professional manager tell you about the U.S. government? That he or she has read the financial statement and annual reports and thinks it's a good investment?

Why do you need diversification when buying government bonds? Isn't one bond backed by the full faith and credit of the U.S. Government as safe as 100 U.S. Government issues? For that matter, isn't it safer than a diversified portfolio of 100 corporate bonds?

Cynical observers have said of some mutual funds that they are "sold, not bought." This may be an overstatement in general, but when it comes to government bond funds, it is a simple fact. In 1988, according to the Investment Company Institute, nearly $80 billion of the roughly $82 billion assets of open-end government income funds were raised by sales representatives. Only $2.5 billion were purchased through direct marketing, that is, without a sales rep.[2]

When you buy a government bond fund, you pay for management you don't need, place your assets in the hands of a third party, and may even lose the state tax deduction associated with ownership of Treasury bonds. To add insult to injury, you don't even have to pay a commission to buy a Treasury bond (see Chapter 15, Treasury Bills and Bonds).

CORPORATE BOND FUNDS

There is a stronger case for a corporate bond fund, although it's still weak unless you don't have the assets to diversify at least a dozen bonds. In theory, analysts can earn their keep in analyzing corporate credit, but if you buy high-quality bonds, their failure rate is practically nil, and as we have seen in the section on bonds in the discount brokerage chapters, both discounters and full-service brokers charge very moderate commissions for bonds. If you buy from a full-service broker at issue, you normally pay no commission; the issuer pays. The same can be said of municipal bonds.

When you buy a bond directly, you are receiving the benefit of an extensive credit analysis by top-drawer professionals

---

[2] Source: Investment Company Institute. (1989). *Mutual fund fact book*. Washington, DC: Author.

without any cost. The credit rating agencies rate the bonds at no charge to the investor; the issuer pays the cost for Moody's, Standard and Poor's, or whatever service is retained to rate the bonds.

The strongest case for using a bond fund is in junk bonds. You need substantial diversification for these high-risk investments. Furthermore, the market is very illiquid and sometimes only trades in large sizes. Junk bond fund managers have not shown that their professional management has been able to improve results, but at least you are getting diversification and access to the market on reasonable terms. Closed-end bond funds can also be attractive when the discount is sufficient, but that is not because the vehicle works well. It is because a sufficient discount will make even an unattractive vehicle attractive.

Bond funds do have one major advantage. They are useful if you want to temporarily park your funds in bonds rather than leave them for the long haul. The reason is that resale costs on certain types of bonds—particularly municipal and junk bonds—can be high. The commission is not high, but the spread between bid and asked could be as high as a few percentage points. If you plan to resell your bonds in a year or two, a bond fund could turn out to be less costly than direct purchase.

CHAPTER 11

Money Market Funds

The first money fund, the Reserve fund, was organized in 1972. It was based on a simple concept. Large investors were able to secure much more attractive rates than small investors by buying certificates of deposit (CDs) in $1 million denominations. If you pooled together a number of small investors, you would have the necessary funds to secure these higher rates and could pass them on to your investors. It was an idea that lingered, but like the mutual fund itself, did not catch on for a time. I remember having lunch in Palo Alto in 1978 with an innovative fellow whose money fund was based on investing in Treasury bills. A year later, when we had dinner in New York, he was justifiably proud that his fund had just passed the $100 million mark.

Meanwhile in Washington, DC another acquaintance, Wayne Silby, had just passed the $10 million mark with his newly launched fund. He knew of the Palo Alto fund and vise versa; it was a small industry where all the players knew each other. He started the fund with a $5000 legal fee paid to an old friend. Not yet 30, he and his partner ran the fund with a low-key laid-back efficiency. A few months later, the business had moved to a brownstone off Dupont Circle where the senior staff retired after work to a hot tub behind the building. (I suggested that disputes could be resolved by collecting the executives in the tub and turning up the heat until unanimous agreement was reached.)

Apparently the funds survived without benefit of my management techniques. Wayne's fund grew, was sold to a major company, and now his Calvert funds invest over one-half billion dollars. The fellow from California did okay too. Jim Benham's 18 funds currently handle close to $6 billion dollars in investor funds.

Money funds have been one of the great success stories of the century. From small beginnings with innovative pioneers like the Reserve fund, Jim Benham, and Wayne Silby, the industry exploded. By the end of the 1980s, close to $400 billion was invested in money funds. Today it literally rivals the banking system in terms of deposits. Most investors are familiar with money funds. They advertise in all the financial papers and their yields are quoted in the press. In a few years, there could be more money in money funds than in traditional bank deposits. The money fund is the new bank of the investor revolution.

In at least one respect, the money market mutual fund is unique: Due to the size of their investments, money funds are often able to secure rates that are better than most individuals could secure directly. To that extent, there is no cost for using a money fund. Its yields are higher than the most common competitive direct investment (bank deposits) and higher than the yields most individuals could secure through direct investment. (One notable exception to this shall be discussed later.) Therefore, it is the one type of mutual fund which pays its own way.

EARNING A HIGHER YIELD

The easiest way to increase yield is to switch from a bank money fund to one of the nationally distributed variety, such as those listed in the Money Market Fund section of the Mutual Funds Directory (Appendix E). For example, on March 18, 1990, a survey cited in the *New York Times* indicated that the average rate on money market accounts for small investors was 6.25%. During that same period, nationally marketed money funds were typically offering over 7.5%, and some were offering as much as 8.4%.

Once you've made the switch from a bank fund to a money market fund, the pickings get slimmer, unless a price war happens to be going on. For example, during the past few years, the top 20% of the nationally marketed money funds yielded only about .2% more annually than the average of such funds, and .7% higher than the bottom 20%. If we didn't already know it, these statistics would tell us that the ability of one manager to earn more than another by better investing is very limited.

More than half the assets of taxable money funds at present are invested in commercial paper, short-term loans to major corporations. Any 30-day commercial paper of a given credit rating will sell for almost exactly the same price as any other. The same is true for other money market instruments. The difference in yields arises almost entirely from differences in expenses.

In other words, for money funds more than any other type of mutual fund, expenses are what counts. The track record does not count because, as we have seen, the investments are so circumscribed that the manager can do very little to improve the yield.

The money market fund directory in Appendix E lists funds that typically offer high yields as a result of low expense ratios. They include taxable and nontaxable, government and corporate. These funds all had expense ratios of .7% or less. Some of them very much less. This places their expenses in roughly the lower 20% of all funds during this period. (Money funds' expense ratios currently average .8%). Sales fees are not a factor since money funds are the one fund where sales fees are virtually never charged.

This list should prove a useful starting point, but it's also a good idea to check for the highest yields in the press. *Changing Times, Money, Barron's,* the *New York Times* and the *Wall Street Journal* are among the many financial magazines and major daily newspapers that regularly compare yields of the major money funds. For those whose assets justify subscribing to a newsletter for the most current information, *Donoghue's* is considered the leading authority in the field (see Appendix D).

PRICE WARS

Checking current yields allows you to take advantage of periodic "price wars" which break out. When a fund sponsor decides they are willing to forego current profits in order to build up the size of the fund, they will absorb part of the normal expenses. This can create very attractive yields during the buildup period, which can last for quite a while. At the time of writing, the Fidelity Spartan Fund and Dreyfus Worldwide Dollar Fund are engaged in such a price war. It is Godzilla vs. King Kong. These are two of the country's largest money funds, run by two of the best-known fund sponsors, and they are offering yields in 8.25–8.5% range while most of the market is .5 to .75% lower. These are the type of opportunities from which the cost-conscious investor can benefit—until peace breaks out.

Unless you are prepared to switch accounts frequently, big funds in price wars are preferable to small ones. When the war ends, the fund with a large asset base will likely continue to offer attractive yields because large funds naturally have lower costs—the economies of scale are pronounced in the fund business. By contrast, a small fund that has failed to gain market share may be forced to *raise* its expenses sharply to cover costs. For this reason, larger funds are emphasized in the Directory. Figure 11.1 shows the yield differentials we have discussed.

Figure 11.1. Comparison of Yields

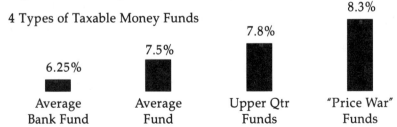

RISK

Beware of funds that offer high yields without unusually low expenses. In a field where investments are so circumscribed, one must be suspicious of funds that are earning more than others. They may be taking higher risks. For example, the SEC permits money funds to buy either of two grades of commercial paper. They are both high grade, but the lower grade of the two includes some companies whose credit is significantly weaker than others.

While defaults on high-grade commercial paper are rare, they are possible. In 1989, two funds are known to have held commercial paper in Integrated Resources, a syndicator, when it filed for bankruptcy. A few others were rumored to have held their paper as well. To their credit, the fund sponsors elected to absorb the loss themselves. Then in March 1990, the Mortgage and Realty Trust defaulted on $150 million in notes, half of them reportedly held by money market funds. Undoubtedly, part of these funds will be recovered, sponsors will probably again elect to absorb all or enough of the loss to assure that no principal is lost, and life will go on as usual. Even a total loss of $75 million is negligible for a $300 billion industry.

The greater risk would be that in a massive financial panic or recession, some of the weaker fund sponsors would be unwilling or unable to absorb the losses. Even then, the loss would likely be small. It is hard to imagine a scenario in which large numbers of top-rated companies suddenly go bankrupt within the short time frame of the typical money fund investment. Those troubled by this risk may prefer to accept a lower yield and invest in a fund that exclusively purchases government or high-grade municipal securities, a certificate of deposit in a bank which is insured by the government agencies up to $100,000, or Treasury bills.

Another theoretical risk would be a rogue fund—a fund run by a crook who flies off with your money. I am not aware that this has ever occurred, but it is one argument for sticking with the larger, better-established funds.

THE CONVENIENCE FACTOR

If you do not have a large balance in a money fund, you may want to accept a lower yield for convenience. Money funds normally offer checking facilities (restricted to checks of a specified minimum) and the convenience of being able to switch between the funds and other bank or brokerage accounts by telephone. If you invest with a mutual fund family, you will probably want to use the fund associated with that fund—as long as its yields are reasonable. For this same reason, many individuals prefer the convenience of their bank money fund.

TREASURY BILLS

Earlier in this chapter, I noted that money funds pay their own way. Unless you have a spare million to invest, they can earn higher rates due to their large investments in commercial paper and similar instruments. This allows them to cover their costs and often earn a higher rate than the typical investor could earn by direct investment.

There is one major exception to this—Treasury bills. While not as convenient as money funds, they are liquid, free from state and local taxes, backed by the full faith and credit of the U.S. Government, and can be purchased without a commission. Frequently they yield more than money funds as well. At the time of writing, the yield on 6-month Treasury bills was 8.24%, higher than almost any money fund in the country. At this same time, the average money fund, according to *Donoghue's*, was yielding 7.67%. By investing directly, you would increase your yield by .7%—approximately 10% more interest income—with the safest investment of all: U.S. Treasury bills. They are discussed at greater length in Chapter 15, Treasury Bills and Bonds.

FOREIGN MONEY FUNDS

Investors who believe that other currencies will appreciate at the expense of the dollar prefer to keep some of their funds in non-dollar denominated currencies. A few funds have sprung up to service this type of investor. This subject is discussed in the next chapter.

CHAPTER 12

International Funds

The outstanding stock funds of the 1980s were mutual funds which invested in international stock. If you invested $10,000 in a typical international fund in 1980, your investment was worth about $58,000 by the end of the decade. By comparison, a similar investment in a typical domestic stock mutual fund was worth about $42,000.

The performance of international funds was so strong that I decided to create a separate ranking category and section in Appendix E for them. Otherwise, if they were lumped together with domestic mutual funds, they would dominate the list of the top 50.

That would present a misleading list. The foreign markets were generally booming during the 1980s, so nearly all the funds with foreign investments did well. The 1990s could be different. Therefore, to make the cut for a listing in the international fund section of the Directory, a stock fund had to outperform its domestic counterpart. Specifically, an international fund had to show appreciation of approximately 160% during the 1985–1990 period to make our international list vs. 110% to make our domestic stock funds list. The permissible expense ratio is also higher for reasons described later.

Otherwise, the selection criterion for stock funds is similar to the criteria for domestic stocks. The stock funds are all no-load or low-load funds whose performance was among the best of all global or international funds during this decade. Their average annual return during this period was a sizzling 22%.

In this chapter, the term international funds is used to include a category of fund which is technically known as a global fund. However, the Directory does indicate which funds are globals and which are true internationals. The difference between them is that global funds may invest in both domestic and international stocks. Sometimes the fund's charter limits investments to specified percentages in each category, for example, not less than 50% international. More frequently, the fund manager exercises discretion about what proportion to invest in domestic vs. international. Therefore, if you want all your investment in a fund to be invested abroad, you would prefer an international fund. If you prefer that the fund manager exercise discretion in deciding whether the domestic or international markets are better, a global fund is more suitable. It comes down to a question of who should decide what percentage of your assets should be allocated abroad: you or the fund manager?

Chapter 4, International Funds, in Appendix E includes stock and bond funds. In the case of bond funds, it was frankly easier to be listed in the international funds chapter than the bond funds chapter. There are not many international bond funds, so all but the highest expense funds were included.

In addition to stock and bond funds, the international funds chapter lists international closed-end funds. They could have been listed under other directories which cover this subject, but from the perspective of investing at a discount, international funds have more in common with each other than with their domestic brethren.

First, their expenses are higher. This reflects the reality of higher commission costs in most foreign markets, less liquidity, and the additional costs of maintaining both foreign and domestic offices (since we only list U.S.-based funds).

International Funds

Second, they all share one common factor exclusively with each other: currency translation. I am reluctant to use the more traditional term "currency risk" because risk implies a one-way street. Currency translation is a two-way street. When you buy an international fund, the fund is acquiring securities denominated in foreign currencies. If the dollar is weak during the period you own the fund, the foreign fund's securities will tend to increase in value. If the dollar is strong, they will tend to decrease.

Whether you ultimately make a profit or loss on a foreign investment then is based on a combination of two factors: the appreciation or depreciation of the value of the securities in their own stock markets and the currency translation factors. Stock market investors are accustomed to volatility, so the addition of one more factor affecting price may not make a great deal of difference. However, bond market investors should be aware that the currency factor may significantly alter their expectations about the certainty of their investment. Both the amount of annual interest and the value of their security will be affected by the currency transaction factor.

INVESTMENT ALTERNATIVES TO MUTUAL FUNDS

Another factor that all international investments have in common is that funds—bonds, stocks, and closed-end—are all probably worth their admittedly high expenses for the novice investor and worthwhile in many instances for the sophisticated investor as well.

The problem for most investors who want to take advantage of the outstanding returns of foreign securities is threefold: lack of knowledge of the securities to buy; lack of knowledge of the mechanism; and the higher expenses for individuals buying foreign stocks.

American Depository Receipts

There is one exception to most of these problems. Certain foreign stocks can be purchased on the New York and American Stock

Exchanges through an instrument known as ADRs—American Depository Receipts. These provide the equivalent of owning a foreign stock without some of the nuisances. The dividends are paid in U.S. dollars, they can be purchased or sold through discount or full-service brokers like any other stock, and if they are a variety known as "sponsored" ADRs, you will receive annual reports and other information similar to those that American investors are accustomed to receiving.

There are approximately 50 ADRs listed on the New York Stock Exchange and a few on the American. Some 75 more trade through the NASDAQ (National Association of Securities Dealers Automated Quotations) system. Those which trade on the exchanges offer excellent liquidity, sometimes better than in their home markets. Over 600 others trade over-the-counter, sometimes very far over-the-counter, in the market known as the "pink sheets." Here one must be careful. The bid/asked spreads can be so wide that they make acquisition unattractive for any but the long-term investor.

It is possible for U.S. investors to buy stocks directly on the foreign markets. The cost is not necessarily prohibitive and may provide a lower cost alternative to mutual funds for the longer-term investor with access to stock recommendations. However, the costs, the clearing procedures, and the extent of information available all vary drastically depending upon the country and the intermediary used to purchase stocks.

CLOSED-END FUNDS

Closed-end funds have developed a special place in international investing. Approximately 25 closed-end funds, primarily trading on the New York Stock Exchange, permit you to invest exclusively in the markets of a range of countries. The funds available include most Western European countries, many Asian and South American countries, and others.

The country fund section of the international funds chapter in the Mutual Funds Directory provides you with information about many of these funds, although new ones seem to sprout each week. If you think the economy of a country will take off, you can invest in it without your funds ever leaving the United States. Their net asset values and premiums or discounts are listed along with other closed-end funds in the papers (see Chapter 13, Closed-End Funds, for further discussion).

FOREIGN CURRENCY FUNDS

Several mutual funds permit investment in interest-bearing deposits in the major foreign currencies. This type of fund is attractive to investors who anticipate a decline in the U.S. dollar versus these currencies. For example, if the dollar declines 10% versus the German mark, and mark deposits yield 8% annually, then your total return in dollars for the year would be approximately 18%. But if you bet wrong, and the dollar appreciates 10% against the mark, then you would end the year with a 2% loss (10% loss on the currency exchange rate less 8% yield).

Until recently, these mutual funds offered the only practical way for investors to directly buy into foreign currencies. You could also indirectly buy in through purchase of foreign stocks, but then you are betting on the foreign stock market. You could open accounts with foreign banks abroad as well, but this involves more red tape and paperwork, as well as distance, than most people wanted to put up with.

The funds typically charge a small up-front load, for example, 1%, and a 1.5% management fee. That charge isn't too steep for an equity mutual fund, but it's high for money funds which almost never charge admission fees and have lower operating costs. No doubt it reflects the higher costs of operating abroad. Paying 1% up front and 1.5% per year is a big bite out of your income in countries such as Japan or Germany, where the interest rates are only 6 to 8% per year. If the yield is 6%, you're paying almost half that to the sponsor in the first year. Even where there is no front-end load, even a 1.5% fee on a 6% income stream is steep.

There is now an alternative for larger investors. You can open a foreign currency account with a major foreign bank in the United States. The largest concentration of such banks is in New York, but there are also many in Los Angeles, San Francisco, Chicago, and the other major financial centers.

There is no charge for opening up your account with the bank, so you get roughly the same yield without paying the costs. By avoiding the middleman, you can increase your return in yens, for example, from 4 to 6.5%. As with a U.S. CD, you can place your funds on deposit for varying periods and normally get slightly higher yields for longer periods. The only catch is that the banks currently impose minimum investments. These levels vary by bank and currency, but you may need to be prepared to invest $25,000 to $50,000 or more to participate.

THE GLOBAL PORTFOLIO

The complexities of a global portfolio are too great to cover in a single chapter of a book whose focus is investing at discount, but there are no great mysteries. It just takes time to learn the ropes. To assist those who want to invest in international stocks, bonds, or mutual funds, Mercer has recently begun to publish a newsletter entitled, *The Global Portfolio*. Readers of this book are welcome to subscribe (see Discount Publications Directory) or write for a sample issue to Mercer Inc., 80 Fifth Ave, Suite 800, New York, NY 10011.

CHAPTER 13

Closed-End Funds

As previously noted, a closed-end fund is a company which raises capital by selling shares and uses the proceeds to buy securities of a designated type; for example, stocks, bonds, or stocks in a specific country. After the initial issue, the stock trades in the open market. Sometimes it trades at a discount to the underlying net asset value, sometimes at a premium. These swings present opportunities, as well as pitfalls, for the unwary.

At one time, closed-end funds were so seldom seen that they were practically a curiosity. This changed in the 1980s. One of the major reasons for its new-found popularity in the late 1980s was the fact that a lot of sales representatives were sitting around with nothing to do. After the stock market crash of 1987, investors were not receptive to new issues of common stock, to put it mildly. The resourceful brokerage industry looked for alternatives to keep their sales forces busy. One of the alternatives that they seized upon were closed-end bond funds.

Bond funds offered the shaken investor a steady and predetermined income—which sounded pretty good after the devastating declines of October 1987—and offered sales reps the chance to earn a commission on selling the new bond funds at issue.

A flood of issues reached the market. The number of closed-end bond funds had reached approximately 150 by the end of 1989. By then, the market was glutted and most of these funds were selling at a discount. This leads us to the first rule for investing at a discount.

DON'T BUY A NEW CLOSED-END FUND

You should avoid buying a new issue closed-end fund the same way you would avoid buying an open-end mutual fund with a sales charge (load). If the fund is sold with an 8% sales fee, you are buying at a premium of 8% since the proceeds to the fund will only be 92% of the amount raised.

Unless it's a very hot issue, the odds are good that the fund will eventually settle down to trade at its net asset value or a discount. In most cases, you can save that sales fee by avoiding the new issue and waiting until it trades at a lower price in the market.

The new issue cost is even worse than it looks. If you bought a new fund at issue and it subsequently trades at a 5% discount, you might think that the decline was 5%. But if you paid an 8% commission, then in effect you bought the fund at an 8% premium, since only 92% of the money invested went to the fund. Therefore, the decline is 5% plus the initial commission—a total of 13%.

There are times when new issues will go to premiums; primarily in very hot isolated issues. But hot issues are rationed, and it's very hard to get shares when they are really hot. Most discounters will not receive any shares for their clients and full-service brokers reserve hot issues for their best clients.

In any event, these hot issues are usually hot for only a short time. Eventually they cool down. In most cases, unless the fund has some kind of franchise, such as being designated the only foreign fund in that country or having an outstanding track record, most funds settle to their natural state. Their natural state is to sell at a discount.

Closed-End Funds

WHEN A DISCOUNT MAY NOT BE A DISCOUNT

Normally, I advocate buying at a discount. However, the typical closed-end fund should not normally be purchased simply because it sells at a discount. While a closed-end fund selling at a discount may well be a good long-term holding, it is not necessarily a bargain nor is it a discount in the sense that the term has been used. It could remain at the same discount to net asset value for years or decades. In that respect, the closed-end fund is similar to the companies that value investors like to buy. Many companies sell at 30 to 40% below the price they would command if they went private or were purchased by another company. Unless and until that occurs, however, that discount will remain.

However, unlike most companies, closed-end funds that suddenly become popular may start selling for large premiums. In one of the most extreme cases, country funds became extraordinarily popular near the end of 1989. Reportedly, Japanese brokerage firms were advising their customers to buy into these funds at almost any cost. The result was that funds which held stocks in European countries and had been selling at discounts or nominal premiums went to huge premiums.

When the discount is appropriate, a closed-end fund offers advantages over open-end funds. For example, if you buy a closed-end fund at a 20% discount, it will earn higher dividends per share than a comparable open fund. That is because the fund earns dividends on $100 in stock while you only invest $80 to buy the fund's stock. This can be a particular advantage with bond funds since it boosts the yield. Bonds funds rarely sell at a 20% discount, but a 10 to 12% discount at times is not unusual.

Another advantage of buying a fund at a discount is that there is a possibility that hostile investors or the fund's own board will decide to turn the fund into an open-end fund. This development has occurred in many cases recently. When the fund converts to an open-end fund, the discount disappears. If the fund had a 20% discount and converts to open-end, the value of your shares would rise, for example, from $80 to $100, providing a tidy 25% profit.

The discount or premium on closed-end funds is typically reported by the funds on Thursday or Friday and is available in the *New York Times* and *Barron's* on Saturday, and the *Wall Street Journal* on Monday. It appears in other financial papers as well. The Net Asset Value is reported as well as the most recent market price and the discount as of that date.

WHEN THE DISCOUNT IS RIGHT

The key to buying closed-end funds is buying when the discount is right. Unfortunately, there are no enduring guidelines. Things may change with market conditions. And the appropriate buy point depends on the fund.

But as a rule of thumb, bond funds are worth considering as a substitute for direct purchase or open-end funds when their discounts exceed 10%. Broadly diversified domestic stock funds become attractive as their discounts approach 20%.

The appropriate premium for country funds is anyone's guess and highly variable depending on the country. If it is an underdeveloped country with a weak currency, such as Brazil or Turkey, a 20% discount may only offer fair value—not a bargain. For a country with a strong currency and growth prospects, such as Germany, a 15% discount could present an attractive buying opportunity.

The patient investor who is looking for value, not the hottest new fund, can frequently take advantage of anomalies in the premiums and discounts among funds. For example, at the time of writing, there were three closed-end funds exclusively buying German stocks: the Germany Fund, the New Germany Fund, and the Future Germany Fund. There were differences among the types of stocks they proposed to buy, but these differences were not material. When I checked the listing, one was selling at a 16.64% premium, the second at a 7.35% discount, and the third at a 14.09% discount. All three were run by the same adviser!

Closed-end funds offer many opportunities to buy stocks or bonds at a real discount, but you need to know when to buy. These rules of thumb below will give you a rough idea, but if you are serious about investing, you need to learn the historical

Closed-End Funds

discount/premium patterns of the funds. Find out what factors drive the discounts or subscribe to a newsletter that will provide suitable information.

If you are interested in foreign or country funds, Mercer will be pleased to provide a sample issue of our newsletter for international investing, *The Global Portfolio*. If domestic stock or bond funds are your interest, several newsletters listed in the Publications Directory cover closed-end funds.

Premium Swamp Expenses

While expenses are as important to a closed-end fund's performance as they are to an open-end fund's, these premium swings swamp the outlook for the fund. It's rather like having a beagle and a St. Bernard sitting in your canoe. You can glance at the beagle from time to time, but you better keep your eyes on the St. Bernard.

If Fund A's annual expense ratio is 1% lower than Fund B's, but Fund A sells at a 15% premium to Fund B, the savings in annual expenses is swamped by the premium differential. It would take 15 years in expense savings to match that premium differential. So keep your eye on the premium. Watch that St. Bernard.

If different funds are selling at close to the same premium, then expenses become more important. To assist in identifying closed-end funds, I have listed some of the larger funds in the closed-end fund section of the Mutual Funds Directory—along with their recent expense ratios.

Part Three

Other Investments and Investment Vehicles

CHAPTER 14

Self-Directed IRAs

You may be surprised to learn that to an investor trading as little as three times per year, the difference between the right and wrong broker for an IRA account is over $7000 at the end of 10 years.

Since funds in your IRA are pretty much equivalent to post-tax dollars unless you are approaching retirement, an investor in the 33% tax bracket would have to earn over $10,000 to keep $7000 after taxes. Over a 20-year period, those pretax savings will exceed $25,000 and the posttax equivalent would be close to $40,000. That's not bad for an investment of a few minutes of your time.

It takes no magic or brilliance to achieve these savings. It's simply a matter of paying attention to the three ways in which you're charged for your self-directed IRAs, then find the bank or broker which is least expensive for your particular situation. Through the power of compound interest and after-tax savings, these seemingly modest savings mount up.

These numbers are based upon Mercer's *1989 Discount IRA Survey,* which surveys over 100 banks and discounters offering self-directed IRAs to determine which ones are least expensive for different users and establish what the potential savings can be.

HOW SELF-DIRECTED IRAs CAN ACHIEVE SAVINGS

These savings are possible with discounters if you use self-directed IRAs. These accounts permit the investor to use the IRA like a brokerage account: to invest in stocks, bonds, or other types of securities.

While the *Survey* focuses on potential savings through stock investments, some self-directed IRA accounts will permit you to invest in a variety of other investments, including mutual funds, option GNMAs, commodity funds, and income-producing limited partnerships. You can't invest on margin in a self-directed IRA, nor buy most collectibles. But the laws limiting the scope of investment change from time to time. In 1987, U.S. Treasury gold and silver coins joined the list of permissible investments, and others may be gradually added.

The percentage of assets in self-directed IRAs grew rapidly throughout the 1980s. This was partly due to the fact that an increasing number of people transferred their IRA funds into self-directed accounts, but also was a result of the rapid appreciation of the type of assets that you can buy through self-directed accounts. These assets appreciated faster throughout the 1980s than they have on average during most periods for the last 50 years.

During the past 50 years, equities have outperformed bonds and bonds have outperformed savings accounts. Certainly there have been periods when this wasn't true. And some people seem to have a knack for buying at the top of the stock market and selling at the bottom. Those people would probably be better off in a bank account. But historically, investors have done better in equities over any extended period, as long as they were patient.

IRAs facilitate long-term investments. Barring an emergency, you know the IRA funds must remain invested. They are

Self-Directed IRAs

not competing with a new car or a round-the-world trip. For that reason they lend themselves to equity investments or other types of investments that are more volatile than savings accounts, but are ultimately likely to be more profitable.

If you just want to buy a certificate of deposit or place your IRA money in a money fund, you don't need a self-directed IRA. But as your annual contributions mount and compound over the years, an increasing number of sophisticated investors will want to take advantage of the greater flexibility and returns afforded by investing through a self-directed IRA.

MAXIMIZING SAVINGS

Self-directed IRAs are typically subject to three types of charges:

1. Set-up costs when you establish the account
2. Annual fees for as long as the account is open
3. Commission charges when you make a purchase or sale

The *Mercer Discount IRA Survey* covers over 100 banks and discount brokers offering self-directed IRAs. The following outline describes these costs as of the *1989 Survey*.

Set-up cost. Range: 0 to $60. This is the least ambiguous of the charges. It is the one-time cost imposed when you initially establish the account. Once it's paid, it's over, and never comes back to haunt you.

Mercer found that some firms impose no set-up charges whatsoever; others charge up to $60 for the same privilege. The least expensive discounters are less than typical full-service firms, but the most expensive discounters charge as much or more than full-service firms.

Annual Fees. Range: 0 to $35 per year. As the term states, these are the fees imposed each year on the account. As in the case of the set-up charges, the least expensive discounters are less than typical full-service firms, but the most expensive discounters charge as much or more than typical full-service firms.

Commissions. Range: $23 to $500 per transaction. Difference for an average transaction: $144. These are the most complicated to compare, since every broker charges a different amount, depending upon the size of the transaction and the number and price of the shares involved.

To determine potential savings, I used the findings of the *Mercer 1989 Stock Commission Survey* to estimate commission charges on stock transactions with a value of $5000 or less. With IRA accounts typically valued at $10,000 to $25,000 in the early 1990s, we can assume that most stock transactions would be $5000 or less, since people don't want to put all their eggs in one basket.

Even though the dollars involved in these transactions are not large, the savings using the right discount broker can be quite striking—as much as $432 less than a typical full-service broker if you happen to be buying 5000 shares at $1, and averaging $144 for the 8 trades under $5000 which we analyzed.

The After-Tax Effect—Magnifies Savings by 50%

Ben Franklin lived before the income tax: Today, a dollar saved is more than a dollar earned. You pay taxes on earnings, but not on savings. If your combined federal, state, and city taxes bring you into the 33% tax bracket, then you would need $1500 in earnings to keep $1000 after taxes. So $1 after taxes is really worth $1.50 pretax.

IRA dollars are not exactly equivalent to posttax dollars, since you will have to pay taxes on them some day. But earning money now and paying taxes on it 20 years from now, while it compounds tax free in between, is almost like having after-tax dollars.

Unless you're approaching retirement, you can look at the savings estimate, and make a mental note that it's worth even more than it looks since you'd have to earn approximately 150% of that amount to end up with those savings.

TIPS ON PICKING AN IRA BROKER

If you're really inactive, you may want to use one of the firms listed in the *1989 Survey* that have no set-up charges for their IRAs (see Table 14.1). Some firms will charge as much as $165 more than others over a 3-year period, not counting interest. And that's before you make a single trade.

Self-Directed IRAs

Or you may want to reconsider whether you really need a self-directed account at this time. If you just want to buy a bank certificate of deposit, or leave your funds in a money fund, you should switch to a non-self-directed account. There is generally no charge or annual fee. And you could always switch back when you're ready to buy securities.

ACTIVE INVESTORS

If you are likely to trade as little as once per year in your account, commissions may be more important than fees. But if you're not sure that you will trade every year, you may want to focus on a reasonably low commission broker with very low fees.

If you're trading more than once per year, commissions are more important than fees and set-up costs. As you take off into the stratosphere of the 5 to 10 times per year traders, you should pay more attention to commissions. With a potential savings of $144 per trade, the greatest savings lie here. The Discount Brokerage Directory (Appendix A) identifies the deep discounters that offer the greatest savings.

Table 14.1. Potential Savings for IRA Investor Making 3 Stock Trades per Year.

This table which shows how an investor can save $7232 in 10 years is calculated as follows:

Assumptions:
1. *The investor would save 80% of the maximum possible savings between the highest and lowest cost discounter on annual fees and set-up costs.*
2. *The investor would save 80% of the average savings measured by the difference between the cost of a full-service broker and the 20 least expensive discount brokers in the latest* Mercer Discount Brokerage Stock Commission Survey.

   By using the 20th least expensive broker instead of the least expensive, I have allowed for the fact that an investor won't always shop for the least expensive trade. Number 20 is a reasonable proxy for a typical deep discounter.
3. *Savings were assumed to be reinvested in a money fund or other account at 8%.*
4. *The equivalent taxable income was developed for a 33% tax bracket taxpayer.*

Listing of Firms with No Set-Up Charge:

1. BANKS (Brokers)

American Security Bank
American Security Investment Services
American Trust & Savings Bank
Ameritrust Co.
Amsouth
Bank of Baltimore
Bank of Boston
Bank of New York
Bank One
Barclays Bank
Central Bank of the South
Central Carolina Bank
Chase Lincoln 1st Brokerage Services
Chase Manhattan Bank
Chemical Bank
Commercial National Bank
Cont Illinois, Natl Bank
Continental Bank
Crestar Bank
Deposit Guaranty Natl Bank
European American Bank
First Bank
First Commercial Trust
First Eastern Bank
First Natl Bank of Commerce
First Natl Bank of Maryland
First Natl Bank of Omaha
First Wisconsin Natl Bank
Merchants Natl Bk & Trust
Meridian Bank
Midlantic Securities Corp.
National Bank of Commerce
National City Bank
NatWest USA Brokerage Serv
Northern Trust Bank
Norwest Bank
Old Kent Bank & Trust
One Valley Bank
Oregon First
People's Bank
Piedmont Trust
Union Bank & Trust Co.
Union Planters Natl Bank
United Bank of Arizona
United Jersey Bank
Valley Bancorporation
West-One Bank

2. DISCOUNT BROKERS

Arbour Securities
Arnold Securities
Atlantic Discount Brokerage
Baker & Co.
Brown & Company
Bull & Bear
Calvert Group
Charles Schwab
Fidelity Investments
First Natl Brokerage Service
First Security Discount Brokerage
First Union Brokerage—NC
Freeman, Welwood & Co.
Harper-Schwerin
Icahn & Co., Inc.
Jack White & Co.
John Finn & Company, Inc.
Kashner Davidson
Marquette De Bary
NEII
Olde Discount
Quick & Reilly
Recom Securities
Richard Blackman & Co.
Robinson Securities
Rodecker & Co.
Roland Francis & Co., Inc.
Sarroff, Sager & Co.
Sentinel Securities, Inc.
Voss & Co.
York Securities

Discount IRA Survey. (1990). New York: Mercer Inc. Reprinted with permission.

*Potential Savings[1]
for IRA Investor—
3 Trades per Year*

Year	1	2	3	4	5	6	7	8	9	10
Initial Fees	$ 48									
Annual Fees	28	$ 29	$ 31	$ 32	$ 34	$ 36	$ 38	$ 39	$ 41	$ 43
Commissions	346	363	381	400	420	441	463	486	511	536
Current Year Savings	422	392	412	432	454	477	501	526	552	580
Previous year savings	0	455	915	1433	2015	2667	3395	4208	5112	6117
Interest at 8%	34	68	106	149	198	251	312	379	453	536
Cumulative Savings	455	915	1433	2015	2667	3395	4206	5112	6117	7232
Equivalent Taxable Income 33% tax bracket[2]	690	1387	2172	3053	4041	5144	6375	7745	9268	10,958

Stock Transaction per Year: 3

(1) Savings are computed as follows:
  a) Annual fees and set-up charges:
     80% of the difference between the highest and lowest broker.
  b) Commission Savings

Commission savings are based upon the latest *Mercer Discount Brokerage Stock Commission Survey.*

They are based on the 8 stock transactions of $5000 or less covered by that Survey.

They are computed by taking the arithmetic average of the difference between the commissions charged by the typical full-service broker and the difference between the commissions charged by the typical full-service broker and the typical deep discount broker.

—defined as the 20th least expensive discounter for each of the 8 trades.

The figure ($144) is then reduced by 20% to allow for possible weighing toward higher priced trades (where discounts are less) and other factors.

The figure ($115) is multiplied by 3 to show typical savings with a deep discounter for an investor making 3 stock trades per year.

(2) This is based on the assumption that funds in an IRA dollars are ultimately taxable.

It is a good approximation for 10 years or longer. For less than 10 years, the accurate figure lies somewhere between the Cumulative Savings and Equivalent Taxable Income, approaching the former as retirement draws closer.

CHAPTER 15

Treasury Bills and Bonds

I offer Exhibit A in support of the proposition that we have become a nation of couch potato investors the glaring example of U.S. Treasury bills. Close to $400 billion dollars is currently invested in money funds, and the assets keep growing, yet Treasury bills are demonstrably superior investments in every way except the one aspect that couch potatoes value above all else: convenience.

Even *there* Treasury bills have made inroads. The Federal Reserve's new Treasury Direct system provides the equivalent of a federal broker. This broker even has 37 convenience offices around the country through which you can do business: the branches of the Federal Reserve System. And it wires interest payments straight into your bank account at no charge. In one major way, it differs from both discount and full-service brokers. This broker is free.

Why then is $400 billion invested in money funds? One reason is that the Federal Reserve probably doesn't have .1% of the advertising budget of the money fund industry, and even if it did, couch potato syndrome has spread across the land. Convenience reigns supreme.

AN INVESTMENT COMPARISON: TREASURY BILLS VS. MONEY FUNDS

Safety

Treasury bills are direct issues and guaranteed by the full faith and credit of the U.S. government. They are widely regarded as the safest investment in the world. With a Treasury Direct account, you have a direct claim against the U.S. government; there is no intermediary.

Most taxable money funds are invested in commercial paper or other obligations of private corporations. You do not have a direct claim against those issuers, but rather against the mutual fund companies. As a group, their safety record has been outstanding, and in normal times, will likely remain that way. But no one can be sure what might happen in the event of a major financial collapse (see Chapter 11, Money Market Funds).

There are mutual funds that buy U.S. government securities, but they pay the same price as individual investors. (There are no discounts for volume purchases in buying from the U.S. government.) The funds then deduct their fee, which typically averages about 10% of the yield (.8% at current levels).

Tax Advantages

The interest from most money funds is subject to local, state, and federal tax. Interest from Treasury bills is not subject to state or local tax.

Also, interest on money funds is taxable in the year it is earned. Treasury bill interest is taxable in the year that the bill matures. For example, if you buy a bill in January 1991 and it matures in January 1992, you will not be taxed on the interest earned until the 1992 tax year. For a money fund, you would pay taxes in 1991.

Yield

With these multiple advantages, you would expect Treasury bills to yield significantly less than money funds. In fact, due to

Treasury Bills and Bonds

the expenses of operating money funds, the yield on Treasury bills is frequently *higher*, even before taking tax advantages into account.

For example, during the first week of April 1990, the yield on 6-month Treasury bills was 8.24%. By comparison, during the same period *Donoghue's* average yield on taxable money funds, with a 45-day average maturity, was 7.67%. Therefore, Treasury bills were paying .57% more than money funds on a pretax basis. For high-tax bracket investors in a high-tax state, Treasury bills probably yielded over a percent more than money funds—a full 15% higher yield after taxes.

Treasury bills are often superior to even tax-free money funds. Their 7-day average yield during this period was 5.42%, and in many cases, this yield would be subject to state and local tax. By comparison, a Treasury bill would yield 5.5 to 5.9% after all federal, state, and local taxes, depending on whether you were in the 28% or 33% bracket.

WHO SHOULD NOT USE TREASURY BILLS

There are really only a few good reasons not to use Treasury bills.

1. You do not have the $10,000 minimum investment required ($1000 for notes and bonds).
2. You may need most of the funds on short notice. (If you will only need part of the funds, then you could place part in a money fund and part in Treasury bills.)
3. The savings are too small to justify the time involved.
4. You are a confirmed, unreconstructed, and unrepentant couch potato.

USING THE TREASURY DIRECT ACCOUNT

To take advantage of this federal broker who charges no commission and offers a safer product with a higher yield, you simply call or write to the nearest Federal Reserve Bank on the list at the end of this chapter. Ask for information about opening a direct deposit account to purchase Treasury bills. The form you

Figure 15.1. Sample 6-Month Treasury Bill Application

FORM PD 5176-2
(January 1986)

TREASURY DIRECT

OMB No. 1535-0069
Expires: 01-31-89

TENDER FOR 26-WEEK TREASURY BILL

TENDER INFORMATION

AMOUNT OF TENDER: $ ____________

BID TYPE (Check One) ☐ NONCOMPETITIVE ☐ COMPETITIVE AT ___ . ___ %

ACCOUNT NUMBER ___ - ___ - ___

INVESTOR INFORMATION

ACCOUNT NAME

ADDRESS

CITY STATE ZIP CODE

TAXPAYER IDENTIFICATION NUMBER

1ST NAMED OWNER ___ - ___ - ___ (SOCIAL SECURITY NUMBER) OR ___ - ___ (EMPLOYER IDENTIFICATION NUMBER)

TELEPHONE NUMBERS

WORK ( ) ___ - ___ HOME ( ) ___ - ___

PAYMENT ATTACHED

TOTAL PAYMENT: $ ____________

CASH (01): $ ____________ CHECKS (02/03): $ ____________

SECURITIES (05): $ ____________ $ ____________

OTHER (06): $ ____________ $ ____________

FOR DEPARTMENT USE

TENDER NUMBER
912794

CUSIP

ISSUE DATE

RECEIVED BY

DATE RECEIVED

EXT REG ☐

FOREIGN ☐

BACKUP ☐

REVIEW ☐

CLASS ☐

NUMBERS

DIRECT DEPOSIT INFORMATION

ROUTING NUMBER

FINANCIAL INSTITUTION NAME

ACCOUNT NUMBER

ACCOUNT NAME

ACCOUNT TYPE (Check One) ☐ CHECKING ☐ SAVINGS

AUTOMATIC REINVESTMENT

1 2 3 4 Circle the number of sequential 26-week reinvestments you want to schedule at this time

AUTHORIZATION

For the notice required under the Privacy and Paperwork Reduction Acts, see the accompanying instructions.

I submit this tender pursuant to the provisions of Department of the Treasury Circulars, Public Debt Series Nos. 1-86 and 2-86 and the public announcement issued by the Department of the Treasury.

Under penalties of perjury, I certify that the number shown on this form is my correct taxpayer identification number and that I am not subject to backup withholding because (1) I have not been notified that I am subject to backup withholding as a result of a failure to report all interest or dividends, or (2) the Internal Revenue Service has notified me that I am no longer subject to backup withholding. I further certify that all other information provided on this form is true, correct and complete.

SIGNATURE

DATE

Courtesy of the U.S. Treasury Department

Treasury Bills and Bonds

will receive is not an intimidating five-page government form to be completed in triplicate, but a simple one-page application. Figure 15.1 is an example of a form used to buy a 6-month Treasury bill.

Now comes the most difficult part. You must submit a certified check when purchasing Treasury bills. This is the one part of the process which seems unnecessarily onerous and downright inhuman. It may break your banker's heart to certify such a large amount leaving your bank account.

When your account form and check, stained with your banker's tears, arrives at the Fed, you will receive a unique account number and what amounts to a brokerage statement. Any time there is activity in your account, you will receive another statement.

THE REINVESTMENT OPTION

One of the pleasant surprises about this account is that you can reinvest (roll) your Treasury bills automatically for up to two years. Looking at the form, you will notice an "automatic reinvestment" line just above the bottom. If you circle number 4, your funds will be automatically reinvested four times in the 6-month bills that you originally purchased.

When the six months are nearly up, you will be sent a notice that the funds will be reinvested. This gives you a chance to change your mind. If you don't, the interest earned on the first six months investment will be wired directly to your bank account at no cost and the principal will be reinvested. No time needed to clip coupons and no risk of lost checks.

You can also purchase 3-month Treasury bills, and automatically roll them up to eight times (two years) or 1-year bills and roll them twice. By renewing your instructions every two years, you can continue to let the government invest for you indefinitely in this manner.

OTHER NOTES AND BONDS

Through the same process, you can purchase government notes, which come in varying maturities up to 10 years, and bonds, which have longer maturities. Whatever you purchase will appear on your combined account statement, which will list all bills, notes, and bonds you hold through the Treasury Direct system.

TIMING

When you buy through the Treasury Direct system, you are actually buying at a government auction. In most cases, this provides a higher yield than buying in the open market because you do not pay the market maker's markup and you do not pay commissions.

These auctions occur weekly for 3-month and 6-month bills, monthly for 1-year bills, and at various times around the year for notes and bonds. The packet that you will receive from the Federal Reserve Board provides a phone number with a recorded message describing forthcoming auction dates.

RESALE

The system is primarily designed for investors who want to hold their Treasury instruments until maturity. If you want to sell before maturity, you must submit a form that requests transfer of your securities to a designated bank or broker. When the transfer is complete, you instruct that bank or broker to sell your security in the open market and pay normal brokerage costs.

For this reason, I suggest that investors not use this system for funds which they may need on short notice. The transfer time plus the costs of resale make money funds more suitable for this purpose.

BUYING BILLS AND NOTES THROUGH A BROKER

If you are dealing in large amounts, or longer maturities, you may find that buying Treasury bonds or bills through a broker is a good compromise between the Treasury Direct system and a money fund. Mercer's *Bonds and Bills Survey* found that bank charges for purchase of Treasury bills typically ranged from $30 to $75. Many offered flat charges regardless of the size of the purchase, but a few charged more as the value increased.

If you pay $50 to purchase a $25,000 1-year Treasury bill, that reduces your effective pretax yield by about .2%, still leaving higher tax bracket payers well ahead of a money fund. As the amounts invested get larger or the maturities longer, the costs of using this method decline. However, if you only want to invest $10,000 in 3-month Treasury bills, you should use either the Treasury Direct method or a money fund. Brokers are not economic for smaller amounts and frequent turnover.

GOVERNMENT NOTES AND BONDS

As previously noted, government bond funds are one of the mutual fund industry's less admirable products. This example will show why this is true. With a government bond fund, you will typically pay .8% per year when you could buy that same security without charge through the Treasury Direct account or for a one-time $30 to $75 charge which, over a decade, amounts to less than .05%, even on a $10,000 purchase.

If you are using a government bond fund for the convenience of check writing, you would do better to set aside the portion which you may need soon in a money fund and use the balance to buy bonds directly.

SAVINGS BONDS

A number of years ago, I worked at the U.S. Treasury Department in Washington. The main office for U.S. Savings Bonds was a few doors down the hall, but it really wasn't considered part of the Treasury by most of us. Frankly it was an embarrassment. The yield was so low that it amounted to a government ripoff of the smallest and least knowledgeable investor.

This situation has changed. Over the last few years, the yield has improved. It is now set at 85% of the yield on 5-year

Treasury notes. You would still do better in Treasury notes, of course, but the savings bond is available in denominations as small as $25, qualifies for many payroll savings plans, and offers other advantages to the small investor.

Furthermore, it's free from city and state tax, so in highly taxed areas, you may actually do better after taxes than you would with a CD. That's pretty good for a $25 investment that carries Uncle Sam's seal of approval.

Effective after 1990, Congress introduced a provision that could make these investments even more attractive, but you won't know if they really are more attractive until your children go to college. Under the new law, interest on savings bonds is tax-free if used to pay college tuition, and if the parents' adjusted gross income is under $60,000 or, in some circumstances, under $90,000. At the current yield, that would be equivalent to a 7% tax-free bond with zero risk since it's guaranteed by the Federal Government and furthermore, keyed to a relatively short-term rate which limits your interim interest loss if interest rates were to move sharply upward.

However, there are two qualifications which make the benefits unpredictable. First, if your child decides to skip college and join the army or see the world, the interest becomes taxable. That's not so bad. You'll be so thrilled at not having to pay $100,000 plus inflation for college tuition that you won't mind parting with a few bucks to Uncle Sam.

The worst part is that the income criterion—the $60,000 or $90,000 number—will be determined at the time your child goes to college! So if you work hard and make your way into the upper brackets, you get to pay both college tuition *and* Uncle Sam. That's not so thrilling.

This is such a silly law that the odds are good it will change, so you should check with your tax adviser at the time that you are thinking about investing in savings bonds.

Listed below are branches of the Federal Reserve system to which you can write or call to establish a Treasury Direct account.

FEDERAL RESERVE OFFICES

Board of Governors

Board of Governors of the Federal Reserve System
20th and Constitution Avenue, N.W.
Washington, DC 20551
(202) 452-3000

Main Offices

ATLANTA
Federal Reserve Bank of Atlanta
104 Marietta Street, N.W.
Atlanta, Georgia 30303
(404) 521-8500

BOSTON
Federal Reserve Bank of Boston
600 Atlantic Avenue
Boston, Massachusetts 02106
(617) 973-3000

CHICAGO
Federal Reserve Bank of Chicago
230 South LaSalle Street
Chicago, Illinois 60690
(312) 322-5322

CLEVELAND
Federal Reserve Bank of Cleveland
1455 East Sixth Street
Cleveland, Ohio 44101
(216) 579-2000

DALLAS
Federal Reserve Bank of Dallas
400 South Akard Street
Dallas, Texas 75222
(214) 651-6111

KANSAS CITY
Federal Reserve Bank of Kansas City
925 Grand Avenue
Kansas City, Missouri 64198
(816) 881-2000

MINNEAPOLIS
Federal Reserve Bank of Minneapolis
250 Marquette Avenue
Minneapolis, Minnesota 55480
(612) 340-2345

NEW YORK
Federal Reserve Bank of New York
33 Liberty Street
New York, New York 10045
(212) 720-5000

PHILADELPHIA
Federal Reserve Bank of Philadelphia
101 Independence Mall
Philadelphia, Pennsylvania 19106
(215) 574-6000

RICHMOND
Federal Reserve Bank of Richmond
701 East Byrd Street
Richmond, Virginia 23219
(804) 643-1250

ST. LOUIS
Federal Reserve Bank of St. Louis
411 Locust Street
St. Louis, Missouri 63102
(314) 444-8444

SAN FRANCISCO
Federal Reserve Bank of San Francisco
101 Market Street
San Francisco, California 94105
(415) 974-2000

Branch Offices

BALTIMORE (Richmond)
502 South Sharp Street
Baltimore, Maryland 21201
(301) 576-3300

BIRMINGHAM (Atlanta)
1801 Fifth Avenue North
Birmingham, Alabama 35202
(205) 252-3141

BUFFALO (New York)
160 Delaware Avenue
Buffalo, New York 14202
(716) 849-5000

CHARLOTTE (Richmond)
401 South Tryon Street
Charlotte, North Carolina 28230
(704) 336-7100

CINCINNATI (Cleveland)
150 East Fourth Street
Cincinnati, Ohio 45201
(513) 721-4787

DENVER (Kansas City)
1020 16th Street
Denver, Colorado 80202
(303) 572-2300

DETROIT (Chicago)
160 Fort Street West
Detroit, Michigan 48231
(313) 961-6880

EL PASO (Dallas)
301 East Main Street
El Paso, Texas 79999
(915) 544-4730

HELENA (Minneapolis)
400 North Park Avenue
Helena, Montana 59601
(406) 442-3860

HOUSTON (Dallas)
1701 San Jacinto Street
Houston, Texas 77002
(713) 659-4433

JACKSONVILLE (Atlanta)
515 Julia Street
Jacksonville, Florida 32231
(904) 632-4400

LITTLE ROCK (St. Louis)
325 West Capitol Avenue
Little Rock, Arkansas 72203
(501) 372-5451

LOS ANGELES (San Francisco)
409 West Olympic Boulevard
Los Angeles, California 90015
(213) 683-8323

LOUISVILLE (St. Louis)
410 South Fifth Street
Louisville, Kentucky 40201
(502) 568-9200

MEMPHIS (St. Louis)
200 North Main Street
Memphis, Tennessee 38103
(901) 523-7171

MIAMI (Atlanta)
9100 N.W. Thirty-Sixth Street Extension
Miami, Florida 33178
(305) 591-2065

NASHVILLE (Atlanta)
301 Eighth Avenue North
Nashville, Tennessee 37203
(615) 259-4006

NEW ORLEANS (Atlanta)
525 St. Charles Avenue
New Orleans, Louisiana 70161
(504) 586-1505

OKLAHOMA CITY (Kansas City)
226 Dean A. McGee Avenue
Oklahoma City, Oklahoma 73125
(405) 235-1721

OMAHA (Kansas City)
2201 Farnum Street
Omaha, Nebraska 68102
(402) 221-5500

PITTSBURGH (Cleveland)
717 Grant Street
Pittsburgh, Pennsylvania 15230
(412) 261-7800

PORTLAND (San Francisco)
915 S.W. Stark Street
Portland, Oregon 97205
(503) 221-5900

SALT LAKE CITY (San Francisco)
120 South State Street
Salt Lake City, Utah 84111
(801) 322-7900

SAN ANTONIO (Dallas)
126 East Nueva Street
San Antonio, Texas 78204
(512) 224-2141

SEATTLE (San Francisco)
1015 Second Avenue
Seattle, Washington 98104
(206) 442-1376

CHAPTER **16**

The Futures Market

You may not know it, but the odds are high that you have seen the futures market at work. It's that unforgettable shot when the TV camera pans across hundreds of people screaming and waving their arms, making strange hand signals. It could be an average day at a Liverpool soccer match, but they're in a large room with numbers flashing on the walls, standing in a circle. These are the commodity pits. As much as any other, this image is the media's picture of capitalism. Most viewers probably assume they are watching the New York Stock Exchange on Wall Street. They don't realize they're often seeing Wall Street's unruly Chicago cousins, the traders in the futures (commodities) markets.

Many TV symbols are appealing but misleading. They don't really hold up under close scrutiny. But the commodities, or futures, markets as they're somewhat interchangeably described, are quite an accurate symbol for the trading markets of capitalism.

The economic system known as capitalism, which Adam Smith laid out in the 1700s was based on the distasteful notion that the best of all systems is built on an explicit recognition of human greed. Perhaps the most serious defect of this philosophy was not to surface until two centuries later when it became apparent that capitalists were at a severe disadvantage on TV talk shows. Capitalists did not come across well advocating Greed while their Socialist opponents argued for the Greater Good of Mankind. This disadvantage has been considerably lessened by the recent collapse of most of those countries who advocated the Greater Good.

Actually, Adam Smith was not a naive fellow. What he foresaw in the 1700s, and his opponents still did not see two centuries later, was that the minister could preach charity from the pulpit, but the congregation was still thinking about how to turn a shilling. Human nature being what it is, the next best thing was to make sure that these greedy folks worked against each other. If they did, Smith figured, the public would benefit. And the best way to keep them at each others' throats, instead of the public's, was a competitive market.

Therefore, it is fitting that these unseemly capitalists, the screaming and waving commodity traders, loudly pursuing their own self-interests, have created what may be the most efficient market in the world. And hence, the best for the consumer (the investor). It is the least expensive way that an individual can trade the markets.

Yet most investors, even most active investors, never will use the commodities markets. And that is just as well. It takes a certain combination of financial means, risk tolerance, trading style, and self-discipline to effectively harness these unruly markets. But for those sophisticated investors who fit this bill, there is a great deal of money to be saved.

These potential savings will be examined in the next section after talking about the more conventional question: How much can you save using a discount commodity broker?

DISCOUNT FUTURES BROKERS

Commissions

If you've followed the discussion of discount stock brokers, you will find the cost advantages similar for discount futures brokers, as commodity brokers are generally known.

The Futures Market

Mercer publishes the *Discount Futures Broker Survey* which compares the commissions and other costs of different discount commodity brokers both with each other and full-service brokers (see The Discount Publications Directory). From the *1989 Survey*, I have compiled the Discount Futures Brokers Directory, which appears in Appendix C. Using some of these brokers, you can save up to 75% of the commission costs charged by a full-service commodity broker.

Commission savings typically vary from about 30 to 75%, depending on which discount brokers and full-service brokers are being compared. Typically, you will pay $85 to $100 per contract for a round trip (buy and sell) contract to a full-service firm, and $30 to $40 to a full-discount commodity broker. So your potential savings is $75 per trade.

So far, the comparisons of discount broker savings discussed have been restricted to those who hold themselves out to the public and deal with individual retail investors. If you're an extremely active trader, verging on a professional, you may be able to negotiate a rate down to about $12 per trade. But don't even think about it unless you're trading 50 to 100 contracts per week.

Commission charges are more uniform among futures brokers than stock brokers, because the charges are typically built around the number of contracts you trade, not the price of those contracts nor their underlying value. And there are far fewer types of contracts than there are stocks.

Noncommission Costs

Unlike stocks, however, the complex margin requirements of futures trading involve significant noncommission costs. The largest of these is the cost of meeting the initial and subsequent margin requirements. The exchanges require that customers put up cash or collateral in order to trade. However, different firms may impose different in-house minimums, and, most importantly from a cost perspective, they impose different types of collateral requirements.

Being required to put up a $10,000 Treasury bill is not really a cost. You will receive interest on the bill. However, some firms will not let you use Treasury bills for smaller investments; they will require that you place some money in non-interest bearing accounts. Or they will require that the funds be placed in a house account which pays less than market interest.

In an 8% market, the loss of interest on $5000 will cost you $400 per year, so you have to review the information you receive from the broker quite carefully to assure that you understand what the noncommission cost will be.

Service and Other Variations

The principal advantage of a full-service broker is that you will receive more service and research than with a discounter. This parallels the variations between discounters and full-service brokers in the stock market, but commodity market brokers are more prone to offer multiple levels of service.

If you want to make all your own trades without advice, then you will get the low rates which are described above. However, if you want some limited forms of advice, many futures discounters will offer a second level of service that is not as steeply discounted. Some will offer a third. This type of variation is not as common among stock discounters.

Otherwise you will find the full panoply of services that is found in the stock discount industry: quote services; computer trading; publications; hotlines; personal account executives, if you want them; and several other small perks not typically found in the stock market firms.

SEVERAL CAVEATS FOR STOCK INVESTORS INTERESTED IN FUTURES

Before explaining the least expensive method of trading that exists, you should be aware of several of the risks and methods of the commodities market that differ from stocks. At the conceptual level, buying a future on a stock index is the same as owning the stocks. But in the real world, you may be in for a few surprises. Some of the differences are listed below.

- The leverage is huge. Typically 10% down versus 50% if you buy stocks on margin. So the value of your contract

The Futures Market

swings may be 5 times as great as a comparable stock investment.
- Margin positions are "marked to the market" every night. You must immediately remit cash to cover your margin call if the market moves against you. This does not mean a gentlemanly stock market week to pay, but rather having cash in your money market to cover whatever is necessary the next morning, or wiring funds to cover it, or being sold out of your position.

No SIPC Safety Net

You need to pay more attention in selecting a futures broker than a stock broker because there is no government agency such as SIPC which guarantees commodity accounts. There is government oversight, but no government guarantees.

You therefore need to be certain that the clearing broker, the one that holds your funds and issues you the monthly statement, is an experienced, well-capitalized firm. As one trader tactfully told me, the commodities market is more concerned with "counterpart risk than customer risk." That means, they want to be sure that one firm does not fail in honoring its commitment to the other.

Actually, this is a kind of Adam Smith consumerism. The major risk in a highly leveraged business is if one major firm fails to pay another. This brings down that second firm, which brings down the third, and so on. Then the whole house of cards could collapse and alot more consumers could get hurt. Still, if you're an investor at the firm which honored its counterpart instead of your account, this will not provide much consolation. Failures have been few and far between, but you don't want to be the next casualty.

When opening an account, you may want to take the further precaution of seeing that any profits you make in excess of margin requirements are moved into a segregated money market account which is held in your name, not the firm's, and therefore is not subject to attachment by the firm's creditors.

But the best insurance is care in selecting the firm. The rule of thumb in the industry is to avoid firms that are clearing agents for options traders or locals—freelance traders who stand in the pits and trade for their own account. These people are notorious in the industry for overtrading and finding themselves unable to meet their obligations. This in turn can jeopardize the safety of your account with the firm.

A well-known name may be worth the price as a form of insurance. But most of the futures brokers associated with well-known names are subsidiaries. The parent is not liable. You are therefore counting on their reputation and unwillingness to let a subsidiary go under rather than any strict legal guarantees. This will probably work well enough as long as the firm's parent is very solvent and the deficit of the subsidiary is of modest proportions. What would happen in a pinch is unknown, but we do have the example of Drexel Burnham Lambert.

According to published reports, when 1990 began, Drexel Burnham paid its employees $350 million in 1989 year-end bonuses, including over $10 million to each of 3 executives. This $49 million was drawn down on an overnight credit line. The next morning, they declared bankruptcy and told their creditors that they could not pay their $100 million debt. This prompted Paul Kangas, the stock commentator whose humorous "Last Word" segment closes out PBS's "Evening Business Report," to display a recent book titled *Wall Street Ethics*. He opened the book. All the pages were blank.

This may be a bit harsh, but it's food for thought. Everything considered, one should not rely on Wall Street, or Chicago, to forego their year-end bonus to pay off clients of a subsidiary.

THE LEAST EXPENSIVE WAY IN THE WORLD TO TRADE STOCKS—IF YOU CAN HANDLE IT

The futures markets offer the least expensive way to trade the market averages.

One of the Chicago Mercantile Exchange's S&P 500 Index contracts at the time of writing was equivalent to approximately $165,000 in stock. Using a discount commodity broker, you can buy and sell that contract for $30. With a typical deep discount broker, buying and selling a basket of 20 stocks worth a total of

The Futures Market

$165,000 would cost over $1650. With a full-service broker, it would be about $7600. Translated into discounts, that means futures brokers offer a discount of 98.2% vs. deep discounters, or 99.6% vs. full-service firms.

The eye doesn't understand these numbers. They are too large. A better way to make the comparison may be to state that the typical deep discounter's commission would cost over 55 times as much as a futures broker; a full-service broker, over 250 times as much.

In addition, the cost of the spread between bid and asking price is much smaller in the futures market than the stock market. The best spread which you could hope to achieve in buying and selling a stock on an exchange would be $1/8$ point in each direction. Since you will often pay more, let's assume a round trip costs $3/8$ point. With the average stock at the end of 1989 selling for approximately $37, this works out to almost exactly 1% more.

The spread is an important transaction cost, but as long as we've been comparing discounters with full-service brokers, or brokers with mutual funds that also pay the same spread, it was a wash. Everyone was paying the same cost, so it did not alter the equation. Now that different marketplaces, commodities vs. stocks, are being compared, the spread becomes relevant. In the futures market, the typical spread on a normal day is about $25 each way on an actively traded contract like the S&P 500. That is a total of $50 for a round trip vs. $1650 for either a full-service or discount broker. Add this factor into the equation and even the best discount stock broker looks incredibly expensive.

In fact, the futures contracts are so efficient as trading vehicles that they are even less expensive for most traders than "free" switching with a mutual fund. Investors who use mutual funds to trade in and out of the stock market pay no commission cost at all, but they do pay the fund's normal expenses.

Using a 1.5% expense ratio for a typical stock fund and .8% for a money market, the investor who switches back and forth will pay an average expense ratio of 1.15%. This assumes the person parks his or her money in each fund for half the year. Based on $165,000 invested, that worked out to an annual bill of

$1900. But since it only costs $80 round trip ($50 for the spread and $30 for the commission), an investor could make more than 20 round trips per year for that price. So if you change your mind about the market less than 20 times per year, a futures account could be a less expensive way to trade than "free" switching privileges with a mutual fund.

THE INTOXICATING EFFECT OF THE FUTURES MARKET

The problem with these low commission rates is that they are intoxicating. Between the low cost of trading and the enormous leverage in the futures market, most individual investors seem to get carried away. It's like playing the $500 chip table at Las Vegas with the house lending you 90 cents on the dollar.

It is well established that most individual investors lose money in the futures market. And with the huge leverage, they lose it very fast; many are washed out within a year. As one person knowledgeable about futures firms told me in jest, "Don't bother to write the check to your account. Write it straight to your broker. The money will be his by the end of the year anyhow."

For this reason, I recommend the lowest cost market in the world only to those individual investors who can stand at the $500 chip table at Vegas with $5000 in their wallets and not reach into their pockets except to pay for drinks.

Don't expect any help from your commodities broker. Discount commodity brokers are much more aggressive than their discount stock broker counterparts. In many cases, you will hear from them often with trading tips, until they determine that they are wasting their time, because you're not biting.

SAVING MONEY AND PROTECTING CAPITAL WITH FUTURES

If you have a substantial portfolio and can resist the temptations of the market and the suggestions from your broker, the futures market may have a place in your portfolio strategy.

The Futures Market

It is not for the long-term investor who buys a stock and holds it through thick and thin, but it is good for the trader who wants to occasionally increase his or her market position for a short time. If you want to play your belief that the market will rise or fall over the next few months, futures are an ideal way. Clearly they are much less expensive than trading individual stocks, and considerably less expensive for a few turnovers per year than parking your money in a mutual fund (with the meter running).

The savings could be substantial; turning over a $165,000 portfolio twice a year even with a typical deep discounter will cost close to $3500 in commissions, plus quite likely an equal amount in the spreads which you don't see. With a futures broker, it will cost $160, spreads included. Assuming that there is some loss of interest during the year because brokers don't credit you with the full interest on your initial deposit, the cost for everything should still be less than $500. The savings potential on commission only is over $3000.

With a mutual fund, your parking costs (annual expenses) are estimated at 1.15% per year, if you spend equal amounts of time in the stock and money fund parking lots at about $2000 per year for a $165,000 portfolio. Savings potential on commissions only: $1500 plus.

For the long-term investor with a substantial portfolio, who occasionally feels the market is overvalued and would like to hedge but doesn't want the cost or capital gains associated with selling off long-term positions, futures are ideal. If you had a $300,000 portfolio in mid-1987 and decided the market was grossly overvalued, but didn't want to pay taxes on $100,000 in long-term gains, you could have sold one contract to hedge half your portfolio, or two to hedge it all.

This will work well as long as you have a diversified portfolio whose performance approximates that of one of the general market indices that trade in the futures market. If your portfolio is dominated by one issue, or invested in a specialized group of stocks, selling futures contracts as a hedge will not work well. The two indexes which are most useful for individual stock investors are the S&P 500 Index which trades on the Chicago Mercantile Exchange and the slightly smaller Blue Chip (Major

Market Index) trading on the Chicago Board of Trade. The S&P 500 tracks the broad market's largest stocks; the Blue Chip is designed to track the Dow Jones.

Unless you are consciously speculating, futures are best suited for the investor with a larger portfolio. The size of the basket of stocks or other securities underlying the most popular futures contracts is typically six figures. There are contracts designed for the smaller investor—not quite as liquid and not quite as cheap—but still very low cost versus buying and selling stocks. But even those contracts are typically in the middle five figures.

Futures is a complex area with many intricacies that can't be addressed in this book. For that reason, several books on the subject of varying sophistication levels are included in the Discount Publications Directory. Further reading is highly recommended before initiating futures trades.

Institutions understand the value of the futures market and use them frequently. It has acquired a bad reputation among individual investors as risky, and with good reason. Many of those individuals who use it are small investors using the leverage to swing for the bleachers, and they wind up striking out. But for the sophisticated individual investor with a larger portfolio, the world's least expensive market should have a place in their portfolio.

CHAPTER 17

Limited Partnerships

In the early 1980s, when tax brackets were high and inflation was rampant, a previously obscure legal creature known as the limited partnership suddenly became popular. As a limited partner, an investor could benefit from tax deductions while limiting his or her liability to the amount of capital invested. The partnerships generally invested in tangible assets, such as real estate or oil and gas, which were expected to appreciate handsomely from double digit inflation.

It has been estimated that over 12 million people invested more than $100 billion in limited partnerships in the 1980s—an astonishing number considering that less than 20 million people bought stocks during that period. Excluding fixed income and savings type accounts, it was probably Americans' second most popular investment in the early 1980s. But with the decline of inflation, weakness in real estate markets, and the crash in oil prices, these partnerships have generally fared poorly. And with the change in the tax law in 1986, many of their future tax benefits were lost. Limited partnerships have literally fallen off the edge of the investment world.

But investment trends come and go. Contrarians would argue that the current unpopularity of limited partnerships bodes well for the future. In any event, no book on investing would be complete without discussion of an investment that attracted 12 million investors in its heyday and may someday rise again.

Frankly, partnerships are a difficult subject to approach from the perspective of a discount. They are not interchangeable: one partnership is not the same as another. When you buy General Motors stock, you're buying the same stock shares from a discounter or full-service broker. The only difference is the transaction cost. But when you compare two real estate partnerships, one partnership may own a better piece of real estate. It's like comparing apples and oranges.

Nevertheless, I believe that there are certain rules that you can follow which will improve your chances of buying into a better partnership. They don't guarantee success, but they are very simple and they do guarantee that you can improve your odds. At their root is the fact that the partnership market is much less efficient than the stock market. Recognizable disparities exist, if you take the time to recognize them.

THE NOT-SO-RANDOM WALK

Some serious students of the stock market believe that you can match the typical fund manager's performance by tacking the stock market page of your newspaper to a wall, throwing a dart at it, and buying the stock where the dart lands. The official title for the dartboard theory is the random walk, and the *Wall Street Journal* has run a semi-tongue-in-cheek monthly article comparing the performance of experts with the *Journal*'s dartboard. Frequently, the dartboard outperforms the pros.

But if you decide to enlist a dart as your investment adviser, make sure you pin the stock pages, not a limited partnership prospectus, on your wall. Even if it's not worth your time to read 50-page annual reports or stock offering memorandums, it is worth your time to read the document which accompanies the limited partnership offering.

The reason that there is some validity behind the dartboard theory in the stock market is that you have a large number of

Limited Partnerships

analysts or investors looking at a comparatively small number of stocks. These stocks all trade in an active secondary market. Therefore, the price of the stock reflects the consensus of informed opinion about what it is worth. While there are many qualifications needed to translate the theory into practice, the underlying concept is sound.

When a new stock issue comes out, there is no public market for that particular stock, but there are many similar stocks out there. If it's a new computer company, analysts know that similar companies in similar fields with similar growth rates are trading at, for example, a price per share equal to 14 times earnings. If the new stock issue is underwritten by a reputable broker, the price may be a little high or a little low, but it must bear some relation to the pricing of existing stocks. The institutions and professionals who are significant purchasers of all but the most speculative and untried new issues know what market price is reasonable, and won't buy unless the offering price is in line.

While there are some limited partnerships that are traded on the major exchanges like stocks, there is no meaningful secondary market for the vast majority of the nearly $100 billion in limited partnership units sold during the 1980s. There are several reasons. Most of these were not businesses, resale was restricted for legal reasons to help assure tax benefits, and most of them were too small to justify an exchange listing.

The typical limited partnership is not sold to professional investors. It is sold to individuals. Surely, many of these individuals are quite sophisticated and must meet eligibility standards to participate in a private placement offering, but there are no analysts out there comparing 20 issues and keeping them in line.

Furthermore, in the case of the larger public offerings, where the amount involved is small and the eligibility requirements minimal, the buyers can be quite unsophisticated. The price is whatever the underwriter decides the traffic will bear. As a result, there is an enormous variation in the quality and pricing of limited partnerships in the same field.

The bottom line is that the dartboard doesn't work for limited partnerships. If you want to invest blind, stick to the stock market (preferably the larger and most widely followed issues). There, Adam Smith's Invisible Hand keeps prices in line.

But the good news is that investors probably can select a partnership that will outperform the average. In other words you can beat the dartboard. Even if you've given up hope of ever learning anything meaningful from a corporation's lengthy annual report, don't throw out the limited partnership prospectus which you receive from the sales rep with the offering documents (known as a private placement memorandum for the smaller private placement offerings).

WEED OUT THE BAD APPLES

Because I've read hundreds of offering documents, I know that there is one almost invariable rule which goes quite contrary to common sense. The worse the deal, the worse the track record of the general partner, the higher the partnership costs. This seems to be the result of some kind of perverse natural selection. The better underwriters will not accept general partners with bad track records, so they are forced to seek out less reputable underwriters who charge more to raise the funds.

But you will sometimes find even reputable underwriters sponsoring bad deals. I remember studying with astonishment one set of oil drilling partnerships. Surprisingly it was sponsored by a substantial financial services company, which lent these partnerships a credibility which they didn't deserve.

Let us call it the D&P (Drill and Pray) oil company. D&P had a high upfront fee, high management fees, and its nonaccounting overhead would soak up 8% of the initial partnership's capital annually. But the most amazing aspect of the document was the track record. It was spelled out in black and white: Over 20 partnerships were organized over several years. Over several years, the average partnership had returned a total of less than 10 cents per dollar invested. And this was during a period when oil prices were rising.

Several years after reading these memorandums, I came across a newspaper article indicating that the president of these companies had embezzled several million dollars. I felt much better. It explained something which puzzled me: How could anyone drill that many wells when oil prices were high without returning at least 10 cents on the dollar? You should have been able to drill at random and produce a better record.

As it happened, I'd had experience in the oil industry, but you didn't need 10 years of experience in the industry to figure out something was wrong here. And you didn't need to know the president was stealing. If you spent an hour reading the document, you would wonder why any sane person would want to invest in this partnership. But thousands of high income investors who should have known better had not spent that hour.

The problem was that they didn't know what sections to read. Faced with 150 pages of legal gobbledygook, most investors just throw up their hand and hope for the best. In reality, if you focus on three sections of the prospectus, you will have learned most of what you need to know.

Upfront Costs: Organization and Sales Costs. How much of every dollar you invest actually makes its way into the investment and how much gets diverted to the sales reps, lawyers, general partners, and others involved in organizing the partnership?

Upfront costs typically include an 8% commission, 2 to 3% for legal costs, plus miscellaneous costs. The general partner, who organized and operates the partnership and has ultimate liability for its debts, also usually receives a fee at closing. The underwriter receives a fee as well as others involved in the offering.

At the peak of their popularity in the early 1980s, average organization costs for oil partnerships were running 17 to 18% and real estate partnerships often ran 25%! This meant that only 75 cents to 83 cents on every dollar invested in the partnership actually made its way into the underlying investment.

Partnerships are also expensive to organize. What is a low organization cost for a partnership would be exorbitant for a mutual fund. If you want to participate, you will have to pay the price. But today, you should think twice about a limited partnership if the organization and sales costs are much over 10%. With 90 cents on the dollar working for you, there's a fighting chance of a decent return.

Management Fees and Overhead. Perhaps only an expert in the field can look at the fees and overhead and tell whether they are reasonable or somewhat high. But an alert reader can tell if they are totally out of line. That is the purpose reading this section; to weed out the rotten apples.

In the D&P partnership, the private placement memorandum clearly indicated that the partnership proposed to charge approximately 20% annually for overhead. This did not include the management fee. This would not be out of line for an active business, but this partnership was primarily a passive investment. It's hard to see how one could subtract 20% annually and still turn much of a profit. Could you do that in the stock market?

You need to ask yourself the basic question: Will the general partner still succeed if the partnership fails? The general partner is entitled to receive some fixed fees for time irrespective of results, just like the salaried executives of any company, but major profits should be tied to results.

Track Record. As the song says, "you don't have to be a weatherman to tell which ways the wind is blowing." If the general partner has formed numerous partnerships over the years which have underperformed the competition, stay away. This seems so obvious, but investors seem to forget. There will be another partnership coming along sooner or later; hold out for the good track record.

The SEC has been quite successful in getting partnership sponsors to disclose material items in the offering documents, warts and all. It's generally all there if you read it. But the SEC has been much less successful in getting investors to read it (you can lead a horse to water . . .).

Reading these three sections won't guarantee that you'll make money in a limited partnership. External factors, such as the price of oil or real estate, may ultimately determine the success of your investment. But carefully reading these warnings will allow you to weed out the lemons and invest in partnerships where the costs are reasonable and you have a decent shot at turning a profit.

THE SECONDARY MARKET

My description of how to select partnership investments focuses on reviewing the offering documents which the SEC requires

Limited Partnerships

accompany all new offerings. That is because until recently, investors could purchase units in a partnership only at its inception. Unlike stocks or bonds, which you can buy at the offering and sell the next day on the exchanges or the over-the-counter market, there was no market for limited partnerships expected. They were primarily designed as long-term investments, to be liquidated when the underlying asset or business was sold. Until that time, the investor was expected to sock his or her investment away in a closet and forget about it.

So if you wanted to invest in a limited partnership, you had to buy into a new one. That is also when the tax advantages were greatest. The largest ones were registered with the SEC and sold through brokers; smaller partnerships were sold through brokers or other financial intermediaries.

In the late 1980s, an informal secondary market for limited partnerships developed. In theory, it should be very attractive for buyers who want to invest at a discount since there is no sales commission, broker/dealer's cost, or partnership's organization costs. If upfront sales and organizational costs in the early 1980s, when most of these were sold, used to average 15 to 25%, there should be huge discounts in purchasing through this secondary market where there are no such costs. Unfortunately, the reality of these secondary markets at present is far less attractive than the theory. Whatever you save in lower organizational costs is offset by the dealer's markup. It's primarily a market for distress sales.

Apparently there are enough anxious sellers among 12 million investors who bought during the 1980s to support this small, informal market. They're willing to sell because many of these partnerships turned out to be disappointing investments, and they'd now like to be rid of them. They were designed to offer tax benefits and hedge against inflation. But inflation moderated, real estate prices leveled or declined, and oil prices crashed. The tax benefits have been received, or if ongoing, their value is diminished due to the decline in the tax brackets and changes in the tax law. So some of their owners want out—at virtually any price.

Apart from the brokers who comprise the market, buyers are rare birds. One dealer to whom I spoke was very pleasant, and very surprised when I expressed an interest buying in oil limited partnerships. He sounded like he'd never heard from a buyer before. They had basically kept whatever units they could buy, or resold in large units to private groups that helped finance the purchase.

It's an odd market when dealers have phone sales representatives combing the country soliciting limited partnership owners to sell their units. When was the last time you had a cold call from a sales rep with a hot tip about something to *sell*?

Most of the market makers restrict themselves to the largest public real estate limited partnerships or a few equipment leasing partnerships. There still is no market for the tens of thousands of private limited partnerships or smaller public ones. But times change. Perhaps it will evolve into more of a two-way market in the future. If you're a sophisticated investor, and want to nose around, some of the firms which currently comprise that market are listed in Table 17.1.

Table 17.1 Secondary Market Limited Partnerships

Bigelow Management Inc. 800/431-7811 (in NY: 212/697-5880)	**MacKenzie Securities** 800/854-8357 (in CA: 800/821-4252)
Chicago Partnership Board Inc. 800/272-6273	**National Partnership Exchange Inc.** 800/356-2739 (in FL: 800/336-2739)
Cuyler & Associates 800/274-9991	**Nationwide Partnership Marketplace** 707/829-1600
Dunhill Equities Inc. 800/937-0550 (in NY: 516/747-5904)	**Pacific Asset Group Inc.** 818/796-6693
EquityLine Properties Inc. 800/327-9990 (in FL: 305/662-4088)	**Partnership Securities Exchange Inc.** 800/736-9797
Equity Resources Group 617/876-4800	**Raymond James & Associates Inc.** 800/248-8863
Frain Asset Management 800/654-6110	**G.K. Scott & Co.** 800/526-1763
Liquidity Fund 800/227-4688	**2nd Market Capital Services** 608/833-7793

THE DO-IT-YOURSELF DISCOUNT

Forming your own limited partnership is not a realistic option for most people. They don't have the time, they don't have the

Limited Partnerships

resources, and they don't have the entrepreneurial bent. That's why they are paying someone else to run it. And that's why this chapter primarily addresses how to find the best, least expensive partnership.

But some people do have the time and the inclination for active investment. They are retired, or their job does not demand all their time, energy, or interests. If you're in this category, and looking for a profitable way to spend your time, you might consider organizing your own limited partnership.

Among all the areas of investment, limited partnerships are probably the most time intensive, the most costly to organize, and, consequently, impose the greatest costs on outside investors. The flip side of that coin is that if you organize your own partnership, the savings are greater than for almost any other type of investment.

This becomes apparent when comparing the cost of investing in a limited partnership to investing in a stock mutual fund. While upfront costs are typically lower today than in the early 1980s, even a good limited partnership typically has 10 to 15% in organizational costs. Management and general partner profit sharing vary enormously depending on the type and size of the investment. Assuming they average 5% annually, on a $50,000 investment the potential savings are $5000 at the outset and $2500 per year.

Let's now assume that you were prepared to spend an equal amount of time investing in stocks. You pore through annual reports and newsletters, you follow the market, you read the financial press. But how much can you save?

If you've read the chapter on mutual funds, then you know that if you shop around you can buy good professional management with zero upfront costs and fees that typically range from $1/2$ to $1 1/2$% per year! The total savings, if you spend 60 hours per week on stocks, is still no more than $1 1/2$% of $50,000—$750 per year. That is only about $1/10$ of the first year cost of a limited partnership and 30% of the ongoing costs.

Managing stocks have their own rewards. Unlike running a limited partnership, you can monitor your stock portfolio from your living room on a rainy afternoon or winter evening, and ease up when the sun is shining. But if you have plenty of time available, there is no comparison in the potential savings.

Limited partnerships are not more expensive because general partners are greedier than Wall Street fund managers. Part of the added expense results from the significant time involved in assembling and running a limited partnership. There are certain irreducible costs that cannot be eliminated because they are part of the nature of the investment in tangible properties.

- The market is quite specialized, so unless you know the investors personally, sales reps must be compensated to raise the capital.
- It takes the general partner time to find the right building or oil well, negotiate the terms, and organize the partnerships. That time must be compensated.
- The lawyers who draft the lengthy limited partnership document do not work for free.
- Finally, the management takes time—collecting rents, dealing with operating problems, and so on. That must be compensated.

Then, when you've finally finished, you must go out and start all over again for the next partnership.

But the real key to why limited partnerships are so much more expensive than mutual funds lies in the economies of scale. It may take a conscientious portfolio manager 50 or 60 hours per week to run a $10 million portfolio, but it doesn't take him any longer to run a $50 million portfolio, or a $1 billion portfolio, for that matter. He or she just adds a few assistants and adds a few zeros to the size of the orders.

Organization costs are much lower for equities as well. Once an open-end fund is formed, it can keep accepting investors forever. Limited partnerships operate under more restrictive legal rules which require a new legal document every time more capital is raised. If the Fidelity Magellan fund had been required to raise capital in this manner, it would have taken 5000 legal closings at $2 million apiece to reach its current size.

You may not have the experience to organize an oil partnership, or the resources to lease an airplane, but most people can become involved in the most popular of limited partnerships—real estate. Here, local knowledge is a great advantage. You may not merely be able to match the track record of the large national syndicators; if you do your homework, you may be able to beat them.

If you don't have the resources to buy a building yourself, start with a few friends and their friends. There's a good chance you can assemble the necessary capital for the right project. I have known several people who started this way, working part-time while holding down another job, and made fortunes. You may not make a fortune, but you'll certainly invest with a handsome do-it-yourself discount and might even have some fun along the way.

CHAPTER **18**

Precious Metals, Discount Coins, and Other Purported Discounts

I'm no expert on precious coins and any inclination to become one was dispelled by my conversations with a nationally advertised coin dealer. I had responded to an ad offering a brochure from a firm which advertised itself as a discount coin dealer. A week later, a sales representative called. I couldn't take his first call, but he caught me on the second round.

"What size discount do you offer?" I asked.
"60% to 80%," he answered.
"60% to 80% off what?" I asked.
"60% to 80% off the retail price of the coin."

I let it drop. Since I don't believe in Santa Claus, I don't believe that firms take out expensive national ads so that their sales reps can hunt you down to sell you a product at 80% below the retail price.

A week later, a second sales rep from the same firm caught me at the office at night. Welcoming a temporary break from work, I asked the same question, "What kind of discount do you offer?" He answered with an example. He cited a certain $20 gold piece that was listed in a national coin magazine. The magazine indicated that the bidding price for the coin was $7600 and the asking price was $7800. He indicated that they would sell it at $7550.

While the story sounded more plausible than his associate who had called the previous week, it still didn't make sense. If the bid was $7600, why spend his nights calling prospects to sell it at $7550?

I realized there is a fundamental problem in trying to apply the term discount to this type of market.

DISCOUNTS VS. BARGAINS

My wife can walk through a store and at 50 feet away spot the one item which is stylish, high quality, and selling at half its normal price. It's probably the one item in the store on which the manager is losing his shirt. If there were a hundred other women like my wife, New York would not be safe for retailers.

She is buying at a much larger discount than I could ever hope to find, but it's not the type of discount we're talking about. A good shopper getting a low price for buying in quantity or finding a car for a fraction of its cost are all examples of saving money. In common language, these are discounts, but they are not the type of discounts that have been discussed in this book.

I would not call these discounts, but bargains. The savings on bargains are potentially much greater than discounts where transaction costs may range from $1/2$ to 8%, rarely more. Bargains can be 60% or greater.

The savings are much greater for bargains, but they are harder to teach. Spotting a bargain requires aptitude and experience. Getting a discount requires no more than going to the right source for information. Like this book.

My focus has been on transactional discounts—ways to keep down the costs of purchasing items. The transaction cost is clearly separated from the underlying price when the purchase is made in an open market by a third-party broker.

Precious Metals, Discount Coins, and Others

If you are buying directly from the seller with no third party in between, the discount on the transaction costs can still be identified if the item being sold is fungible and has a price which can clearly be identified in the open market. In the financial market, the instruments are all fungible. One share of General Motors is identical to any other share. A $10,000 Treasury bill is identical to any other of similar denomination and maturity.

In most of the financial markets, you can fix the price to within a fraction of a point. The spread between the bid and asked may range from $1/8$ to $1/2$ on the stock exchanges, to $1 or $2 in the less liquid over-the-counter stocks, to several dollars on junk bonds. But there is a price which can generally be fixed with great precision.

COLLECTIBLES

Collectibles, such as rare coins, stamps, paintings, and antiques are not fungible. One Picasso is not like another; each is very different. They may be sufficiently similar to group together (coins and diamonds are graded) but they're all different, and you really need to be knowledgeable in the field to be sure that the coin the dealer is offering for $7550 is truly similar in all meaningful respects to the $7800 coin advertised in the paper.

When you start dealing in collectibles where the price is uncertain and the quality varies, the term discount is out of place. The price differences resulting from quality and market variations swamp the impact of any discount which may exist. In collectibles, we have passed from the world of discounts into the world of bargains. How to spot a bargain is beyond the scope of this book.

Precious Metals and Modern Precious Coins

While rare coins fall into the collectibles area, gold and silver bullion and modern day precious coins like Krugerrands and Maple Leafs are a different story. They are fungible and their price can be readily established in the open market. Modern precious coins and bullion that meet designated standards for purity will sell at the same price in the markets around the world, plus or minus the transaction price.

There are some discount brokers and discount banks that do offer precious metals at a discount. They won't be calling you at night to tell you about their bargains, but they will charge less than you may have been accustomed to paying to purchase them.

You can identify these firms by looking at the section titled Investment Products in the profiles of the banks and brokers listed in the Discount Brokerage Directory. Some of these firms will list precious metals or coins among the products they offer. I don't identify the deep discounters among this group, because the sample is not large enough, but some offer lower costs than others. A few phone calls will establish which of these discounters offers the best prices for your intended purchase.

If you are a large-scale purchaser, you may also want to review the costs of buying a commodity contract for gold and silver and taking delivery at the expiration date. This is not commonly done, but in sufficient size, can sometimes result in uncommonly large savings.

CHAPTER 19

Shareholder Discounts and Privileges

One of the greatest privileges of share ownership in the 1980s was the right to greenmail. You bought 10% of the stock, threatened a takeover, and walked away with a tidy tip from management for your gentlemanly agreement to leave them alone. Not quite blackmail. Greenmail.

On the other hand, if you don't have the spare $50 million needed to play this game, you will be pleased to learn that you don't always have to settle for a glossy, full-color picture of the chairman of the board. Some companies take good care of their shareholders without any threats.

Would you like to buy $100,000 worth of stock without paying a dime's commission? What about a 10 to 50% discount on some of the best-known hotels, resorts, and products in the country? These are the types of benefits available from certain companies that like to treat their shareholders right.

Shareholder benefits fall into several categories: Annual Meeting Goodies, Product and Service Discounts, Dividend Reinvestment Plans, and Voluntary Stock Purchase Plans.

ANNUAL MEETING GOODIES

This is probably the most frequently offered and least valuable of the perks. The IRS won't even let you deduct the cost of going to the meeting. But you could learn something about your company, possibly receive a few samples of company products, and occasionally get a free lunch, disproving the old adage that there is no such thing as a free lunch.

PRODUCT AND SERVICE DISCOUNTS

Many companies offer discounts on the company's products. They do this to create a bond between the company and its shareholders. The company wants shareholders who will identify with it and take pride in its products, not just an interest in the latest quarterly earnings.

Frequently, they will require that the shareholder be registered, rather than hold the shares in street name. This means that you will need to have your broker deliver to you some of the shares of stock which you own, if you don't already hold it directly. The rewards are well worth the small inconvenience if you own stock in the right companies. Here are a few of the more interesting shareholder discounts that I have found.

Marriott Hotels. Marriott offers its registered shareholders discounts at Marriott hotels and Marriott-owned hotels. One share will suffice provided it's registered. The discounts apply to Friday and Saturday night stays at three of their chains. Representative discounts range from $10 off per night at the Marriott hotels to a whopping 50% off at the Residence Inn chains, or a stay at the Courtyard hotels for $39 to $59 per night.

Prime Motor Inns. This company, which now also owns the former Ramada chain, offers shareholders a 25 to 50% discount at many of its hotels on Fridays and Saturdays on an availability basis.

Ralston Purina. Cupcakes, Twinkies, and Ding Dongs are offered at its annual meeting, but for the more active investor, this company offers discounts at its Keystone Colorado ski resort. Shareholders can get discount coupons at certain times of the year for themselves and the entire family.

Shareholder Discounts and Privileges 171

Disney. Discounts at Disneyland and Disney World are offered to shareholders.

Even the keys to the Magic Kingdom are available at a discount to the shareholder with the right password. If you are a registered shareholder, you can receive information from the shareholder discounts section at 714/490-3200. Don't bother to call here if you're not registered, only the registered will receive information.

Brown Forman began offering its shareholders discounts on its famous Lenox china a few years ago. Now it's become a tradition. Every September, the company mails out a listing of a dozen or so holiday gift items which shareholders can buy at a 50% discount!

Tandy, parent company of the well-known Radio Shack stores, has been offering its shareholders across-the-board 10% discounts at holiday time in recent years. The offer comes out in a shareholder letter that arrives each November and is good until the year's end.

Pfizer offers a substantial discount on certain cosmetics at year-end.

Squibb offers a discount on Charles of the Ritz products.

General Mills gives you 25% off at its Red Lobster restaurants.

Subject to Change

In many cases, management tends to view these discounts as management prerogatives which may be changed or eliminated. Therefore, you will want to contact the company or read your latest annual report to see that the discount is still being offered. If you are interested in further information on the subject, you may want to see the *Mercer Shareholder Discount Survey* (see the Discount Publications Directory).

DIVIDEND REINVESTMENT PLANS

The best-known of the company stock purchase plans is a dividend reinvestment plan. This permits investors to reinvest their dividends in company stock without paying any brokerage commission. It is offered by many companies. A smaller number of companies not only permit reinvestment without commissions, but they offer a discount on the cost of the new shares that you purchase with your dividends. These are also listed in the *Mercer Shareholder Discount Survey.*

VOLUNTARY INVESTMENT PLANS— THE ULTIMATE DISCOUNT

What is less well known is that many companies permit shareholders with as little as one share of stock to buy large quantities of stock with absolutely zero commission.

If you own one share of stock, you can currently buy up to $60,000 worth of Phillip Morris, $100,000 of Martin Marietta, or $120,000 of Phillips Petroleum every year free of charge. This is a fitting note on which to end this book. Investing $100,000 without paying a dime's commission must be the ultimate discount.

Appendices

APPENDIX A

The Discount Brokerage Directory

The information contained in this Directory is excerpted from the *Mercer 1989 Discount Financial Directory*[1] (see Appendix D, The Discount Publications Directory).

Chapter 1 (The Discount Brokers) provides the names, addresses, and 17 key facts about non-bank discount brokers. You will find this useful in identifying firms, assessing the types of services they offer, finding out the manner in which they offer the service to the public, and understanding the operational structure of the firm.

Chapter 2 (The Bank Brokers) provides facts about many of the banks that are currently offering discount brokerage. These profiles cover a somewhat different set of facts, but can be used in the same manner.

THE DIRECTORY'S METHODOLOGY

The information contained in this Directory is based on surveys of discount brokers (non-bank and bank) conducted since our

---
[1] Reprinted with permission from Mercer, Inc.

first survey in 1983 and updated during the fall of 1989 and winter of 1990. Letters containing the profiles of each discount or bank brokerage firm were prepared by Mercer's staff and sent to each firm for review and correction. These were followed up with telephone discussions where considered useful. While the information contained in this Directory has been obtained from reliable sources and is believed to be correct, Mercer cannot guarantee the accuracy of the contents. In some cases, space limitations preclude complete discussion of commission and account requirements. Furthermore, changes occur over time. Therefore, **I strongly urge readers to request the latest information from the broker before making an investment decision.**

CHAPTER 1

The Discount Brokers

This section provides key facts about virtually every substantial non-bank discount brokerage firm in the country. The areas which are covered are listed below.

(1) *Name and address.* The address listed is that of the principal office.

(2) *Telephone numbers.* The local number and the toll-free number, if available, are included. Where the firm has several local numbers, the number listed is for new accounts.

(3) *Other office locations.* Notes which other cities house offices; provides an indication of the firm's scope.

(4) *Insurance protection.* All firms should provide the standard $500,000 insurance offered by the SIPC. This covers securities and up to $100,000 cash in brokerage accounts. Where supplemental coverage is provided, the amount of that coverage is listed.

(5) *Order handling.* There are two basic methods used to service customers. One is to assign a specific account executive to each account; the other is to use a team system. This section tells you which system each firm uses and whether that firm uses registered representatives exclusively to take orders.

(6) *Clearinghouse.* This section identifies the clearinghouse (wholesale vendor) used.

(7) *Firm's exchange membership.* Membership on the New York Stock Exchange or other exchanges are listed. NASD membership, which tends to be standard, is not listed.

(8) *Special account requirements.* This section notes out-of-the-ordinary account requirements of two types: (1) initial account requirements, such as cash required to be in the account before making a trade, and (2) ongoing account requirements. Options may be subject to account limitations more restrictive than those noted here.

(9) *Commission structure.* If the designation "DD" appears, this indicates that the firm is designated as a deep discounter. This means that the broker has been identified as one of the 30 independent brokers with the lowest average cost for either the sample of trades averaging approximately $6000 (LO) or $13,000 (HI). If the firm appears on both lists, then both are listed, for example, DD (HI, LO). The source is the *Mercer 1989 Discount Brokerage Survey* (see Appendix D).

Also indicated is the type of cost system. Mercer has coined the terms for the two types of commission structures used: Those who charge on the basis of the value of the transaction are termed "valuebrokers." Those who charge strictly according to the number of shares traded are termed "sharebrokers."

(10) *Minimum charge.* The minimum charges required for investment (if any) are noted.

(11) *Margin interest costs.* The method and level of the charges is described.

(12) *Interest paid on cash balances.* The amount being paid or method for calculating interest and the minimum balance necessary for the client to receive interest are noted.

(13) *Investment products.* Identifies which investment products are offered by the firm.

(14) *Additional charges.* This includes costs such as delivery charges, limit order surcharges, and so on.

(15) *Date firm established.* The date when the firm was established (it may have begun to offer discount brokerage services later).

(16) *States where licensed to do business.* A category which is subject to frequent change and does not necessarily preclude occasional stray accounts in other states.

(17) *Services.* Describes publications or other services provided to assist the investor in making investment decisions.

(18) *Notes.* Highlights unusual features.

Andrew Peck Associates, Inc.
32 Broadway
New York, NY 10004

Telephone Numbers:

    Toll-Free (nationwide)   800/221-5873
    Local   212/363-3770

Other Office Locations: None

Insurance Protection: SIPC, $500,000 with $9.5 million additional

Order Handling: Team system

Clearinghouse: Securities Settlement Corp.

Firm's Exchange Membership: None

Special Account Requirements: Deposit for first transaction

Commission Structure: Sharebroker, DD (HI)

Minimum Charge: Stocks, $50; Options, $50

Margin Interest Costs: Negotiable on large debits

Interest Paid on Cash Balances (Rate and Minimum):   2% below broker's call rate; $2000 minimum

Investment Products: Stocks; Bonds; Options

Additional Charges: $25 for wiring funds and courtesy transfers; $35 for exchanges or tender offers

Date Firm Established: 1979

States Where Licensed to Do Business: Most states

Note: Offers a "Savings in Size" program for investors who consistently trade 3000 shares or more, charging $0.03/share (listed; $100 minimum) or $0.02/share (OTC; $75 minimum)

Arbour Securities
85 Church Street
New Haven, CT 06510

Telephone Numbers:

    Toll-Free (in-state)   800/922-4506
    Local   203/776-1910

Other Office Locations: None

Insurance Protection: SIPC, with $2.5 million additional

Order Handling: Team system

Clearinghouse: U.S. Clearing Corp.

Firm's Exchange Membership: None

Special Account Requirements: None

Commission Structure: Sharebroker

Minimum Charge: Stocks, $40; Options, $40

Margin Interest Costs: Information not available

Interest Paid on Cash Balances
(Rate and Minimum):   Money market fund; $1000 first deposit; $100 minimum increments

Investment Products: Information not available

Additional Charges: Information not available

Date Firm Established: 1979

States Where Licensed to Do Business: Information not available

Arnold Securities, Inc.
830 Second Avenue South
Minneapolis, MN 55402

Telephone Numbers:

    Toll-Free (out-of-state)   800/328-4076
    Toll-Free (in-state)   800/292-4135
    Local   612/339-7040

Other Office Locations: None

Insurance Protection: SIPC, $500,000

Order Handling: Team system

Clearinghouse: Swiss American Securities, Inc.

Firm's Exchange Membership: None

Special Account Requirements: None

Commission Structure: Sharebroker

Minimum Charge: Stocks, $35; Options, $35

Margin Interest Costs:

$ Borrowed	Broker's Call+
Up to $10,000	$1 \tfrac{1}{2}$%
$10,000–$30,000	$1 \tfrac{1}{4}$%
$30,000–$50,000	1%
$50,000–$75,000	$\tfrac{3}{4}$%
Above $75,000	$\tfrac{1}{2}$%

Interest Paid on Cash Balances
(Rate and Minimum): 2% below broker's call rate; $2000 minimum balance

Investment Products: Stocks; Bonds; Options; IRAs; Mutual Funds

Additional Charges: None

Date Firm Established: 1976

States Where Licensed to Do Business: Information not available

Atlantic Discount Brokerage Services Corp.
7 East Baltimore Street
Baltimore, MD 21202

Telephone Numbers:

    Toll-Free (nationwide)   800/634-4935
    Local   301/244-3541

Other Office Locations: Bethesda, MD

Insurance Protection: SIPC, up to $500,000 (limited to $100,000 cash); Aetna Casualty and Surety Co., up to $2 million

Clearinghouse: Fidelity Brokerage Services, Inc.

Firm's Exchange Membership: Information not available

Special Account Requirements: None

Commission Structure: Valuebroker

Minimum Charge: $40

Margin Interest Costs: Annual rate varies from a minimum of $1/4\%$ to a maximum of 2% above broker's call money rate, depending on the amount of the debit balance

Interest Paid on Cash Balances (Rate and Minimum):   Money market rates; $100 minimum

Investment Products: Stocks; Options; IRAs

Services: Special research rooms

Additional Charges: Legal items $25 per transfer

Date Firm Established: 1984

States Where Licensed to Do Business: Maryland, Pennsylvania, Virginia

Note: Subsidiary of The Bank of Baltimore

K. Aufhauser & Company, Inc.
112 West 56 Street
New York, NY 10019

Telephone Numbers:

    Toll-Free (nationwide)   800/645-9486
    Local   212/246-9431

Other Office Locations: None

Insurance Protection: SIPC, $500,000 plus $10 million additional

Clearinghouse: Pershing & Co., Division of Donaldson, Lufkin & Jenrette

Firm's Exchange Membership: National Futures Association

Special Account Requirements: Information not available

Commission Structure: Sharebroker

Minimum Charge: Stocks, $45; Options, $45

Margin Interest Costs: Variable

Interest Paid on Cash Balances
(Rate and Minimum): Competitive with money market rates

Investment Products: Information not available

Additional Charges: Small service change for transfers, etc.

Date Firm Established: 1982

States Where Licensed to Do Business: California, Connecticut, Georgia, Illinois, Maryland, Michigan, New Jersey, New York, Ohio, Oklahoma, Texas

The Discount Brokerage Directory   185

**Baker & Co., Inc.
Baker Building
1940 East Sixth Street
Cleveland, OH 44114**

Telephone Numbers:
    Toll-Free (out-of-state)   800/321-1640
    Toll-Free (in-state)   800/362-2008
    Local   216/696-0167

Other Office Locations: Sarasota, FL

Insurance Protection: SIPC, $500,000 plus $2 million additional

Order Handling: Team system and 12 account executives

Clearinghouse: Cowen & Co.

Firm's Exchange Membership: NYSE

Special Account Requirements: None

Commission Structure: Valuebroker, DD (LO)

Minimum Charge: Stocks, $35; Options, $35

Margin Interest Costs:

$ Borrowed	Broker's Call+
Up to $9999	2 1/4%
Reduced 1/4% every $9999 to $30,000 debit	

Interest Paid on Cash Balances (Rate and Minimum): Money market funds available

Investment Products: Information not available

Additional Charges: None

Date Firm Established: 1971

States Where Licensed to Do Business: Florida, Illinois, Indiana, Massachusetts, Michigan, New York, Ohio, Pennsylvania

Barry W. Murphy & Co., Inc.
270 Congress Street
Boston, MA 02210

Telephone Numbers:

    Toll-Free (nationwide)   800/221-2111
    Local   617/426-1770

Other Office Locations: None

Insurance Protection: SIPC, $500,000 plus Aetna, $2 million

Order Handling: Account executive assigned

Clearinghouse: Broadcort Capital Corp., a subsidiary of Merrill, Lynch, Pierce, Fenner & Smith

Firm's Exchange Membership: None

Special Account Requirements: None

Commission Structure: Sharebroker, DD (HI, LO)

Minimum Charge: Stocks, $25; Options, $20

Margin Interest Costs:

Borrowed	Broker's Call+
Up to $9999	$2 1/4$%
$10,000–$19,999	2%
$20,000–$29,999	$1 3/4$%
$30,000–$49,999	$1 1/2$%
Above $50,000	$3/4$%

Interest Paid on Cash Balances
(Rate and Minimum):   Summit fund; $1000 minimum

Investment Products: Stocks; Bonds; Options; IRAs

Additional Charges: None

Date Firm Established: 1975

States Where Licensed to Do Business: Most states; also, 27 other countries

Berlind Securities, Inc.
One North Broadway
White Plains, NY 10601

Telephone Numbers:

    Toll-Free (in-state)   800/942-1962
    Local   914/761-6665

Other Office Locations: Greenwich, CT

Insurance Protection: SIPC, $500,000 with $10 million additional

Order Handling: Account executive assigned

Clearinghouse: Securities Settlement Corp.

Firm's Exchange Membership: None

Special Account Requirements: None

Commission Structure: Sharebroker

Minimum Charge: Stocks, $35; Options, $35

Margin Interest Costs: Information not available

Interest Paid on Cash Balances
(Rate and Minimum): 3% below broker's call rate; $2500 minimum

Investment Products: Information not available

Additional Charges: Information not available

Date Firm Established: 1979

States Where Licensed to Do Business: Information not available

Bidwell & Company
209 S.W. Oak Street
Portland, OR 97204

Telephone Numbers:

    Toll-Free (out-of-state)   800/547-6337
    Toll-Free (in-state)   800/452-6774
    Local   503/790-9000

Other Office Locations: Beaverton, OR

Insurance Protection: SIPC, $500,000; $10 million upon request

Order Handling: Team system

Clearinghouse: Self

Firm's Exchange Membership: Pacific Stock Exchange, Midwest Stock Exchange

Special Account Requirements: None

Commission Structure: Sharebroker, DD (HI, LO)

Minimum Charge: Stocks, $20; Bonds, $50; Options, $30

Margin Interest Costs: Prevailing market rates

Interest Paid on Cash Balances
(Rate and Minimum): Prevailing money market rates, $1 interest/month minimum

Investment Products: Stocks; Bonds; Options; IRAs

Services: Research facilities

Additional Charges: Certificate delivery charge, $2.50; Legal transfer, $20

Date Firm Established: 1977

States Where Licensed to Do Business: Idaho, Oregon, Washington

Brokers Exchange, Inc.
Arcadia Office Park
6941 North Trenholm Road
Columbia, SC 29206

Telephone Numbers:

    Toll-Free (out-of-state)   800/845-0946
    Toll-Free (in-state)   800/922-0960
    Local   803/738-0204

Other Office Locations: Maryland, South Carolina, Virginia

Insurance Protection: SIPC, $100,000 for cash plus $2.5 million for securities

Order Handling: Account executive assigned

Clearinghouse: Shatkin Lee Securities

Firm's Exchange Membership: None

Special Account Requirements: None

Commission Structure: Valuebroker

Minimum Charge: Stocks, $35; Options, $35

Margin Interest Costs: Information not available

Interest Paid on Cash Balances
(Rate and Minimum): Current money market rates

Investment Products: Stocks; Bonds; Options; IRAs

Additional Charges: $10 additional commission charge

Date Firm Established: 1981

States Where Licensed to Do Business: Alabama, District of Columbia, Georgia, Maryland, South Carolina, Virginia

Brown & Company
20 Winthrop Square
Boston, MA 02110

Telephone Numbers:

    Toll-Free (nationwide)   800/225-6707
    Local   617/742-2600

Other Office Locations: Orlando, FL; Chicago, IL; New York, NY; Philadelphia, PA

Insurance Protection: SIPC, $500,000

Order Handling: Team trading

Clearinghouse: Self

Firm's Exchange Membership: NYSE, AMEX, Philadelphia Stock Exchange

Special Account Requirements: $10,000 in cash or securities to open an account; to trade: buying power or securities must be in the account on trade date.

Commission Structure: Sharebroker, DD (HI, LO)

Minimum Charge: Stocks, $25 + $.04/share; Options, $21

Margin Interest Costs: Ranges from broker's call rate to $1/2\%$ below broker's call rate, depending on amount borrowed

Interest Paid on Cash Balances
(Rate and Minimum): Depends on market conditions; often less than money market rates.

Investment Products: Stocks; Bonds; Options; IRAs

Additional Charges: $10 charge for transfer and delivery of securities

Date Firm Established: 1960

States Where Licensed to Do Business: All states

Bruno, Stolze & Company, Inc.
425 N. New Ballas Road
P.O. Box 27359
St. Louis, MO 63141-1759

Telephone Numbers:

Toll-Free (Midwest)	800/325-1332
Toll-Free (in-state)	800/392-1378
Local	314/569-3900
Other	Call collect

Other Office Locations: None

Insurance Protection: SIPC, $500,000 plus $9.5 million

Order Handling: Team system (all registered representatives)

Clearinghouse: Securities Settlement Corp.

Firm's Exchange Membership: None

Special Account Requirements: None

Commission Structure: Value/Sharebroker

Minimum Charge: Stocks, $35; Options, $30

Margin Interest Costs:

$ Borrowed	Broker's Call+
Up to $10,000	$2 1/4$%
$10,000–$30,000	2%
$30,000–$50,000	$1 1/2$%
Above $50,000	$1 1/4$%

Interest Paid on Cash Balances
(Rate and Minimum): 4% below broker's call rate; $2500 minimum

Investment Products: Stocks; Bonds; Options; Mutual Funds; IRAs; Real Estate Trusts; Public Storage

Services: Boardroom/research library; financial workshops; research reports; information booklets; financial planners

Additional Charges: None

Date Firm Established: 1975

States Where Licensed to Do Business: Florida, Illinois, Missouri

Bull & Bear Securities, Inc.
11 Hanover Square
New York, NY 10005

Telephone Numbers:

    Toll-Free (nationwide)   800/262-5800
    Local   212/742-1300

Other Office Locations: None

Insurance Protection: SIPC, $500,000 plus Aetna, $2 million

Order Handling: Ernst & Co.

Clearinghouse: Ernst & Co.

Firm's Exchange Membership: New York Futures Exchange, Municipal Securities Rulemaking Board

Special Account Requirements: Naked options, $100,000 minimum; spreads, $10,000 minimum

Commission Structure: Valuebroker

Minimum Charge: Stocks, $39; Options, $39

Margin Interest Costs:

$ Borrowed	Broker's Call+
Up to $24,999	2 1/2%
$25,000–$49,999	2%
$50,000–$89,999	1 1/2%
Above $90,000	1%

Interest Paid on Cash Balances (Rate and Minimum):   Broker loan minus 2 1/2%; $100 minimum

Investment Products: Information not available

Additional Charges: None

Date Firm Established: 1984

States Where Licensed to Do Business: All states

The Discount Brokerage Directory

Burke Christensen & Lewis Securities, Inc.
303 West Madison
Chicago, IL 60606

Telephone Numbers:

Toll-Free (out-of-state)	800/621-0392
Toll-Free (in-state)	800/621-0392
Local	312/346-8283

Other Office Locations: Cleveland, OH; Detroit, MI; Minneapolis, MN; Milwaukee, WI

Insurance Protection: SIPC, $500,000

Order Handling: Team trading

Clearinghouse: Self

Firm's Exchange Membership: Midwest Stock Exchange

Special Account Requirements: None

Commission Structure: Valuebroker, DD (HI, LO)

Minimum Charge: Stocks, $30; Options, $30

Margin Interest Costs:

$ Borrowed	Broker's Call+
All amounts	1%

Interest Paid on Cash Balances
(Rate and Minimum): Linked to 3-month Treasury bill rate

Investment Products: Stocks; Bonds; Options; IRAs

Additional Charges: Securities delivery fee, $15; Wire TRF, $15

Date Firm Established: 1973

States Where Licensed to Do Business: 35 states

W.T. Cabe & Co.
1270 Avenue of the Americas
Rockefeller Center
New York, NY 10020

Telephone Numbers:

    Toll-Free (out-of-state)   800/223-6555
    Local   212/541-6690

Other Office Locations: None

Insurance Protection: SIPC, $500,000

Order Handling: Registered representatives assigned

Clearinghouse: Self

Firm's Exchange Membership: Information not available

Special Account Requirements: None

Commission Structure: Valuebroker

Minimum Charge: Stocks, $40; Options, $40

Margin Interest Costs: 1% above prime rate

Interest Paid on Cash Balances
(Rate and Minimum):   Money market fund; $5000 minimum

Investment Products: Stocks; Bonds; Options; IRAs; Mutual Funds

Services: Library; research

Additional Charges: None

Date Firm Established: 1973

States Where Licensed to Do Business: Connecticut, New York, Pennsylvania

Calvert Securities Corporation
51 Louisiana Avenue, N.W.
Washington, DC 20001

Telephone Numbers:

    Toll-Free (nationwide)   800/368-2700 or -2750
    Local   202/783-0759

Other Office Locations: None

Insurance Protection: SIPC, $500,000 plus $2 million additional

Order Handling: Team system (registered representatives only; assigned upon request)

Clearinghouse: Robert W. Baird & Co., Inc.

Firm's Exchange Membership: None

Special Account Requirements: Information not available

Commission Structure: Value/Sharebroker

Minimum Charge: Stocks, $45; Options, $45

Margin Interest Costs:

$ Borrowed	
All amounts	Broker's Call + 2%

Interest Paid on Cash Balances (Rate and Minimum):   Calvert Group Fund; $2000 initial deposit

Investment Products: Stocks; Bonds; Options

Additional Charges: Information not available

Date Firm Established: 1983

States Where Licensed to Do Business: Most states

CoreStates Securities Corp.
P.O. Box 13429
Philadelphia, PA 19101-3429

Telephone Numbers:

    Toll-Free (nationwide)   800/222-0124
    Local   215/973-6208

Other Office Locations: None

Insurance Protection: SIPC

Order Handling: DirecTrade

Clearinghouse: National Financial Services Corp.

Firm's Exchange Membership: None

Special Account Requirements: None

Commission Structure: Valuebroker

Minimum Charge: Stocks, $35; Options, $35

Margin Interest Costs: Information not available

Interest Paid on Cash Balances
(Rate and Minimum):   Cash sweep available

Investment Products: Stocks; Bonds; Options

Additional Charges: None

Date Firm Established: 1984

States Where Licensed to Do Business: New Jersey, Pennsylvania

S.C. Costa Company, Inc.
320 South Boston Avenue
West Lobby
Tulsa, OK 74103

Telephone Number:

    Local   918/582-0110

Other Office Locations: None

Insurance Protection: SIPC, $500,000

Order Handling: Team system (account executive assigned on request)

Clearinghouse: Southwest Securities

Firm's Exchange Membership: None

Special Account Requirements: None

Commission Structure: Valuebroker

Minimum Charge: Stocks, $38; Options, $38

Margin Interest Costs: Information not available

Interest Paid on Cash Balances
(Rate and Minimum): $6\ 3/4\%$ (floating rate); $200 minimum

Investment Products: Stocks; Bonds; Options

Additional Charges: None

Date Firm Established: 1975

States Where Licensed to Do Business: Oklahoma

Downstate Discount Brokerage, Inc.
Pinellas Shopping Center
825 West Bay Drive
Largo, FL 33540

Telephone Number:
Local   813/586-3541

Other Office Locations: None

Insurance Protection: SIPC, $500,000

Order Handling: Team system

Clearinghouse: Swiss American Securities, Inc.

Firm's Exchange Membership: None

Special Account Requirements: None

Commission Structure: Valuebroker, DD (HI, LO)

Minimum Charge: Stocks, $.08/share on first 500 shares; Options, $31.50

Margin Interest Costs:

$ Borrowed	Broker's Call +
Up to $10,000	$2\,1/4\%$
$10,000–$20,000	2%
$20,000–$30,000	$1\,3/4\%$
$30,000–$50,000	$1\,1/2\%$
Above $50,000	$3/4\%$

Interest Paid on Cash Balances
(Rate and Minimum):   Varies with broker call; no minimum

Investment Products: Stocks; Bonds; Options; Unit Trusts; Mutual Funds; GNMAs; Precious Metals

Services: Library available including Value Line and other market letters. *Dow Jones News Service* and *Moody's Research* are displayed electronically.

Additional Charges: None

Date Firm Established: 1980

States Where Licensed to Do Business: Florida

Exchange Services, Inc.
P.O. Box 7471
Richmond, VA 23221

Telephone Numbers:
   Toll-Free (in-state)   800/552-2120
   Local   804/288-5522
Other Office Locations: None
Insurance Protection: SIPC, $500,000
Order Handling: Team system
Clearinghouse: Self
Firm's Exchange Membership: National Securities Clearing Corp.
Special Account Requirements: Cash in advance of purchases; security delivery in advance of sales
Commission Structure: Valuebroker
Minimum Charge: Stocks, $23; Options, not traded
Margin Interest Costs: No margin trading
Interest Paid on Cash Balances
(Rate and Minimum):   Approximately 2% less than short-term U.S. Government bond rate; $25 minimum balance
Investment Products: Stocks; Bonds; IRAs
Additional Charges: $10 per issue for delivery or receipt of securities; $1.25/month custodial fee per security issue (maximum custodial fee is $5 per month regardless of number of issues held in customer's account)
Date Firm Established: 1980
States Where Licensed to Do Business: Connecticut, Delaware, District of Columbia, Florida, Georgia, Maryland, New York, North Carolina, Pennsylvania, South Carolina, Virginia, West Virginia

Fidelity Brokerage Services, Inc.
161 Devonshire Street
Boston, MA 02110

Telephone Numbers:
    Toll-Free 800/225-1799
    Local   617/423-0116
                 617/523-1919

Other Office Locations: Nationwide

Insurance Protection: SIPC, $500,000; Aetna Casualty & Surety, $2 million

Order Handling: Team system

Clearinghouse: Self and Pershing & Co., Division of Donaldson, Lufkin & Jenrette

Firm's Exchange Membership: All major U.S. stock exchanges

Special Account Requirements: None

Commission Structure: Valuebroker

Minimum Charge: Stocks, $36; Options, $36

Margin Interest Costs:

$ Borrowed	Broker's Call+
Up to $9999	2%
$10,000–$24,999	1 1/2%
$25,000–$49,999	1%
$50,000–$99,999	1/2%
Above $100,000	1/4%

Interest Paid on Cash Balances (Rate and Minimum): Variable rate; $1000 minimum

Investment Products: Stocks; Bonds; Options; Mutual Funds; IRAs; Government Securities; Precious Metals; Unit Investment Trusts; Insurance

Services: Fidelity Video Library; Fidelity Investors Express, to research stocks via *Dow Jones News Retrieval* and to place trades online via PC terminal

Additional Charges: $25 fee for transferring security to other than account holder

Date Firm Established: 1946

States Where Licensed to Do Business: All states

First Institutional Securities Corp.
470 Colfax Avenue
Clifton, NJ 07013-1675

Telephone Numbers:
    Toll-Free (out-of-state)   800/526-7486
    Local   201/778-9700

Other Office Locations: None

Insurance Protection: SIPC, $500,000

Order Handling: Information not available

Clearinghouse: National Financial Services Corp.

Firm's Exchange Membership: Information not available

Special Account Requirements: Information not available

Commission Structure: Valuebroker

Minimum Charge: Stocks, $45; Options, $45

Margin Interest Costs: Information not available

Interest Paid on Cash Balances
(Rate and Minimum):   Information not available

Investment Products: Information not available

Additional Charges: Yes, for legal transfer items and odd lots

Date Firm Established: Information not available

States Where Licensed to Do Business: Information not available

First National Brokerage Services
1822 Douglas Street
Omaha, NE 68102

Telephone Numbers:

    Toll-Free (nationwide)   800/228-3011
    Local   402/346-5965

Other Office Locations: Los Angeles, CA; St. Louis, MO

Insurance Protection: SIPC, $500,000

Order Handling: Team system (16 registered representatives)

Clearinghouse: Ameritrade, Inc.

Firm's Exchange Membership: Information not available

Special Account Requirements: None

Commission Structure: Sharebroker, DD (HI, LO)

Minimum Charge: Accutrade, 3 cents a share commission—$48 minimum; standard schedule; stocks, $29; options, $25

Margin Interest Costs:

$ Borrowed	Broker's Call +
Up to $10,000	2%
$10,000–$24,999	1 1/2%
$25,000–$49,999	1 1/4%
Above $50,000	1%

Interest Paid on Cash Balances (Rate and Minimum):   2% below broker's call rate; $1000 minimum

Investment Products: Stocks; Bonds; Options; IRAs; Mutual Funds

Additional Charges: $2 handling fee per trade on the $29 commission rate; no handling fee on the Accutrade program

Date Firm Established: 1971

States Where Licensed to Do Business: All states, plus District of Columbia

Note: First National offers two systems for charges on trading stocks. One system allows the client to talk directly to a broker. With the other, Accutrade, a touchtone phone allows you to key in trades with a flat fee of 3 cents a share. It is available 24 hours a day, 7 days a week, toll-free.

First Union Brokerage Services
Division: First Union Securities Corp.
301 South College Street, 17th Floor
Charlotte, NC 28202

Telephone Numbers:

Toll-Free (out-of-state)	800/334-9406
Toll-Free (in-state)	800/532-0367
Local	704/374-6927

Other Office Locations: Florida: Hallandale, Boca Raton, Palm Beach, Pompano Beach, Clearwater, Miami, Bay Harbor, Miami Beach, Orlando, Jacksonville; Georgia: Augusta, Savannah, Atlanta; North Carolina: Winston-Salem, Wilson

Insurance Protection: SIPC, $500,000 plus additional $10 million

Order Handling: Team system

Clearinghouse: Pershing & Company

Firm's Exchange Membership: None

Special Account Requirements: None

Commission Structure: Value/Sharebroker

Minimum Charge: Stocks, $38; Options, $38

Margin Interest Costs:

$ Borrowed	Broker's Call +
Up to $10,000	2 1/4%
$10,000–$19,999	2%
$20,000–29,999	1 3/4%
$30,000–$49,999	1 1/2%
Above $50,000	3/4%

Interest Paid on Cash Balances (Rate and Minimum): Current money market rates

Investment Products: Information not available

Additional Charges: None

Date Firm Established: 1980 (Firm purchased by First Union National Bank on December 15, 1980)

States Where Licensed to Do Business: Florida, Georgia, North Carolina, South Carolina, Kentucky, Tennessee, Virginia

Freeman Welwood & Co., Inc.
2800 Century Square
1501 Fourth Avenue
Seattle, WA 98101

Telephone Numbers:

    Toll-Free (out-of-state)   800/426-1160
    Toll-Free (in-state)   800/542-7884
    Local   206/382-5353

Other Office Locations: Honolulu, HI; Portland, OR; Spokane and Tacoma, WA

Insurance Protection: SIPC, $500,000

Order Handling: Team system

Clearinghouse: Self

Firm's Exchange Membership: Midwest Stock Exchange, Pacific Stock Exchange, Options Clearing Corp., and correspondent of NYSE member

Special Account Requirements: Cash in advance for low dollar stocks and options

Commission Structure: Valuebroker

Minimum Charge: Stocks, $29; Options, $29

Margin Interest Costs:

$ Borrowed	Broker's Call +
Up to $10,000	2%
$10,001–$50,000	$1^{1}/_{2}$%
$50,001–$100,000	1%
Above $100,000	$^{1}/_{2}$%

Interest Paid on Cash Balances (Rate and Minimum):   Linked to short-term interest rates

Investment Products: Information not available

Additional Charges: None

Date Firm Established: 1972

States Where Licensed to Do Business: Alabama, California, Hawaii, Idaho, Montana, Oregon, Washington

Harper-Scherwin/Securities Research, Inc.
936-A Beachland Boulevard
Vero Beach, FL 32960

Telephone Numbers:

    Toll-Free (out-of-state)   800/327-3156
    Local   305/231-6689

Other Office Locations: Danbury, CT; Florida: Gainesville, Jacksonville, Stuart, Winter Park, Melbourne, Tampa; Richmond, VA

Insurance Protection: SIPC, $500,000 plus $2 million additional

Order Handling: Team system (account executive assigned on request)

Clearinghouse: J.C. Bradford

Firm's Exchange Membership: None

Special Account Requirements: None

Commission Structure: Sharebroker, DD (HI, LO)

Minimum Charge: Stocks, $30; Options, $28

Margin Interest Costs: Information not available

Interest Paid on Cash Balances
(Rate and Minimum): Tied to Treasury bill rate; $4000 minimum initial deposit

Investment Products: Stocks; Bonds; Options; Foreign Securities

Services: Research; portfolio strategy; economic forecasting

Additional Charges: None

Date Firm Established: 1973

States Where Licensed to Do Business: Information not available

Heritage Investment Securities, Inc.
505 Fifth Avenue South
Naples, FL 33940

Telephone Number:
  Local   813/263-1110

Other Office Locations: None

Insurance Protection: SIPC, $500,000 plus $8 million additional

Order Handling: Account executive assigned

Clearinghouse: Securities Settlement Corp.

Firm's Exchange Membership: None

Special Account Requirements: None

Commission Structure: Sharebroker, DD (HI)

Minimum Charge: Stocks, $30; Options, $30

Margin Interest Costs: Broker's call + 2%

Interest Paid on Cash Balances
(Rate and Minimum):   Money market rates; no minimum; $100 increments

Investment Products: Stocks; Bonds

Additional Charges: None

Date Firm Established: 1980

States Where Licensed to Do Business: Florida

Icahn & Co., Inc.
1370 Avenue of the Americas
New York, NY 10019

Telephone Numbers:

   Toll-Free (out-of-state)   800/223-2188
   Local   800/634-8518

Other Office Locations: Information not available

Insurance Protection: SIPC, $500,000 plus $2 million additional

Clearinghouse: Cowan & Co.

Firm's Exchange Membership: NYSE, AMEX

Special Account Requirements: None

Commission Structure: Sharebroker, DD (HI, LO)

Minimum Charge: Stocks, $40; Options, $40

Margin Interest Costs:

$ Borrowed	Broker's Call+
Up to $9999	$2 1/4\%$
$10,000–$19,999	2%
$20,000–$29,999	$1 3/4\%$
$30,000–$49,999	$1 1/2\%$
Above $50,000	$3/4\%$

Interest Paid on Cash Balances (Rate and Minimum): $2000 minimum balance

Investment Products: Stocks; Bonds; Options; IRAs

Additional Charges: Information not available

Date Firm Established: 1976

States Where Licensed to Do Business: Information not available

Illinois Company Investments, Inc.
30 North LaSalle Street
Chicago, IL 60602

Telephone Numbers:

    Toll-Free (out-of-state)   800/323-6166
    Toll-Free (in-state)   800/942-0850
    Local   312/897-7100

Other Office Locations: Florida: Sarasota, Tampa; Illinois: Barrington, Chicago, Oak Brook, Rockford, Waukegan; Indiana: Indianapolis, Munster; Michigan: Birmingham, Grand Rapids; Ohio: Rocky River, Lima, Toledo; Wisconsin: Oconomowoc

Insurance Protection: SIPC, $500,000 plus $2 million additional

Order Handling: Account executive assigned

Clearinghouse: Swiss American Securities

Firm's Exchange Membership: NYSE, Midwest Stock Exchange

Special Account Requirements: Information not available

Commission Structure: Sharebroker

Minimum Charge: Stocks, $34 + .03/share; Options, $34 + .03/contract

Margin Interest Costs: Information not available

Interest Paid on Cash Balances (Rate and Minimum): Money market fund; $2000 minimum

Investment Products: Stocks; Bonds; Options; Unit Trusts; Limited Partnerships; Government Securities

Additional Charges: Information not available

Date Firm Established: 1977

States Where Licensed to Do Business: Information not available

Jack White & Company, Inc.
9191 Towne Centre Drive
Suite 220
San Diego, CA 92122

Telephone Numbers:

    Toll-Free (nationwide)   800/233-3411
    Local   619/587-2000

Other Office Locations: None

Insurance Protection: SIPC, $500,000 plus $9.5 million additional

Order Handling: Team system

Clearinghouse: Pershing & Co., Division of Donaldson, Lufkin & Jenrette

Firm's Exchange Membership: None

Special Account Requirements: None

Commission Structure: Valuebroker

Minimum Charge: Stocks, $33; Options, $33

Margin Interest Costs:

$ Borrowed	Broker's Call+
All amounts	1/2%

Interest Paid on Cash Balances
(Rate and Minimum):   Money market rates

Investment Products: Stocks; Bonds; Options; IRAs; Mutual Funds; Commodities

Services: S&P company fact sheets are available at no charge

Additional Charges: None

Date Firm Established: 1975

States Where Licensed to Do Business: All states

John Finn & Company, Inc.
932 Dixie Terminal Building
Cincinnati, OH 45202

Telephone Numbers:

    Toll-Free (nationwide)   Call collect
    Local   513/579-0066

Other Office Locations: None

Insurance Protection: SIPC, $500,000

Order Handling: Team system

Clearinghouse: Robert A. Baird, Inc.

Firm's Exchange Membership: None

Special Account Requirements: None

Commission Structure: Sharebroker

Minimum Charge: Stocks, $35; Options, $35

Margin Interest Costs: $ Borrowed   Broker's Call+
    All amounts   1%–2% sliding

Interest Paid on Cash Balances
(Rate and Minimum): Money market rate; $1000 minimum initial deposit

Investment Products: Stocks; Bonds; Options; IRAs; Mutual Funds

Additional Charges: None

Date Firm Established: 1975

States Where Licensed to Do Business: Florida, Kentucky, Ohio, Indiana

John Howard Discount Brokerage, Inc.
200 South Orange Avenue
Livingston, NJ 07039

Telephone Numbers:

Toll-Free (in-state)	800/222-0797
Local	201/533-7551

Other Office Locations: None

Insurance Protection: SIPC, $500,000

Order Handling: Information not available

Clearinghouse: Swiss American Securities, Inc.

Firm's Exchange Membership: Information not available

Special Account Requirements: Information not available

Commission Structure: Sharebroker

Minimum Charge: Stocks, $40; Options, $35

Margin Interest Costs:

$ Borrowed	Broker's Call+
Up to $10,000	$1 \frac{1}{2}$%
$10,000–$30,000	$1 \frac{1}{4}$%
$30,000–$50,000	1%
$50,000–$75,000	$\frac{3}{4}$%
Above $75,000	$\frac{1}{2}$%

Interest Paid on Cash Balances (Rate and Minimum): Money market rates on balances greater than $2000

Investment Products: Stocks; Bonds; Options; IRAs

Additional Charges: Information not available

Date Firm Established: 1986

States Where Licensed to Do Business: Most states

Note: John Howard Discount Brokerage, Inc. is a wholly owned subsidiary of the Howard Savings Bank

Kashner Davidson Securities Corp.
77 South Palm Avenue
Sarasota, FL 34236

Telephone Numbers:

    Toll-Free (nationwide) 800/678-2626
    Local 813/951-2626

Other Office Locations: Venice, FL

Insurance Protection: SIPC, $500,000 plus $2 million additional

Order Handling: Account executive assigned

Clearinghouse: Regional Clearing Corp.

Firm's Exchange Membership: None

Special Account Requirements: None

Commission Structure: Sharebroker

Minimum Charge: Stocks, $45; Options, $45

Margin Interest Costs:

$ Borrowed	Broker's Call+
Up to $10,000	1 1/2%
$10,000–$30,000	1 1/4%
$30,000–$50,000	1%
Above $50,000	1/2%

Interest Paid on Cash Balances (Rate and Minimum): Money market fund; $1000 minimum initial deposit

Investment Products: Stocks; Bonds; Options; IRAs; Mutual Funds; Insurance

Services: Research available including S&P and Value Line

Additional Charges: None

Date Firm Established: 1969

States Where Licensed to Do Business: Information not available

Kennedy, Cabot & Co.
9465 Wilshire Boulevard
Beverly Hills, CA 90212

Telephone Numbers:

Toll-Free (out-of-state)	800/252-0090
Toll-Free (in-state)	800/257-2045
Local	213/550-0711

Other Office Locations: California: San Francisco, San Diego, Palm Desert, Santa Monica, Long Beach, Fresno, Newport Beach, Riverside, Orange, Encino, Monterey Park; Hawaii

Insurance Protection: SIPC, $500,000 plus $10 million additional

Order Handling: Team system; 28 traders

Clearinghouse: Securities Settlement Corporation

Firm's Exchange Membership: None

Special Account Requirements: None

Commission Structure: Sharebroker, DD (HI, LO)

Minimum Charge: Stocks, $20; Options, $30

Margin Interest Costs:

$ Borrowed	Broker's Call+
Up to $100,000	$1/2\%$
Above $100,000	$1/4\%$

Interest Paid on Cash Balances
(Rate and Minimum): Treasury rate; $1000 minimum

Investment Products: Stocks; Bonds; Options; Mutual Funds

Additional Charges: None

Date Firm Established: 1960

States Where Licensed to Do Business: All states

R.F. Lafferty & Co.
50 Broad Street
New York, NY 10004

Telephone Numbers:

    Toll-Free (out-of-state)   800/221-8514
    Toll-Free (in-state)   800/522-5653
    Local   212/269-6636

Other Office Locations: None

Insurance Protection: SIPC, $500,000 plus $2 million additional

Order Handling: Account executive assigned

Clearinghouse: N.B. Clearing Corp.

Firm's Exchange Membership: Information not available

Special Account Requirements: Deposit requested prior to first transaction for new accounts

Commission Structure: Sharebroker, DD (HI, LO)

Minimum Charge: Stocks, $50; Options, $50

Margin Interest Costs: Broker's call + $1/2$%

Interest Paid on Cash Balances
(Rate and Minimum): Information not available

Investment Products: Stocks; Options; IRAs

Additional Charges: None

Date Firm Established: 1946

States Where Licensed to Do Business: Most states

Marquette de Bary Co., Inc.
488 Madison Avenue
New York, NY 10022

Telephone Numbers:

    Toll-Free (nationwide) 800/221-3305
    Local 212/644-5300

Other Office Locations: None

Insurance Protection: SIPC, $500,000 plus $2 million additional ($10 million available)

Order Handling: Team system (registered representative assigned on request)

Clearinghouse: Paine, Webber, Jackson & Curtis, Inc.

Firm's Exchange Membership: None

Special Account Requirements: None

Commission Structure: Sharebroker, DD (LO)

Minimum Charge: Stocks, $20; Options, $25

Margin Interest Costs:

$ Borrowed	Broker's Call+
Up to $100,000	¾%
Above $100,000	Negotiable

Interest Paid on Cash Balances (Rate and Minimum): Money market rate through Paine, Webber, Jackson & Curtis Cash Fund; $5000 initial deposit; $500 minimum

Investment Products: Stocks; Bonds; Options; IRAs; Keoghs; Foreign Currency Options; Precious Metals

Services: Provides news retrieval information

Additional Charges: $20 service charge for transfer of securities from one account to another not related to a commission generating trade

Date Firm Established: 1962

States Where Licensed to Do Business: All states

The Discount Brokerage Directory

Marsh Block & Co.
50 Broad Street
New York, NY 10004

Telephone Numbers:

Toll-Free (out-of-state)	800/366-1500
Toll-Free (fixed income)	800/366-1200
Local	212/514-6400
Local (fixed income)	212/363-8330

Other Office Locations: Delaware; Ohio; Smyrna Beach, FL

Insurance Protection: SIPC, $500,000 plus $2 million additional

Order Handling: Account executive assigned

Clearinghouse: Asiel & Co.

Firm's Exchange Membership: None

Special Account Requirements: None

Commission Structure: Valuebroker

Minimum Charge: Stocks, $25; Options, $25

Margin Interest Costs: $1/2$% or 2% above broker's call depending on account

Interest Paid on Cash Balances
(Rate and Minimum): Broker's call rate less 3%; $1000 minimum

Investment Products: Stocks; Bonds; Options; IRAs

Additional Charges: None

Date Firm Established: 1969

States Where Licensed to Do Business: Information not available

Max Ule
with Meyers, Pollock, Robbins, Inc.
170 Broadway, Suite 505
New York, NY 10038

Telephone Numbers:

Toll-Free (out-of-state)	Call collect
Toll-Free (in-state)	800/223-6642
Local	212/766-2610

Other Office Locations: None

Insurance Protection: SIPC, $500,000 plus $2 million additional

Order Handling: Team system

Clearinghouse: Mabon, Nugent & Co.

Firm's Exchange Membership: None

Special Account Requirements: $1000 minimum equity on options

Commission Structure: Sharebroker

Minimum Charge: Stocks, $35; Options, $35

Margin Interest Costs:

$ Borrowed	Broker's Call+
All amounts	$1 1/2\%$

Interest Paid on Cash Balances (Rate and Minimum): Money market rates; $1000 minimum

Investment Products: Stocks; Bonds; Options; IRAs; GNMAs; Mutual Funds; Unit Investment Trusts

Services: Access to Max Ule on CompuServe or with Tickerscreen

Additional Charges: None

Date Firm Established: 1945

States Where Licensed to Do Business: Connecticut, New Jersey, New York

Muriel Siebert & Co., Inc.
444 Madison Avenue
New York, NY 10022

Telephone Numbers:

    Toll-Free (nationwide)   800/USA-0711
    Local   212/644-2400

Other Office Locations: None

Insurance Protection: SIPC, $500,000 plus $2 million additional

Order Handling: Team system; VIPs assigned a broker

Clearinghouse: Q & R Clearing Corp.

Firm's Exchange Membership: NYSE, AMEX

Special Account Requirements: Depends on account

Commission Structure: Sharebroker

Minimum Charge: Stocks, $34; Options, $34

Margin Interest Costs: Variable up to 2% above broker's call

Interest Paid on Cash Balances
(Rate and Minimum): Money market fund; $2000 minimum balance

Investment Products: Stocks; Bonds; Options; IRAs; Government Securities (GNMAs, CATS); Unit Investment Trusts; Tax Shelters

Additional Charges: Information not available

Date Firm Established: 1967

States Where Licensed to Do Business: All states

NEIE Discount Brokerage Services
P.O. Box 1828
Boston, MA 02205

Telephone Numbers:

    Toll-Free (nationwide)   800/634-5000
    Local   Use 800 number

Other Office Locations: Maine; New Jersey

Insurance Protection: SIPC, $500,000 plus $2 million additional

Order Handling: Team system

Clearinghouse: Q & R Clearing Corp.

Firm's Exchange Membership: None

Special Account Requirements: None on cash accounts; cash in advance of purchase in option account

Commission Structure: Valuebroker

Minimum Charge: Stocks, $35; Options, $35

Margin Interest Costs: Information not available

Interest Paid on Cash Balances (Rate and Minimum):   None

Investment Products: Information not available

Additional Charges: None

Date Firm Established: 1982

States Where Licensed to Do Business: Connecticut, Florida, Maine, Massachusetts, New Hampshire, New Jersey, New York, Vermont

Olde Discount Stockbrokers
The Olde Building
751 Griswold Street
Detroit, MI 48226-3274

Telephone Numbers:

    Toll-Free (out-of-state) 800/626-PLAN
    Local 313/961-6666

Other Office Locations: Nationwide

Insurance Protection: SIPC, $500,000

Order Handling: Team system; account executive assigned upon request

Clearinghouse: Self

Firm's Exchange Membership: NYSE, AMEX, Midwest Stock Exchange, Pacific Stock Exchange, and Chicago Board Options Exchange

Special Account Requirements: None

Commission Structure: Sharebroker

Minimum Charge: Stocks, $40; Options, $40

Margin Interest Costs:

$ Borrowed	Broker's Call+
Up to $20,000	1%
$20,000–$50,000	1/2%
Above $50,000	1/4%

Interest Paid on Cash Balances (Rate and Minimum): Rates vary with current short-term money market rates; $1000 minimum

Investment Products: Stocks; Bonds; Options; IRAs; Mutual Funds

Services: The OLDE Report—a nationwide telephone recording, updated hourly, with stock market information.

Additional Charges: Minimal for special transfers

Date Firm Established: 1971

States Where Licensed to Do Business: All states

OvestMarine Brokerage Service
Division of Marine Midland Securities, Inc.
90 Broad Street
New York, NY 10004

Telephone Numbers:

    Toll-Free (nationwide)   800/255-0700
    Local   212/612-1090

Other Office Locations: None

Insurance Protection: SIPC, $500,000 plus $10 million additional

Order Handling: Team system (all registered representatives)

Clearinghouse: Pershing & Co.

Firm's Exchange Membership: None

Special Account Requirements: None

Commission Structure: Sharebroker

Minimum Charge: Stocks, $35; Options, $35

Margin Interest Costs:

$ Borrowed	Broker's Call+
Up to $9999	2 1/4%
$10,000–$19,999	2%
$20,000–$34,999	1 1/2%
$35,000–$54,999	1%
$55,000–$74,999	3/4%
Above $75,000	1/2%

Interest Paid on Cash Balances
(Rate and Minimum):   Money market rates; $500 minimum

Investment Products: Information not available

Additional Charges: Information not available

Date Firm Established: 1977

States Where Licensed to Do Business: Florida, Michigan, New Jersey, New York, Nevada

Note: Division of Marine Midland Securities

Pace Securities, Inc.
225 Park Avenue
New York, NY 10017

Telephone Numbers:

    Toll-Free (out-of-state)   800/221-1660
    Local   212/490-6363

Other Office Locations: None

Insurance Protection: SIPC, $500,000 plus $2 million additional

Order Handling: Team trading plus management; supervision on trading desk

Clearinghouse: Cowen & Co.

Firm's Exchange Membership: NYSE, AMEX, Municipal Securities Rulemaking Board

Special Account Requirements: None

Commission Structure: Sharebroker, DD (HI, LO)

Minimum Charge: Stocks, $35; Options, $35

Margin Interest Costs:

$ Borrowed	Broker's Call+
Up to $9999	2 1/4%
$10,000–$20,000	2%
$20,000–$30,000	1 3/4%
$30,000–$50,000	1 1/2%
Above $50,000	3/4%

Interest Paid on Cash Balances
(Rate and Minimum): Money market fund (Dreyfus) or Credit Interest Program within account; $2000 minimum deposit

Investment Products: Stocks; Bonds; Options; IRAs; Mutual Funds; GNMAs; FNMAs

Services: Research

Additional Charges: None

Date Firm Established: 1980

States Where Licensed to Do Business: Connecticut, District of Columbia, Delaware, Florida, Illinois, Minnesota, New Jersey, New York, Pennsylvania, Rhode Island, Tennessee, Texas

Pacific Brokerage Services, Inc.
5757 Wilshire Blvd., Suite 3
Los Angeles, CA 90036

Telephone Numbers:

    Toll-Free (out-of-state)   800/421-8395
    Toll-Free (in-state)   800/421-3214
    Local   213/939-1100

Other Office Locations: San Francisco, CA; Boca Raton, FL; Chicago, IL; New York, NY; Dallas, TX

Insurance Protection: SIPC, $500,000 (excess $2 million)

Order Handling: Team system

Clearinghouse: Self, Member NSCC, DTC

Firm's Exchange Membership: NYSE, AMEX, Midwest Exchange, Pacific Stock Exchange

Special Account Requirements: None

Commission Structure: Sharebroker, DD (HI, LO)

Minimum Charge: Stocks, $25; Options, $25

Margin Interest Costs:

$ Borrowed	Broker's Call +
Up to $25,000	1%
$25,001–$100,000	1/2%
Above $100,001	0%

Interest Paid on Cash Balances (Rate and Minimum):   Money market fund; no minimum

Investment Products: Stocks; Bonds; Options

Services: S&P reports are available to clients upon request

Additional Charges: None

Date Firm Established: 1976

States Where Licensed to Do Business: All states

Parsons Securities, Inc.
Le Veque Tower
50 West Broad Street, Suite 1960
Columbus, OH 43215-3380

Telephone Numbers:

    Toll-Free (nationwide)   800/282-2756
    Local   614/224-0038

Other Office Locations: None

Insurance Protection: SIPC, $500,000 plus $10 million additional

Order Handling: Team system

Clearinghouse: Securities Settlement Corp.

Firm's Exchange Membership: Information not available

Special Account Requirements: Information not available

Commission Structure: Valuebroker

Minimum Charge: Stocks, $35; Options, $35

Margin Interest Costs: Information not available

Interest Paid on Cash Balances
(Rate and Minimum):   1% below broker's call rate; $100 minimum

Investment Products: Stocks; Bonds; Options; IRAs; Real Estate Limited Partnerships; Equipment Leasing Limited Partnerships

Additional Charges: Information not available

Date Firm Established: 1978

States Where Licensed to Do Business: Ohio

Peremel & Co., Inc.
Discount Stock Brokers
One North Charles Street, Suite 407
Baltimore, MD 21201

Telephone Numbers:

    Toll-Free (nationwide)   800/635-2279
    Local   301/539-7171

Other Office Locations: None

Insurance Protection: SIPC, $500,000; plus London Underwriters, $10 million additional

Order Handling: Account executive assigned

Clearinghouse: Securities Settlement Corp.

Firm's Exchange Membership: Philadelphia Stock Exchange

Special Account Requirements: None

Commission Structure: Sharebroker

Minimum Charge: Stocks, $40; Options, $40

Margin Interest Costs: Negotiable

Interest Paid on Cash Balances
(Rate and Minimum):   Money market fund; $1000 minimum

Investment Products: Stocks; Bonds; Options

Additional Charges: None

Date Firm Established: 1970

States Where Licensed to Do Business: Maryland

Quick & Reilly, Inc.
120 Wall Street
New York, NY 10005-3982

Telephone Numbers:

    Toll-Free (out-of-state)   800/221-5220
    Toll-Free (in-state)   800/522-8712
    Local   212/943-8686

Other Office Locations: Nationwide

Insurance Protection: SIPC, $500,000 plus $2 million additional

Order Handling: Account executive assigned

Clearinghouse: Q & R Clearing Corp.

Firm's Exchange Membership: NYSE

Special Account Requirements: None

Commission Structure: Sharebroker

Minimum Charge: Stocks, $35; Options, $35

Margin Interest Costs:

$ Borrowed	Broker's Call+
Up to $5000	2%
$5000–$9999	$1^{3}/_{4}$%
$10,000–$14,999	$1^{1}/_{2}$%
$15,000–$19,999	$1^{1}/_{4}$%
$20,000–$24,999	1%
Above $25,000	$^{3}/_{4}$%

Interest Paid on Cash Balances (Rate and Minimum):   Money market fund; $1000 initial deposit; $100 increments

Investment Products: Stocks; Bonds; Options; IRAs; GNMAs; Mutual Funds; Option Income Funds; Tax-Free Unit Trusts; Estate Liquidation

Services: Free gift of the book *Stock Market Blueprints* to all clients; QuickQuote.

Additional Charges: None

Date Firm Established: 1974

States Where Licensed to Do Business: All states

Recom Securities, Inc.
200 Metro Bank Building
Minneapolis, MN 55402

Telephone Numbers:

    Toll-Free (nationwide)   800/328-8600
    Local   612/339-5566

Other Office Locations: None

Insurance Protection: SIPC, $500,000 plus additional insurance up to $2 million, securities only

Order Handling: Team system

Clearinghouse: Q & R Clearing Corp.

Firm's Exchange Membership: Information not available

Special Account Requirements: Deposit of 25%

Commission Structure: Sharebroker

Minimum Charge: Stocks, $30; Options, $30

Margin Interest Costs:

$ Borrowed	Broker's Call+
Up to $5000	2%
$5000–$9999	$1 \frac{3}{4}$%
$10,000–$14,999	$1 \frac{1}{2}$%
$15,000–$19,999	$1 \frac{1}{4}$%
$20,000–$25,000	1%
Above $25,000	$\frac{3}{4}$%

Interest Paid on Cash Balances
(Rate and Minimum): Money market fund; $2000 initial deposit; $100 increments

Investment Products: Stocks; Bonds; Options

Additional Charges: Information not available

Date Firm Established: 1977

States Where Licensed to Do Business: Information not available

Richard Blackman & Co., Inc.
Route 17 at Route 4, Suite 10
P.O. Box 929, NY 10601
Paramus, NJ 07652

Telephone Numbers:

    Toll-Free (nationwide)   800/631-1635
    Local   201/368-0800

Other Office Locations: New Jersey: Morristown, Princeton, West Caldwell, Fort Lee

Insurance Protection: SIPC, $500,000 plus Aetna, $2 million

Order Handling: Team system

Clearinghouse: National Financial Services Corp.

Firm's Exchange Membership: None

Special Account Requirements: None

Commission Structure: Sharebroker, DD (HI, LO)

Minimum Charge: Stocks, $25; Options, $25

Margin Interest Costs:

$ Borrowed	Broker's Call+
Up to $9999	2%
$10,000–$24,999	$1\frac{1}{2}$%
$25,000–49,999	1%
Above $50,000	$\frac{1}{2}$%

Interest Paid on Cash Balances
(Rate and Minimum): Money market rate; $1000 first deposit; $250 thereafter

Investment Products: Stocks; Bonds; Options; IRAs

Additional Charges: None

Date Firm Established: 1977

States Where Licensed to Do Business: New Jersey, New York

Note: Richard Blackman & Co., Inc. is a wholly owned subsidiary of United Jersey Bank Financial Corporation.

Robert Thomas Securities, Inc.
Division of Raymond James Financial Group
741 North Milwaukee Street
Milwaukee, WI 53202

Telephone Numbers:

    Toll-Free (in-state) 800/242-1523
    Local 414/273-2255

Other Office Locations: None

Insurance Protection: SIPC, $500,000 plus Lloyd's of London $5 million additional

Order Handling: Team system or individual broker

Clearinghouse: Raymond James, Inc.

Firm's Exchange Membership: NYSE

Special Account Requirements: None

Commission Structure: Sharebroker

Minimum Charge: Stocks, $30; Options, $30

Margin Interest Costs:

$ Borrowed	Broker's Call+
Up to $35,000	$1 1/2$%
Above $35,000	1%

Interest Paid on Cash Balances (Rate and Minimum): Money market fund: $1000 minimum; credit interest program: $100 minimum

Investment Products: Stocks; Bonds; Options; IRAs; Mutual Funds; Annuities; Unit Trusts; Gold/Silver Certificates; Insurance; Limited Partnerships (Real Estate, Cable Television, Equipment Leasing)

Additional Charges: Information not available

Date Firm Established: 1980

States Where Licensed to Do Business: Information not available

Robinson Securities
Division: John Dawson & Associates, Inc.
Eleven South La Salle Street
Chicago, IL 60603

Telephone Numbers:

    Toll-Free (out-of-state) 800/621-2840
    Toll-Free (in-state) 312/346-7711(collect)
    Local 312/346-7711

Other Office Locations: Des Moines, IA

Insurance Protection: SIPC, plus blanket bond; various amounts fidelity bonds in various states

Order Handling: Team system (all registered representatives)

Clearinghouse: Midwest Clearing Corp.

Firm's Exchange Membership: Midwest Stock Exchange

Special Account Requirements: Account application on file and approved prior to first trade. Cash on hand (or in money market) and securities on hand, prior to buying or selling options

Commission Structure: Value/Sharebroker, DD (HI, LO)

Minimum Charge: Stocks, $28; Options, $28

Margin Interest Costs:

$ Borrowed	Broker's Call+
Up to $19,999	1½%
$20,000–$49,999	1¼%
$50,000–$99,999	1%
$100,000–$249,999	½%
Above $250,000	¼%

Interest Paid on Cash Balances
(Rate and Minimum): Money market fund (Alliance Group); $100 minimum

Investment Products: Stocks; Bonds; Options; IRAs

The Discount Brokerage Directory

Additional Charges: $30 per issue for accommodation transfers; $10 "legal item" deposits; $20 per bank wire of funds

Date Firm Established: 1972

States Where Licensed to Do Business: California, Connecticut, Delaware, Georgia, Hawaii, Illinois, Indiana, Iowa, Kansas, Kentucky, Michigan, Minnesota, Missouri, New Mexico, North Carolina, Ohio, Oklahoma, Pennsylvania, Tennessee, Texas, West Virginia

Rodecker & Company Investment Brokers, Inc.
4000 Town Center, Suite 101
Southfield, MI 48075-1497

Telephone Number:

    Local   313/358-2282

Other Office Locations: None

Insurance Protection: SIPC, $500,000; plus Aetna, $2 million

Order Handling: Account executive assigned

Clearinghouse: Cowen & Co.

Firm's Exchange Membership: None

Special Account Requirements: None

Commission Structure: Valuebroker

Minimum Charge: Stocks, $50; Options, $50

Additional Transaction Charges: None

Margin Interest Costs:

$ Borrowed	Broker's Call+
All amounts	$1/2\%$ — 2%

Interest Paid on Cash Balances
(Rate and Minimum): $1/2\%$ below broker's call rate; $2000 minimum balance

Investment Products: Stocks; Bonds; Options; IRAs; Limited Partnerships (Real Estate, Oil/Gas, Equipment Leasing); Unit Trusts; Investment Counseling

Services: Research department

Additional Charges: None

Date Firm Established: 1976

States Where Licensed to Do Business: Colorado, Florida, Michigan, New Jersey, New York, Ohio

Roland Francis & Co., Inc.
Discount Securities Brokerage
8893 La Mesa Blvd., Suite C
La Mesa, CA 92041

Telephone Number:

    Local   619/464-2346

Other Office Locations: None

Insurance Protection: SIPC, $500,000; $2 million additional

Order Handling: Account executive on duty

Clearinghouse: Wedbush Morgan Securities, Inc.

Firm's Exchange Membership: None

Special Account Requirements: None

Commission Structure: Valuebroker

Minimum Charge: Stocks, $38; Options, $38

Margin Interest Costs: Interest rate in effect at the time

Interest Paid on Cash Balances
(Rate and Minimum):   Current market rates; interest not paid if below $2 month

Investment Products: Information not available

Additional Charges: Information not available

Date Firm Established: 1979

States Where Licensed to Do Business: California

T. Rowe Price Discount Brokerage
100 East Pratt Street
Baltimore, MD 21202

Telephone Numbers:

Toll-Free (nationwide)	800/225-7720
Local	301/625-7720

Other Office Locations: None

Insurance Protection: SIPC, $500,000 plus $9.5 million additional

Order Handling: Team system

Clearinghouse: Pershing & Co.

Firm's Exchange Membership: None

Special Account Requirements: None

Commission Structure: Valuebroker

Minimum Charge: Stocks, $35; Options, $35

Margin Interest Costs:

$ Borrowed	Broker's Call+
Up to $9999	2%
$10,000–$29,999	1 1/2%
$30,000–$49,999	1%
Above $50,000	1/2%

Interest Paid on Cash Balances
(Rate and Minimum): Sweep accounts: Money market rates; Cash accounts: None

Investment Products: T. Rowe Price Family of Mutual Funds

Additional Charges: None

Date Firm Established: Discount Brokerage: 1984; T. Rowe Price Investment: 1937

States Where Licensed to Do Business: All states

Royal/Grimm & Davis, Inc.
20 Exchange Place
New York, NY 10005

Telephone Numbers:
    Toll-Free (out-of-state)   800/221-5195
    Toll-Free (in-state: except NYC)   800/426-6970
    Local   212/943-7960

Other Office Locations: None

Insurance Protection: SIPC, $500,000; plus $10 million additional

Order Handling: Team system (account executive assigned upon request)

Clearinghouse: Securities Settlement Corp.

Firm's Exchange Membership: NYSE

Special Account Requirements: None

Commission Structure: Sharebroker, DD (HI, LO)

Minimum Charge: Stocks, $30; Options, $30

Margin Interest Costs:

$ Borrowed	Broker's Call+
Up to $10,000	$1 3/4$%
$10,000–$30,000	$1 1/2$%
$30,000–$50,000	1%
Above $50,000	$3/4$%

Interest Paid on Cash Balances
(Rate and Minimum): 2% below broker's call rate; $2000 minimum

Investment Products: Stocks; Bonds; Options; IRAs

Services: S & P reports

Additional Charges: None

Date Firm Established: 1962

States Where Licensed to Do Business: Connecticut, Florida, New Jersey, New York, Pennsylvania

Russo Securities, Inc.
170 Broadway
New York, NY 10038

Telephone Number:

Local   212/962-7482

Other Office Locations: None

Insurance Protection: SIPC, $500,000

Order Handling: Information not available

Clearinghouse: Herzog Heine Geduld

Firm's Exchange Membership: NYSE

Special Account Requirements: Information not available

Commission Structure: Sharebroker, DD (HI, LO)

Minimum Charge: Stocks, $35; Options, $35

Margin Interest Costs: Information not available

Interest Paid on Cash Balances
(Rate and Minimum):   Information not available

Investment Products: Information not available

Additional Charges: Information not available

Date Firm Established: 1979

States Where Licensed to Do Business: New Jersey, New York

St. Louis Discount Securities, Inc.
200 South Hanley, Lobby Suite 103
Clayton, MO 63105

Telephone Numbers:

    Toll-Free (out-of-state)   800/726-7401
    Toll-Free (in-state)   800/726-7401
    Local   314/721-7400

Other Office Locations: None

Insurance Protection: SIPC, $500,000 plus $9.5 million additional

Order Handling: Team system

Clearinghouse: Securities Settlement Corp.

Firm's Exchange Membership: None

Special Account Requirements: None

Commission Structure: Sharebroker, DD (HI, LO)

Minimum Charge: Stocks: Round lot minimum, $33; Add lot minimum, $28; Options, $30

Margin Interest Costs:

$ Borrowed	Broker's Call+
Up to $10,000	3%
$10,000–$30,000	2 3/4%
$30,000–$50,000	2 1/4%
Above $50,000	2%

Interest Paid on Cash Balances (Rate and Minimum): 2% below broker's call

Investment Products: Stocks; Options, Corporate Bonds, Mutual Funds

Additional Charges: $1.50 per transaction

Date Firm Established: 1980

States Where Licensed to Do Business: Illinois, Missouri

Charles Schwab
The Schwab Building
101 Montgomery Street
San Francisco, CA 94104

Telephone Numbers:

    Toll-Free (nationwide)   800/648-5300
    Local   415/627-7000

Other Office Locations: Nationwide

Insurance Protection: SIPC, $500,000 plus $2 million additional

Order Handling: Team system

Clearinghouse: Self

Firm's Exchange Membership: All principal stock exchanges and option exchanges

Special Account Requirements: None

Commission Structure: Valuebroker

Minimum Charge: Stocks, $39; Options, $39

Margin Interest Costs:

$ Borrowed	Broker's Call+
Up to $25,000	$1 \frac{1}{2}\%$
$25,000–$50,000	1%
Above $50,000	$\frac{1}{2}\%$

Interest Paid on Cash Balances (Rate and Minimum): Initial deposit of $1000 in cash

Investment Products: Stocks; Bonds; Options; IRAs; Mutual Funds; Unit Investment Trusts

Additional Charges: None

Date Firm Established: 1975

States Where Licensed to Do Business: All states

The Discount Brokerage Directory

Scottsdale Securities, Inc.
12801 Flushing Meadow Drive
St. Louis, MO 63131

Telephone Numbers:

    Toll-Free (nationwide)   800/888-1980
    Local   314/965-1555

Other Office Locations: Phoenix, AZ; Springfield, MO; Dayton, OH

Insurance Protection: SIPC, $500,000

Order Handling: Information not available

Clearinghouse: Information not available

Firm's Exchange Membership: Information not available

Special Account Requirements: Information not available

Commission Structure: Sharebroker, DD (HI, LO)

Minimum Charge: Stocks, $29; Options, $27

Margin Interest Costs: Information not available

Interest Paid on Cash Balances
(Rate and Minimum):   Information not available

Investment Products: Stocks; Bonds; Options

Additional Charges: $1 for postage/handling; $20 additional for legal items

Date Firm Established: 1980

States Where Licensed to Do Business: Information not available

Seaport Securities Corporation
19 Rector Street
New York, NY 10006

Telephone Numbers:

    Toll-Free (out-of-state) 800/221-9894
    Local 212/482-8689

Other Office Locations: None

Insurance Protection: SIPC, $500,000 plus $2 million additional

Order Handling: Team system

Clearinghouse: Q & R Clearing Corp.

Firm's Exchange Membership: NYSE

Special Account Requirements: None

Commission Structure: Sharebroker, DD (HI, LO)

Minimum Charge: Stocks, $34; Options, $34

Margin Interest Costs:

$ Borrowed	Broker's Call+
Up to $4999	2%
$5000–$9999	1 3/4%
$10,000–$14,999	1 1/2%
$15,000–$19,999	1 1/4%
$20,000–$24,999	1%
Above $25,000	3/4%

Interest Paid on Cash Balances (Rate and Minimum): Money market fund available

Investment Products: Stocks; Bonds; Options; IRAs; Mutual Funds; Unit Investment Trusts

Services: Provides Standard & Poor's, Value Line, and company annual reports at no extra charge

Additional Charges: None

Date Firm Established: 1980

States Where Licensed to Do Business: California, Connecticut, District of Columbia, Florida, Georgia, Illinois, Maryland, Massachusetts, Michigan, New Hampshire, New Jersey, New York, Ohio, Pennsylvania, Rhode Island, Texas, Virginia

J.D. Seibert & Company, Inc.
20 West Ninth Street
Cincinnati, OH 45202

Telephone Numbers:

Toll-Free (in-state)	513/224-9100
Local	513/241-8888

Other Office Locations: None

Insurance Protection: SIPC, $500,000 plus $2 million additional

Order Handling: Account executive assigned

Clearinghouse: U.S. Clearing Corp.

Firm's Exchange Membership: None

Special Account Requirements: None

Commission Structure: Value/Sharebroker

Minimum Charge: Stocks, $40; Options, $40

Margin Interest Costs:

$ Borrowed	Broker's Call+
Up to $4999	2%
$5000–$9999	$1\,3/4\%$
$10,000–$14,999	$1\,1/2\%$
$15,000–$19,999	$1\,1/4\%$
$20,000–$24,999	1%
Above $25,000	3/4%

Interest Paid on Cash Balances
(Rate and Minimum): Money market fund; $1000 initial deposit; $100 increments

Investment Products: Stocks; Bonds; Options; Mutual Funds

Services: *Standard & Poor's Stock Guides* are available to clients

Additional Charges: None

Date Firm Established: 1979

States Where Licensed to Do Business: Information not available

The Discount Brokerage Directory

Sentinel Securities, Inc.
555 Fifth Avenue
New York, NY 10017

Telephone Numbers:

    Toll-Free (nationwide)   800/447-4566
    Local   212/953-4444

Other Office Locations: None

Insurance Protection: SIPC, $500,000 plus $2 million additional

Order Handling: Direct lines to executing brokers

Clearinghouse: Q & R Clearing Corp.

Firm's Exchange Membership: AMEX

Special Account Requirements: None

Commission Structure: Sharebroker, DD (HI, LO)

Minimum Charge: Stocks, $35; Options, $35

Margin Interest Costs:

$ Borrowed	Broker's Call+
Up to $4999	2%
$5000–$9999	$1 3/4$%
$10,000–$14,999	$1 1/2$%
$15,000–$19,999	$1 1/4$%
$20,000–$24,999	1%
Above $25,000	$3/4$%

Interest Paid on Cash Balances (Rate and Minimum): Credit balances maintained in Alliance Capital Reserves at current market rates

Investment Products: Stocks; Bonds; Options; IRAs; Government Securities (GNMA); Mutual Funds

Additional Charges: None

Date Firm Established: 1988

States Where Licensed to Do Business: All states

Note: Sentinel offers two account types. The Regular Account, for normal traders, charges 15 cents/share with a $35 minimum. The second, SuperSaver, for high-volume traders, charges 5 cents/share with a $60 minimum.

Shearman Ralston, Inc.
100 Wall Street
New York, NY 10005

Telephone Numbers:

    Toll-Free (nationwide)   800/221-4242
    Local   212/248-1160

Other Office Locations: Fort Lee, NJ; Huntington, NY

Insurance Protection: SIPC, $500,000

Order Handling: Team system (all registered representatives assigned upon request)

Clearinghouse: Q & R Clearing Corp.

Firm's Exchange Membership: None

Special Account Requirements: None

Commission Structure: Sharebroker

Minimum Charge: Stocks, $30; Options, $20

Margin Interest Costs: Variable

Interest Paid on Cash Balances
(Rate and Minimum): Money market fund; $500 minimum balance

Investment Products: Stocks; Bonds; Options; IRAs

Additional Charges: None

Date Firm Established: 1976

States Where Licensed to Do Business: Information not available

Shochet Securities, Inc.
Discount Stock Brokers
1484 E. Hallandale Beach Boulevard
Hallandale, FL 33009

Telephone Numbers:

    Toll-Free (out-of-state)   800/327-1536
    Toll-Free (in-state)   800/940-4567
    Local   305/454-0304

Other Office Locations: South Miami, FL

Insurance Protection: SIPC, $500,000 plus $9.5 million additional

Order Handling: Account executive assigned

Clearinghouse: Securities Settlement Corp.

Firm's Exchange Membership: None

Special Account Requirements: None

Commission Structure: Sharebroker

Minimum Charge: Stocks, $37; Options, $37

Margin Interest Costs: Negotiable

Interest Paid on Cash Balances (Rate and Minimum):   Money market fund (Kemper); $1000 initial deposit; $100 increments

Investment Products: Stocks; Bonds; Options; IRAs; Mutual Funds; Government Securities

Additional Charges: None

Date Firm Established: 1980

States Where Licensed to Do Business: Florida, New Jersey, New York

The Discount Brokerage Directory

Spear Securities, Inc.
510 West Sixth Street
Suite 525
Los Angeles, CA 90014

Telephone Numbers:

    Toll-Free (out-of-state)   800/821-1902
    Toll-Free (in-state)   800/252-9011
    Local   213/626-4221

Other Office Locations: Fresno and San Francisco, CA

Insurance Protection: SIPC, $500,000

Order Handling: Account executive assigned

Clearinghouse: Self

Firm's Exchange Membership: Pacific Stock Exchange

Special Account Requirements: None

Commission Structure: Valuebroker

Minimum Charge: Stocks, $38; Options, $38

Margin Interest Costs:

$ Borrowed	Broker's Call+
Up to $9999	$2\frac{1}{2}$%
$10,000–$29,999	$2\frac{1}{4}$%
$30,000–$49,999	$1\frac{3}{4}$%
$50,000–$99,999	$\frac{3}{4}$%
Above $100,000	$\frac{1}{2}$%

Interest Paid on Cash Balances
(Rate and Minimum): Money market rates; $2000 minimum

Investment Products: Information not available

Additional Charges: None

Date Firm Established: 1983

States Where Licensed to Do Business: All states

StockCross, Inc.
One Washington Mall
Boston, MA 02108

Telephone Numbers:

    Toll-Free (out-of-state)   800/225-6196
    Toll-Free (in-state)   800/392-6104
    Local   617/367-5700

Other Office Locations: Honolulu, HI

Insurance Protection: SIPC, $500,000

Order Handling: Team system (registered representatives only)

Clearinghouse: Self

Firm's Exchange Membership: NYSE, AMEX, Boston Stock Exchange

Special Account Requirements: None

Commission Structure: Sharebroker, DD (HI, LO)

Minimum Charge: Stocks, $25; Options, $20

Margin Interest Costs:

$ Borrowed	Broker's Call+
Up to $25,000	1%
Above $25,000	0%

Interest Paid on Cash Balances (Rate and Minimum): Money market fund; $3000 minimum

Investment Products: Stocks; Bonds; Options; IRAs

Additional Charges: $10 additional fee for limit orders

Date Firm Established: 1971

States Where Licensed to Do Business: Information not available

The Discount Brokerage Directory

The Stock Mart
Division: William O'Neil & Co., Inc.
11915 La Grange Avenue
Los Angeles, CA 90025

Telephone Numbers:

    Toll-Free (out-of-state)   800/421-6563
    Toll-Free (in-state)   800/352-7442
    Local   213/820-3090

Other Office Locations: None

Insurance Protection: SIPC, $500,000 plus $2 million additional

Order Handling: Account executives available

Clearinghouse: Broadcort Capital Corp., a wholly owned subsidiary of Merrill Lynch, Pierce, Fenner & Smith

Firm's Exchange Membership: NYSE, AMEX, Pacific Stock Exchange

Special Account Requirements: $10,000 minimum equity to open account-in funds and/or securities; all stock is held in street name

Commission Structure: Sharebroker, DD (LO)

Minimum Charge: Stocks, $30; Options, $30

Margin Interest Costs:

$ Borrowed	Broker's Call+
Up to $10,000	$2 1/4\%$
$10,000–$19,999	2%
$20,000–$29,999	$1 3/4\%$
$30,000–$49,999	$1 1/2\%$
Above $50,000	$3/4\%$

Interest Paid on Cash Balances
(Rate and Minimum): Summit Cash Reserve Fund; $5000 initial deposit

Investment Products: Information not available

Services: With confirmation of each security purchase, The Stock Mart will send a copy of its *Instant Daily Graph*

Additional Charges: None

Date Firm Established: 1964

States Where Licensed to Do Business: Arizona, California, Colorado, Connecticut, Florida, Illinois, New Jersey, New Mexico, New York, Ohio, Oregon, Pennsylvania, Texas, Utah, Washington, Wisconsin

Texas Securities, Inc.
4200 South Hulen
Suite 536
Fort Worth, TX 76109

Telephone Numbers:

    Toll-Free (nationwide)   800/772-3111
    Local   817/732-0130

Other Office Locations: None

Insurance Protection: SIPC, $500,000

Order Handling: Team system

Clearinghouse: Southwest Securities, Inc.

Firm's Exchange Membership: Information not available

Special Account Requirements: Information not available

Commission Structure: Sharebroker

Minimum Charge: Stocks, $40; Options, $40

Margin Interest Costs: All amounts borrowed at prime rate

Interest Paid on Cash Balances
(Rate and Minimum): Prime rate less 1%; $200 minimum

Investment Products: Stocks; Bonds; Options; Commodities; IRAs; Mutual Funds; Government Securities; Precious Metals; Insurance Investments; Real Estate Unit Trusts; International Securities

Services: Some original research primarily on regional companies and growth stocks. Also provides research from outside sources.

Additional Charges: None

Date Firm Established: 1978

States Where Licensed to Do Business: All states

Thomas F. White & Co., Inc.
1 Second Street
Suite 1040
San Francisco, CA 94105

Telephone Numbers:

    Toll-Free (nationwide)   800/66-WHITE
    Local   415/764-1900

Other Office Locations: Scottsdale, AZ; Beverly Hills, Chico, Concord, Escondido, Fremont, Fresno, Sacramento, Hemet, Hollister, Larkspur, Palo Alto, San Mateo, CA; Stamford, CT; Vero Beach, FL; Elkhart and Lafayette, IN; Rochester, MI; Toledo, OH; Erie, PA; Houston and San Antonio, TX

Insurance Protection: SIPC, $500,000

Order Handling: Registered representative assigned

Clearinghouse: Self

Firm's Exchange Membership: Pacific Stock Exchange

Special Account Requirements: None

Commission Structure: Valuebroker

Minimum Charge: Stocks, $30; Options, $35

Margin Interest Costs:

$ Borrowed	Broker's Call+
Up to $10,000	2%
$10,000–$30,000	1½%
$30,000–$50,000	1%
Above $50,000	¾%

Interest Paid on Cash Balances
(Rate and Minimum):   2% below broker's call rate; $500 minimum

Investment Products: Stocks; Bonds; Options; IRAs; Government Securities (specializing in tax-free municipals); Mutual Funds; Unit Trusts Foreign Securities; Partnerships; Insurance

Services: Supplies free monthly publication, *White Paper on Municipal Bonds*

Additional Charges: Postage charges only

Date Firm Established: 1978

States Where Licensed to Do Business: Arizona, California, Colorado, Connecticut, Florida, Hawaii, Iowa, Kansas, Michigan, Missouri, Nevada, New Mexico, North Dakota, Ohio, Pennsylvania, Tennessee, Texas, Utah, Wisconsin, Wyoming

Tradex Brokerage Service, Inc.
20 Vesey Street
New York, NY 10007

Telephone Numbers:

    Toll-Free (nationwide)   800/522-3000
    Local   212/233-2000

Other Office Locations: Miami, FL; Houston, TX

Insurance Protection: SIPC, $500,000 plus $10 million additional

Order Handling: Team system

Clearinghouse: Security Settlement

Firm's Exchange Membership: NYSE

Special Account Requirements: None

Commission Structure: Sharebroker, DD (HI, LO)

Minimum Charge: Stocks, $25; Options, $25

Additional Transaction Charges: $1.50 per transaction (insurance, mail, handling)

Margin Interest Costs: Broker's call + 1%

Interest Paid on Cash Balances
(Rate and Minimum):   Broker's call 2%, $250 minimum; (IRA & Keogh, no minimum amount)

Investment Products: Stocks; Bonds; Options; IRAs; Commodities

Additional Charges: None

Date Firm Established: 1979

States Where Licensed to Do Business: California, Connecticut, Delaware, Florida, Georgia, Illinois, Indiana, Kentucky, Louisiana, Maryland, Massachusetts, Michigan, New Jersey, New York, Pennsylvania, Tennessee, Texas, Virginia

Tuttle Securities
Twelve Mony Plaza
Syracuse, NY 13202

Telephone Numbers:
  Toll-Free (in-state)   800/962-5489
  Local   315/422-2515

Other Office Locations: None

Insurance Protection: SIPC, $500,000 plus $10 million additional

Order Handling: Team system

Clearinghouse: Pershing & Co., Division of Donaldson, Lufkin & Jenrette

Firm's Exchange Membership: None

Special Account Requirements: None

Commission Structure: Sharebroker

Minimum Charge: Stocks, $35; Options, $35

Additional Transaction Charges: None

Margin Interest Costs:

$ Borrowed	Broker's Call+
Up to $9999	2 1/4%
$10,000–$29,999	2%
$30,000–$49,999	1 1/2%
Above $50,000	3/4%

Interest Paid on Cash Balances
(Rate and Minimum): Money market rates; $500 minimum

Investment Products: Stocks; Bonds; Options; Lease Investments; IRAs; Real Estate Limited Partnerships

Services: Tuttle provides independent research on 4500 companies, through Standard & Poor's and other sources

Additional Charges: None

Date Firm Established: 1976

States Where Licensed to Do Business: New York

Voss & Co., Inc.
6320 Augusta Drive
Suite 1200
Springfield, VA 22150-5097

Telephone Numbers:

    Toll-Free (out-of-state)   800/426-8106
    Toll-Free (in-state)   800/426-8106
    Local   703/569-9300 or -8300

Other Office Locations: None

Insurance Protection: SIPC, $500,000 plus $2 million additional

Order Handling: Account executive/registered rep assigned

Clearinghouse: Clearing Corp.

Firm's Exchange Membership: National Futures Association

Special Account Requirements: None

Commission Structure: Value/Sharebroker, DD (HI, LO)

Minimum Charge: Stocks, $38.50; Options, $40

Margin Interest Costs: $1/2\%$–2% above broker's call, depending on size of debit balance

Interest Paid on Cash Balances
(Rate and Minimum): Alliance Money Reserves; $100 minimum

Investment Products: Stocks; Bonds; Options; IRAs; Futures; Precious Metals; Commodities; Mutual Funds; Government Securities

Services: Standard & Poor's; Value Line; access to daily Gelderman research reports; commodity brochures and charts on request; free use of Touchquote®, an automated 24-hr quote service with all accounts; quarterly newsletter

Additional Charges: None

Date Firm Established: 1973

States Where Licensed to Do Business: California, Colorado, District of Columbia, Florida, Illinois, Maryland, Massachusetts, Nebraska, New York, North Carolina, Oklahoma, Pennsylvania, Texas, Virginia, West Virginia

The Wall Street Discount Corporation
100 Wall Street
New York, NY 10005

Telephone Numbers:

    Toll-Free (out-of-state)   800/221-7990
    Toll-Free (in-state)   800/842-4255
    Local   212/747-5100

Other Office Locations: None

Insurance Protection: SIPC, $500,000 plus $2 million additional

Order Handling: Team system

Clearinghouse: Ernst & Co.

Firm's Exchange Membership: NYSE

Special Account Requirements: None

Commission Structure: Sharebroker, DD (HI, LO)

Minimum Charge: Stocks, $35; Options, $35

Additional Transaction Charges: None

Margin Interest Costs:

$ Borrowed	Broker's Call+
Up to $25,000	$2 1/4\%$
$25,000–$100,000	$1 1/2\%$
Above $100,000	$1/2\%–1\%$

Interest Paid on Cash Balances
(Rate and Minimum): $2 1/2\%–1/2\%$ below broker's call rate, depending on size of balance; $1000 initial deposit

Investment Products: Information not available

Additional Charges: None

Date Firm Established: 1978

States Where Licensed to Do Business: California, Connecticut, Delaware, Florida, Illinois, Maryland, Massachusetts, Michigan, Minnesota, Nevada, New Jersey, New York, North Carolina, Ohio, Pennsylvania, Texas, Wisconsin

The Discount Brokerage Directory

Waterhouse Securities, Inc.
44 Wall Street
New York, NY 10005-2489

Telephone Numbers:

Toll-Free (out-of-state)	800/327-7500
Toll-Free (in-state)	800/522-7500
Local	212/344-7500

Other Office Locations: Los Angeles and San Francisco, CA; Washington, DC; Miami, FL; Atlanta, GA; Chicago, IL; Boston, MA; Detroit, MI; St. Louis, MO; Philadelphia, PA; Dallas, TX; Seattle, WA

Insurance Protection: SIPC, $500,000

Order Handling: Account executive assigned

Clearinghouse: Self

Firm's Exchange Membership: NYSE, AMEX, Midwest Stock Exchange

Special Account Requirements: Information not available

Commission Structure: Sharebroker, DD (HI, LO)

Minimum Charge: Stocks, $35; Options, $31.25

Margin Interest Costs:

$ Borrowed	Broker's Call+
Up to $50,000	1%
Above $50,000	1/2%

Interest Paid on Cash Balances (Rate and Minimum): Money market fund; $1000 minimum initial deposit

Investment Products: Stocks; Bonds; Options; IRAs; Government Securities

Services: Provides each client a package of information from S&P's including: company reports, stock guides, special editions of S&P's *The Outlook,* and a tax guide.

Additional Charges: None

Date Firm Established: 1978

States Where Licensed to Do Business: Information not available

Whitehall Securities, Inc.
1021 Avenue of the Americas
New York, NY 10018

Telephone Numbers:
    Toll-Free (out-of-state)   800/223-5023
    Toll-Free (in-state)   Call collect
    Local   212/719-5522

Other Office Locations: None

Insurance Protection: SIPC, $500,000 plus $9.5 million additional

Order Handling: Registered representative assigned

Clearinghouse: Securities Settlement Corp.

Firm's Exchange Membership: Information not available

Special Account Requirements: None

Commission Structure: Sharebroker, DD (HI)

Minimum Charge: Stocks, $50; Options, $50

Margin Interest Costs: Information not available

Interest Paid on Cash Balances
(Rate and Minimum): $2500 minimum

Investment Products: Stocks; Bonds; Options; IRAs; Government Securities; Tax Shelters

Additional Charges: None

Date Firm Established: 1982

States Where Licensed to Do Business: All states

Wisconsin Discount Securities Corporation
2050 W. Good Hope Road
Milwaukee, WI 53209

Telephone Numbers:

    Toll-Free (out-of-state)   800/537-0239
    Toll-Free (in-state)   800/242-9196
    Local   414/352-5050

Other Office Locations: None

Insurance Protection: SIPC, $500,000

Clearinghouse: Securities Settlement Corp.

Firm's Exchange Membership: Information not available

Commission Structure: Sharebroker

Minimum Charge: Stocks, $30; Options, $30

Margin Interest Costs: Available

Interest Paid on Cash Balances
(Rate and Minimum): Money market fund

Investment Products: Stocks; Bonds; Options; Commodities

Additional Charges: Information not available

Date Firm Established: 1977

States Where Licensed to Do Business: Colorado, Florida, Illinois, Wisconsin

York Securities
160 Broadway (East Building)
New York, NY 10038

Telephone Numbers:

    Toll-Free (nationwide)   800/221-3154
    Local   212/349-9700

Other Office Locations: None

Insurance Protection: SIPC, $500,000 plus $2 million additional

Order Handling: Team system

Clearinghouse: Q & R Clearing Corp.

Firm's Exchange Membership: NYSE, AMEX, National Futures Assoc., NY Option Exchange, Commodities Futures Trading Commission Registrant

Special Account Requirements: None

Commission Structure: Sharebroker, DD (HI, LO)

Minimum Charge: Stocks, $35; Options, $35

Margin Interest Costs:

$ Borrowed	Broker's Call+
Up to $4999	$1\,3/4\%$
$5000–$9999	$1\,1/2\%$
$10,000–$14,999	$1\,1/4\%$
$15,000–$19,999	1%
Above $20,000	$3/4\%$

Interest Paid on Cash Balances (Rate and Minimum):   Money market

Investment Products: Stocks; Bonds; Options; Index Futures; Commodities; Government Securities; IRAs; Mutual Funds

Services: S&P's *Stock Guide* and company reports available

Additional Charges: None

Date Firm Established: 1979

States Where Licensed to Do Business: Most states

Young, Stovall and Company
9627 South Dixie Highway
Suite 101
Miami, FL 33156

Telephone Numbers:

    Toll-Free (in-state)   800/433-5132
    Local   305/666-2511

Other Office Locations: Dade and Broward, FL

Insurance Protection: SIPC, $500,000

Order Handling: Account executive assigned

Clearinghouse: Q & R Clearing Corp.

Firm's Exchange Membership: None

Special Account Requirements: Information not available

Commission Structure: Sharebroker

Minimum Charge: Stocks, $35; Options, $35

Margin Interest Costs: Varies depending on amount borrowed

Interest Paid on Cash Balances
(Rate and Minimum): Variable

Investment Products: Stocks; Bonds; Options; IRAs; Mutual Funds; GNMAs; Unit Trusts

Services: Maintains current research on 8000 securities; also maintains a research library

Additional Charges: None

Date Firm Established: 1980

States Where Licensed to Do Business: Florida

CHAPTER 2

The Bank Brokers

The banks which are profiled were selected from cities throughout the country, both large and small, and range from money center and regional banks to medium size and community banks. Each of them, in common with hundreds of other banks offering discount brokerage services, integrate banking and brokerage services to varying degrees. This means that trades can usually be settled through a variety of demand deposit accounts, and dividends and interest can often be credited in various ways. The areas which are covered are listed below.

(1) *Name and Address.* The address listed is that of the principal office.

(2) *Telephone Numbers.* The local number and a toll-free number, where it is available, are listed.

(3) *Deposits.* Total bank deposits, which are an indication of size, are noted.

(4) *Name of Service.* This identifies the name of the discount brokerage service which has been established by the bank.

(5) *Order Handling.* There are two basic methods used to transact customer orders and handle customer inquiries. One method is to assign a particular account executive. The other is to use a team system, which means that orders and inquiries are handled by whichever person is available. This section tells you which system is used.

(6) *Commission Structure.* If the designation "DD" appears, this indicates that the bank is designated as a deep discounter. This means that the bank has been identified as one of the 40 banks with the lowest average cost among bank brokers for either the sample of trades averaging approximately $6000 (LO) or $13,000 (HI). If the firm appears on both lists, then both are listed, for example, DD (HI,LO).

Also indicated is the type of cost system. Mercer has coined the terms for the two types of commission structures used: Those who charge on the basis of the value of the transaction are termed "valuebrokers." Those who charge strictly according to the number of shares traded are termed "sharebrokers."

(7) *Settlement Accounts.* Describes the accounts out of which securities trades may be settled. Typically, they include checking, savings, and NOW accounts.

(8) *Brokerage Vendor.* Most financial institutions currently offering discount brokerage services do so through contractual arrangements with correspondent brokers or banks (vendors) who provide discount brokerage services. This entry identifies the correspondent broker or bank providing such services.

(9) *Investment Products.* Identifies which investment products are offered by the firm.

(10) *Services.* Publications or other services provided to assist the investor in making investment decisions are listed.

American Security Bank
1501 Pennsylvania Avenue, N.W.
A-1/334
Washington, DC 20013

Telephone Number: Local   202/624-4560
Deposits: $3.6 billion
Name of Service: American Security Investment Services, Inc.
Order Handling: Team system
Commission Structure: Valuebroker
Settlement Accounts: Various options available
Brokerage Vendor: BHC Securities, Inc.
Investment Products: Stocks; Bonds; Options; IRAs; Mutual Funds; Government Securities; Unit Investment Trusts
Note: Offers self-directed IRAs, Keoghs, and retirement plans

American Trust & Savings Bank
895 Town Clock Plaza
Dubuque, IA 52004-0938

Telephone Number: Local   319/582-1841
Deposits: $255 million
Name of Service: Discount Brokerage Service
Order Handling: Team system
Commission Structure: Valuebroker, DD (HI, LO)
Settlement Accounts: American Trust checking or money market account
Brokerage Vendor: Automated Brokerage Services
Investment Products: Information not available
Note: Offers self-directed IRAs

Ameritrust Co.
900 Euclid Avenue
P.O. Box 94556
Cleveland, OH 44101-4556

Telephone Numbers: Toll-Free (out-of-state)   800/634-4029
                     Toll-Free (in-state)   800/634-8639
                     Local   216/687-8400

Deposits: $6 billion
Name of Service: AmeriTrust Investor Services
Order Handling: Team system
Commission Structure: Valuebroker, DD (HI, LO)
Settlement Accounts: Information not available
Brokerage Vendor: National Financial Services Corp.
Investment Products: Stocks; Bonds; Options; Government Securities

Amoskeag Bank
875 Elm Street
P.O. Box 6060
Manchester, NH 03108-6060

Telephone Numbers: Toll-Free (nationwide)   800/637-3202
                     Local   603/624-3406
Deposits: $856 million
Name of Service: SBS Discount Brokerage Service
Order Handling: Team system
Commission Structure: Valuebroker
Settlement Accounts: Any Amoskeag bank account
Brokerage Vendor: National Financial Services Corp.
Investment Products: Stocks; Bonds; Options

AmSouth
P.O. Box 830329
Birmingham, AL 35282

Telephone Numbers: Toll-Free (nationwide)   800/444-2425
                     Local   205/581-7585
Deposits: $4.4 billion
Name of Service: AmSouth Investment Services, Inc.
Order Handling: Account executive assigned
Commission Structure: Valuebroker
Settlement Accounts: AmSouth checking account
Brokerage Vendor: National Financial Services Corp.
Investment Products: Stocks; Bonds; Options; IRAs; Mutual Funds

The Arizona Bank
101 N. 1st Avenue
P.O. Box 2511
Phoenix, AZ 85002

Telephone Numbers: Toll-Free (nationwide) 800/842-4004
                   Local   602/262-4700
Deposits: $1.97 billion
Name of Service: Security Pacific Investment, Inc.
Order Handling: Account executive assigned
Commission Structure: Valuebroker
Settlement Accounts: Checking or savings account
Brokerage Vendor: Southwest Securities
Investment Products: Stocks; Bonds; Options; IRAs; Mutual Funds; Precious Metals; Government Securities

Atlantic Bank of New York
960 Avenue of the Americas
New York, NY 10001

Telephone Numbers: Toll-Free (nationwide) 800/622-2998
                   Local   212/695-5400
Deposits: $811 million
Name of Service: Discount Brokerage Service
Order Handling: Information not available
Commission Structure: Valuebroker, DD (HI)
Settlement Accounts: Checking or savings account
Brokerage Vendor: Olde Discount Corporation
Investment Products: Stocks; Bonds; Options; IRAs; Mutual Funds

Bank IV
100 North Broadway
P.O. Box 4
Wichita, KS 67201-0004

Telephone Number: Local 316/261-4445
Deposits: $1.14 billion

Name of Service: Bank IV Discount Brokerage American Brokerage Services, Inc.
Order Handling: Account executive assigned
Commission Structure: Sharebroker
Settlement Accounts: Checking or savings account
Brokerage Vendor: Olde Discount Corporation
Investment Products: Stocks; Bonds; Options; Government Securities; Mutual Funds; IRAs; Unit Investment Trusts

Bank of Baltimore
P.O. Box 896
Baltimore, MD 21203

Telephone Numbers: Toll-Free (in-state) 800/492-1653
  Local 301/244-3541
Deposits: $22 billion
Name of Service: Atlantic Discount Brokerage Services Corporation
Order Handling: Team system
Commission Structure: Valuebroker, DD (HI, LO)
Settlement Accounts: Bank of Baltimore checking, savings, or money market account
Brokerage Vendor: National Financial Services Corp.
Investment Products: Stocks; Bonds; Options; IRAs; Mutual Funds
Services: Research rooms available

Bank of Boston
100 Federal Street 01-1B-02
P.O. Box 1860
Boston, MA 02110

Telephone Numbers: Toll-Free (nationwide) 800/356-0008
  Toll-Free (in-state) 800/548-8002
  Local 617/434-5860
Deposits: $22 billion
Name of Service: BancBoston Brokerage Inc.
Order Handling: Team system

Commission Structure: Valuebroker
Settlement Accounts: Bank of Boston checking/NOW or First Rate account
Brokerage Vendor: National Financial Services Corp.
Investment Products: Stocks; Bonds; Options; IRAs; Mutual Funds; Government Securities; Futures; Unit Investment Trusts; Precious Metals

Note: Offers self-directed IRAs, Keoghs, and other retirement plans

Bank of Delaware
300 Delaware Avenue
P.O. Box 8744
Wilmington, DE 19899

Telephone Numbers: Toll-Free (out-of-state)   800/722-1172
                     Toll-Free (Kent or Sussex County)   800/922-0102
                     Local   302/429-7100
Deposits: $1.3 billion
Name of Service: Christina Brokerage Services
Order Handling: Account executive assigned
Commission Structure: Valuebroker
Settlement Accounts: Checking account
Brokerage Vendor: Bradford Broker Settlement, Inc.
Investment Products: Information not available

Bank of Hawaii
111 South King Street
P.O. Box 2900
Honolulu, HI 96846

Telephone Number: Local   808/537-8621
Deposits: $4.4 billion
Name of Service: Bankoh Brokerage Service
Order Handling: Team system
Commission Structure: Valuebroker
Settlement Accounts: Any Bank of Hawaii account

Brokerage Vendor: Information not available
Investment Products: Information not available

**Bank of New England
P.O. Box 1070
Boston, MA 02103**

Telephone Numbers: Toll-Free (nationwide)   800/343-5015
                    Local   617/722-6444
Deposits: $29 billion
Name of Service: New England Discount Brokerage, Inc.
Order Handling: Team system
Commission Structure: Valuebroker, DD (HI)
Settlement Accounts: Information not available
Brokerage Vendor: National Financial Services Corp.
Investment Products: Stocks; Bonds; Options; IRAs; Unit
                       Investment Trusts; Mutual Funds

**Bank of New York
48 Wall Street
New York, NY 10286**

Telephone Numbers: Toll-Free (nationwide)   800/255-8282
                    Local   212/804-2080
Deposits: $15 billion
Name of Service: BNY Personal Brokerage, Inc.
Order Handling: Registered representatives
Commission Structure: Valuebroker
Settlement Accounts: Bank of New York checking account
Brokerage Vendor: National Financial Services Corp.
Investment Products: Stocks; Bonds; Options; Government
                       Securities; Mutual Funds; IRAs

**Bank of Oklahoma
Robinson at Robert S. Kerr Avenue
P.O. Box 24128
Oklahoma City, OK 73124**

Telephone Numbers: Toll-Free (in-state)   800/522-3415
                    Tulsa   405/743-4457
                    Local   405/272-2105

Deposits: $1.6 billion
Name of Service: Investor Brokerage/MPACT Brokers
Order Handling: Team system
Commission Structure: Valuebroker
Settlement Accounts: Bank of Oklahoma account
Brokerage Vendor: National Financial Services Corp.
Investment Products: Information not available

Bank One
10 East Market Street
Indianapolis, IN 46277

Telephone Number: Local 317/639-7897
Deposits: $2.8 billion
Name of Service: Bank One Securities, Inc.
Order Handling: Team system
Commission Structure: Valuebroker
Settlement Accounts: Checking account
Brokerage Vendor: Dominick & Dominick, Inc.
Investment Products: Information not available

Bank One Milwaukee, N.A.
P.O. Box 974
Milwaukee, WI 53201

Telephone Numbers: Toll-Free (nationwide) 800/336-6006
                         Local 414/765-2100
Deposits: $1.7 billion
Name of Service: Bank One Wisconsin Investment Services Corporation
Order Handling: Team system
Commission Structure: Valuebroker
Settlement Accounts: Bank account
Brokerage Vendor: National Financial Services Corp.
Investment Products: Stocks; Bonds; Options

Bankers Trust Company
One Bankers Trust Plaza
27th Floor
New York, NY 10006

Telephone Numbers: Toll-Free (nationwide)   800/445-0081
                     Local   212/250-5600
Deposits: $56.4 billion
Name of Service: The Wall Street Account
Order Handling: Team system
Commission Structure: Valuebroker, DD (HI)
Settlement Accounts: Money market account
Brokerage Vendor: BT Brokerage Corporation
Investment Products: Stocks; Bonds; Options; IRAs; Mutual Funds; Government Securities

Bankwest, N.A.
420 S. Pierre
P.O. Box 998
Pierre, SD 57501-0998

Telephone Number: Local   605/224-7391
Deposits: $115 million
Name of Service: Discount Brokerage Service
Order Handling: Team system
Commission Structure: Valuebroker
Settlement Accounts: Checking or savings account
Brokerage Vendor: Security Pacific Brokers Financial Clearing and Services Corp.
Investment Products: Stocks; Bonds; Options; Government Securities; Mutual Funds; IRAs; Unit Trusts; Precious Metals; Foreign Securities

Barclays Bank
P.O. Box 200
Great Neck, NY 11022

Telephone Numbers: Toll-Free (nationwide)   800/632-4455
                     Local   516/482-7482

Deposits: $80 billion
Name of Service: Barclays Brokerage Services
Order Handling: Account executive assigned
Commission Structure: Valuebroker, DD (HI, LO)
Settlement Accounts: Information not available
Brokerage Vendor: Pershing & Company, Division of Donaldson, Lufkin & Jenrette
Investment Products: Stocks; Bonds; Options; IRAs; Government Securities; Mutual Funds; Unit Investment Trusts; Precious Metals; Foreign Securities
Services: S&P company reports are available

Barnett Bank
Barnett Center
625 North Flagler Drive
West Palm Beach, FL 33401

Telephone Numbers: Toll-Free (nationwide) 800/BARNETT
         Local 305/832-1200
Deposits: $1.6 billion
Name of Service: Barnett Brokerage Service
Order Handling: Team system
Commission Structure: Valuebroker
Settlement Accounts: Any Barnett account
Brokerage Vendor: Securities Settlement Corporation
Investment Products: Stocks; Bonds; Options; Mutual Funds; Unit Investment Trusts

BayBanks, Inc.
175 Federal Street
Boston, MA 02110

Telephone Numbers: Toll-Free (nationwide) 800/451-9600
         Local 617/695-0088
Deposits: $10 billion
Name of Service: BayBanks Brokerage Services, Inc.
Order Handling: Team system
Commission Structure: Valuebroker

Settlement Accounts: Checking or savings account
Brokerage Vendor: Pershing & Company, Division of Donaldson, Lufkin & Jenrette
Investment Products: Stocks; Bonds; Options; IRAs; Mutual Funds
Note: Offers self-directed IRAs and Keoghs

The Boatmen's National Bank of St. Louis
P.O. Box 236
St. Louis, MO 63166

Telephone Numbers: Toll-Free (nationwide) 800/262-8636
　　　　　　　　　　Local　　　　　　　　　 314/444-3000
Deposits: $3 billion
Name of Service: Boatmen's Investment Services
Order Handling: Information not available
Commission Structure: Valuebroker
Settlement Accounts: Any Boatmen's account
Brokerage Vendor: Dominick & Dominick, Inc.
Investment Products: Stocks; Bonds

Boone County National Bank
8th and Broadway
P.O. Box 678
Columbia, MO 65205

Telephone Number: Local 314/874-8535
Deposits: $250 million
Name of Service: Boone County National Bank Brokerage Services
Order Handling: Information not available
Commission Structure: Valuebroker
Settlement Accounts: Information not available
Brokerage Vendor: Information not available
Investment Products: Information not available

The Bowery
110 East 42nd Street
New York, NY 10017

Telephone Numbers: Toll-Free (nationwide) 800/333-4437
                    Local   212/953-8300
Deposits: $5.1 billion
Name of Service: Griffin Financial Services
Order Handling: Information not available
Commission Structure: Valuebroker
Settlement Accounts: Information not available
Brokerage Vendor: Information not available
Investment Products: Stocks; Bonds; Options; IRAs; Mutual Funds; Precious Metals; Insurance; Medicare/Nursing Care

Broadway National Bank
1177 N.E. Loop 410
P.O. Box 17001
San Antonio, TX 78286

Telephone Number: Local 512/824-0444
Deposits: $371 million
Name of Service: Broadway Brokerage Services
Order Handling: Team system
Commission Structure: Valuebroker
Settlement Accounts: Checking or money market investment account
Brokerage Vendor: National Financial Services Corp.
Investment Products: Information not available

Capital Bank
P.O. Box 2710
Baton Rouge, LA 70821

Telephone Number: Local 504/927-1220
Deposits: $426 million
Name of Service: Capital Bank Discount Brokerage Service
Order Handling: Team system

Commission Structure: Valuebroker
Settlement Accounts: Checking, NOW, or money manager account
Brokerage Vendor: Depositors Discount Brokerage Service
Investment Products: Information not available

Casco Northern Bank, N.A.
One Monument Square
P.O. Box 678
Portland, ME 04104

Telephone Number: Local   207/774-8221
Deposits: $1.2 billion
Name of Service: Brokerage Service Program
Order Handling: Team system
Commission Structure: Valuebroker
Settlement Accounts: Checking, NOW, or variable market rate account
Brokerage Vendor: Fidelity Brokerage Service, Inc.
Investment Products: Information not available

Centerre Bank
800 Market Street
P.O. Box 14979
St. Louis, MO 63178

Telephone Number: Local   314/554-7777
Deposits: $4 billion
Name of Service: Market Street Securities, Inc.
Order Handling: Personal broker
Commission Structure: Valuebroker
Settlement Accounts: Information not available
Brokerage Vendor: Pershing & Company, Division of Donaldson, Lufkin & Jenrette
Investment Products: Information not available

The Discount Brokerage Directory

Central Bank of The South, N.A.
P.O. Box 127
Huntsville, AL 35804

Telephone Numbers: Toll-Free (nationwide) 800/523-6117
                    Local   205/532-6011
Deposits: $2.3 billion
Name of Service: Central Brokerage Services
Order Handling: Account executive assigned
Commission Structure: Valuebroker, DD (LO)
Settlement Accounts: Any account
Brokerage Vendor: Wall Street Clearing Company
Investment Products: Stocks; Bonds; Options; IRAs; Mutual Funds; Unit Trusts

Central Carolina Bank
111 Corcoran Street
Durham, NC 27702

Telephone Numbers: Toll-Free (nationwide) 800/533-1200
                    Local   916/683-7777
Deposits: $1.2 billion
Name of Service: Investor Service Center
Order Handling: Team system
Commission Structure: Valuebroker, DD (HI)
Settlement Accounts: Information not available
Brokerage Vendor: National Financial Services Corp.
Investment Products: Information not available

Charleston National Bank
Charleston National Plaza
P.O. Box 1113
Charleston, WV 25324

Telephone Number: Local 304/348-5606
Deposits: $315 million
Name of Service: Discount Brokerage Services
Order Handling: Team system
Commission Structure: Valuebroker

Settlement Accounts: Checking account
Brokerage Vendor: National Financial Services, Inc.
Investment Products: Information not available

Chase Lincoln First
P.O. Box 22974
Rochester, NY 14692

Telephone Numbers: Toll-Free (out-of-state)   800/833-8595
                    Toll-Free (in-state)   800/462-4655
                    Local   716/258-6803
Deposits: $3.02 billion
Name of Service: Chase Lincoln First Service Brokerage Services, Inc.
Order Handling: Team system
Commission Structure: Valuebroker
Settlement Accounts: Checking or money market account
Brokerage Vendor: National Financial Services Corp.
Investment Products: Information not available
Note: Offers self-directed IRAs

Chase Manhattan Bank
One Chase Manhattan Plaza
New York, NY 10081

Telephone Numbers: Toll-Free (nationwide)   800/621-3700
                    Local   212/619-3333
Deposits: $94.8 billion
Name of Service: Rose & Company, One Financial Place, Chicago, IL 60605
Order Handling: Team system (registered representatives assigned upon request)
Commission Structure: Valuebroker DD (HI, LO)
Settlement Accounts: Information not available
Brokerage Vendor: Self
Investment Products: Information not available

Chemical Bank
277 Park Avenue
New York, NY 10172

Telephone Number: Local 212/310-4264
Deposits: $56.6 billion
Name of Service: Chemical Securities, Inc.
Order Handling: Team system
Commission Structure: Sharebroker
Settlement Accounts: Checking account
Brokerage Vendor: Pershing & Company, Division of Donaldson, Lufkin & Jenrette
Investment Products: Stocks; Bonds; Options; IRAs; Mutual Funds; Municipal Securities; Government Securities; Unit Trusts
Services: Bimonthly market newsletter
Note: Offers self-directed IRAs and Keoghs

Citibank
399 Park Avenue
New York, NY 10043

Telephone Numbers: Toll-Free (nationwide) 800/248-4472
Local 212/736-8170
Deposits: $121.5 billion
Name of Service: Citicorp Brokerage Service
Order Handling: Team system
Commission Structure: Valuebroker
Settlement Accounts: Any account
Brokerage Vendor: B.H.C. Securities, Inc.
Investment Products: Stocks; Bonds; Options; IRAs; Mutual Funds; Government Securities
Services: "Direct Access," a service allowing on-line trading and access to *Dow Jones News* with a personal computer (available in the NY Metro area)

Citizens and Southern Bank
33 North Avenue
Suite 1800
Atlanta, GA 30308

Telephone Number: Local   404/897-3200
Deposits: $14 billion
Name of Service: Citizens and Southern Securities Corporation
Order Handling: Personal broker
Commission Structure: Valuebroker
Settlement Accounts: Checking or savings account
Brokerage Vendor: Broadcort Capital Corporation
Investment Products: Information not available

Colorado National Bank of Denver
P.O. Box 5168
Denver, CO 80217

Telephone Numbers: Toll-Free (outside Metro Denver)   800/321-1472
                     Local   303/892-4137
Deposits: $959 million
Name of Service: Colorado National Brokerage, Inc.
Order Handling: Team system
Commission Structure: Valuebroker
Settlement Accounts: Checking or savings account
Brokerage Vendor: BHC Securities, Inc.
Investment Products: Information not available
Special Requirements: Trading open to Colorado residents only

Comerica Bank
Fort at Washington Boulevard
Detroit, MI 48275

Telephone Numbers: Toll-Free (nationwide)   800/327-7911
                     Toll-Free (Michigan only) 800/327-5965
                     Local   313/222-5580

Deposits: (Parent) $10.3 billion
Name of Service: Comerica Brokers, Inc.
Order Handling: Team system
Commission Structure: Valuebroker, DD (HI)
Settlement Accounts: Comerica Bank checking, savings, or money market account
Brokerage Vendor: National Financial Services Corp.
Investment Products: Stocks; Bonds; Options; IRAs; Mutual Funds
Note: Offers self-directed IRAs

Commerce Bank of St. Louis
P.O. Box 15201
St. Louis, MO 63110

Telephone Numbers: Toll-Free (states bordering MO)   800/821-2182
Toll-Free (Kansas City)   816/234-2416
Local   800/772-SAVE
Deposits: $1.5 billion
Name of Service: Commerce Brokerage Services, Inc.
Order Handling: Team system
Commission Structure: Valuebroker
Settlement Accounts: Checking, NOW, super-NOW, or insured money market account
Brokerage Vendor: National Financial Services Corp.
Investment Products: Information not available

Commercial National Bank
601 Minnesota Avenue
Kansas City, KS 66101

Telephone Number: Local   913/573-1007
Deposits: $255 million
Name of Service: Commercial National Bank Discount Brokerage Service
Order Handling: Team system
Commission Structure: Valuebroker

Settlement Accounts: CNB checking, money market, or super-NOW account
Brokerage Vendor: Securities Settlement Corporation
Investment Products: Information not available

The Connecticut Bank and Trust Company
One Constitution Plaza
Hartford, CT 06115

Telephone Number: Local   203/244-5000
Deposits: $14 billion
Name of Service: New England Brokerage Service
Order Handling: Account executive assigned
Commission Structure: Valuebroker
Settlement Accounts: Checking or NOW account
Brokerage Vendor: Fidelity Brokerage Services, Inc.
Investment Products: Information not available

Connecticut National Bank
777 Main Street
Hartford, CT 06115

Telephone Number: Local   203/728-4848
Deposits: $7 billion
Name of Service: CNB Discount Brokerage, Inc.
Order Handling: Team system
Commission Structure: Valuebroker, DD (LO)
Settlement Accounts: Checking account or direct payment
Brokerage Vendor: National Financial Services Corp.
Investment Products: Stocks; Bonds; Options; IRAs; Mutual Funds

Continental Bank
Centre Square
1500 Market Street
Philadelphia, PA 19102

Telephone Numbers: Toll-Free (nationwide)   800/222-2024
                   Local   215/564-7575

Deposits: $14.4 billion
Name of Service: Midlantic Securities Corporation
Order Handling: Team system
Commission Structure: Valuebroker, DD (HI, LO)
Settlement Accounts: Checking, NOW, or money market account
Brokerage Vendor: BHC Securities, Inc.
Investment Products: Stocks; Bonds; Options; IRAs; Mutual Funds

Note: Part of the Midlantic Corporation (201/321-8171; 800/272-1354)

Continental Bank and Trust
P.O. Box 30177
Salt Lake City, UT 84130

Telephone Number: Local 801/534-6086
Deposits: $260 million
Name of Service: Discount Brokerage Service
Order Handling: Team system
Commission Structure: Valuebroker
Settlement Accounts: Checking or savings account
Brokerage Vendor: Financial Clearing & Services Corp. (Security Pacific Brokers, Inc.)
Investment Products: Stocks; Bonds; Options; Government Securities; Mutual Funds; Precious Metals

Continental Illinois National Bank
and Trust Company of Chicago
231 South LaSalle Street
Chicago, IL 60697

Telephone Numbers: Toll-Free (nationwide) 800/621-1095
　　　　　　　　　Toll-Free (in-state) 800/572-7008
　　　　　　　　　Local 312/923-0412
Deposits: $32.4 billion
Name of Service: Continental Brokerage Services, Inc.
Order Handling: Team system

Commission Structure: Valuebroker
Settlement Accounts: Checking or money market account
Brokerage Vendor: National Financial Services Corp.
Investment Products: Stocks; Bonds; Options; Government Securities; Mutual Funds; IRAs; Unit Investment Trusts
Services: *S&P MarketScope* and *ADP NewsBeat* available at no extra charge

Crestar Bank
P.O. Box 596
Richmond, VA 23205

Telephone Numbers: Toll-Free (nationwide)   800/368-5003
                    Local   804/782-7030
Deposits: $6.2 billion
Name of Service: Crestar Securities
Order Handling: Team system
Commission Structure: Valuebroker, DD (HI)
Settlement Accounts: Deposit account/Check
Brokerage Vendor: National Financial Services Corporation
Investment Products: Stocks; Bonds; Options; IRAs; Mutual Funds; Gov't Securities; Eurodollars
Services: Financial, trust, estate, and retirement planning

Delaware Trust Company
900 Market Street Mall
P.O. Box 1109
Wilmington, DE 19899

Telephone Numbers: Toll-Free
                      (out-of-state)   800/232-4600 x7175
                    Toll-Free (in-state)   800/292-9596 x7175
                    Local   302/421-7175
Deposits: $951 million
Name of Service: Delaware Trust Discount Brokerage
Order Handling: Account representatives
Commission Structure: Valuebroker
Settlement Accounts: Information not available

Brokerage Vendor: National Financial Services Corp.
Investment Products: Information not available

Deposit Guaranty National Bank
P.O. Box 1200
Jackson, MS 39215-1200

Telephone Numbers: Toll-Free (nationwide) 800/821-8774
 Toll-Free (in-state) 800/227-0625
 Local 601/968-4922
Deposits: $2.4 billion
Name of Service: Perform Brokerage Services
Order Handling: Team system
Commission Structure: Valuebroker
Settlement Accounts: Information not available
Brokerage Vendor: National Financial Services Corp.
Investment Products: Stocks; Bonds; Options; IRAs; Government Securities

The Dime Savings Bank of New York
589 Fifth Avenue
New York, NY 10017

Telephone Number Local 212/326-6021
Deposits: $6.7 billion
Name of Service: INVEST
Order Handling: Team system
Commission Structure: Valuebroker
Settlement Accounts: None
Brokerage Vendor: Pershing & Company, Division of Donaldson, Lufkin & Jenrette
Investment Products: Information not available

Dominion Bank
P.O. Box 13327
Roanoke, VA 24040

Telephone Numbers: Toll-Free (states bordering VA) 800/423-1956
 Toll-Free (in-state) 800/572-2221

Deposits: $600 million
Name of Service: Dominion Brokerage Services
Order Handling: Information not available
Commission Structure: Valuebroker, DD (HI, LO)
Settlement Accounts: Checking, savings, or money market; investment account is optional except for options accounts
Brokerage Vendor: National Financial Services Corp.
Investment Products: Stocks; Bonds; Options; IRAs; Mutual Funds; Coins

European American Bank
European American Bank Plaza
Uniondale, NY 11555-2021

Telephone Number: Local 516/296-5859
Deposits: $6 billion
Name of Service: EAB Securities, Inc.
Order Handling: Information not available
Commission Structure: Valuebroker, DD (HI)
Settlement Accounts: Information not available
Brokerage Vendor: Information not available
Investment Products: Stocks; Bonds; Options

Fidelity Bank
Broad & Walnut Streets
Philadelphia, PA 19109

Telephone Numbers: Toll-Free (out-of-state) 800/235-7600
                   Toll-Free (in-state)   800/523-9972
                   Local   215/985-6300
Deposits: $9 billion
Name of Service: Fidelcor Brokerage Services
Order Handling: Information not available
Commission Structure: Sharebroker
Settlement Accounts: Information not available
Brokerage Vendor: Information not available
Investment Products: Information not available

Fifth Third Securities, Inc.
36 East Fourth Street
Suite 916
Cincinnati, OH 45202

Telephone Numbers: Toll-Free (nationwide) 800/334-0483
                            Local 513/621-1341
Deposits: Information not available
Name of Service: Fifth Third Securities, Inc.
Order Handling: Team system
Commission Structure: Valuebroker
Settlement Accounts: Any bank account, in-house money market account
Brokerage Vendor: BHC Securities, Inc.
Investment Products: Stocks; Bonds; IRAs; Government Securities; Unit Investment Trusts; Mutual Funds; Gold Eagle Coins; Municipal Bonds
Services: On-line *Dow Jones News* or *S&P MarketScope* available; sweep accounts
Note: Offers self-directed IRAs and other retirement plans

First Alabama Bank
P.O. Box 10247
Birmingham, AL 35202

Telephone Number: Local 205/326-7008
Deposits: $750 million
Name of Service: First Alabama Investments, Inc.
Order Handling: Team system
Commission Structure: Valuebroker
Settlement Accounts: Checking or money market account
Brokerage Vendor: Pershing & Company, Division of Donaldson, Lufkin & Jenrette
Investment Products: Information not available

First American Bank of Georgia, N.A.
2000 River Edge Parkway
Atlanta, GA 30328

Telephone Numbers: Toll-Free (out-of-state) 800/221-3506
                    Toll-Free (in-state)   800/282-1093
                    Local   404/951-4482
Deposits: $460 million
Name of Service: Discount Brokerage Service
Order Handling: Team system
Commission Structure: Valuebroker
Settlement Accounts: NBG checking
Brokerage Vendor: Pershing & Company, Division of Donaldson, Lufkin & Jenrette
Investment Products: Stocks; Bonds; IRAs

First Bank Minneapolis
1700 Soo Line Building
P.O. Box 522
Minneapolis, MN 55480

Telephone Numbers: Toll-Free (nationwide) 800/328-1534
                    Toll-Free (in-state)   800/247-0230
                    Local   612/343-1570
Deposits: $5.8 billion
Name of Service: FBS Brokerage Services
Order Handling: Team system
Commission Structure: Valuebroker
Settlement Accounts: First Bank account optional
Brokerage Vendor: National Financial Services Corp.
Investment Products: Stocks; Bonds; Options; Government Securities; IRAs; Mutual Funds; Unit Investment Trusts

First Bank of North Dakota
P.O. Box 1980
Fargo, ND 58107-1980

Telephone Numbers: Toll-Free (nationwide) 800/328-1534
                    Toll-Free (in-state)   800/247-0230
                    Local   701/280-3500

Deposits: $226 million
Name of Service: FBS Brokerage Services
Order Handling: Team system
Commission Structure: Valuebroker
Settlement Accounts: First Bank account
Brokerage Vendor: National Financial Services Corp.
Investment Products: Information not available

First Capital Bank
P.O. Box 528
Concord, NH 03301

Telephone Number: Local 603/225-4300
Deposits: $244 million
Name of Service: Discount Brokerage
Order Handling: Information not available
Commission Structure: Valuebroker
Settlement Accounts: Information not available
Brokerage Vendor: Information not available
Investment Products: Information not available

First Citizens Bank
Trust Department
P.O. Box 151
Raleigh, NC 27602

Telephone Numbers: Toll-Free (in-state) 800/368-4420
                   Local   919/755-7437
Deposits: $2.6 billion
Name of Service: First Citizens Bank Discount Brokerage
Order Handling: Team system
Commission Structure: Valuebroker
Settlement Accounts: Automatically charged and credited to your account
Brokerage Vendor: Pershing & Company, Division of Donaldson, Lufkin & Jenrette
Investment Products: Information not available

First City National Bank of Houston
P.O. Box 4662
Houston, TX 77210

Telephone Numbers: Toll-Free (nationwide) 800/392-8989
                                    Local   713/658-7000
Deposits: Over $13 billion
Name of Service: First City Brokerage Company
Order Handling: Team system
Commission Structure: Valuebroker, DD (HI)
Settlement Accounts: Checking or money market account or sweep into a Fidelity Fund
Brokerage Vendor: National Financial Services Corp.
Investment Products: Stocks; Bonds; Options; Government Securities; Mutual Funds; IRAs; Precious Metals; Unit Investment Trusts; Physical Coins/Metals; Limited Partnerships
Services: Access to *Dow Jones News* and *S&P MarketScope*

First Commercial Trust
P.O. Box 1471
Little Rock, AR 72203

Telephone Numbers: Toll-Free (nationwide) 800/643-6411
                                  Toll-Free (in-state)   800/222-8866
                                  Local   501/371-7100
Deposits: $797 million
Name of Service: Bank Brokerage Services
Order Handling: Team system
Commission Structure: Valuebroker, DD (HI, LO)
Settlement Accounts: Savings or checking account
Brokerage Vendor: Olde & Co., Inc.
Investment Products: Information not available

The Discount Brokerage Directory 299

First Eastern Bank
P.O. Box L
11 West Market Street
Wilkes-Barre, PA 18773

Telephone Numbers: Toll-Free (out-of-state)   Call collect
                     Toll-Free (in-state)   800/432-8012
                     Local   717/826-8443
Deposits: $1.9 billion
Name of Service: First Eastern Brokerage Services, Inc.
Order Handling: Information not available
Commission Structure: Valuebroker
Settlement Accounts: Any account
Brokerage Vendor: Pershing & Company, Division of Donaldson, Lufkin, & Jenrette
Investment Products: Stocks; Bonds; Options; Government Securities; Unit Investment Trusts; Precious Metals; IRAs; Mutual Funds
Services: *Dow Jones News, S&P Marketscope* & *Pershing Research* available on-line; *Value Line Investment Survey, S&P Outlook, Barron's, Wall Street Journal* & quote terminal in lobby

First Fidelity Bank
810 Broad Street
Newark, NJ 07192

Telephone Number: Local   201/565-3200
Deposits: $12 billion
Name of Service: First Fidelity Brokers, Inc.
Order Handling: Account executive assigned
Commission Structure: Valuebroker
Settlement Accounts: Checking, NOW, or money market account
Brokerage Vendor: Q & R Clearing Corporation
Investment Products: Information not available

FirsTier Bank
P.O. Box 82504
Lincoln, NE 68501

Telephone Numbers: Toll-Free (out-of-state)   800/228-5888
                     Toll-Free (in-state)   800/742-4407
                     Local   402/471-1472
Deposits: $994 million
Name of Service: FirsTier Brokerage, Inc.
Order Handling: Registered representatives
Commission Structure: Valuebroker, DD (LO)
Settlement Accounts: FirsTier checking or money market
Brokerage Vendor: Pershing & Company, Division of Donaldson, Lufkin & Jenrette
Investment Products: Stocks; Bonds; Options; Government Securities; IRAs; Mutual Funds

First Interstate Bancorp of California
707 Wilshire Boulevard
Los Angeles, CA 90017

Telephone Numbers: Toll-Free (nationwide)   800/222-0468
                     Local   213/239-4000
Deposits: $21 billion
Name of Service: First Interstate Discount Brokerage*
Order Handling: Team system
Commission Structure: Valuebroker
Settlement Accounts: Any First Interstate bank account
Brokerage Vendor: Lomas Clearing Corporation
Investment Products: Stocks; Bonds; Options; Government Securities; IRAs; Mutual Funds; Unit Trusts; Precious Metals

*Brokerage service is in Texas at 713/225-3839 or 800/392-5218

First Interstate Bank of Billings
401 N. 31st Street
P.O. Box 30918
Billings, MT 59116-0918

Telephone Numbers: Toll-Free (out-of-state) 800/222-0468
　　　　　　　　　　Toll-Free (in-state) 800/332-7091
　　　　　　　　　　Local 406/255-5235
Deposits: $270 million
Name of Service: First Interstate Discount Brokerage
Order Handling: Team system
Commission Structure: Valuebroker
Settlement Accounts: Any First Interstate bank account
Brokerage Vendor: National Financial Services Corp.
Investment Products: Stocks; Bonds; Options; Government Securities; IRAs; Mutual Funds; Unit Trusts; Precious Metals

First Interstate Bank of Des Moines, N.A.
P.O. Box 817
Des Moines, IA 50304

Telephone Numbers: Toll-Free (nationwide) 800/222-0468
　　　　　　　　　　Local 515/245-7135
Deposits: $341 million
Name of Service: Discount Brokerage Services
Order Handling: Account executive assigned
Commission Structure: Valuebroker
Settlement Accounts: First Interstate Bank Account
Brokerage Vendor: Lehman Brothers, Kuhn Loeb
Investment Products: Stocks; Bonds; Options; Government Securities; IRAs; Mutual Funds; Unit Trusts; Precious Metals

First Interstate Bank of Great Falls
425 First Avenue North
P.O. Box 5010
Great Falls, MT 59403

Telephone Numbers: Toll-Free (nationwide)   800/222-0468
                     Local   406/761-1750
Deposits: $95.5 million
Name of Service: First Interstate Discount Brokerage
Order Handling: Team system
Commission Structure: Valuebroker
Settlement Accounts: Checking or savings account
Brokerage Vendor: National Financial Services Corp.
Investment Products: Stocks; Bonds; Options; Government Securities; IRAs; Mutual Funds; Unit Trusts; Precious Metals

First Interstate Bank of Idaho
700 West Idaho Street
Box 57
Boise, ID 83757

Telephone Number: Local   208/327-2000
Deposits: $746 million
Name of Service: First Interstate Discount Brokerage
Order Handling: Team system
Commission Structure: Valuebroker
Settlement Accounts: Checking or savings account
Brokerage Vendor: National Financial Services Corp.
Investment Products: Stocks; Bonds; Options; Government Securities; IRAs; Mutual Funds; Unit Trusts; Precious Metals

First Interstate Bank of Nevada
1 East First Street
P.O. Box 11007
Reno, NE 89520

Telephone Number   Local   702/784-3000
Deposits: $2 billion

The Discount Brokerage Directory 303

Name of Service: First Interstate Discount Brokerage
Order Handling: Team system
Commission Structure: Valuebroker
Settlement Accounts: Checking or savings account
Brokerage Vendor: National Financial Services Corp.
Investment Products: Stocks; Bonds; Options; Government Securities; IRAs; Mutual Funds; Unit Trusts; Precious Metals

First National Bank
Drawer 1186
Sioux Falls, SD 57117-1186

Telephone Number: Local 605/335-5100
Deposits: $221 million
Name of Service: Investment Account
Order Handling: Registered representatives
Commission Structure: Valuebroker
Settlement Accounts: Deposit account at First National Bank
Brokerage Vendor: Depositor's Discount Brokerage Services
Investment Products: Information not available

First National Bank in Albuquerque
P.O. Box 1305
Albuquerque, NM 87103-1305

Telephone Numbers: Toll-Free (in-state) 800/826-3910
                   Local   505/765-4500
Deposits: $948 million
Name of Service: BHC Securities, Inc.
Order Handling: Information not available
Commission Structure: Valuebroker
Settlement Accounts: First National Bank in Albuquerque account is optional
Brokerage Vendor: BHC Securities, Inc.
Investment Products: Stocks; Bonds; Options; Government Securities; IRAs; Mutual Funds; Precious Metals
Note: Offers self-directed IRAs and other retirement plans

First National Bank in Wichita
105 N. Main Street
Box One
Wichita, KS 67201-9956

Telephone Number   Local   316/268-1111
Deposits: $700 million
Name of Service: First Brokerage Service
Order Handling: Team system
Commission Structure: Valuebroker
Settlement Accounts: Any FNB account including money market account
Brokerage Vendor: Bankers System Brokerage Services
Investment Products: Stocks; Bonds; Options; IRAs; Gold; Government Securities; Mutual Funds
Note: Offers self-directed IRAs, Keoghs, and QRPs

The First National Bank of Chicago
One First National Plaza
Chicago, IL 60670

Telephone Numbers: Toll-Free (out-of-state)   800/537-4938
                     Toll-Free (in-state)   800/621-6592
                     Local   312/732-4414
Deposits: $33 billion
Name of Service: First Chicago Investment Services
Order Handling: Team system
Commission Structure: Valuebroker
Settlement Accounts: First Chicago Bank account or by check
Brokerage Vendor: Pershing & Company, Division of Donaldson, Lufkin & Jenrette
Investment Products: Stocks; Bonds; Options; Government Securities; IRAs; Mutual Funds; Unit Trusts; Precious Metals
Note: Offers self-directed IRAs, Keoghs, and other retirement plans

First National Bank of Commerce
P.O. Box 61239
New Orleans, LA 70161-1239

Telephone Numbers: Toll-Free (Louisiana)   800/462-9511
                    Toll-Free (Mississippi) 800/535-9601
                    Local   504/561-1594
Deposits: $2.5 billion
Name of Service: First Commerce Investment Services
Order Handling: Team system
Commission Structure: Valuebroker, DD (HI, LO)
Settlement Accounts: Any First National Bank of Commerce checking or savings account
Brokerage Vendor: National Financial Services Corp.
Investment Products: Stocks; Bonds; Options; IRAs; Mutual Funds
Note: Offers self-directed IRAs, Keoghs, and other retirement plans

First National Bank of Maryland
P.O. Box 13044
Baltimore, MD 21203

Telephone Numbers: Toll-Free (out-of-state) 800/638-6115
                    Toll-Free (in-state)   800/492-2117
                    Local   301/244-4900
Deposits: $3.9 billion
Name of Service: First Maryland Brokerage Corp.
Order Handling: Information not available
Commission Structure: Valuebroker
Settlement Accounts: Information not available
Brokerage Vendor: National Financial Services Corp.
Investment Products: Stocks; Bonds; Options; IRAs; Mutual Funds

First National Bank of Omaha
One First National Center
Omaha, NE 68102-1596

Telephone Numbers: Toll-Free (out-of-state) 800/228-4411
                    Toll-Free (in-state)   800/642-9907
                    Local   402/341-0500
Deposits: $692 million
Name of Service: First Bankcard Center-Investment Services
Order Handling: Team system
Commission Structure: Valuebroker
Settlement Accounts: Brokerage account can be linked to a First National Bank of Omaha Market Rate checking account
Brokerage Vendor: National Financial Services Corp.
Investment Products: Stocks; Bonds; Options; Mutual Funds; Unit Trusts
Note: Offers self-directed IRAs and Keoghs

First of America Bank
211 South Rose
Kalamazoo, MI 49007

Telephone Number: Toll-Free (nationwide) 800/643-6718
Deposits: $12.5 billion
Name of Service: First of America Brokerage Service, Inc.
Order Handling: Team system
Commission Structure: Valuebroker, DD (HI, LO)
Settlement Accounts: Checking or First of America bank account
Brokerage Vendor: National Financial Services
Investment Products: Stocks; Bonds; Options; Unit Trusts; Gov't Securities; Mutual Funds

First Pennsylvania Bank
P.O. Box 13669
Philadelphia, PA 19101

Telephone Numbers: Toll-Free (out-of-state) Call collect
                    Toll-Free (in-state)   800/342-0009
                    Local   215/786-8500

Deposits: $4 billion
Name of Service: First Pennsylvania Investments Company
Order Handling: Team system
Commission Structure: Valuebroker, DD (HI, LO)
Settlement Accounts: Checking or NOW account
Brokerage Vendor: National Financial Services Corp.
Investment Products: Stocks; Bonds; Options; IRAs

First Security Bank
P.O. Box 30011
Salt Lake City, UT 84130

Telephone Numbers: Toll-Free (states bordering Utah) 800/453-3703
Toll-Free (in-state) 800/421-1190
Local 801/350-5030
Deposits: $5.5 billion
Name of Service: First Security Discount Brokerage
Order Handling: Registered traders
Commission Structure: Valuebroker
Settlement Accounts: Information not available
Brokerage Vendor: BHC Securities, Inc.
Investment Products: Information not available

First Security National Bank & Trust Co.
One First Security Plaza
Lexington, KY 40507

Telephone Numbers: Toll-Free (nationwide) 800/432-9268
Local 606/231-2300
Deposits: $1.01 billion
Name of Service: First Security Brokerage Co. of Kentucky
Order Handling: Account executive
Commission Structure: Valuebroker, DD (HI, LO)
Settlement Accounts: Any First Security checking or Financial Manager account or by check on client's own account
Brokerage Vendor: National Financial Services Corp.
Investment Products: Stocks; Bonds; Options; IRAs; Mutual Funds; Units

Note: Offers self-directed IRAs, Keoghs, and other retirement plans

First Tennessee Bank
4655 Poplar
Memphis, TN 38117

Telephone Numbers: Toll-Free (nationwide) 800/238-1111
                       Local 901/523-5900
Deposits: $4.3 billion
Name of Service: First Tennessee Discount Brokerage
Order Handling: Team system
Commission Structure: Valuebroker
Settlement Accounts: Checking account
Brokerage Vendor: National Financial Services Corp.
Investment Products: Information not available

First Union National Bank
One First Union Center CMG-18
Charlotte, NC 28288

Telephone Numbers: Toll-Free (nationwide) 800/334-9406
                                             800/532-0367
                       Local 704/374-6927
Deposits: $27 billion
Name of Service: First Union Investment Services, Inc.
Order Handling: Account executive assigned
Commission Structure: Valuebroker
Settlement Accounts: Checking or Market Access account
Brokerage Vendor: Cowen & Co.
Investment Products: Stocks; Bonds; Options; IRAs; Mutual Funds; Unit Trusts; Government Securities; Gold/Silver; Insurance
Services: Trust service; investment newsletter

First Valley Bank (Lehigh Securities)
P.O. Box 2228
Lehigh Valley, PA 18001

Telephone Numbers: Toll-Free (nationwide) 800/245-4487
Local 215/437-5543
Deposits: $1.7 billion
Name of Service: Lehigh Securities
Order Handling: Information not available
Commission Structure: Valuebroker
Settlement Accounts: Information not available
Brokerage Vendor: Self-clearing
Investment Products: Stocks; Bonds; Mutual Funds; Unit Trusts; Limited Partnerships

First Wachovia Bank and Trust
P.O. Box 110
Winston-Salem, NC 27102-0110

Telephone Number: Toll-Free (nationwide) 800/462-7538
Deposits: $17.3 billion
Name of Service: First Wachovia Brokerage Service
Order Handling: Team system
Commission Structure: Sharebroker, DD (LO)
Settlement Accounts: Checking or savings
Brokerage Vendor: Information not available
Investment Products: Stocks; Bonds; Options; Government Securities; IRAs; Mutual Funds
Note: Offers self-directed IRAs and other retirement plans

First Wisconsin National Bank
P.O. Box 954
Milwaukee, WI 53201-9985

Telephone Number: Local 414/765-4321
Deposits: $3 billion
Name of Service: Elan Investment Services
Order Handling: Team system
Commission Structure: Sharebroker

Settlement Accounts: Savings or checking account
Brokerage Vendor: Pershing & Company, Division of Donaldson, Lufkin & Jenrette
Investment Products: Stocks; Bonds; Options; Government Securities; IRAs; Mutual Funds; Unit Trusts; Precious Metals

Fleet Bank
P.O. Box 922
Providence, RI 02901

Telephone Numbers: Toll-Free (out-of-state) 800/225-5211
Toll-Free (in-state) 800/462-1231
Local 401/278-6900
Deposits: $5 billion
Name of Service: Fleet Brokerage Services, Inc.
Order Handling: Team system
Commission Structure: Valuebroker
Settlement Accounts: Money market, statement savings, or checking account
Brokerage Vendor: National Financial Services Corp.
Investment Products: Information not available

Florida National Bank
225 Water Street
FNB Tower
Jacksonville, FL 32231

Telephone Numbers: Toll-Free (out-of-state) 800/367-5386
Toll-Free (in-state) 800/342-2049
Local 904/359-5111
Deposits: $7.8 billion
Name of Service: Florida National Brokerage Services, Inc.
Order Handling: Team system
Commission Structure: Valuebroker
Settlement Accounts: Any account
Brokerage Vendor: National Financial Services Corp.
Investment Products: Stocks; Bonds; Options; Government Securities; Mutual Funds; IRAs

**Harris Bank
111 West Monroe Street
P.O. Box 755
Chicago, IL 60690**

Telephone Numbers: Toll-Free (nationwide) 800/251-2121
                    Local   312/461-6000
Deposits: $6 billion
Name of Service: Harris Brokerage Services
Order Handling: Account executive assigned
Commission Structure: Valuebroker, DD (HI, LO)
Settlement Accounts: Checking, savings, or money market account
Brokerage Vendor: National Financial Services Corp.
Investment Products: Stocks; Bonds; Options; IRAs; Mutual Funds

**Hibernia National Bank
440 North Third Street
P.O. Box 3597
Baton Rouge, LA 70821**

Telephone Number: Local 504/381-2000
Deposits: $714 million
Name of Service: Hibernia Investment Securities
Order Handling: Team system
Commission Structure: Valuebroker
Settlement Accounts: Any Fidelity account
Brokerage Vendor: Depositors Discount Brokerage Service
Investment Products: Information not available

**Howard Savings Bank
200 South Orange Avenue
Livingston, NJ 07039**

Telephone Numbers: Toll-Free (in-state) 800/222-0797
                    Local   201/533-7551
Deposits: $3.7 billion
Name of Service: John Howard Discount Brokerage

Order Handling: Team system
Commission Structure: Sharebroker
Settlement Accounts: Information not available
Brokerage Vendor: Swiss American Securities, Inc.
Investment Products: Information not available

Huntington National Bank
41 South High Street
Columbus, OH 43287

Telephone Numbers: Toll-Free (nationwide) 800/322-4600
                   Local   614/463-4200
Deposits: $5.4 billion
Name of Service: Huntington Discount Brokerage
Order Handling: Team system
Commission Structure: Sharebroker
Settlement Accounts: Checking or money market account
Brokerage Vendor: Pershing & Company, Division of
                  Donaldson, Lufkin & Jenrette
Investment Products: Information not available

Idaho First National Bank
P.O. Box 7009
Boise, ID 83727

Telephone Number: Local 208/383-7162
Deposits: $2.18 billion
Name of Service: Discount Brokerage Service
Order Handling: Team system
Commission Structure: Valuebroker
Settlement Accounts: Checking or savings account
Brokerage Vendor: Financial Clearing & Services Corp.
                  (Security Pacific Brokers, Inc.)
Investment Products: Stocks; Bonds; Options; Government
                     Securities; Mutual Funds; Precious
                     Metals

Irving Bank Corporation
One Wall Street Brokerage, Inc.
P.O. Box 1010
Scarsdale, NY 10583

Telephone Numbers: Toll-Free (out-of-state)   800/631-9255
                     Toll-Free (in-state)   800/872-4015
                     Local (Irving Trust)   212/635-1111
Deposits: $12.6 billion
Name of Service: One Wall Street Brokerage, Inc.
Order Handling: Information not available
Commission Structure: Valuebroker
Settlement Accounts: Information not available
Brokerage Vendor: Information not available
Investment Products: Stocks; Bonds; Options; Mutual Funds

Jackson County Bank
125 S. Chestnut
Box 1001
Seymour, IN 47274

Telephone Number: Local   812/522-3607
Deposits: $92 million
Name of Service: Jackson County Bank's Depositors
                   Brokerage Service
Order Handling: Team system
Commission Structure: Valuebroker
Settlement Accounts: Checking, savings, or NOW Account
Brokerage Vendor: Depositors Discount Brokerage Service
Investment Products: Information not available

Key Bank
60 State Street
P.O. Box 1973
Albany, NY 12207

Telephone Numbers: Toll-Free (out-of-state)   800/527-2770
                     Toll-Free (in-state)   800/777-7880
                     Local   518/486-8061

Deposits: $2 billion
Name of Service: Key Brokerage Company
Order Handling: Team system
Commission Structure: Valuebroker
Settlement Accounts: Check or Key Bank checking, or money market account
Brokerage Vendor: National Financial Services Corp.
Investment Products: Stocks; Bonds; Options; IRAs

Key Bank of Idaho
P.O. Box 2800
Boise, ID 83701

Telephone Numbers: Toll-Free (nationwide)   800/533-1200
                     Local   208/334-7250
Deposits: $473 million
Name of Service: Investor Service Center
Order Handling: Team system
Commission Structure: Valuebroker
Settlement Accounts: Checking account
Brokerage Vendor: Fidelity Brokerage Services, Inc.
Investment Products: Information not available

LaSalle National Bank
135 South LaSalle Street
Chicago, IL 60603

Telephone Numbers: Toll-Free (nationwide)   800/782-1522
                     Toll-Free (in-state)   800/572-0410
                     Local   312/443-2870
Deposits: $1 billion
Name of Service: LaSalle Brokerage Services, Inc.
Order Handling: Team system
Commission Structure: Valuebroker, DD (HI)
Settlement Accounts: LaSalle National bank account
Brokerage Vendor: National Financial Services Corp.
Investment Products: Stocks; Bonds; Options; IRAs; Government Securities; Mutual Funds
Services: S&P reports available at no cost

Lehigh Securities
P.O. Box 2228
Lehigh Valley, PA 18001

See **First Valley Bank**

Liberty National Bank
416 West Jefferson
P.O. Box 32500
Louisville, KY 40232

Telephone Numbers: Toll-Free (nationwide) 800/542-2265
                    Local   502/566-2406
Deposits: $2 billion
Name of Service: Banker's Investment Group, Inc.
Order Handling: Team system
Commission Structure: Value/Sharebroker
Settlement Accounts: Checking account
Brokerage Vendor: BHC Securities, Inc.
Investment Products: Stocks; Bonds; Options; Mutual Funds
Note: Offers self-directed IRAs, Keoghs, and other retirement plans

Mbank
300 West Fifth
Suite 800
Austin, TX 78701

Telephone Number: Local 214/748-9183
Deposits: $3.3 billion
Name of Service: MPACT
Order Handling: Team system
Commission Structure: Valuebroker
Settlement Accounts: MPACT Management Account, IRA, Keogh
Brokerage Vendor: MPACT Brokers
Investment Products: Information not available

M & T Bank
One M & T Plaza, Third Floor
P.O. Box 1357
Buffalo, NY 14240

Telephone Numbers: Toll-Free (in-state)   800/544-2300
                     Local   716/842-5200
Deposits: $2.3 billion
Name of Service: M & T Discount Brokerage Services
Order Handling: Information not available
Commission Structure: Valuebroker
Settlement Accounts: Checking or savings account
Brokerage Vendor: National Financial Services Corp.
Investment Products: Stocks; Bonds; Options; IRAs; Mutual Funds

Manufacturers Hanover
270 Park Avenue
Fourth Floor
New York, NY 10017

Telephone Numbers: Toll-Free
                      (nationwide)   800/MH STOCK
                     Local   212/286-5846
Deposits: $60.6 billion
Name of Service: Manufacturers Hanover Brokerage Services
Order Handling: Team system
Commission Structure: Valuebroker, DD (HI, LO)
Settlement Accounts: Information not available
Brokerage Vendor: Pershing & Company, Division of Donaldson, Lufkin & Jenrette
Investment Products: Information not available

Marine Midland Bank
90 Broad Street
New York, NY 10004

Telephone Number: Local   212/612-1090
Deposits: $17 billion

The Discount Brokerage Directory 317

Name of Service: OvestMarine Brokerage Service
Order Handling: Team system
Commission Structure: Valuebroker DD (HI)
Settlement Accounts: Checking account
Brokerage Vendor: Pershing & Company, Division of Donaldson, Lufkin & Jenrette
Investment Products: Stocks; Bonds; Options; Government Securities; IRAs; Precious Metals; Mutual Funds; Unit Trusts; GNMAs; Annuities

Mellon Bank
1 Mellon Bank Center
Pittsburgh, PA 15258

Telephone Numbers: Toll-Free (out-of-state) 800/527-8635
Toll-Free (in-state) 800/422-1157
Local 412/234-7002
Deposits: $31.5 billion
Name of Service: InvestNet
Order Handling: Through trades or correspondent bank
Commission Structure: Valuebroker, DD (HI)
Settlement Accounts: Bank account
Brokerage Vendor: Self-clearing
Investment Products: Stocks; Bonds; Options; Mutual Funds; Commercial Paper; Precious Metals; IRAs; Keoghs; Corporate Retirement Plans

Merchants National Bank & Trust Co.
One Merchants Plaza
Suite 301E
Indianapolis, IN 46255

Telephone Numbers: Toll-Free (in-state) 800/382-9414
Local 317/267-3711
Deposits: $2 billion
Name of Service: Folio/One Brokerage Service
Order Handling: Team system

Commission Structure: Valuebroker, DD (HI, LO)
Settlement Accounts: Checking or bank account
Brokerage Vendor: National Financial Services Corp.
Investment Products: Stocks; Bonds; Options; IRAs; Mutual Funds

The Merchants Trust Company
164 College Street
P.O. Box 1009
Burlington, VT 05401

Telephone Number: Local   802/865-1833
Deposits: $451 million
Name of Service: Merchant's Brokerage Service
Order Handling: Team system
Commission Structure: Valuebroker
Settlement Accounts: Any account
Brokerage Vendor: Olde Discount Corporation
Investment Products: Stocks; Bonds; Mutual Funds; IRAs
Services: Trust management; estate planning

Meridian Bank
35 North Sixth Street
P.O. Box 7922
Reading, PA 19603

Telephone Numbers: Toll-Free (out-of-state)   Call collect
                    Toll-Free (in-state)   800/321-1331
                    Local   215/320-3214
Deposits: $7 billion
Name of Service: DBS Discount Brokerage Services
Order Handling: Team system
Commission Structure: Valuebroker, DD (HI, LO)
Settlement Accounts: Checking, savings, or Money Rate Savings account
Brokerage Vendor: Q & R Clearing Corporation
Investment Products: Stocks; Bonds; Options; Mutual Funds
Note: Offers self-directed IRAs

Midlantic Securities Corp.
Metro Park Plaza
Edison, NJ 08818

Telephone Number: Toll-Free (nationwide) 800/222-2024
Deposits: $18 billion
Name of Service: Midlantic Securities Corp.
Order Handling: Team system
Commission Structure: Valuebroker
Settlement Accounts: NOW or checking account
Brokerage Vendor: BHC Securities
Investment Products: Information not available
Note: Offers self-directed IRAs

National Bank of Alaska
P.O. Box 196127
Anchorage, AK 99519-6127

Telephone Number: Local 907/265-2734
Deposits: $874 million
Name of Service: Discount Brokerage Service
Order Handling: Registered representatives
Commission Structure: Valuebroker
Settlement Accounts: Information not available
Brokerage Vendor: Financial Clearing & Services Corp.
Investment Products: Information not available

National Bank of Commerce
13th & O
P.O. Box 82408
Lincoln, NE 68501

Telephone Number: Local 402/434-4270
Deposits: $385 million
Name of Service: NBC Discount Brokerage Service
Order Handling: Team system
Commission Structure: Valuebroker
Settlement Accounts: Designated NBC account
Brokerage Vendor: Depositors Discount Brokerage Service

Investment Products: Stocks; Bonds; Options
Note: Offers self-directed IRAs; Keoghs, and other retirement plans

National Bank of Detroit
Genesee Towers - Suite 1215
One East First Street
Flint, MI 48502-1937

Telephone Numbers: Toll-Free (nationwide)   800/621-0414
                     Toll-Free (Michigan)   800/621-1648
                     Local   313/225-1779
Deposits: $9.7 billion
Name of Service: NBD Securities, Inc.
Order Handling: Team system
Commission Structure: Sharebroker, DD (HI)
Settlement Accounts: Information not available
Brokerage Vendor: BHC Securities, Inc.
Investment Products: Stocks; Bonds; Options; IRAs; Mutual Funds

National Bank of Georgia
P.O. Box 1234
Atlanta, GA 30371-1401

Telephone Numbers: Toll-Free (nationwide)   800/241-0541
                     Local   404/951-4000
Deposits: $460 million
Name of Service: Discount Brokerage Service
Order Handling: Team system
Commission Structure: Valuebroker
Settlement Accounts: NBG checking
Brokerage Vendor: Pershing & Company, Division of Donaldson, Lufkin, & Jenrette
Investment Products: Information not available

The Discount Brokerage Directory 321

National Bank of Washington
4340 Connecticut Avenue, N.W.
Washington, DC 20008

Telephone Number: Local 202/537-2004
Deposits: (Parent) $1.5 billion
Name of Service: Washington Brokerage Services, Inc., 1100 17th Street, N.W., Washington, DC 20036
Order Handling: Series & registered representatives
Commission Structure: Valuebroker, DD (HI, LO)
Settlement Accounts: NBW checking, NOW, money market, or savings account
Brokerage Vendor: Swiss American Securities, Inc.
Investment Products: Stocks; Bonds; Options; Government Securities; IRAs; Mutual Funds; Unit Investment Funds
Services: Various news publications available at main office. Also, *Dow Jones News Retrieval, Value Line Survey, S&P Stock-Bond Guides,* and *Mutual Fund Forecaster*

National City Bank
National City Center
P.O. Box 5756
Cleveland, OH 44101-0756

Telephone Numbers: Toll-Free (in-state) 800/848-5006
Local 216/575-3495
Deposits: $4.6 billion
Name of Service: BHC Securities, Inc. at Bankers Investor Services
Order Handling: Team system
Commission Structure: Valuebroker, DD (HI, LO)
Settlement Accounts: National City Deposit account is optional
Brokerage Vendor: BHC Securities, Inc.
Investment Products: Information not available

National City Bank of Minneapolis
75 South Fifth Street
P.O. Box E 1919
Minneapolis, MN 55480

Telephone Numbers: Toll-Free (in-state) 800/247-0311
                    Local   612/340-4600
Deposits: $378 million
Name of Service: National City Securities
Order Handling: Team system
Commission Structure: Valuebroker
Settlement Accounts: Cash or National City bank account
Brokerage Vendor: Information not available
Investment Products: Information not available

National Westminster Bank USA
175 Water Street
New York, NY 10038-4924

Telephone Number: Local 212/602-1800
Deposits: $11.1 billion
Name of Service: NatWest USA Brokerage Services
Order Handling: Registered representatives
Commission Structure: Valuebroker, DD (HI)
Settlement Accounts: Cash or National Westminster account
Brokerage Vendor: National Financial Services Corp.
Investment Products: Stocks; Bonds; Options; IRAs; Mutual Funds; Unit Trusts

Norstar Bank of Commerce
67 Wall Street
New York, NY 10005

Telephone Numbers: Toll-Free (nationwide) 800/221-5088
                    Local   212/806-2700
Deposits: $427 million
Name of Service: Norstar Brokerage
Order Handling: Team system
Commission Structure: Sharebroker

Settlement Accounts: Information not available
Brokerage Vendor: N.B. Clearing Corporation
Investment Products: Information not available

Northeastern Bank of Pennsylvania
Wyoming Avenue & Spruce Street
Scranton, PA 18503

Telephone Number: Local   717/961-7098
Deposits: $1.7 billion
Name of Service: The Investment Account
Order Handling: Team system
Commission Structure: Valuebroker
Settlement Accounts: Checking, Money Market Access, savings, or NOW account at Northeastern
Brokerage Vendor: BHC Securities, Inc.
Investment Products: Stocks; Bonds; Options; IRAs; Mutual Funds; Gold/Silver Bullion

Northern Trust Company
200 West Madison Street
Chicago, IL 60606

Telephone Numbers: Toll-Free (out-of-state)   800/621-2253
                   Local   312/407-6800
Deposits: $9.4 billion
Name of Service: Northern Trust Brokerage, Inc.
Order Handling: Account executive assigned
Commission Structure: Valuebroker
Settlement Accounts: Any Northern Trust bank account
Brokerage Vendor: Clearing at Omnibus Basic with Pershing & Co.
Investment Products: Stocks; Bonds; Options; Government Securities; Mutual Funds; IRAs; Unit Investment Trusts
Services: S&P company information provided

Northwest Bank Des Moines, N.A.
666 Walnut Street
P.O. Box 837
Des Moines, IA 50304

Telephone Numbers: Toll-Free (nationwide) 800/447-3266
Toll-Free (Minnesota) 800/322-0073
Toll-Free (Minneapolis/
St. Paul) 612/372-0797
Local 515/245-3221
Deposits: $98 million
Name of Service: Norwest Brokerage Services
Order Handling: Registered representatives
Commission Structure: Valuebroker, DD (HI)
Settlement Accounts: Information not available
Brokerage Vendor: BHC Securities, Inc.
Investment Products: Information not available

Old Kent Bank & Trust Company
1 Vandenberg Center
Grand Rapids, MI 49503

Telephone Numbers: Toll-Free (nationwide) 800/652-4232
Toll-Free (in-state) 800/442-1500
Local 616/774-4300
Deposits: $8.2 billion
Name of Service: Old Kent Discount Brokerage
Order Handling: Team system
Commission Structure: Valuebroker
Settlement Accounts: Any bank account
Brokerage Vendor: BHC Securities, Inc.
Investment Products: Stocks; Bonds; Options; Mutual Funds
Note: Offers self-directed IRAs

One Valley Bank, N.A.
One Valley Square
P.O. Box 1793
Charleston, WV 25326

Telephone Number: Local   304/348-7256
Deposits: $800 million
Name of Service: Discount Brokerage Service
Order Handling: Information not available
Commission Structure: Sharebroker, DD (HI)
Settlement Accounts: Checking, savings, or money market account
Brokerage Vendor: Olde Discount Brokerage
Investment Products: Stocks; Bonds; Options; Government Securities; Mutual Funds; IRAs
Note: Offers self-directed IRAs, Keoghs, and other retirement plans

Oregon First Bank
P.O. Box 2888
Portland, OR 97208

Telephone Number: Local   503/248-6080
Deposits: $239 million
Name of Service: Discount Brokerage Service (DBS)
Order Handling: Team system
Commission Structure: Valuebroker
Settlement Accounts: Checking or savings account
Brokerage Vendor: Introducing Broker: Security Pacific Brokers Inc./Clearing Broker: Financial Clearing & Services Corp.
Investment Products: Stocks; Bonds; Options; Government Securities; Mutual Funds; IRAs; Precious Metals

Peoples Bank
1414 Fourth Avenue
P.O. Box 720
Seattle, WA 98111

Telephone Numbers: Toll-Free
    (out-of-state)   800/426-0648 x5670
    Toll-Free (in-state)   800/552-7138 x5670
    Local   206/344-5670
Deposits: $2.1 billion
Name of Service: Discount Brokerage Services
Order Handling: Team system
Commission Structure: Valuebroker, DD (HI, LO)
Settlement Accounts: Checking, savings, NOW account, money market account
Brokerage Vendor: National Financial Services Corp.
Investment Products: Information not available

Piedmont Trust
P.O. Box 4751
Martinsville, VA 24115-4751

Telephone Number: Local   703/632-2971 x238
Deposits: $432 million
Name of Service: Piedmont Investor Services
Order Handling: Information not available
Commission Structure: Valuebroker, DD (LO)
Settlement Accounts: Deposit account
Brokerage Vendor: Information not available
Investment Products: Information not available
Note: Offers self-directed IRAs and other retirement plans

Pittsburgh National Bank
Pittsburgh National Building, 25th Floor
5th Avenue & Wood Street
Pittsburgh, PA 15265

Telephone Numbers: Toll-Free (out-of-state)   800/352-2204
    Toll-Free (in-state)   800/PNB-0123
    Local   412/355-2082

Deposits: $7.4 billion
Name of Service: PNB Brokerage Services, Inc.
Order Handling: Team system
Commission Structure: Valuebroker
Settlement Accounts: Information not available
Brokerage Vendor: BHC Securities, Inc.
Investment Products: Information not available

Planters Bank
Trust Department
P.O. Box 1220
Rocky Mount, NC 27802

Telephone Number: Local   919/977-8211
Deposits: $723 million
Name of Service: Discount Brokerage Services
Order Handling: Information not available
Commission Structure: Valuebroker
Settlement Accounts: Information not available
Brokerage Vendor: Uvest
Investment Products: Information not available

Provident Bank
1 East 4th Street
Cincinnati, OH 45269

Telephone Number: Local   513/579-2365
Deposits: $1 billion
Name of Service: Provident Securities & Investment Co.
Order Handling: Registered representatives
Commission Structure: Valuebroker
Settlement Accounts: Information not available
Brokerage Vendor: Information not available
Investment Products: Stocks; Bonds; Options; IRAs; Precious Metals; Government Securities

Pulaski Bank and Trust Company
5800 R Street
P.O. Box 7299
Little Rock, AR 72207

Telephone Number: Local   501/661-7700
Deposits: $122 million
Name of Service: Discount Investment Brokerage
Order Handling: Team system
Commission Structure: Valuebroker, DD (LO)
Settlement Accounts: Checking account
Brokerage Vendor: Stephens Financial Services Clearing
Investment Products: Information not available

Security Pacific Bancorporation Northwest
Security Pacific Bank Tower
1301 Fifth Avenue
P.O. Box 91061
Seattle, WA 98111-9161

Telephone Numbers: Toll-Free (in-state)   800/858-0518
                                    Local   206/621-6141
Deposits: $9.26 billion
Name of Service: Security Pacific Investments, Inc., A Washington Corporation
Order Handling: Team system
Commission Structure: Valuebroker
Settlement Accounts: Checking, savings, or money fund account
Brokerage Vendor: Southwest Securities, Inc.
Investment Products: Stocks; Bonds; Options; Government Securities; Mutual Funds; IRAs; Precious Metals

Security Pacific National Bank
155 North Lake Avenue; Suite 160
P.O. Box 7000
Pasadena, CA 91101

Telephone Numbers: Toll-Free (nationwide)   800/272-4060
                                    Local   818/578-0606

Deposits: $47.5 billion
Name of Service: Security Pacific Brokers, Inc.
Order Handling: Team system; registered reps
Commission Structure: Valuebroker
Settlement Accounts: Checking or savings account
Brokerage Vendor: Financial Clearing & Services Corp.
Investment Products: Information not available

Shawmut Bank
One Federal Street
Boston, MA 02211

Telephone Numbers: Toll-Free (nationwide) 800/343-8903
          Local   617/292-2000
Deposits: $5 billion
Name of Service: Shawmut Brokerage Services, Inc.
Order Handling: Team system
Commission Structure: Valuebroker
Settlement Accounts: Checking, savings, or NOW Account
Brokerage Vendor: National Financial Services Corp.
Investment Products: Stocks; Bonds; Options; Mutual Funds

Signet Bank
7 North Eighth Street
P.O. Box 25339
Richmond, VA 23260-5339

Telephone Numbers: Toll-Free (in-state) 800/368-9999
          Local (brokerage) 804/771-7326
          Local (bank)   804/644-2682
Deposits: $4.3 billion
Name of Service: Signet Investment Corporation
Order Handling: Team system
Commission Structure: Valuebroker
Settlement Accounts: Information not available
Brokerage Vendor: Information not available
Investment Products: Stocks; Bonds; Options

**South Carolina National Bank
101 Greystone Boulevard
Columbia, SC 29226**

Telephone Numbers: Toll-Free (nationwide) 800/922-9008
                    Local   803/771-3511
Deposits: $1.1 billion
Name of Service: SCN Discount Brokerage Services
Order Handling: Team system
Commission Structure: Valuebroker
Settlement Accounts: Checking or savings account
Brokerage Vendor: National Financial Services Corp.
Investment Products: Stocks; Bonds; Options

**South Shore Bank
1400 Hancock Street
Quincy, MA 02169**

Telephone Numbers: Toll-Free (in-state) 800/462-6262
                    Local   617/847-3100
Deposits: $782 million
Name of Service: Multibank Brokerage Service
Order Handling: Team system
Commission Structure: Valuebroker
Settlement Accounts: Checking, NOW, or Better Money Market account
Brokerage Vendor: Dominick Investors Service Corp.
Investment Products: Stocks; Bonds; Mutual Funds; Precious Metals; Unit Trusts; Government Securities

**Southeast Bank, N.A.
P.O. Box 012500
Miami, FL 33101**

Telephone Numbers: Toll-Free (out-of-state) 800/351-5544
                    Toll-Free (in-state)   800/432-7283
                    Toll-Free (Broward County) 305/467-2510
                    (Dade County)   305/375-7400
                    Toll-Free   Call collect

Deposits: $9.6 billion
Name of Service: Southeast Bank Brokerage Service
Order Handling: Team system
Commission Structure: Valuebroker
Settlement Accounts: Checking or savings account
Brokerage Vendor: National Financial Services Corp.
Investment Products: Stocks; Bonds; Options; Mutual Funds

SouthTrust Bank
P.O. Box 2554
Birmingham, AL 35290-0100

Telephone Numbers:	Toll-Free (nationwide)	800/843-8618
	Toll-Free (Southeast)	800/633-6260
	Toll-Free (in-state)	800/821-5268
	Local	205/254-5949

Deposits: $1.9 billion
Name of Service: SouthTrust Brokerage Services, Inc.
Order Handling: Information not available
Commission Structure: Valuebroker
Settlement Accounts: Any SouthTrust deposit account
Brokerage Vendor: BHC Securities, Inc.
Investment Products: Information not available

Sovran Bank
One Commercial Place
Norfolk, VA 23501

Telephone Numbers:	Toll-Free (in-state)	800/572-3090
	Local	804/441-4955

Deposits: $14 billion
Name of Service: Investor Services
Order Handling: Team system
Commission Structure: Valuebroker, DD (LO)
Settlement Accounts: Checking account or cashier's check
Brokerage Vendor: Pershing & Company, Division of Donaldson, Lufkin & Jenrette
Investment Products: Stocks; Bonds; Options; Precious Metals

The State First National Bank
Box 8000
State Line Plaza
Texarkana, TX 75502-5975

Telephone Number: Local   214/773-4541
Deposits: $297 million
Name of Service: Discount Brokerage Services
Order Handling: Information not available
Commission Structure: Valuebroker
Settlement Accounts: Information not available
Brokerage Vendor: Information not available
Investment Products: Information not available

Summit Bank
915 S. Clinton Street
P.O. Box 2345
Fort Wayne, IN 46801-2345

Telephone Numbers: Toll-Free (in-state)   800/552-6655
                     Local   219/427-8492
Deposits: $1 billion
Name of Service: Summcorp Financial Services, Inc.
Order Handling: Information not available
Commission Structure: Valuebroker
Settlement Accounts: Information not available
Brokerage Vendor: BHC Securities, Inc.
Investment Products: Stocks; Bonds; Options; Government Securities; Precious Metals; Unit Investment Trusts

Sunburst Bank
Investments Department
P.O. Box 23053
Jackson, MS 39225-3053

Telephone Number: Local   601/226-3141
Deposits: $1 billion
Name of Service: Discount Brokerage Service

Order Handling: Team system
Commission Structure: Valuebroker
Settlement Accounts: Checking account
Brokerage Vendor: Fidelity Brokerage Services, Inc.
Investment Products: Information not available

SunTrust Bank
25 Park Place
P.O. Box 4418, Center 708
Atlanta, GA 30302

Telephone Numbers: Toll-Free (nationwide WATS) 800/874-4770
Local 404/581-1777
Toll-Free Call collect

Deposits: $27 billion
Name of Service: SunTrust Securities, Inc.
Order Handling: Information not available
Commission Structure: Sharebroker
Settlement Accounts: Information not available
Brokerage Vendor: BHC Securities, Inc.
Investment Products: Information not available
Note: Offers self-directed IRAs and other retirement plans

SunWest Bank
P.O. Box 25500
Albuquerque, NM 87125-0500

Telephone Numbers: Toll-Free (out-of-state) 800/334-5577
Toll-Free (in-state) 800/545-0765
Local 505/765-2200

Deposits: $2.48 billion
Name of Service: Bankers Systems Brokerage Services at SunWest Bank
Order Handling: Team system
Commission Structure: Valuebroker
Settlement Accounts: Checking, savings, or money market fund
Brokerage Vendor: Bankers Systems Brokerage

Investment Products: Stocks; Bonds; Options; Mutual Funds
Note: Offers self-directed IRAs

Sussex Trust
P.O. Box 311
Georgetown, DE 19947-0311

Telephone Number: Local   302/856-4600
Deposits: $330 million
Name of Service: Discount Brokerage Service
Order Handling: Team system
Commission Structure: Valuebroker
Settlement Accounts: Checking or savings account
Brokerage Vendor: Financial Clearing & Services Corp.
Investment Products: Stocks; Bonds; Options; Mutual Funds
Note: Offers self-directed IRAs, Keoghs, and other retirement plans

Trust Company Bank
P.O. Box 4418, Center 708
25 Park Place
Atlanta, GA 30302

Telephone Numbers: Toll-Free (Florida)   800/874-4770
                     Toll-Free (in-state)   800/572-1777
                     Local   404/588-1777
Deposits: $2.3 billion
Name of Service: SunTrust Securities, Inc.
Order Handling: Team system
Commission Structure: Sharebroker
Settlement Accounts: Checking account
Brokerage Vendor: BHC Securities, Inc.
Investment Products: Information not available

Union Bank
445 South Figueroa Street
Los Angeles, CA 90071

Telephone Numbers: Toll-Free (nationwide)   800/634-1100
                     Local   213/236-7919

Deposits: $9.5 billion
Name of Service: Market Investment Services
Order Handling: Investment services representative assigned
Commission Structure: Valuebroker
Settlement Accounts: Checking, savings, or money market account
Brokerage Vendor: Market Investment Services Corp.
Investment Products: Stocks; Bonds; Options; Government Securities; Mutual Funds

Union Bank and Trust Co.
P.O. Box 2191
60 Commerce Street
Montgomery, AL 36104

Telephone Number: Local 205/265-8201; x200
Deposits: $359 million
Name of Service: Union Bank's Discount Brokerage Service
Order Handling: Information not available
Commission Structure: Valuebroker, DD (LO)
Settlement Accounts: Union Bank checking account
Brokerage Vendor: Stephens Financial Services Clearing Division
Investment Products: Information not available

Union National Bank of Little Rock
P.O. Box 1541
Little Rock, AR 72203

Telephone Numbers: Toll-Free (in-state) 800/482-8450
                   Local 501/378-4000
Deposits: $430 million
Name of Service: Union's Discount Brokerage Service
Order Handling: Team system
Commission Structure: Valuebroker
Settlement Accounts: Checking account
Brokerage Vendor: Stephens Financial Services Clearing Division
Investment Products: Information not available

Union Planter's National Bank of Memphis
P.O. Box 387
Memphis, TN 38147

Telephone Numbers: Toll-Free (nationwide)   800/238-7125
                     Local   901/756-3500
Deposits: $1.5 billion
Name of Service: Union Planter's Brokerage Services
Order Handling: Team system
Commission Structure: Valuebroker
Settlement Accounts: Checking account
Brokerage Vendor: Union Planter's Brokerage Services
Investment Products: Information not available
Note: Offers self-directed IRAs, Keoghs, and other retirement plans

United Bank of Arizona
P.O. Box 2908
Phoenix, AZ 85062-2908

Telephone Numbers: Toll-Free (in-state)   800/824-0767
                     Local   602/248-1280
Deposits: $2.2 billion
Name of Service: UB Brokerage of Arizona
Order Handling: Information not available
Commission Structure: Sharebroker, DD (HI)
Settlement Accounts: Information not available
Brokerage Vendor: Information not available
Investment Products: Information not available

United Jersey Banks
United Jersey Bank Building
90 Nassau Street, CN 843
Princeton, NJ 08540

Telephone Numbers: Toll-Free (Connecticut, New York,
                       and Pennsylvania)   800/631-1635
                     Local   201/368-0800
Deposits: $6.7 billion

Name of Service: Richard Blackman & Co.
Order Handling: Account executive
Commission Structure: Sharebroker, DD (HI, LO)
Settlement Accounts: Cash or United Jersey Bank account
Brokerage Vendor: Ernst & Co.
Investment Products: Information not available
Note: See Richard Blackman Company in the Discount Brokers Section

United Missouri Bank
P.O. Box 232
Kansas City, MO 64141

Telephone Number: Local   816/842-2222
Deposits: $1.4 billion
Name of Service: United Missouri Brokerage Services, Inc.
Order Handling: Team system
Commission Structure: Valuebroker, DD (HI)
Settlement Accounts: Any deposit account
Brokerage Vendor: National Financial Services Corp.
Investment Products: Information not available

U.S. National Bank of Oregon
111 SW Fifth T-9
P.O. Box 5060
Portland, OR 97204

Telephone Numbers: Toll-Free (out-of-state)   800/547-6556
                    Toll-Free (in-state)   800/452-4448
                    Local   503/225-4705
Deposits: $8.6 billion
Name of Service: US Brokerage Services, Inc.
Order Handling: Team system
Commission Structure: Valuebroker, DD (HI, LO)
Settlement Accounts: Bank or checking account
Brokerage Vendor: BHC Securities, Inc.
Investment Products: Stocks; Bonds; Options; IRAs; Government Securities; Mutual Funds; Precious Metals; Unit Trusts

Valley Bancorporation
Valley Bank Plaza
P.O. Box 239
Appleton, WI 54912-0239

Telephone Numbers: Toll-Free (in-state) 800/242-3342
 Local 414/738-3860
Deposits: $3 billion
Name of Service: Valley Securities
Order Handling: Team system
Commission Structure: Sharebroker, DD (LO)
Settlement Accounts: Savings or checking account
Brokerage Vendor: National Financial Services Corp.
Investment Products: Stocks; Bonds; Options; Government Securities; Mutual Funds; IRAs; Unit Trusts
Note: Offers self-directed IRAs

Vermont National Bank
P.O. Box 1308
Burlington, VT 05402-1308

Telephone Number: Local 802/863-8909
Deposits: $527 million
Name of Service: Depositors Discount Brokerage Service
Order Handling: Information not available
Commission Structure: Valuebroker, DD (LO)
Settlement Accounts: Information not available
Brokerage Vendor: Information not available
Investment Products: Information not available

VNB Investment Services, Inc.
Subsidiary of Valley National Bank of Arizona
Valley Bank Center
P.O. Box 71
Dept. A742
Phoenix, AZ 85001

Telephone Number: Local 602/261-2905
Name of Service: Direct Brokerage Services

Order Handling: Team system
Commission Structure: Valuebroker
Settlement Accounts: Deposit account with Valley National Bank of Arizona
Brokerage Vendor: Pershing & Company, Division of Donaldson, Lufkin and Jenrette
Investment Products: Information not available

Washington Trust Bank
P.O. Box 2127
Spokane, WA 99210-2127

Telephone Number: Local   509/455-4202
Deposits: $419 million
Name of Service: Discount Brokerage
Order Handling: Team system
Commission Structure: Valuebroker
Settlement Accounts: Savings or checking account
Brokerage Vendor: Pershing & Company, Division of Donaldson, Lufkin & Jenrette Securities Corp.
Investment Products: Stocks; Bonds; Options; Gold/Silver Coins

Wells Fargo Bank
P.O. Box 7701
San Francisco, CA 94120-9886

Telephone Number: Toll-Free (nationwide)   800/TRADERS
Deposits: $33 billion
Name of Service: Wells Fargo Brokerage Service
Order Handling: Team system
Commission Structure: Valuebroker
Settlement Accounts: Savings, checking, or money market account
Brokerage Vendor: Westnet and Pershing, Division of Donaldson, Lufkin & Jenrette
Investment Products: Information not available
Special Account Requirements: Brokerage available to California residents only

Wilmington Trust
Wilmington Trust Center
Rodney Square North
Wilmington, DE 19890

Telephone Numbers: Toll-Free (nationwide)   800/441-7120
                                        Local   302/651-1000
Deposits: $1.9 billion
Name of Service: Wilmington Brokerage Services
Order Handling: Team system
Commission Structure: Valuebroker
Settlement Accounts: Checking account
Brokerage Vendor: National Financial Services Corp.
Investment Products: Stocks; Bonds; Options; Government Securities; Mutual Funds; GNMAs; Unit Investment Trusts

Worthen Bank and Trust Company, N.A.
Worthen Bank Building
P.O. Box 1681
Little Rock, AR 72203

Telephone Numbers: Toll-Free (in-state)   800/482-8484
                                        Local   501/378-1287
Deposits: $639 million
Name of Service: Discount Brokerage Service
Order Handling: Team system
Commission Structure: Valuebroker, DD (LO)
Settlement Accounts: Checking account
Brokerage Vendor: Stephens Financial Services Clearing Division
Investment Products: Stocks; Bonds; Options; Gold/Silver

Zions First National Bank
1 South Main Street
13th Floor
Salt Lake City, UT 84111

Telephone Numbers: Toll-Free (out-of-state)   800/843-9758
                                        Local   801/524-4711

Deposits: $2.3 billion
Name of Service: Zion's Discount Brokerage, Inc.
Order Handling: Team system
Commission Structure: Valuebroker
Settlement Accounts: Checking or money market account
Brokerage Vendor: Pershing & Company, Division of Donaldson, Lufkin & Jenrette Securities Corp.
Investment Products: Stocks; Bonds; Options; Government Securities; Mutual Funds

APPENDIX B

Everything You Ever Wanted to Know About Discount Brokerage... and More

While some readers just like to get their feet wet, others want to immerse themselves into a subject. They want to learn everything they can until they develop a sense of mastery. This Appendix is dedicated to those readers.

This Appendix is adapted and updated from selected chapters of *70% Off: The Investor's Guide to Discount Brokerage.*[1] It was the first book published on the subject of discount brokerage, and to this day remains the only book exclusively dedicated to that subject.

While a few chapters may be of less interest today than they were in 1984 and some of the numbers have changed, the core chapters remain surprisingly current. Discount brokers have added new products and a few new gadgets, but the basic technology, mechanism, and merits of discount brokerage remain surprisingly constant. Often the best ideas are the simplest, and these often do not change.

---

[1] *Note:* Adapted from *70% Off: The Investor's Guide to Discount Brokerage* (1984). New York: Facts on File. Reprinted with permission.

The following is an annotated Table of Contents.

1. *To Switch or Not to Switch.* Explores whether you should kick the full-service habit and switch to a discount broker.
2. *The Emergence of the Discount Broker.* Discusses a bit of American history that wasn't covered in high school Civics.
3. *Making It On Your Own.* Provides assistance for those venturing out into the investment world on their own.
4. *Essential Mechanics.* Introduces you to order execution and a lady called DOT.
5. *Evaluating Brokerage Firm Features.* . . . because the investor does not live by commissions alone.
6. *The Art of Dealing with a Discounter.* Teaches one of the lesser known arts.
7. *Features and Services.* Shows you how to get your frills with a no-frills broker.
8. *Frills.* More of the above.
9. *SIPC Protection.* Chapter 9 is a reprint of a brochure published by the Securities Investor Protection Corporation (SIPC) which explains how their organization protects the stock investor.

CHAPTER 1

To Switch or Not to Switch

If you are agonizing over whether to switch from a full-service broker to a discounter, this chapter may help. You are attracted by the potential savings, but concerned with leaving the comfort of your current broker and venturing into the unknown. Let those of firm resolve pass on. This chapter is dedicated to the undecided.

Actually, many investors, perhaps most investors, use both a discounter and a full-service broker. They use a discounter for the trades they originate themselves and a full-service broker when their recommendations appeal.

Discount brokers are not for everyone. But is a discount broker for you? If you are really in the market to make money, if you are prepared to take some initiatives to make more, then in most cases, the answer is a resounding "yes." Unfortunately, many investors who should unquestionably use a discount broker, in the end will not. They cannot break the habit. They cannot face that moment of truth when they must say "Buy!" without the reassurance of a soothing voice on the other end of the phone.

However, since you have taken the money to buy and the time to read this book, you are presumably not crippled by such indecision. You are interested in discount brokerage, but don't want to rush into a new area without evaluating the merits.

The first question that you must answer is the most difficult. It requires the most demanding type of honesty, self-honesty. The other questions can be resolved later (whether a discount house is safe, convenient to use, offers other valued services, and so on). In all likelihood, you will satisfy yourself on these questions. This first question is the tough one.

Try to step back from your relationship with your broker—forget whether you like or dislike him or her, whether you could bring yourself to confess that you are changing accounts, or any other stray thoughts that come to mind. Answer this question: Is your broker really an asset, a liability, or just a neutral order-taker?

Is your broker a liability, unpleasant, unhelpful to deal with, and usually wrong? Or very pleasant, very helpful, but has that knack for recommending that one stock which, seemingly in defiance of all known laws of probability, plunges while all those about it are rising? In this clear-cut case, whether or not you switch to a discounter, you will not stay with this broker long. You're just marking time. This bit of self-examination will simply speed up the inevitable.

On the other hand, if your broker is a real asset, commission savings alone should not compel you to leave. The question then becomes, How great an asset is he or she? You are paying a fee. That fee is hidden in the high commission costs. Is your broker worth enough to justify that added cost? We will examine this case in detail in the next chapter.

Finally, we come to order-takers. One of the hardest relations to sever is that between the investor and the friendly order-taker. This person is normally very decent, pleasant, and is ready to chat whenever you call. You are never able to blame him or her for a bad decision because this person is just placing your orders. And yet, as much as you may dislike removing your account, can you really justify continuing to pay two to five times the commission charged by a good discounter for the continuing pleasure of his or her company?

Unfortunately, most brokers do not fall into just one of these clear-cut, black-and-white categories. You may not find this question as easy to answer as it first appears. To hone your skills, let's begin with a clear-cut example. This is a tale of two brokers. The first is called George, to protect his family; they may be innocent. The second is called Bill, because his name is Bill.

I inherited George when I was twenty-one. He came with the portfolio my father asked me to manage. Dad believed in training with "live bullets." He thought the best way to learn to manage a portfolio was to manage one. George was employed by an extremely large brokerage firm. Its name would be familiar to anyone reading this book. He called me twice a day and talked in terms that were very impressive to a junior at college. "It looks like we're hitting a support level today. It's time to buy," George would say. Or, "Better sell, the market looks toppy." Or, "Money supply looks like it'll be down. We could be caught underinvested."

I certainly didn't want my friends to think that I would hold onto a stock when the market was "toppy," failed to buy at a support level, or would be caught with my money supply down. So at the end of our one-minute phone call, when George would tell me to buy or to sell, I would usually buy or sell.

Every afternoon, around quarter to five, I'd go down to the big newsstand in Harvard Square to wait for the afternoon newspaper with the closing market prices. The same crowd used to assemble there every afternoon. The others didn't look much like students. I think they were waiting for the racing results. At the time, I looked down on them. After all, I was an investor; they were just gamblers. Alas, time blunts youth's sharp distinctions. To be sure, the stock market is more respectable. Laying your money down on a horse makes you a gambler; laying it on a stock makes you an investor. But the motivation behind the act may not be so very different. I didn't understand my motivation very well. George did.

He would call me up to tell me about a "hot one, a real winner" that could "break out and lead the market. The odds are good," he would say, "the market is closing strong," or "You could double your money in no time with this one."

Years later, I was in a brokerage firm's boardroom watching the stock tape play across the screen in the front of the room. The market was strong that day. A young fellow in a fit of enthusiasm, watching the strong up-ticks on his stock, yelled out "Go! Go! Go!" I thought of George. Whenever George finished one of his one-minute sales pitches, he would ask me, breathlessly, if I wanted to buy. Or sell. Or buy the one I sold yesterday. Or sell the one I bought the day before. If I didn't agree, he would sound miffed or angry, as though I was wasting his time. As though he had better things to do with that minute than talk to some college kid. I didn't like to say no.

One day I decided to make the pilgrimage to New York City to meet George in person. We had previously only spoken by phone. I prepared for that meeting like a lawyer studying for the New York Bar exam. I examined the balance sheets of stocks his firm had recommended, memorized price/earnings ratios, analyzed the composition of sales revenues. With reams of paper and notes in my green bookbag, I went to the Big City to meet George.

I started out to impress him by asking a clever question about a stock he had once recommended. It didn't register. He did not recall recommending it. So I asked about the book value of a second stock; he didn't remember it either. I asked about the relative growth rate of a third; it had slipped his mind. It continued like this for a half an hour. But if you think that George was embarrassed, you're wrong. He was downright insulted. Why was I wasting his time with these trivial questions when the market was hot? I wasn't the most alert 21-year-old around, but it gradually dawned on me that something was wrong. I stopped trading much with George after that. About six months later, I finally worked up the courage to move the account elsewhere.

On the other hand, there are brokers like Bill. He had come to the securities industry late in life. Closing fast on 50, he found that 20 years pursuing a life in religion and music would not put his four children through college. So he became a broker. For years people were skeptical. But he gradually compiled a record that dispelled their skepticism and attracted a large following.

Bill is everything one could possibly want in a broker. He is a man of great integrity and good judgment. He is responsive to questions, pleasant, and does his homework exceedingly well—not simply passing on his research department's recommendations but also ferreting out small companies or special situations. When Bill makes a strong recommendation, I usually concur. "How can I argue with a man of God," I ask, "who also makes 30 percent per year?"

Bill works for a full-commission firm. I maintain an account there of moderate size. The firm offers no discounts, and I have never asked for one. If you use a full-commission house and have a broker like Bill, stick with it. Count yourself lucky. You will not meet many Bills in a lifetime; I have met one.

The decision whether to switch to a discount brokerage house would not be difficult if brokers were made from two molds: one named George and one named Bill. You would always switch in the first case; never, in the second. Alas, life seldom presents such easy choices.

If you do meet a broker made from one of these molds when you walk in the door of your local firm, the odds are unfortunately in favor of your meeting a George. The explanation is nine words long: People like Bill are rare, and the cream rises.

The top brokers have long since been promoted or no longer handle small or walk-in accounts. The real life Bill no longer accepts small accounts. Once in a while you might catch a rising star shortly after he or she joins the firm and before an eventual promotion. But the odds of a chance encounter with the young Bernard Baruch are not great.

The broker you will meet is likely to be intelligent and have a certain amount of training, far more than in decades past. Some of the larger brokerage firms provide excellent in-house training for their personnel. Much of this training is directed toward helping the broker to better advise clients. Much of it is also directed toward the bottom line—helping the broker to sell his or her clients.

Each broker who is on commission must also take a registered-representatives exam. This exam does ensure a certain minimum level of competence among those selling securities to the public. But speaking from experience, it is fair to state that something less than an encyclopedic knowledge will suffice to pass that exam.

ONE DOZEN LAME EXCUSES—AND A FEW GOOD ONES—FOR NOT OPENING AN ACCOUNT WITH A DISCOUNT BROKER

The Lame Ones

1. *I don't have time to watch my stocks, so I need a paid broker to keep an eye on them.*

Your broker, if typical, has about 300 clients. He or she is not losing much sleep watching your particular portfolio. Unless this broker's track record is good, there are many other ways to get a good babysitter for your portfolio.

2. *I have made quite a bit of money with my broker over the last few years.*

So has everyone, with or without a broker. In the great bull market that began in August 1982, you could have done well picking stocks with a ouija board. However, if your broker has the averages, and you are satisfied, he or she is worth keeping.

3. *Why should I use a discount broker and pay for advice when I can get it free from my regular broker?*

Because you cannot get it free. If there are still any free lunches in this competitive world, they are not being served on Wall Street. You are paying in the form of inflated commissions. It is there just as surely as if it were spelled out on your monthly statement. Even a moderate investor may find it much less expensive, and possibly more profitable, to use an advisory service. Their record can be checked. Their annual cost is spelled out, and unlike commissions, is tax-deductible.

4. *You get better prices when you buy stocks with a regular broker.*

You do not. Every order is essentially executed in the same manner through a form of auction system on the floor of the exchange. The price does not depend on your broker.

5. *I don't need to switch to a discount broker because I got a discount from my full-commission broker.*

There are discounts, and there are *discounts*. Many full-commission brokers will negotiate discounts with their active customers. Each firm has its own policy. If you are a good account, your broker probably has authority to negotiate about a 25% discount. If you are an extraordinarily good account, generating some $10,000 per year or more in commissions, your broker may be able to get his or her office manager's permission to go to 40 percent.

But with the right discount broker, you would not be paying $10,000 per year in commissions. You would be paying $3000 or less. The savings will depend on your specific broker and trading pattern, but even a very good individual account, receiving a good discount from his or her conventional broker, will end up paying the broker twice as much as a good discounter would be paid. And at this level, twice as much means a difference of thousands of dollars per year.

But few investors are such good accounts that they can command a 40 percent discount from a conventional broker. Even good customers typically will not get any more than 20 to 25%. At this level, you are paying three to four times as much as you would with the right discounter. For all practical purposes, you are getting no discount.

6. *My broker customizes my portfolio to suit my needs.*

The concept of a "customized" portfolio was developed by an advertising genius, not a financial one. You can pick stocks that don't move much compared to the rest of the market and some that do. You can get stocks that pay higher or lower dividends. You can diversify your portfolio among different industries. But that's about it. It is easy to do all this yourself. The newspaper publishes the dividend rate every day; also the range for the year which tells you how much it has moved. With very little work, and no money, you can do this for yourself.

7. *With my regular broker I get the inside track when his or her firm makes a "buy" recommendation.*

Do you have some reason to believe that you are the first person out of 300 clients that is called? For that matter, are you sure that you are among the first 50? And is your broker among the first on his or her firm's calling list? That is unlikely because the "buy" recommendation typically goes out from the firm's research department over the wire to hundreds or thousands of the firm's brokers at roughly the same time. If anyone gets the word early, it's probably the big institutional clients. By the time your broker gets the news of the "buy," it is already stale. By the time that you get your phone call, it is history.

8. *Why trouble over a few bucks in commissions anyway?*

If you trade 100 shares on leap years only, it is not worth the trouble. But if you trade much more than this, it is.

But if you're in a position where you can look $5000 in extra commissions square in the eye and say it doesn't matter, it probably doesn't to you. Then again, if you're in that position, probably nothing much else matters anyway. You've bought the wrong book.

9. *I don't have any time to spend on stocks.*

If you really mean that you do not have any time for stocks, you should not use a broker at all, unless his or her record is proven. Sell your stocks. Place the proceeds in a good low-load mutual fund. And go back to whatever you were doing.

10. *An investment advisory publication costs a lot of money.*

Not necessarily, although you may pay roughly $100 to $300 per year for a good one. But since that fee is tax deductible, it only costs a taxpayer in the 33% bracket $70 to $200 per year after taxes. With the right discount broker, an investor could save the annual subscription on a single $10,000 transaction, or several smaller ones.

Furthermore, as a reader of this book, you're entitled to a break on some of them (see the Discount Publications Directory.).

11. *You can't tell whether an investment-advisory publication will do as well as an established full-commission broker.*

Actually, the opposite is correct. The better services publish their records. And others make their living grading such services. On the other hand, few brokerage firms really put their recommendations to a test. Some put their recommendations into a monitored portfolio form, with purchases and sales duly entered.

But most put their recommendations into formats which do not lend themselves to accurate measurement and comparison.

One analytical group set out to measure the brokerage houses' performance. It caused quite a ruckus. In the end they were unable to do so. They just could not get the brokerage houses to participate in a system that would make their records subject to real scrutiny. The brokers did not want anyone making recommendations about the quality of their recommendations.

12. *An investment advisory publication takes time to read and use.*

The better ones are quite clear, readable, and not at all time-consuming. You can pick one whose methods fit your time requirements.

By now it should be clear that leaving your broker will not leave you out in the cold. You will be forced neither to spend long, lonely evenings researching stocks in the downtown library nor to stay forever in the good graces of your cousin Herbert for stock tips.

Well-established advisory publications, with records tested and measured over a period of time in a manner that few brokers' records ever are, will recommend when to buy and sell stocks. Some discount brokers provide these without charge. But even if you have to pay, that cost, for most investors who read this book, will be repaid many times through commission savings. And your stock performance may improve, to boot.

Now that I've exhausted the lame excuses for staying with a full-commission broker, lets look at . . .

The Good Ones

Most investors would be better off using a discount broker for at least some of their trades. Some would not. Assuming that you are otherwise satisfied with your current broker, here are a few good reasons to stick with him or her:

1. *You trade so little that it doesn't make much difference.*

Even if you could save 70% on your commissions, it wouldn't make much difference. The savings would not justify the trouble of a move.

2. *Your average trade size is small (not much more than a $35 commission per trade with your current full-commission broker).*

This is the one type of transaction where large savings may not be possible. Certain discount houses may even be more expensive than certain full-commission firms for very small-sized transactions.

Even the better discount brokers typically have minimum costs of $25 to $35 for stock trades. This is probably $5 to $10 lower than most conventional brokers, but certainly not in itself sufficient to justify a move. Discount brokers can't save you much here because there is no fat to cut at this price level. You're just paying for the firm's processing the trade.

When you reflect for a moment, it is remarkable that you can place an order, have it transmitted to the floor, executed, confirmed back to you, transferred to you, and the stock held, in most cases, at your broker's cost more or less indefinitely—all for $25 or $30. It is a tribute to the economies produced by computers and the efficiency of the stock market that it can all be done at this price. (Actually, in some cases, it cannot. Many brokers, especially conventional ones with their higher overheads, are really losing money at this price. They are willing to absorb this loss to keep your business. They hope to make it up on larger trades where profit margins are high.)

3. *Your full-commission broker runs a portfolio for you on a discretionary basis and does all the trades; you never initiate any. Even compared to the better investment advisory services, his or her record is good.*

Great! Stick with this broker. And tell your friends.

4. *You are in the enviable position described above, except you do initiate some trades on your own.*

Open a second account with a discount broker exclusively for those trades which you initiate.

5. *Your Uncle George is a broker. He already has your account. The prospect of Aunt Matilda's stony silence at Thanksgiving dinner if you switched accounts is more than you could endure.*

This excellent reason demands no further explanation.

CHAPTER 2

The Emergence of the Discount Broker

THE FIRST BROKERS WERE DISCOUNTERS

Back in 1792, a gang of merchants used to hang out near a buttonwood tree on a walled street in lower Manhattan. They would trade a few Continental bonds, tell a few Indian jokes, and drink a lot of tea. When they weren't trading jokes or bonds, they would grumble about their competitors—the auctioneers

"You have to deal with the auctioneers because they have a monopoly on securities sales, but I wouldn't want my sister to marry one," they would say. Or, "Monopolies like the auctioneers' are evil, un-American, and should be abolished."

Then things changed. The regulars started spending an awful lot of time at Corre's Hotel and talking in unusually low voices, considering that they were New York traders. And you didn't hear much about the evils of monopoly any more. Clearly, something was afoot.

Some of the Buttonwood crowd had decided to stop grumbling about the auctioneers and do something about them.

The secret meetings at Corre's Hotel aimed to break the auctioneers' trading monopoly by establishing one of their own. Theirs would be an exclusive market where only members could trade securities.

Of course, there were detractors. "What? Are you kidding? New York isn't some big-league city like Philadelphia. They already have a stock exchange down there. Who wants to trade in the boonies—on Wall Street—when they can trade in Philadelphia?"

But the proponents of the new organization were not to be caught flatfooted by such arguments. They carefully marshaled their response.

"Dummy! It takes two days to get to Philadelphia. And the telephone isn't going to be invented for 80 years. The locals will have to deal with us, as long as we stick together."

The details of these debates are unknown but the outcome is clear. We know that on May 17, 1792, two dozen merchants, following a few weeks of secret meetings at Corre's Hotel, signed an agreement. It said:

> We the subscribers, brokers for the Purchase and Sale of Public Stock, do hereby solemnly promise and pledge to ourselves, to each other, that we will not buy or sell from this day for any person whatsoever, any kind of Public Stock at less than one-quarter of one percent Commission on the Specie value and that we will give preference to each other in our Negotiations. In Testimony whereof we have set out hands this 17th day of May at New York, 1792.

Today we call the the organization founded that day the New York Stock Exchange. You might say that their charter, the so-called Buttonwood Agreement, sets forth the first recorded commission schedule in American history—one-quarter percent across the board.

For the next 100 years, any broker on the New York Stock Exchange would quote you the same rate as any other to within a few cents. That rate was fixed by the Exchange, and everyone had to abide by it. No discounts were allowed. So you might say they were full-commission brokers.

But let us not jump to hasty conclusions. If you go to a good discount broker, on a number of common trades, a good approximation of the rate that you will pay is one-quarter percent—the rate established in 1792! Maybe the founding fathers of the New York Stock Exchange were discounters after all.

DISCOUNT BROKERS TODAY

People may not realize the historical significance of the discount rates, but they do know a good buy when they see one. Discount brokerage is one of the fastest growing segments of the securities industry. Over a million investors are known to use discount brokers. Their rapidly growing ranks currently include some very large firms, with national offices and billions of dollars under management. And their ranks have recently swelled through entry of more than 2000 banks and thrifts offering discount brokerage services.

They already hold billions of dollars in securities in their vaults. Their clients this year will account for close to 20% or more of the nation's retail stock trading. Belatedly, they have won acceptance and respect.

It was not always so. A few short years ago, they were seen as poor cousins of the conventional brokerage firms. And they were viewed with suspicion. People wondered, "How can they offer such low prices?" "There must be something wrong. What's the catch?"

A close look at the industry reveals that there is no catch. The cost savings that allow them to discount rates are no mystery, as we shall see later. The mystery, if there is one, is why investors had to wait so long to get a discount.

Doubtless the answer is that 180 years of custom dies hard. The system of fixed commission rates endured the buffeting of the free market for nearly two centuries. It also survived repeated legal challenges that claimed the fixed-rate system was an unlawful form of price fixing.

The courts agreed that it was price-fixing but concluded that it was not unlawful. What would normally be a violation of the antitrust laws, the courts decided, was legal because it was sanctioned by the government agency responsible for regulating the securities industry, the SEC.

Discount-company brochures tend to credit the SEC with ending fixed exchange rates. They cite its May Day decision in evidence, but this is too kind. (Or perhaps it is just the normal deference of the regulated to the regulator.) The SEC, one of the most respected regulatory agencies, tolerated the fixed-price system for 40 years. In view of the length of this span, embracing every administration from Roosevelt to Nixon, this tolerance cannot be attributed to partisan politics. Evidently the agency was simply loath to tamper with a system that had worked well for nearly two centuries. One would like to think that in the end, they saw the light. Technically this is accurate. The fixed-rate system was indeed ended by the SEC's May Day decision of May 1, 1975. No doubt, that decision took some courage to make. But it also took years of prodding.

The real credit for bringing down the fixed-rate system belongs not to the government but to the forces of the marketplace, "the invisible hand" as Adam Smith used to call it. It works in strange ways. In this case, the end of the system was forced from within, by some of those who had prospered most under it.

An end to fixed exchange rates was proposed in 1969 by no less an Establishment figure than the president of the New York Stock Exchange himself. His proposal won the immediate support, if not prior approval, of Merrill Lynch and Salomon Brothers, two of the real powerhouses of Wall Street. One can only admire them. No one had prospered more under the existing system. In a few decades, these firms came out of nowhere to pre-eminence in their respective fields. Yet they saw the handwriting on the wall and were willing to risk radical change. What drove them to this decision was the specter of losing their largest clients—the institutions.

Before World War II, institutions were not the great force in the stock market that they are today. The individual investor reigned. But in the 1950s and 1960s, the coffers of the great institutional pension funds, trust funds, and others began to overflow. These funds had to find a home somewhere. The trustees and fund managers looked for suitable investments. With bonds paying only a few percent, they looked with favor on the stock market. It was liquid, income-producing, and considered suitable for fiduciary investments.

The great postwar bull market rolled through the 1950s into the 1960s, setting one high after another. And the institutional funds rolled in. Year after year, the institutional share of stock ownership grew, until it came to comprise the nation's dominant shareholders. But if stocks increasingly found favor in their eyes, the stock commissions increasingly came to rankle. The institutions felt that they were being overcharged. But under the fixed-rate system, they had no real choice. Every broker was bound to charge the same amount.

The structure basically mandated a commission proportionate to value. If you paid a $50 commission for 100 shares of stock, you would pay roughly a $500 commission for 1000 shares. Or a $5000 commission for 10,000 shares. But these commission costs bore no realistic relation to the cost of the trade. It did not cost the brokerage firm much more to trade 1000 shares than 100, but the commissions were almost 10 times as high. Since the institutions were typically making the largest purchases, they fared the worst. And they knew it.

They bided their time, waiting for a suitable opportunity. Eventually it arrived. It was known as the "third market." The New York Stock Exchange was the first market. The American Stock Exchange was the second. The trading in the over-the-counter market of stocks listed on the exchanges came to be known as the "third market."

It operated principally through substantial brokerage firms who elected not to join the established exchanges. This left them free of the rate-fixing restrictions imposed on exchange members. If you had a "seat" on the New York Stock Exchange, you had to charge the rate fixed by the Exchange for buying a thousand shares of General Motors. But if you owned 1000 General Motors shares, and were not a member of the Exchange, you could sell at whatever commission you liked.

Thus, networks of dealers, not belonging to the exchanges, began to accumulate stocks or transact purchases or sales outside the exchanges. In effect they charged lower commissions. In accordance with the practice of the over-the-counter market, the lower commission was built into the price rather than charged as a separate commission.

The institutions loved low commissions. They left the exchanges by droves. The third market grew faster than crabgrass. Soon the conventional brokers began to fear that the third market would eventually become the first market.

It was at this point that the president of the New York Stock Exchange dropped his bombshell proposing the abandonment of fixed commissions. Henceforth, he proposed, supply and demand would determine commission rates. This was hardly a revolutionary concept in the rest of the country, where competition was the rule and price-fixing, illegal. But to an industry where 180 years of fixed rates had prevailed, it was a radical notion indeed.

True, the Exchange had been inching toward change: lower rates for orders over 1000 shares were introduced in 1969, but this move to end fixed exchange rates was unexpected. It engendered tremendous controversy. It split the brokerage community right down the middle.

On one side were the Merrill Lynches and Salomon Brothers. The big firms basically supported the change. Perhaps they had more foresight. Or perhaps they just stood to gain most and lose least. In the competitive market of negotiated rates, the Merrills and "Sollys" of the brokerage world stood the best chance of survival.

The smaller firms were scared. Without the wall of fixed rates, they felt their survival would be threatened. Diminished profit margins, better capitalized competitors—it was a frightening specter. And their prospective gains from these changes were small. Why should they care about losing the institutional business they had never really had?

The SEC did not know how to react to this radical proposal. In the time-honored tradition of government agencies, it waffled. Then in 1971, at the request of the securities industry, it opted for limited deregulation. Commissions on orders for $500,000 or more were thrown open for negotiation. But this was not enough to satisfy the institutions. A year later, therefore, the industry came back and asked that the deregulation level be dropped to $300,000. The request was granted.

But it was a case of too little, too late for the old guard. Once-revolutionary ideas were gaining acceptance with the passage of time, even in the stodgy securities industry. Deregulation was an idea whose time had come. The SEC, belatedly but to its credit, decided to bite the bullet. After a trial period of negotiated commissions which began in 1974, it decided to go all out. Wall Street had long praised free enterprise and competition. Now it would have the opportunity to practice it.

On May 1, 1975, the Securities and Exchange Commission invoked the power vested by Congress and ordered an end to rate fixing on the stock exchanges. (As cautiously as the SEC moved, it was a wild-eyed radical by governmental standards. The Canadian government did not deregulate rates until April 1983—eight years later.)

But when this bombshell decision landed, it was less with a bang than a thud. To be sure, it was heard loudly enough at the institutional end of the Street. The institutions immediately demanded and received heavy discounts. They had the clout to come into their broker's office, bang on the table, and demand that their rates be cut in half. Or by 90%. If not, they could take their business next door.

In reality, the transition to discount rates for the institutions took place with less fanfare. The institutions had the clout. They knew they had the clout. The brokers knew they had the clout. Therefore, everyone could dispense with the banging of tables.

Not so for the individual investor, who was not accustomed to negotiating with his or her friendly local broker. Even if he or she were so inclined, the clout wasn't there. It was the bull market of the early 1976. Business was going swimmingly. With the rising market bringing in the customers, there was no inducement to start a price war. Any individual banging on the table would be shown the door.

Thus, for all the radical change, commissions for the individual remained the same. The time was not yet ripe. But the seeds of change had been planted. The May Day decision, which most small brokers viewed with foreboding, was seen by some of the more innovative ones as an opportunity. This included some who had pioneered a form of discount brokerage in the third market. Perhaps the established firms would not give the individual investor a discount, but these firms were different. They would offer discounts. You would not have to plead or threaten to get it. Everyone who opened an account would receive a discount. Moreover, you would know the size of that discount in advance. Even before you decided whether to open an account. It would be spelled out on a published schedule which you would receive upon request and review in advance.

The first discount brokerage firms were pretty much a bare-bones affair. The firms provided nothing much more than execution of the trades; anything else was often unavailable or available only at additional cost. Like any new industry, it had its innovative pioneers and it had its fringe element. The latter received more publicity than the former. The conventional brokers watched and waited to see if the discounters would last. They did. Technology was on the discount broker's side. So was the SEC. In May 1976, a year after its May Day decision, the SEC set forth another rule which required floor brokers, those actually on the trading floor, to negotiate their commissions as well.

While not so widely publicized as the May Day decision, it proved very important to the development of the discount industry. It gave the new firms access to the floor on terms and with skills at least comparable to the Big Boys and often better.

Advancing technology helped, too. As computerization progressed, the cost of trading and support facilities, for example, back-office recordkeeping, was driven lower and lower. And the newer firms were able to acquire the most advanced computer technology; indeed they often pioneered it.

CHAPTER 3

Making It On Your Own

Like learning to speak in prose, selecting your own investments is not nearly as hard as it sounds. There are legions of advisers, paid and unpaid, ready to help you. The better ones tell you precisely when to buy or sell a specific stock. Such advice is neither hard to follow nor time-consuming. And track records of some advisers are good and can be verified. We'll discuss the details in this chapter.

You don't have to make a black-and-white choice between a discounter and a full-commission broker. Many investors elect to use both a discount broker and a conventional broker. They will use a conventional broker when they are following recommendations which that broker initiated, and a discount broker when they are following recommendations initiated by themselves or other sources. In this way, they have the best of both worlds.

Some investors, full-commission brokers fear, may have more than the best of both worlds. They use full-commission brokers to find out which stock to buy, and then place the order with a discount broker to cut costs. No doubt this does happen. It may well be a widespread practice; there is really no way to tell. It is quite understandable why full-commission brokers would feel aggrieved if they believed that their services were being appropriated without compensation. Some investors, however, might differ as to what compensation is adequate—whether it is fair to give some or all of one's business to a broker in exchange for advice. One can only assume that most investors have a sense of what is fair under the circumstances, and that they act upon it.

But most investors, sooner or later, begin to make at least some decisions on their own, or on the basis of some recommendation from a person or publication. Think back. Haven't you initiated some transactions? Called your broker to buy or sell a particular stock when you thought the timing was right? Bought on the recommendation of a friend? Or perhaps you have a good relationship with a conventional broker, but sometimes want to try your hand at buying stocks? However, you don't want to do it with all your funds until you find out how well the stock you pick performs. Under these circumstances, a second account with a discount broker is a natural decision.

So if you would like to ease your way into investing on your own, to test the water before jumping in, having two accounts is a good, conservative way to make a transition. Then, after a period of time, you can compare the results in both accounts and decide which way is better.

FEAR OF FAILURE

Don't let fear of making the wrong decision prevent you from trying. Selecting stocks is not like piloting a plane, where inexperience can be fatal. The risk of making a mistake is a lot less than you may think. Therefore, if a friend whom you trust tells you IBM is a good buy, and you think so too, don't be too concerned that this independent choice will be worse than whatever your broker is recommending. There are several reasons that should help allay this concern.

Most importantly, you are not really buying blind when you buy an actively traded stock. That price which you see in the paper represents the price which thousands of people who follow that stock think—and bet—that it is worth. You know that this is true because if most people thought it was worth more, they would buy more, and the price would go up. The reverse would happen if they thought it was overpriced; then the price would drop.

If you look at IBM in the morning paper and see that it traded 200,000 shares at $100 per share, that means buyers paid out $20 million for IBM yesterday. That much cash on the table means that at least a few institutions or others with expert advice felt it was a good buy at that price. So you will be in good company if you buy.

On the other hand, it is sobering to consider that if $20 million was bought, there was an equally well-advised group of persons who decided to sell $20 million of IBM that day. They did not think it was a good buy. Two groups of experts, opposite conclusions. That's why there are no guarantees. But you never assumed there were, or you would not have waited so long to begin. It will come as no surprise to you then to learn that a substantial body of evidence points to an abundance of one factor among outstanding investors—luck.

It is also a fact that the value of picking the right stock is normally much overrated. A study undertaken a few years back suggested that most stock market profits did not come from picking precisely the right stock. Most of the profits came from going into the market at the right time and buying stocks in the right industry. The specific stock itself was not as important as the other two factors.

There is actually a school of market theorists, usually known as the "Random Walk" group, who think that the market is such a perfectly adjusted mechanism that all good performance, in the long run, is basically attributable to luck—random movements of stock prices.

The most fervent disciples of the Random Walk school would say that over the long run, you can pick stocks by throwing darts at the stock market pages of your newspaper and investing in those companies where the darts hit. This will save you a lot of time, they would say, a lot of bother, and the results will be as good as your broker or anyone else could produce.

The Random Walk theory is not so popular anymore nor is it proving to be so accurate in the current bull market. Apparently stock movement tends to be random in markets that fall or just mill around. But in bull markets, at least in the early stages, stock selection seems to help. The Random Walk is out. Stock selection is back.

This is bad news for Monday night sports fans. It means that homework probably helps. It's back to the books. No more dazzling the neighbors at cocktail parties with stocks you secretly selected with a set of darts, while telling yourself that you're at the forefront of economic theory. However, the good news is that if you do your homework, you may outperform a monkey armed with darts. Or your broker.

Before investing on your own, you should be familiar with the mechanics of the marketplace. Undertake whatever preparation you can to try to get a jump on the market. There are many excellent books concerning the stock market that can help you understand the mechanics and principles of investing. There are also numerous books in a different category. They don't teach principles or mechanics, but a specific "system" that will help you get rich quick, or something more modest—like turn a 100 percent per year profit with no risk. Other than the obvious observation that the author is getting rich quick through book sales, not his or her system, I would leave you with one guiding principle.

It is a new theory I have developed to account for the failure of the Random Walk theory, and to help you analyze future theories and "systems" as you pore through learned tomes or get-rich-quick books. In all modesty, this theory is not only a theoretical tour de force, but an invaluable practical tool. In fact, it is sort of the General Relativity Theory of stock market analysis. It covers every possible contingency. It is called Random Walk Theory of Theories and it says that stock theories, like stock prices, are subject to random movements over time. Sometimes they work; sometimes they don't. (It applies to this theory as well.)

This means that after you have completed reading a few of the better books in the field, you can pick the rest by random selection. It has one practical shortcoming. Your local bookstore owner will wonder why you're throwing darts at the "Investor's" shelf.

I have read quite a few of these books in my time. Some of them are useful for specialized areas, such as options, or specialized situations. But as for general principles of investment, I have been able to distill two.

1. Diversification is the only immutable principle of conservative investment

The way it works is surprising. Ten stocks in your portfolio are vastly safer than one or two. Fifteen are somewhat safer than ten. But 100 stocks are not really much safer than 15. This assumes that the stocks are in different industries. Else, they may tend to move together. If your 15 stocks are all local telephone companies spun off from Ma Bell, someone may ring your bell.

2. Don't trade any more than necessary

The sting is a lot less at 70% off. But if you trade three times as often, you're back where you started, just as surely as if you were paying full commissions. And the tax bite on short-term gains is so high that you often have to earn almost $2 to equal a $1 of long-term gains (over one year).

Let me give you a pointer on how to handle inside tips. First, very calmly, without any sudden movements, back away from the telephone. For the next half-hour stay at least 50 feet from any device through which you might communicate with your broker. This is the danger period. After that, if you're a person of iron discipline, you can check out the stock on the remote chance that you've been told something that every broker on the Street doesn't already know. Nothing, absolutely nothing can make intelligent people lose their judgment so completely as the belief that they are getting an inside tip. I speak from experience. Real inside tips are great; they're also generally illegal. Be careful.

If what you have just learned scares you, you should not be in the stock market. If it does not, then don't be afraid to place an order yourself, just because you do not have the reassurance of a broker's soothing voice on the other end of the phone. With a little preparation, your odds are at least as good as your broker's, and your services come for a lot less.

PUBLICATIONS

There are numerous publications, some of which you may already be reading, that can provide you with good "buy" recommendations. These are discussed in Chapter 3, Investment Advice for the Independent Investor. Reading these magazines once a week or once a month, you can pick up enough recommendations to establish a diversified portfolio. And if the editors of the periodicals have done their job, then you are hearing the advice of the best people in their field.

Don't be surprised if a lot of the recommendations that you read in these publications also crop up in your broker's recommended stocks. Wall Street can be an incestuous community. Brokers' best ideas often come from other brokers.

RESEARCH

If you are blessed with a good investment library in your city, and inclined to invest the time, it is astonishing what you can find there. Investment services with subscription costs aggregating thousands of dollars annually are available without cost at a good library. Here you will find virtually every research tool that you will ever need. Many brokerage firms probably don't have research facilities as complete as a good, big city library.

TELEVISION

A number of excellent television programs are identified in Chapter 3 of this book, Investment Advice for the Independent Investor.

CHAPTER 4

Essential Mechanics

If it's not the best-kept secret in the brokerage business, then it's certainly the least advertised fact: No matter where you place your trade, Merrill Lynch or the smallest discounter, it's all likely to be handled by a computer named DOT. You ought to know about DOT, and some other essential mechanics of the computer age, if you're to decide what's worth paying for in a broker and what is not.

Let's assume you're ready to trade. You have read this book, reviewed your trading pattern, and found the right broker for yourself. Now you want to open an account, but you're concerned that it will be a lot of trouble and you're not looking forward to giving your current broker the bad news. Don't despair. You are wrestling with the type of problem for which American merchandising is world-renowned. Did you think that the folks who brought you "life" insurance for death, the 800-number, and MasterCard were going to desert you now?

Certainly not. Opening an account with a financial institution is governed by the First Rule of Transfer, to which there are no known exceptions. No matter how many regulations they have, no matter how many complications you raise, you will always, always find it's easy to put money *in*. Call up your broker's 800-number, tell him or her you want to start trading as soon as possible, and even the slowest broker will get moving with a speed that would leave a jaguar in the dust. You fill in a few lines on a form, and unless you've been convicted for murder (or worse—bankruptcy) you'll be in business within the week. Some firms will actually let you buy the same day you call, if they can check out your bank references.

If you're buying stock, it's normally not necessary to have the cash in the account in advance, even for your first purchase. So you can open your account first, place a purchase order when you are ready, and pay when it is executed. (Some houses may require a modest minimum to open the account. Check the Discount Brokerage Directory for details.)

The next piece of good news is that you don't have to tell your current broker that you're leaving. You just request a transfer form from your new broker, fill it in, and he or she takes care of the rest. The form is sent to your old broker by your new broker, and the securities are automatically transferred. You don't have to be the bearer of bad tidings.

However, don't transfer any securities that you might want to sell in the next month, because the transfer of securities out of a financial institution is covered by the inexorable Second Rule of Transfer. No matter what pains you take to comply with the rules for transfer out, no matter how carefully you fill in each and every line of the form, is is always hard to move assets *out*. Expect a wait. Expect excuses. Be patient.

Your account is now open. You're authorized to trade, and you've just told your broker to buy at the current market price 300 shares of Plum Computer, a hot new stock which has moved out of the Silicon Valley near San Francisco, and after a sojourn on some lesser exchanges, has taken up residence on the Big Board (the New York Stock Exchange).

If you've always believed that "you get what you pay for," you're about to learn a lesson of the computer age. That rule may still be valid for horses, cigars, wine, and ketchup. But computer products are fungible. Stripped of bells and whistles, advertisements and myths, stock buying for the individual is about as personalized as social security checks. The customer who pays Merrill Lynch $150 to buy Plum Computer, and the customer who pays $40 to a good discounter, both have their orders handled in the same manner, by the *same* computer.

The broker writes your Plum Computer order on a slip, which is then punched into a computer, an electronic order-routing system named DOT (Designated Order System). It doesn't matter whether you deal with Merrill in Albuquerque, or a discounter in Orlando, the order goes into DOT, which is owned and operated by the New York Stock Exchange, not by any particular brokerage firms. DOT currently handles New York Stock Exchange market orders up to 30,000 shares (limit orders up to 100,000 shares) and its capacity keeps growing. The over-the-counter market and some of the other exchanges have their own highly computerized systems as well.

From your broker's office, the order travels over the wires to an electronic switch down in lower Manhattan known as the "Common Message Switch," operated by the Securities Industries Automation Corporation. This switch tells your order where to go—politely.

But suppose you're not satisfied with using the same system as everyone else, and you're not even satisfied with paying four times as much to a full-commission broker who claims to be getting you "better execution" than a discounter. You want the fastest execution possible, and as a person of means, you're prepared to pay whatever it costs, so you buy a seat on the New York Stock Exchange. The day arrives when you're ready to beat everyone else and, in particular, your mousy brother-in-law, Herbert Peebles, who quietly but stubbornly insists that he can do quite well with some ridiculously cheap discounter. Well this time, you tell yourself, Herbert is in for a surprise. You have an ace in the hole. What Herbert doesn't know is that you have gone to Hertz and rented O. J. Simpson for the day as your floor trader.

Herbert and you place the Plum Computer order simultaneously. Seconds later, Herbert's order is punched into DOT and O.J. receives your call. He tears out from the telephone banks, which line the walls of the Exchange, and heads straight across the Exchange floor for the Plum Computer trading post, scattering brokers left and right as he goes. Even by O.J.'s standards, he covers the 50 yards in good time. He whips out your order and hands it to the Plum specialist, who thinks it best not argue with this unorthodox floorbroker, and quickly enters the order. Your triumph over Herbert, you feel, is complete.

Not quite. You see, Herbert won. His order was executed first. His order did not have to travel over telephone lines to the side of the Exchange, and then by hand over 50 yards to the Plum specialist's trading post. His order appeared on the specialist's desk at essentially the same time as it was punched into the DOT line in his broker's office. So I ask you, if O.J. Simpson couldn't get your order executed first, can Merrill Lynch?

Once entered, all orders are handled in the same way through a prescribed open auction system or, in the case of a limit order, through an entry on the specialists' books. It's a tribute to the efficiency of the Exchange mechanism and the DOT system that the average DOT order is executed within 30 seconds. It's monitored daily and specialists who don't measure up are informed that they had better shape up. A computer also tells DOT's monitors if a DOT limit order on a specialist's books fails to execute when it should. If this happens, the specialist can't leave the floor that day until this discrepancy is explained.

The day after your order is executed, a confirmation slip is sent out to you by either the broker or his or her clearinghouse. The average investor doesn't hear much about clearinghouses, but you should know the term. It is significant. In fact, it may be the real secret weapon of the discount brokerage industry. Many discount brokers, and full-commission brokers as well, use a clearinghouse to handle all their back-office work and sometimes their executions as well. This allows the discount broker to specialize in the order-taking business, keep its overhead down, and let a large established clearinghouse handle all the paperwork, often holding the securities as well.

When you open an account, you will often find that you are instructed to fill out an application form and send checks to someone other than the broker whose name is on the door. That someone is the clearinghouse. It is often the clearinghouse that holds your securities and provides margin as well. Even when you don't make out the check to the clearinghouse, your broker may well have a clearinghouse handle the paperwork, and possibly the executions as well. The alternative is to handle it in-house, usually with the aid of a computer service bureau.

Clearinghouses tend to be large, well-capitalized firms, often bigger than all but the largest brokers. The major conventional brokerage firms normally execute through their own clearing subsidiaries, while discount brokers frequently work through large independent clearinghouses or subsidiaries of full-commission brokers. This can create an anomalous situation where the full-commission client is not only paying much more for the same execution through the DOT system, but also, adding insult to injury, receiving confirmation and monthly statements back from the same clearinghouse.

I don't want to leave you with the impression that there is no difference at all between or among discount brokers and conventional brokers. There is. Mercer has tracked a number of different brokers and finds that some have much clearer monthly statements than others. Some are much faster in reporting trades than others, and there can be differences in the timing and execution of non-DOT trades. There are many other fine distinctions as well, some of which are covered in the Discount Brokerage Directory. But these fine points will not matter much to the average investor, and there is no evidence that the conventional firms have an edge.

In fact, whatever difference there is seems to favor discounters. This and other surprising conclusions were revealed in a survey of active investors conducted by the *Wall Street Journal* in 1981. Slightly more than half the investors who used both discount and full-commission firms found no real difference between them with respect to speed and executing orders or accuracy of confirmations and statements. But of those who did, two-thirds thought that discount brokers provided speedier executions, and about 60% thought they provided more accurate confirmations and statements, proving that in the computer age, what you pay for is not necessarily what you get.

CHAPTER 5

Evaluating Brokerage Firm Features

There are various ways to evaluate the features and services of a firm. I offer a three-part approach to help you break down the mass of information into digestible form. First, those services and features which are translatable into dollars and cents in a fairly direct way, for example, a volume discount, will be examined. It cannot be laid out in a commission schedule, since each reader's trading volume differs, but you know how much you trade and can decide how it affects your overall cost. These are "hard dollar" features.

In contrast are features that have a dollar value, but are hard to tag with an exact price, for example, advisory services. You can generally buy these services elsewhere, but you might not and if you did, they would not be precisely the same. Hence, "soft dollar" features.

The third category has no real price tag. The features affect how you feel about the firm. How comfortable you are dealing with them. They are often subjective, but as in any relationship, important to consider. These are "non-dollar" features.

HARD DOLLAR FEATURES

1. Commission Structure and Additional Features or Additional Charges. The hardest of the hard features. These are almost part of the commission schedule, but can't be included there since their impact varies according to the trading patterns of each investor. As I've said before, if you study no other hard dollar sections, study these.

Among the type of variations covered here are volume or "round trip" discounts for active traders; limit order surcharges for cautious ones, and pre-market-hour discounts for early rising ones. These variations can typically raise or lower the cost of dealing with that firm by 5 to 20% depending on your trading pattern. That is why it is important that you check out these sections carefully.

Designation as a deep discounter in the Directory is based on commissions made in normal fashion during market hours, without volume discounts or surcharges. If you are a large trader, and the firm offers a volume discount, you can reduce the estimated commission charge. If you normally use limit orders, and the firm charges for them, increase the estimated cost accordingly. You'll find all kinds of odd little charges listed in this section as well.

2. Margin Interest. A very significant item if you use much margin. Note that some firms charge several percent more than others.

3. Interest on Cash Balances. Speaks for itself, but if a money fund is listed as being offered under this section, be sure to find out whether your funds will be automatically "swept" in or whether you must keep track and request transfers personally.

4. Toll-Free Lines. Hard dollars if you call your broker often.

SOFT DOLLAR FEATURES

One of the features that I very much like in one firm is what they call a "quote" line. This enables me to call in on a toll-free line from any telephone to get the current quotations—bid, asked, volume, and so on.

Most firms let you call your broker and ask for quotes. But for me, a call under these circumstances, no matter how polite your broker, creates a certain psychological pressure to buy. In this case, however, it is not even possible to place an order when calling this line. Therefore, there is no buying pressure, however subtle.

This feature could be placed under the "non-dollar" heading for this reason. But, in my case, it is also possible to place a soft dollar figure on this service, because it serves as a kind of substitute for installing a quote machine in my office.

If I installed a quotation machine, it would cost at least $500 per month. And then, I could only use it when I was in the office. So I would gladly pay a few dollars more for this specific feature.

Soft dollar features appear in the profiles primarily in two places—Research and Investment Advice, and Additional Features and Charges.

The additional features are an oddball group of features, like the one described above. They vary too much to offer any generalizations.

Research and advisory services tend to be of three types:

1. None. Quite common. This tells it like it is.
2. Rundown on specific company upon request.

    If you request a report on a specific company you will get a one-page write-up prepared by a reputable investment advisory service, usually Standard and Poor's, sometimes Value Line. Since a subscription to one of these services would cost several hundred dollars, this is a nice "freebie." On the other hand, you don't get the whole service, just the specific report.

    This service is most helpful to the investor who does not invest often. Without charge, it can be determined whether these reputable services agree with your view.
3. Extensive advisory services.

    Despite the discount broker's reputation for "no-frills," a small number of houses provide a surprising amount of frills along with discount market letters, full services, libraries with hundreds or thousands of dollars worth of advisory services, and even live discussions with key personnel or research analysts. So if you shop around, you can have your cake and eat it too.

NON-DOLLAR FEATURES

Many of these can only be judged by personal experience. Is the firm pleasant to deal with? Do they make many errors? Do they correct them politely and efficiently when they do? How do you like talking with them on the phone? Do you get through quickly?

Only those characteristics that can be put down in advance on paper can be dealt with here. For most people, the most important non-dollar features of this type are size and locality. These are both important features to many investors. But in the brokerage industry, they are not as important as elsewhere.

Size

Size says something about a firm. As the saying goes, you can fool all of the people some of the time, and some of the people all of the time, but you can't fool all of the people all of the time. If a firm has grown large, a great many people must be pleased with what it offers, no small achievement in a field as competitive as discount brokerage.

Up to this point, there has been a heavy concentration of investors in the largest firms. Some estimates have concluded that $2/3$ of the investors deal with the top 3 firms. For some transactions, you will find, the largest firms also offer some of the best commission rates. In this case, you can stick with size and still get value.

Size as an indication of stability is important. Even if your funds are not in jeopardy with a start-up firm—since it is insured by SIPC—you still might want assurances of stability which size provides. You want to be sure that their systems run smoothly, that their operation clicks, and that they will still be selling securities at a discount next year, not insurance.

You would have every reason to want to check out a newer, smaller firm more carefully than a national one. A good new local firm might offer you very good service. They might very well be trying harder. But if you are getting a very cheap rate from a firm which is very new it could also prove very temporary. They might price themselves low initially to attract business, then raise their prices later—like every new bargain restaurant that I have ever discovered in New York City. There is nothing wrong with taking advantage of a temporary bargain, but stay wary. Be prepared to move on when they start referring to Pete, their short-order cook, as their chef, Pierre.

On the other hand, size alone in a discount broker has much less to commend itself than in most business. You are buying a uniform product, with the risk largely insured by SIPC, and the quality pretty much the same.

For the normal moderate-sized order, no broker, discount or full-commission, can really get you a better price. The trade occurs in an open auction market, on the floor of the exchange, with the orders normally forwarded directly to the auction point by computer.

As to speed of execution, accuracy of reports back, and the like, there is no reason to routinely suppose that a big firm is better. Most discount firms are highly computerized. Computers at small firms work as fast as computers at big ones. The computer is really the great leveler. Technology has eliminated many of the differences that may once have existed among firms in these areas. And the plummeting price of computers has put good ones within the reach of every firm, and discount brokers were among the first to take advantage of this. As to management, a capable owner active in the business runs as tight a ship as any on land. You need only visit to see this.

Finally, many firms that are small clear through a clearinghouse that is quite large. The clearinghouse holds your funds, executes your orders, and sends you all confirmations and monthly reports. In many respects, you are really a client of the clearinghouse, with the discount broker acting as a retail branch. The clearinghouse is listed on each profile. Any firm should provide you with detailed information about its clearinghouse, including the latest financial statement. So before you reject an otherwise suitable firm because it is small, check out the clearinghouse, consider what has been said above, and then decide.

Locality

Locality ranks right along with size as the non-dollar items that people value most. People like to deal with a firm that is nearby. That is natural. You like to be able to drop by the office, to "kick the tires," so to speak. You may also prefer to deal with local people. We cannot speak for your preference in dealing with local people. That is a personal matter. If you are willing to pay a premium, if need be, then it is a personal decision with which no one could argue.

In some parts of the country, you may not have to pay any premium at all. You may have an excellent firm in your area, even if you are not in one of the major financial centers. The brokers listed as deep discounters indicate that good value is not restricted to the financial centers. Some of the firms on these lists are in Nebraska, Wisconsin, Virginia, or Florida, to name a few. And many of the largest firms have local branches with whom you can deal. In other parts of the country, however, you may have to pay a substantial premium to deal with a local firm. If that is the case, you may want to reexamine your view.

Buying and selling stock is a telephone business. There really is no reason to meet with your broker, unless you enjoy his or her company. With a toll-free 800- number you can call New York or California for less than the cost of a local call.

I live in New York but my principal brokers at present are in New Jersey, Boston, and Florida. I have found one difference in dealing with out-of-state brokers. The mail seems to arrive from Orlando much faster than it does from Wall Street, one mile away.

Ask yourself whether there really is some sound reason that you should pay a large premium, if that is the case, for dealing with a local broker in cases where out-of-state ones are much less expensive.

CHECKING OUT THE BROKER

The final step is to call up the brokers that you have identified in the profiles, and ask for their rate schedule, descriptive brochure, and their financial statement or that of their clearinghouse. Don't be afraid to call up as many brokers as you might reasonably consider using. That is what a toll-free number is for. It doesn't cost anything, and you will not be hounded by sales reps forever after if you do not decide to open an account.

It is important that you make your final decision after reviewing this information from various brokers. Don't call up just one broker who looks best in the Directory. Call up all your finalists, and maybe even some semi-finalists.

There are several reasons for this approach. First, some of the features or commissions could have changed since this book was prepared in the winter of 1990. Discount brokers do change their schedules from time to time—once a year would be a good guess. While these changes are unlikely to be so radical that they would change your fundamental view of a house, they could make a difference in selecting among finalists.

Then, too, while I have tried very hard for accuracy, there just might be a mistake. So before you lay your money down, check it out.

CHAPTER 6
The Art of Dealing with a Discounter

For those who use their broker often, there are a few tips that I pass along in the belief that it will make your life with a discounter easier and, possibly, more profitable. Some of these suggestions are specific to dealing with a discounter; others, no doubt, could be used with any broker.

THE TELEPHONE

Life with any broker begins with the phone. No one can consider him- or herself a master of dealing with a discounter until achieving complete mastery over Alexander Bell's marvelous, infernal creation.

One occasionally reads horror stories about how long it takes to get through on a line to a discounter. I read one story where the author, a full-commission broker as I recall, claimed that his friend called into a discounter and rang "78 times" before he got an answer. In my experience, that won't happen, but you may encounter two other types of delays if you call during certain hours: a busy signal or a recorded voice that assures you that your call will be answered shortly. About the seventh time that you are reassured of a quick answer, that reassurance can sound unconvincing.

There are a number of ways to deal with this problem. Let's begin with the *time* of day when you call. The worst time is lunchtime for most discounters. The problem is that the line gets clogged with "quoters," people who do not intend to place an order but want quotes. So if you're placing a limit order where you don't need to know the exact price at the time you place it, try to avoid calling at lunch. You can always reach your broker before the market opens without delay, and some firms' lines are open for orders well into the night, sometimes even around-the-clock. Becoming a captive audience for a recording, however, is not the worst fate. Once you've reached the recording stage, you're more than halfway home. Although it may seem interminable, I have always found that in fact you will get a live human voice on the line within a period of a few seconds to two or three minutes. Far worse than a recording is a busy signal. Especially that second busy signal when you call again. That is when you know with certainty that the stock you want to sell is dropping at two points per minute and will be declared bankrupt by the time your broker answers. There is one simple solution to this problem: keep dialing. I don't mean a civilized call every three minutes, as Ma Bell's ads counsel you to do when encountering a busy signal. I mean dial ferociously. Redial immediately as soon as you hear the busy signal. If that's too hard on your fingertips, then for about $100 and change, you can get a Panasonic dialer, or something similar, that will automatically dial any one of 64 numbers, make your life easier in general, and allow you to place roughly 10 calls per minute with the push of a button. It is a constant source of amazement to me that I will almost always get through, even at high noon, by the third or fourth call.

Behind this almost mystical result lies the logic of statistics. When Ma Bell's ad tells you to dial every three minutes if you encounter a busy signal, it assumes that you're calling another individual or small business with one or two phone lines. But many discounters have a dozen lines or more. The average time to place an order or get a quote is short, so one of these lines is becoming free every few seconds. That is why constant dialing works. By the third or fourth call, the law of averages has triumphed over the telephone company.

If you're really concerned with this problem, and haven't selected a broker yet, it's not a bad idea to test call their number at different times during the day for several days. This should give you an idea of whether it's likely to be a serious problem.

If you're already using a broker and have begun to find busy lines to be a real problem, you have a few alternatives. First, try out the multidialing telephone remedy. If that doesn't work, or you find it too much of a nuisance, then find out whether your broker has other branches with toll-free 800-numbers. If so, check to see whether the branch phones are less busy. I use one broker whose Boston branch is often busy but whose Florida branch almost never is. Most discounters will let you place an order through any of their branches, so this is a feasible solution.

Your ultimate resort, if this problem persists, is to switch brokers. There are enough good discounters around with free lines that you don't have to put up with one that is constantly busy. But if you're otherwise happy with your firm, you might talk with the manager about the problem, and ask whether they are taking any steps to remedy it. It is possible that the problem is temporary, in which case you may opt to bear with them. A temporary problem of this type can arise during periods of rapidly rising stock trading because discounters are staffed lean, a consequence of low overhead and subsequent low commissions. As a result, a sudden surge in volume can find them temporarily understaffed. On the other hand, they can adjust very quickly. Once an individual is hired, he or she can be trained to give quotations almost immediately and take orders in less than a month. Thus, there is no reason that a well-run firm should be overly busy for long.

ORDERS, QUOTES, AND INFORMATION

If you haven't used a discount firm before, then you may find them a bit more hurried and less friendly at first than your current friendly broker. They will not engage you in an extended conversation or tell you the latest jokes. It's not that they are really less friendly. It's just that they don't have time. They are generally polite and efficient. But leisurely banter is one of the amenities that went out when the commissions went down.

If this bothers you, then you might prefer a firm where you deal with a specific broker. Some firms automatically assign a particular account executive to you (see the Order Handling category in the Discount Brokerage Directory). But even where they use a team system, where you're assigned the first account executive who's free, the firm will usually agree to your request to deal with a specific individual. After calling up a few times and talking to different account executives, you should be able to spot those individuals who can handle the pressure of rapid order-taking while still remaining pleasant. Account executives whom you like can certainly make stock investment more pleasant, even if they can't make it more profitable.

Another possibility is to switch from a hurried main office to a branch, if your broker has a branch outside one of the larger cities. They often operate under less pressure, and as a result can be a bit more civilized than the main office.

When placing orders you will find that your orders will be taken slightly faster if stated in the particular sequence which that firm uses, and your quotes will go much faster if you know the stock's symbol in advance. For options, some brokers will also ask the name of the exchange on which the option is trading. None of these matters are earthshaking and won't make much difference unless you're practically a day trader. But they will help business go a bit smoother.

If you're trading stock or options that are not too active, and you need quick follow-up to determine whether your order was executed, note the time and ask for the volume and price range of that day. (How to use this information to track your orders in cases where the broker can't give you a quick report will be described later.)

With many firms you can also request information about your account at this point—the number of shares or options you own, the amount of cash, your debit balance, the latest trade, or other information. This and other information appears on the screen which your account executive sees, or can be pulled up at your request.

He or she is typically seated in a little cubbyhole with a desk in a trading room, rather like stalls in a college library, or around a large table with a number of other account executives. Your order is typically written down on a ticket, or possibly typed directly into an electronic machine, and a shorthand backup copy by hand is recorded in a notebook, called a "blotter," to guard against mistakes.

A further check against errors is the beep you will likely hear from time to time—the familiar signal that the FCC requires to inform the speaker that his or her conversation is being recorded. It is a normal precaution that discounters take to assure that any misunderstandings can be corrected, and no doubt is very effective in discouraging both order-giver and order-taker from making errors. Nonetheless you may well feel at a disadvantage: They have their beeper going and you don't have yours.

Once, I did have a problem that I thought was not receiving proper attention. In a fit of pique, egged on by the discovery of a beeping device on my new telephone answering machine, I decided that if it worked for them it would work for me. I called my broker with my own machine beeping away. By chance, mine was in almost perfect synch with theirs. Every few seconds, mine would beep; then theirs would beep, as if in reply. The broker and I talked back and forth in normal tones, pretending to ignore this electronic dialogue in the background, which sounded like a jam session between extraterrestrials.

I no longer recall what the problem was, but it was speedily resolved and my recording device has been unemployed from that day forth, a tribute to both the low error rate among discounters and the enduring psychic satisfaction of revenge.

Order Follow-up

You've done it. You've placed your order. Now what happens? Virtually any market order placed for a stock trading on the New York Stock Exchange should execute within two minutes of the time that the order reaches the floor of the Exchange. As noted earlier, such orders are normally handled by the Exchange's

DOT computer system and better than 80% of such orders are executed within this two-minute time frame. (The greatest exceptions would be hot stocks with high volatility.) Add one or two minutes for your stock order to be punched into the computer and you will see why this type of order can be executed readily within three to five minutes of the time you place it. However, it usually takes a few more minutes before the report of that execution gets back to your broker.

While the trades on the DOT system are all executed within the same time frame, reporting those trades back to you is another matter. Some brokers can do it within a few minutes; others take quite a bit of time. Many discounters will offer to call you back to report the price at which your trade was executed, but don't sit around your phone waiting for a call back right after you've placed the order. Unless it's a slow day, they're too busy handling incoming trades to give you that callback during trading hours (10 A.M. to 4 P.M. Eastern Standard Time), so the callbacks are usually made after the markets close.

Once you've placed a market order, it's not of any operational significance to know the price or time of execution. You know it must have been executed, since it was a market order, but you can't do anything about the price. However, a limit order is different. You don't know whether it was executed, yet you may have other actions that depend upon its execution. If it was not executed, perhaps you want to change the limit price. If it was executed, perhaps you wish to take some other action, like selling a call or another stock. In these instances, where it is important to find out quickly whether your limit order was executed, you'll have to take some action.

Most of the time, with a good broker, all you need do is call back within a reasonable time. If your limit order is "at the market," where there is reasonable expectation of a quick fill, then you might ask the broker how long he or she thinks it will take to find out whether you were "done." This can vary, depending on the market volume that day, but the brokers are the ones who have the best feel for the current report-back time. If it is especially important to find out quickly whether there has been an execution, let the broker know and he or she may be able to help by keeping an eye out or even calling back.

Sometimes the broker will not get a prompt callback with a report on a limit order for some time. This occurs quite often with options, or on days with high trading volume. I've never been able to pinpoint the cause of such delays. My secret suspicion is that despite their legendary reputation for hard work, almost approaching that of the Japanese, computers take coffee breaks. Be that as it may, you may be left in limbo for an hour with only your own resourcefulness to find out whether your order has been executed.

You begin with one clue. You know that a limit order, unless you specified that you would only accept a minimum number of shares or options contracts, must be executed if the stock or option price pierces your limit. If you followed my earlier suggestion of asking for the price information at the time you placed your trade, then you can often determine whether your order is executed simply by asking the broker to tell you whether his or her quote machine shows that the day's high price (for a sell order) or low price (for a buy order) pierced your limit after your order was placed. Quote machines are usually quite accurate and timely, even when reports on specific trades are not coming back so fast from the floor. If you offered to buy 200 shares at $35, then if the price moved to $35 1/8 after your order went in, your order must have been executed. If not, it violated stock and option exchange rules.

The real pros among you will recognize that this does not tell you what happens if your price was touched, but not pierced. In that situation, you generally can't tell from the price alone whether the shares or contracts trading at the limit price were yours or someone else's whose order was "ahead of you." That is when volume helps. With an inactively traded stock, you can sometimes infer an execution if the daily volume increased by precisely the amount of your order. This is even more practical with options that are not too active, especially if your broker has the type of quote machine that lists the time and amount of each option trade. In that instance, you can be quite confident that an execution in your amount, at your price, occurring around the time you placed your order, was none other than yours.

Another effective, but nasty, way to get a report back on your order is to cancel it. I don't recommend this, don't do it myself, and advise you that spurious cancellations will win you no friends with your broker; but I report what brokers have told me, in the spirit of good reporting. I don't know why cancellation triggers reports on executions so quickly, but I suspect that it has something to do with a combination of exchange rules and irate customers who are legitimately trying to get their order cancelled, and get angry at their broker when they can't. Thus, spurious cancellations ride the coattails of sincere annoyance and get quick treatment.

Let me end this chapter on a high note, for those of you distressed at the nuisance which the above procedures entail, by telling you that there is a very easy and legitimate procedure for handling a variation of the situation described above. Sometimes you really don't need to know whether your order was executed, or need to cancel your order, but simply want to change your limit because the price of the stock has changed. You can do this with a "subject to" order.

I don't know whether that is its real name, or whether there is any name for this type of order, but I do know from experience that brokers will revise the limit price "subject to" execution of the prior order. If you placed your previous order to sell Electrohydrolaser Computer class B at $30\,1/2$ and now want to go to 32 because they have just announced a brand new electrohydrolaser computer, you can do so. If the order has already executed, you can't change it, but if it has not, your limit order price will go up. This is really what you're trying to do anyhow, so you're not hurt by not knowing until later in the day precisely what happened. But be certain to emphasize that this is subject to prior execution, not in addition to. Otherwise you may end up selling the same stock twice.

The final stage of the art of dealing with your broker is your confirmation and monthly reports. These will be addressed in a later chapter.

CHAPTER 7

Features and Services

**GETTING YOUR FRILLS WITH A
NO-FRILLS BROKER**

Once upon a time, discount brokers came without frills. You bought the transactions and paid for everything else. As you know by now, life has changed. Discounters still offer discounts but they also offer frills. You're already familiar with some of these because they've been discussed briefly in earlier chapters. Now I will go into greater depth, analyzing some that especially merit your attention, as well as others that are unique to discounters, like the team account executive system.

Account Executives

An account executive in a discount firm is not to be confused with a broker in a full-commission house. The account executive receives no commission, and that's a big difference. It means no account churning, no unsolicited phone calls, and often, a different type of personality.

Many account executives in discount firms are registered representatives, who have served for a year or two as a commissioned broker. But they didn't like it much, or weren't good at sales. They enjoy dealing with people, but not selling them. Others have never been commissioned brokers. They come out of the operational side of the brokerage firm. They were the people who placed the orders or handled the back-office work for the commissioned sales reps.

It is not the least of the discount broker's benefits that their account executives are not sales reps. Some investors treat registered representatives as advisers whereas in fact their qualifications lie in sales. A bad account executive can sell you bad stocks, and sell them to you often. Or as a financial adviser at a Big Eight accounting firm put it: "The biggest risk in dealing with a registered representative at a full-service firm is that they will offer their advice."

An account executive at a discount firm has a much more restricted role. His or her function is primarily to take orders, accurately, quickly, and politely. Bad ones will at worst be brusque and a bit impolite. Good ones, however, can be very pleasant and helpful in terms of providing a feel for the marketplace, although they will not offer recommendations. But if you're friendly, and he or she doesn't sound too impatient, you can ask about volume, market direction, or what type of stocks people are buying.

Without the restraints and incentives provided by a commission, personality plays a larger role. Full-commission brokers will be friendly, since their bread and butter depends upon it. Discount brokers' do not. Therefore, their behavior depends more on their natural personality, compounded by the pressures of the moment.

The account executive at a discount broker may or may not be a registered representative, who has passed a national securities examination. Some discount firms have a policy of hiring only registered representatives; others do not. In my experience, it makes no difference to the experienced investor, although it is possible that a registered representative could better field the questions that a novice might have. If it matters to you, under Order Handling in the Discount Brokerage

Directory, I noted firms that prefer, or only use, registered representatives.

Discount brokerage firms use one of two account-executive systems: some assign a specific individual as the account executive; others use a team system where any one of a group of account executives may answer the phone and take your order. Some firms use a hybrid system in which they use a team system but will permit you to request and use a specific account executive. Both approaches have their merits; it is really a question of your personal preferences, and, as with full-service firms, the qualities of the particular account executive.

The merits of the assigned account executive system are normally billed as "personalized attention," while those of the account team are said to be "no waiting." The truth is that the account team is probably more for the brokerage houses' convenience than yours. But that doesn't mean that some people won't prefer it.

I have used both systems and find it hard to generalize about which system is better. It depends on the people and the firm. Personally, I have a slight preference for the account executive system with a good account executive. He or she tends to take a more personalized interest, knows your account number, and can run interference with the back office on a bookkeeping problem, or if you're being threatened with a margin call because the mail is slow and your check has not arrived. The account executive may know which stocks you're following and pass on information about them. If you really get friendly, on a slow day, he or she may even tell you jokes and pass on bad tips, just like your regular broker used to do.

A typical conversation with a good account executive might go something like this:
"Good morning, this is Mark Coler calling for John Smith."

A few seconds pause while they put John on. Sometimes, you may be put on hold, but if he is busy, someone else will volunteer to handle your order.

If I had just been calling for a quote, and learned that John was busy, then I might ask whoever answered the phone for that quote. Usually that person is a bit more junior and tries to screen simple quote requests.

"Good morning, Mark, How are you?"

"Not bad, are you getting rich on those Merrill calls you bought?"

"Not yet, but I'm working on it."

"Well before you get too rich to talk to me, how's the market doing?"

"A bit slow, only 20 million shares so far today. We did almost 30 million at this time yesterday. What can I do for you?"

"Where is Amerada? I am interested in the stock and the February 30 calls."

"Amerada, let's see. Do you know the symbol and what exchange the options trade on?"

"The symbol is AHC and the exchange is Philly, I think." (The Philadelphia Options Exchange.).

"Let me try that." A pause while he tries the symbol on his quote machine. "Yes, that's right."

From there on, John and I will exchange primarily factual information concerning the bid, volume, and price range. The conversation will conclude with my stating the order precisely, and John reading it back to me as written.

A conversation with a firm that uses a team system would be a bit different. You are assigned an account number and your order is taken by one of a group of people who answer the phones. If you are placing orders frequently, you will get to know who the different people are.

I dial my 800- number toward noon, and get a recorded announcement: "Hello. Thank you for calling Union Brokerage Services. We're sorry, all of our representatives are busy right now. But if you'll stay on the line, someone will be with you as soon as possible."

Thirty or 45 seconds after this recorded announcement, a representative picks up the line. "Hello, Union Brokerage, this is Mary speaking. Can I help you?"

"Yes, I would like to place an order. My account number is 058-968-454."

Other firms might ask for my name first. This particular firm works from the account number. A pause follows while they check the account number in their computer banks. One or two of the representatives will know my voice but the others will have to check to be sure.

Everything You Ever Wanted to Know . . .

"Is this Mark Coler?"

"Yes, it is."

"How can I help you?"

"Can you give me the price of IBM, please."

"Yes, the price is 121 and $1/4$."

"Can you give me bid, asked, and size please?"

"Yes, bid is 121 to 121 $1/2$. Size is 25 by 100."

"Thank you, I would like to place an order."

"Does this cancel or replace a previous order?"

"No, it does not."

The order procedure will then proceed along the lines previously described. At the end, the representative will inquire:

"Would you like us to call back with a report if anything is done on the trade?"

"Yes, please. You can reach me at (212) 343-4721."

"Thank you, Mr. Coler."

While individual firms differ, these conversations may give some of the flavor of dealing with two types of discount houses. The first firm uses an account executive system with a good account executive. The latter, a relatively impersonal firm with a team system. Many discounters may fall somewhere between.

You will note that in both cases, the order placing process is a bit more direct, to the point, than with a normal broker. That reflects what we have said about the working environment in a discount firm. They are there primarily to place orders efficiently, and unless it's a slow day, you're expected to place them promptly.

You will also note the request for the stock symbol and option exchange. Discount brokers usually ask you about the symbol of the stock that you are trading. If you don't have it they'll look it up, but it goes faster all around if you do. If you're placing orders often, and don't know the symbols, you can ask them to send you a Standard and Poor's book or other reference that lists symbols.

The request for the name of the exchange arises solely in options trading. There are four principal option exchanges. With some types of quotation equipment, it is necessary to know the exchange in order to enter the request for option quotes. You can find out the exchange by just checking your morning paper.

In theory a team system is faster. In fact, it probably is a bit faster, but not much. In a well-run account-executive system firm, the account executives will cover each other's clients when they're busy, although the degree of enthusiasm may vary and service levels are prone to a decline when your account executive is on vacation.

In truth it probably doesn't matter a great deal which type of firm you use unless you're very active, very sociable, or very antisocial. If you're the kind of person who doesn't like to leave messages on an answering machine, you probably won't like to leave orders with an impersonal team-system firm. On the other hand, if you habitually snarl at your dog in the morning or just don't feel you have time for small talk, you may be better off with the more impersonal approach of the team system.

SIPC Insurance

One of the more civilizing developments in the brokerage industry has been the advent of the Securities Investor Protection Corporation. To be sure, it takes some of the thrill out of knowing whether you will get you money back if the ABC Brokerage House goes under. But it does make life a bit more relaxed knowing that a quasi-governmental agency with a deep pocket stands behind ABC Securities in the event of a problem.

Whether you are dealing with a discount house or a nondiscount house, you should be dealing with one that is insured by SIPC. If they are dealing with the public, they should be insured. SIPC insurance can be identified by the SIPC symbol which normally appears on the letterhead, or in the application forms that you will receive.

SIPC is inexpensive to join. The fees are nominal, and accordingly there is no material cost to you in dealing with a firm that is a member. It is an inexpensive but, I believe, necessary form of insurance in dealing with any brokerage house.

The Securities Investor Protection Corporation was created by an act of Congress: The Securities Investor Protection Act of 1970. The impetus for the creation of the corporation was the paperwork crisis which overtook the industry at that time. With the peaking of the market in mid-1969, the volume of trading rose to levels which were overloading the back offices of the brokerage firms.

In those days volume averaged 11 to 12 million shares per day, about the volume during the first half-hour of a typical opening today. But without computers, it was crushing and placed a strain with which many of the back offices were unable to cope. Coming at a time when the market was falling sharply, the apparent inability of many houses to keep up with their paperwork alarmed the already jittery public. It created the appearance that the market was getting out of control, and that brokerage houses might be in worse financial condition than they were acknowledging.

Nor was it strictly for appearances. The trading system creates an interlocking network of credits and balances owed between firms as a result of their trades. If a few large firms were in serious difficulty, but delays in the back office slowed disclosure of this condition, then other firms trading with them could be dragged down too—the domino effect.

So in 1970, Congress passed an act that created SIPC. While the Securities Investor Protection Corporation is not an actual member of the family of government agencies, it is certainly a first cousin. It is run by a seven-member board of directors. Five of these, including the chairman and vice-chairman, are appointed directly by the President of the United States with the approval of the Senate. The two remaining board members are appointed from the U.S. Treasury Department and the Federal Reserve Board.

The Securities and Exchange Commission has certain oversight and regulatory functions with respect to SIPC. Its operations and financial conditions are also reviewed by another organization with statutorily delegated authority, the National Association of Securities Dealers, Inc. (NASD).

In the event that SIPC must cover a default by a member firm, it can look to several sources for its financing. First, it has acquired a fund over the past decade through contributions from its broker-dealer members. That fund is maintained at a minimum level of $150 million through occasional assessments against gross revenues and a nominal membership charge. Changes currently in the works may shortly increase this minimum.

This should be more than adequate to cover any default by even a large broker. But if it is not, and additional funds are necessary to protect customers and maintain confidence in the United States securities markets, the Corporation may draw down up to $1 billion from the U.S. Treasury. To repay this loan, SIPC has statutory authority to impose a kind of tax on securities trading.

SIPC Insurance is carried by virtually every firm that will buy stocks for the public and insures up to $500,000 at present. This coverage applies to each account that you have with separate brokers. Thus, if you have $500,000 with broker A and $500,000 with broker B, your total SIPC coverage would equal $1,000,000.

This $500,000 coverage will cover securities or any combination of cash and securities provided that the cash component does not exceed $100,000. Thus, if you have $500,000 in securities with a firm, you are covered. If you have $400,000 in securities and $100,000 in cash, you are covered.

However, if you had $110,000 in cash and $390,000 in securities, you might lose $10,000 because the insurance would only cover the first $100,000. This limitation is apparently designed to keep SIPC's cash coverage in line with that provided by government agencies for banks and savings and loan associations. So your cash with a bank is insured to the extent of $100,000 and your funds with a broker are insured to the same level.

If cash left with your broker is placed with a money fund associated with your broker, rather than left as a free credit balance in the account itself, this would not be subject to the $100,000 limit. Therefore, you could leave more than $100,000 with your broker, provided you limit the account balance to $100,000—which you would want to do in any event because interest rates in money funds are usually higher.

In the case of an actual bankruptcy, your coverage in practice would be a bit broader than the insurance limits suggest. One reason is that the cash assets of the defaulting brokerage house would be divided up first, before the $100,000 insurance protection was invoked.

Another is that any stocks with the broker that were registered in your name, or in the process of being registered, would legally be yours. You would only need the insurance to cover those stocks which were not registered in your name—which were held in "street name."

Finally, if you have a margin account with $700,000, of which $200,000 was purchased with funds borrowed from the brokerage house on margin, you would be fully covered. SIPC would look to the net balance, $700,000 less $500,000, and cover that $500,000 debit.

For most readers, the least of your concerns is whether you can safely keep $100,000 in cash, let alone $500,000 in securities in your account. But I have treated these aspects in detail to show that you really have a great deal of leeway in terms of the insurance protection afforded the account. This shall be discussed later in connection with the desirability of taking delivery of securities that you purchase.

While SIPC has never failed to cover losses in a bankruptcy, it has not always covered itself with glory by the speed with which it has wound up affairs. Especially in the case of the larger bankruptcies, it has taken months and, in some instances, over a year to give investors their securities back. During this time, the securities are frozen with the investor unable to sell them. In a declining market, this can be a serious problem. The stock which was worth 50 at the time of bankruptcy might be down to 35 when you got the securities back. (Of course, in a rising market, it might be the other way around.) Responding to this criticism, SIPC has initiated steps which are expected to lead to automatic liquidation of all option positions, the most volatile of securities. Other changes are afoot which will, hopefully, cause SIPC to add future speed to current certainty.

Additional Insurance

If you are an individual investor, it is unlikely that you will be concerned that $500,000 insurance is insufficient. But if you are managing a corporate or fiduciary account, that may well be a concern. If so, then you will be pleased to learn that many discount houses do provide additional insurance typically up to $2.5 million, higher in some instances. This additional insurance is normally issued by an insurance company, like Aetna or Continental. The added insurance functions as back-up insurance. When the SIPC insurance level is exceeded, the secondary insurance company provides the balance up to its stated coverage amount.

If you are concerned with the coverage of this insurance, or any of the other features which I will discuss in this chapter, you can find out what each firm offers by checking out the firm profile, and having your lawyer review the scope of the additional coverage. I suggest a lawyer because if you are concerned with $2.5 million coverage, you're not too concerned with paying a lawyer.

Advisory Support Services

This section really deserves a chapter in itself, and so I gave it one. Chapter 3 discussed the variety of ways in which you may receive professional assistance in selecting your equity investments. These include general financial publications that carry recommendations, advisory service newsletters that provide both generalized advice about market timing and specific advice about market selection, and other services. You may wish to review that chapter if you currently rely on your broker's recommendations in selecting stocks.

Most discount firms don't provide much by way of investment advice, but a few provide a surprising amount, newsletters, and discount commissions too.

Types of Orders

The average investor is acquainted with two orders: buy and sell. And every investor with a bit of experience knows that he or she can place an order to buy General General at 35, or sell it at 40, without realizing that a limit order is being placed, with a 35 or 40 limit.

If you have done a bit if trading, you know the difference between a day order and a good-till-cancelled order. These are both self-explanatory. The day order is removed from the books at the end of each day. The good-till-cancelled order (G.T.C.) stays on the books until it is cancelled. You can usually use both although some exchanges do not permit G.T.C. orders for option spread transactions.

The placing of a trade is really an art. It is far more complicated than the simplicity of a buy or sell would suggest. A professional will never place an order without getting bid, asked, and size (the amount of stock offered on the asked side and demanded on the bid side). He or she will seldom use a good-till-cancelled order, and will not routinely use market orders—the most familiar order to the novice investor.

If you are an infrequent investor, it does not matter which type of orders a particular brokerage house accepts, since all will accept the basic types of orders described above. But if you are an advanced investor or trader, there are some types of orders that not all firms will handle. You should check to be sure that the firm you are using offers the full complement.

For example, some firms do not like to "work" some of the more exotic orders. So if you are an aficionado of exotica, such as not-held trades where your broker is expected to exercise a certain amount of discretion, check to be certain that the house will handle them. Similarly, with respect to spread transactions in options, some houses will accept spreads on a G.T.C. basis; some only if they're close to the market; some, not at all. In short, *caveat expert:* Let the expert beware that some firms won't handle his favorite exotica.

Of significance to a growing number of people are the premiums imposed on certain orders by some firms. Check the Special Features and Additional Charges categories of the firms listed in the Discount Brokerage Directory to ascertain whether the firm imposes an additional charge for limit or G.T.C. orders, or offers an additional discount for day trades, 30-day round trips, or the like. It may help you to make or save a few shekels.

Quotation Lines—A Pet Favorite

This is a service unique to discounters, and not many of them at that, but it's one of my favorite little frills. A quotation line is a special number that you can call, usually a toll-free 800-number, where you can get several quotes on the stock, option, or bond of your choice.

If you tried to buy this service, it could cost you $500 per month. That is the approximate cost of a quotation machine that will provide current quotations. To be sure, it would be better than a quote line if you're a pro, but not much for normal investors; and then again, a quote machine is helpful only when you're sitting with it in your office. If your office is located in a city where the machine can be installed, the cost is $5000 per year.

In a very small number of cities, you can buy a portable quote machine, which is good, but lags the market by 15 minutes, does not cover all types of markets, and only provides limited types of quotations. Cost: $600 per year.

With a quote line, you can call from anywhere—a client's office, your home, or any phone booth. You can call in 10 times a day if you like (and if you trade with some frequency so that you're not labeled a quote abuser), subject only to a quotation limit of say five quotes per call. With a quote line, you will have available to you the same information as practically any broker in any full-commission house in the country. Cost: free.

Sure, you can call other discount brokers and ask for quotes. If you are calling once per day and asking for four to five quotes, this may not be a problem. But if you are calling frequently or, heaven forbid, calling a full-commission broker for quotes, you may find that two irresistible pressures to buy will be brought to bear. Guilt and greed could combine to make this a very expensive call.

But the quote line. That is free. This wonderful service will be around as long as too many investors don't give their account numbers out to too many brothers-in-law who call in too many times and make the discounters who offer it decide that it is too expensive.

THE PRICE OF PROGRESS

The rise of the discount broker has not been completely without its costs. One casualty is the disappearance of the old style board room, a victim of high rents.

In the old days, you used to be able to sit around and watch the electric ticker tape go by in the front of the room. To the trader, watching his or her stock offered the thrill of the racetrack. But to the unitiated, the repetitive figures on the tape had a hypnotically calming effect. It could make the benighted observer, like the eight-year-old that I was at the time, wonder at the cause of all the commotion in the room with this magical machine.

I remember best the board rooms in Florida where my grandfather wintered. They hummed with activity and diverse characters, retired people, traders, and a few passersby drawn by the lighted sign outside which recorded the hourly peregrinations of the Dow Jones Average. It was like the local neighborhood drugstore, a watering hole, with the comfortingly predictable cast of characters—the regulars always there.

Once the board room was literally a board room. Clerks would rush back and forth jotting down prices in chalk on a large board set up in front of the room. This was succeeded by the electric ticker tape, which itself was replaced by the electronic screen.

Now, in discount houses at least, the board room itself is gone or reduced to efficient but inhospitable dimensions. At $50 per square foot in some cities, few discounters can afford the board room. Even full-commission brokers have trimmed down the seating in their board rooms to a few token seats.

So if you are looking for a friendly, warm place, like the neighborhood drugstore, to spend some time on a winter's day, don't check the discount houses. Like the counter at your neighborhood drugstore, the board room is disappearing. Progress is not without its price.

CHAPTER 8

Frills

Do you consider margin a dirty word? Is it synonymous with irresponsibility or worse? Does it suggest gamblers losing bets and losing their shirts?

Would it surprise you to know that margin is probably the least expensive form of financing available to most consumers in the United States today? Properly used (an important caveat), it can be a very valuable tool.

MARGIN

Margin is a loan made to you by the brokerage house, using your stocks or bonds as collateral to guarantee repayment. Just as a bank will give you a mortgage for an amount equal to 70 or 80% of the value of your house, so will the brokerage house lend you a specified percentage of the value of your securities.

In general, discount brokerage firms offer margin on much the same terms as full-commission houses. Discounters as a group are no bargain here because the discount house must pay the same terms as any other brokerage firm to borrow the funds to cover your margin loans.

However, some discount firms offer exceptional values—as much as 2 to 3% below other full-commission firms or other discount firms. You can find which ones these are by looking at the listing for Margin Interest Costs in the Discount Brokerage Directory. This listing gives you detailed borrowing rates for each firm for every level of borrowing.

The percentage of the value of the securities that the firm is permitted to lend to you is established, in a general way, by the Federal Reserve Board. From time to time the Board will change this percentage. Typically, it might be 50% of the initial value of exchange listed stocks, 50 to 70% for corporate bonds, and 90% for Treasury bills.

Assuming that your portfolio consists of $10,000 in stock, $10,000 in corporate bonds, and $10,000 in government bonds, then you would be able to borrow $5000 on your stocks, $7000 on your corporate bonds, and $9000 on your Treasury bills. That is a total loan of $21,000 on securities worth $30,000.

This is the cheapest loan you are likely to find unless you have a rich and amiable relative. In March 1990, for example, you would pay an interest rate of about 9–11% for this loan, depending on which broker you used and the actual size of the loan—it generally gets cheaper when the loan gets larger.

Let's do some comparison shopping to see what you would have paid elsewhere. First, let us try to get a loan from our local bank. The prime rate at the major banks on this day was 10. But, the prime is the rate that is charged only to the bank's biggest and best customers, so you are likely to pay $1\,1/2$ to $2\,1/2\%$ over prime, since you are not General Motors.

So instead of 12%, you will probably pay $12\,1/2$–14%. Then, there may be some hidden fees on top of that. For example, you may have to pay a one time 1% financing fee, or something similar. And some banks might ask you for compensating balances—a polite way to describe your money in their account without interest.

That is the type of bank loan you might be able to get on a large or well-secured borrowing. Normally, it's much more than that. For example, I have an overdraft line with Citicorp. This is basically an unsecured loan. The rate of interest that Citicorp charged on this same date was about 18%.

Nor is the Citicorp rate out of line. If you borrowed on your credit card, for example, or paid your charges late, you would pay that rate, if not higher. Eighteen percent was about the correct rate for unsecured consumer loans. A consumer finance company would charge considerably more.

Of course, this assumes that you can get a bank loan. An old saw says that banks only lend to people who don't need the money. This may be a bit harsh on bankers, but it's not far from the truth. With collateral you should be able to get a loan, but at best, a bank loan is a time-consuming process.

So unless you have some special term-lending facilities available, a company loan program, or an insurance policy with loan value for example, you are unlikely to be able to borrow anywhere else at the same rate.

For ease of borrowing, nothing matches a margin loan. You simply instruct your broker to put your securities in a margin account, sign your name to a routine margin form, and the funds will be advanced.

Furthermore, unlike virtually every other form of loan, there is no repayment schedule. As long as your securities do not fall sharply in value, you simply pay interest. That is automatically deducted by your broker each month and the amount of the charge shows up on your monthly reports. It is an eternal loan.

Two aspects of the margin loan have given it a bad name. First, when you place your stocks in a margin account, the brokerage firm has a claim on your securities in much the same way that a bank has a mortgage on your home. To secure the ability to execute its claim, the brokerage firm places your securities in street name. This means they are technically an asset of the brokerage firm until you withdraw the securities from the margin account.

From a legal standpoint, this is really not much different from making a deposit with a bank. When you place your money with a bank, it technically becomes the bank's money. You then have a claim against the bank for the amount that you deposited.

Everything You Ever Wanted to Know . . .

But if the bank should go bankrupt before you withdrew your money, then you could lose it.

In the bad old days, brokerage firms were shakier than banks, and the banks, before FDIC insurance, were a bit shaky themselves. Since securities in a margin account are considered an asset of the firm, then if the firm goes down, your securities go with it. This did little to enhance the popularity of margin accounts.

Since the advent of the Securities Investor Protection Act of 1970, however, brokerage accounts have been insured. While investors could experience inconvenience, and delays in releasing the securities could be a problem in declining markets, the securities are not in jeopardy within the insured limits.

The other reason margin has gotten a bad name is through people who borrow on margin to the hilt. There are certain circumstances where it actually makes sense to borrow almost every last dollar, but generally it does not, unless you're prepared to calmly liquidate your stocks in the event that you receive a margin call.

The margin call occurs when there is a sharp decline in the value of your securities. Then the amount of coverage on your loan declines below prescribed limits and the brokerage firm is required under Federal law to ask you to put up additional collateral to compensate for the decline. If you were unable to do so within a reasonable period of time, they would be required to sell whatever amount of stocks is necessary in order to reduce the margin loan to the percentages specified by the Federal Reserve Board. If you are margined to the hilt, and the stocks fall sharply, this is your fate. The broker has no choice.

But don't let this prospect prevent you from taking advantage of perhaps the biggest bargain in the loan market. Just don't be greedy. If you borrow the maximum, then it would not take a very great decline in the stock market to reach the point where you must put up extra funds, or be sold out of your stocks. But if you borrow modestly, 10 to 25% instead of 50 to 70%, then your risk of being forced out of your stocks by a market decline is small, since it would take a huge decline to create a margin call. For example, if you borrow 10%, then your stock would have to decline by something like 80% in value to force a margin call.

That would be equivalent to a 1000-point decline in the Dow-Jones Industrial Average!

Even borrowing to the hilt can be a prudent coarse of action. Let us suppose that I can borrow $10,000 at any time from a bank overdraft line or a credit card. Or I could borrow $10,000 from my broker by borrowing close to the maximum. Which makes more sense?

The answer is borrowing to the hilt. The reason is that I'm only going to pay my broker 10 to 11% interest (in the current market) whereas the rate on the overdraft or credit cards is around 18%. Borrowing from my broker, I will save about 7% or $700 per year. There will never be a margin call if my stocks go up, stay the same, or go down slightly. If they go down sharply, I still have my overdraft and credit cards to meet the margin call. Even in this worst-case scenario I'll at least have saved interest during the time before my stocks dropped.

This approach really works, as long as you use the borrowed money to meet cash needs. If used to buy more stocks, then it is no longer borrowing but speculation. In that case, your hot stock tips had better be hot.

If you're interested in considering margin, then you will want to know the current margin rate. This rate is normally equal to a money market rate, known as broker's call, plus a surcharge imposed by the lending institution. This parallels the practice in the banking industry, where the rate you pay is equal to prime plus a specific percentage. Since the broker normally has to pay the current broker's call rate to obtain the money that is lent to you, his or her profit is earned through the spread, the surcharge.

This surcharge is generally based on a graduated scale. The more funds borrowed, the lower the surcharge. Thus, for example, you might pay 2% for the first $10,000, 1 1/2% for the next $20,000 borrowed, and so forth. Usually, the surcharge drops to less than 1% for sums in excess of $50,000. The surcharge which each broker imposes is listed in the profile, in the Margin Interest Cost category in the Discount Brokerage Directory.

Now that you know the surcharge, you need to find out the current broker's call rate. Papers with financial sections generally have a little box somewhere labeled "money rates" or something similar. There, among the other listings for CDs, Fed Funds and the like, you will find broker's call. (Prime rate is listed here too, useful for that occasional brokerage house whose surcharge is applied to prime instead of broker's call.) You will note that broker's call is normally below prime, and listed as a range rather than a single rate, for example $9 １/２$ to $10 １/２\%$. Unless otherwise specified, you may safely assume that brokers will base their rates on the high end of this range.

Any margin interest you pay is tax deductible up to $10,000. Amounts in excess of that are not deductible in a single year against ordinary income, but may be used to offset other investment income.

Two fine points could raise minor complications on your tax returns. First, if you have government securities in your margin account, the interest that you pay with respect to those securities is deductible against Federal tax but probably not against your state tax. Second, you should be certain that no municipal securities are placed in your margin account, and that you do not create the appearance of borrowing from margin specifically to buy municipal bonds. In the first case, the IRS will disallow the margin interest deduction. In the second instance, they may disallow the margin interest deduction if a causal relationship is established between the margin loan and the bond purchase, that is, you borrowed to buy the bond.

INTEREST

The previous section discussed how much interest you pay to the brokerage house for borrowing their money. Here, I will talk a bit about the amount of interest that the brokerage house pays you for the use of your money.

Did you know that income on clients' credit balances is one of the largest sources of income for the major brokerage firms? In some years, this interest has surpassed commissions as the major source of income. Unless you want to do your bit to strengthen the bottom line of your broker's financial statement, it pays to keep your eye on your credit balances to make sure that they are earning interest.

As noted earlier, in discussing the First and Second Laws of Transfer, watching your credit balance begins with making sure that you get timely credit for deposits. During the day that I wrote this section, I made six phone calls, trying to find out why a prominent broker had not credited my account with $20,000 transferred to them 11 days ago from another account within the same branch of the same bank. Last month, they were unable to locate another large check for which they had given me a receipt. I have never found them to make a similar error in my favor. But perhaps there is justice in all this, because this prominent broker is a full-commission broker. I don't use their trading services but find their cash management account convenient and have been too lazy to date to switch.

Assuming that the money has been properly credited to your brokerage account, you will receive interest at one of three different rates: credit balance rates, money fund rates, or zero. To avoid the zero rate, don't leave funds in your account unless your broker pays interest on free credit balances. These are simply funds left in your brokerage account. Some pay zero on these funds; others pay a credit balance rate, like 5 to 6%, at least on funds above a certain minimum level. The third rate is the highest—the money fund rate. This is currently below 10% but in high interest periods it has exceeded 15%. Most brokerage firms either have their own in-house money funds or can transfer your funds into an associated money fund if you ask for it. Ask for it! Where else will you earn extra cash so easily?

Opening an account is easy. You receive a prospectus that describes the fund and various signature cards. You will also likely receive a choice of added conveniences, like a telephonic transfer which permits you to transfer funds back and forth between your money fund and your bank account.

If you keep a fair amount of money with your broker, and are in a high tax bracket to boot, then you might ask whether they have a tax-free money fund, which sometimes pays a slightly higher posttax rate. There is not much point in shopping between your broker's money fund and others, since most funds earn their income in similar ways, are subject to similar governmentally imposed limitations on their expenses, and therefore offer roughly the same yield.

Now that you know about the three types of rates, the trick to learn is how to keep your funds earning the best of them. First, ask whether your brokerage firm automatically transfers your credit balances or not. Some firms, for example, will sweep balances in excess of $500 into a money fund each week. If they do not, then it's up to you to regularly move your cash balance into the right accounts. Even if your broker promises to keep an eye on your cash balance, remember that he or she is pretty busy. Check it out yourself.

However, if you find that a large sum of money has been allowed to remain in a non-interest bearing account for an extended period of time, despite your instructions to the contrary, don't be afraid to complain. And don't stop with lodging a complaint. Ask for reimbursement of your lost interest. This is one area where you may well succeed in securing the brokerage firm's voluntary agreement to reimburse you.

In this type of situation, you have a good chance of being reimbursed. The reason is not legal, but economic. This is not a zero-sum game in which your gain is their loss. For in this case, the brokerage firm was actually earning money on your funds. You are simply asking them to return the interest that they were earning on *your* money. I once got a client a $1000 reimbursement when his brokerage firm made this kind of error. Come to think of it, the firm is the very same one making the same error on my deposit today. It's not hard to see why they earn so much interest each year.

CUSTODIAL SERVICE

Virtually all brokerage firms, discount and nondiscount, will hold your securities for you. Most investors would be well advised to leave their securities with their broker for safekeeping. It is quite safe and much easier. Having securities delivered to you is cumbersome and may involve an additional delivery charge.

In normal times, it is hard to see any good reason why investors would want to take delivery of securities, unless they simply wish to keep their assets private or feel better with them in their own bank vault than in their brokers'. These securities are insured up to $500,000 by SIPC, and if not left in a margin account, are legally segregated from the broker's securities and not subject to the claims of creditors, even in a bankruptcy. They're also less likely to be lost.

REPORTING

The basic reporting requirements are mandated by Federal regulatory requirements. Therefore, you will receive roughly the same two forms from any broker. The first is a small rectangular slip that you receive after each trade. This slip is usually known as a confirm, since it is a confirmation that a trade was executed. It is typically accompanied by a carbon copy which you remit to the broker with payment if you have made a purchase.

The second is the report on your holdings and trades executed during the past month. Not surprisingly, this is known as the monthly report. While the confirm has probably not changed much, the computer has made the monthly report an increasingly readable and valuable document.

The computer has made possible the inclusion on the monthly report of all types of additional information that would not previously have been practical to include. For example, the valuation of each stock in your portfolio and of the total portfolio is included. It has become increasingly common to list equity value, dividends and interest for the year to date, and assorted other information such as current yield on bonds.

There is a fair degree of variation in the format of the monthly report, made possible by the flexibility of the computer. If you are undecided among several brokers, you might ask each to send you a copy of the monthly report. With a large account, some reporting formats are distinctly more clear and informative than others.

Confirms are a different story. The important point is not whether they are readable, but rather that you read them. You should look at the confirm as soon as it is received. You will note somewhere on the back of the confirm, in the fine print, a statement that you should report errors as soon as possible, and that all trades will be considered final if you have not reported an error within that time. Many firms will also offer telephone confirmations which is convenient, and may help spot simple execution mistakes, but they are not legally binding.

Whether or not this fine print is really legally binding on you, it is a very good idea to report any errors promptly. This is simply a practical matter. A mistake reported quickly has a better chance of being settled amicably because the market has not had much time to change. It would take a very understanding broker to agree to delete a purchase claimed to be in error 30 days later, after the stock had dropped $10.

So you should certainly read the information on the front of the confirm quickly. But too much reading could prove to be a bad thing. If you read the fine print on the back of the original confirm, printed in nearly invisible ink, and hidden between the original confirm and the carbon copy, you may quit trading and take up something safer, like knitting. It informs you of matters such as the firm's right to sell off your securities without notice to cover monies due, to lend your securities to other brokerage houses (if not registered in your name), and that your check is not considered paid until the proceeds are received.

This is a clear case of legal overkill. The attorneys drafting the provisions have given the brokerage houses so much authority that, taken at face value, they would preclude you from buying stocks. As far as I can tell, the conditions spelled out on the back are impossible to comply with, at least if you're counting on the New York City mail to get your check there on time. I once made a calculation and decided that if I mailed a check the day I received my confirm, and they cashed it the day it arrived, it would clear five business days *after* they had the right to liquidate my stock. But since I've never had a broker do this, I can only suppose that they are a bit more reasonable than their attorneys.

OTHER SERVICES

A variety of other services are offered by discount brokers. These include discounts on business publications, commission rebates that are available toward the rental of quotation machines, and other services. Some are quite intriguing. Others are the industry's equivalent of banking's free toasters with each deposit.

OTHER INVESTMENTS

The "financial supermarket" concept which has taken hold with the major conventional brokerage firms has increasingly spread to the discount houses. If you choose, a discount house will bombard you with the same type of investment opportunities that any conventional firm will.

Depending upon the firm, these include IRAs, Keogh plans, municipal bonds, oil drilling programs, real estate investments, and whatever other types of investments are currently in vogue. My casual observation has been that those offered by discount houses are neither perceptibly better nor worse than those offered by conventional firms.

I could list them all, but why do so? You bought this book to learn how to save a great deal of money without compromising quality. Perhaps even improve it. Now you know how to do this, using a discount broker. But when it comes to other investments, discounters can't save you 70% off. They're neither less nor more expensive than anyone else. When the author can no longer help you do it better or cheaper, it's time to stop writing and move on.

CHAPTER 9

SIPC Protection

One of the factors which makes discount stock brokerage so attractive is the Securities Investor Protection Corporation which provides insurance protection up to $500,000 for stock investors.

The following is reprinted from the November 1988 edition of a brochure provided to the public by SIPC, (SIPC, Securities Investor Protection Corporation. 1988. *How SIPC Protects You.* Washington, DC).

FOREWORD

The Securities Investor Protection Corporation (SIPC) protects customers of registered securities broker-dealers, thereby promoting confidence in United States securities markets. Though created by the Securities Investor Protection Act of 1970 (15 U.S.C. § 78aaa et seq., as amended), SIPC is neither a government agency nor a regulatory authority. It is a nonprofit, membership corporation, funded by its member securities broker-dealers.

This text answers the most frequently asked questions about how claims are satisfied when securities customers of a member need SIPC protection. Of course, SIPC does not protect against losses from the rise or fall in market value of your investment. It does, however, provide important protections against certain losses if an SIPC member fails financially and is unable to meet obligations to its securities customers.

While providing a basic explanation, this (booklet) does not offer definitive answers to questions about specific situations. Such answers depend upon interpretations, administrative decisions and court actions.

NO PERSON MAY BY ANY REPRESENTATION, INTERPRETATION OR OTHERWISE AFFECT THE EXTENT OF THE COVERAGE PROVIDED CUSTOMERS' ACCOUNTS BY THE ACT OR THE RULES ADOPTED THEREUNDER BY SIPC OR THE SEC.

November, 1988
Third Edition

BASIC PROTECTION

1. What is SIPC's basic protection?

SIPC protects securities customers of member broker-dealers. If a member fails financially, SIPC may ask a federal court to appoint a trustee to liquidate the firm and protect its customers, or, in limited situations involving smaller firms, SIPC may protect the customers directly. In both cases, protection of securities customers is similar.

The trustee and SIPC may arrange to have some or all customer accounts transferred to another SIPC member broker-dealer. Customers whose accounts are transferred are notified promptly and permitted to deal with the new firm or subsequently transfer their accounts to firms of their own choosing. Accounts so transferred are subject to the limitations of protection discussed below. This procedure minimizes disruption in customers' trading activities. In many cases (for example, where

Everything You Ever Wanted to Know . . . 415

failed firms' records are inaccurate), account transfers are not feasible. SIPC then protects customer accounts in the following manner:

Customers of a failed firm receive all securities registered in their names or in the process of being so registered and which are not by endorsement or otherwise in negotiable form.

Customers receive, on a pro rata basis, all remaining customer cash and securities held by the firm.

After the above distribution, SIPC's funds are available to satisfy the remaining claims of each customer up to a maximum of $500,000, including up to $100,000 on claims for cash (as distinct from claims for securities). When a customer has sold a security, any claim with respect to that transaction would be subject to the $100,000 limit of protection for cash.

Any remaining assets after payment of liquidation expenses may be available to satisfy any remaining portion of customers' claims on a pro rata basis with other creditors.

2. *Who is a "customer" protected under the Act?*

"Customers" are persons with claims for securities received, acquired or held by the firm from or for the securities accounts of such persons for safekeeping, with a view to sale, to cover consummated sales, pursuant to purchases, as collateral security, or for purposes of effecting a transfer. Persons who have cash on deposit with a firm for the purpose of purchasing securities or as a result of sales thereof are also considered "customers."

Cash on deposit with an SIPC member for the purpose of earning interest or for any purpose other than purchasing securities is neither included within a customer's "net equity" nor protected under the Act (see question 3).

A person is not considered a "customer" under the Act to the extent that his claim (a) is for cash or securities which, by contract, agreement, or understanding, or by operation of law, is part of the capital of the firm or is subordinated to the claims of creditors of the firm, or (b) arises out of transactions with a foreign subsidiary of the firm (see question 18 for a discussion of customers who are ineligible to receive money from SIPC).

3. What property does SIPC protect?

Customers' cash and securities. Most types of securities, such as notes, stocks, bonds and certificates of deposit, are covered. No protection, however, is provided for unregistered investment contracts or for any interest in gold, silver or other commodity, or commodity contract, or commodity option. It is important to remember, however, that SIPC protection does not cover decline in the market value of securities.

Cash balances are protected under the Securities Investor Protection Act if the money was deposited or left in a securities account for the purpose of purchasing securities. This is true whether or not the broker pays interest on the cash balances. Of course, cash balances maintained solely for the purpose of earning interest are not protected.

SIPC presumes that cash balances are left in securities accounts for the purpose of purchasing securities. It would require substantial evidence to the contrary to overcome this presumption. Standing alone, the fact that a cash balance was earning interest and was not used to purchase securities for a considerable period of time, say several months, would not be sufficient to overcome the presumption.

4. What are protected "securities?"

In addition to notes, stocks, bonds, debentures and certificates of deposit, for the purposes of applying SIPC protection, the term "security" also includes any publicly registered investment contract or certificate of participation or interest in any profit-sharing agreement or in any oil, gas, or mineral royalty or lease. Additionally, warrants or rights to purchase, sell or subscribe to the securities mentioned above and any other instrument commonly referred to as a security are protected under SIPA.

5. Does SIPC protect money market funds?

Shares of money market funds, although often thought of by investors as cash, are in fact securities when such funds are organized as mutual funds. When held by an SIPC member in a customer's securities account, such fund shares are protected as any other covered security.

Everything You Ever Wanted to Know . . .

6. Why is cash protection limited to $100,000?

Three Federal Government agencies have similar limitations on cash claims: the Federal Deposit Insurance Corporation established by Congress in 1933 to insure bank deposits; the Federal Savings and Loan Insurance Corporation established by Congress in 1934; and, the National Credit Union Administration's share insurance program authorized in October 1970. All limit cash protection to $100,000.

7. May a customer have protected accounts with more than one SIPC member?

Yes. The accounts with each SIPC member are protected within the limits described (in this booklet).

8. May a customer have more than one protected account with the same SIPC member?

Yes, where a customer holds accounts with the same SIPC member in separate capacities. For example, if he deals with the member for himself and also maintains accounts as a trustee for another person under certain trust arrangements, he would be deemed a different customer in each capacity. A customer having several different accounts must be acting in a good faith separate capacity with respect to each.

An investor might, for example, have one account in his or her name and maintain a joint account with his or her spouse, providing each possesses authority to act with respect to the entire account.

All such accounts, however, must meet the requirements of SIPC rules identifying accounts of "separate" customers of SIPC members. Copies of these rules may be obtained by writing to SIPC and requesting the "Series 100 Rules."

A person who in a **single** capacity has several different accounts with the same firm, for example, cash and margin, would be considered a single customer for purposes of applying the $500,000/$100,000 limits.

9. How does SIPC's Fund protect customers?

The examples below apply to claims remaining **after** the return to customers of securities registered in their names and **after** the pro rata distribution of "Customer Property" held by the firm (see question 1).

—A remaining claim is for $400,000 in securities. The claim would be satisfied in full.

—A customer has a claim for $400,000 in securities in an individual account and for $500,000 in securities in a joint account with his or her spouse, as to which each has full authority. The spouse also has an individual account in which there is a claim for $400,000 in securities. All three claims would be fully covered.

—A customer has a claim for $730,000 in securities in a margin account, but he owes the broker $230,000, on those securities. The customer's "net equity" would be $500,000 and would be fully covered. With the trustee's approval, the customer may pay the $230,000 and receive the $730,000 in securities (see question 17).

—A remaining claim is for $420,000 in securities and $100,000 in cash. All but $20,000 would be covered.

—A remaining claim is for $30,000 in securities and $110,000 in cash. The claim would be covered to the amount of $130,000 ($30,000 for securities and $100,000 for cash).

—A customer has a claim for $550,000 in securities and $120,000 in cash. The claim would be covered to the amount of $500,000 (the maximum).

In the last three examples, any portion of the claim remaining may be satisfied in part from assets of the failed firm if any are available for distribution to creditors.

CUSTOMER PROTECTION PROCEEDINGS

10. How do customers learn that their broker has been placed in liquidation?

Notice will be published in one or more newspapers of general circulation and a copy together with a claim form mailed to each customer's address as it appears from the broker's books and records.

11. To whom does a customer submit a claim form?

Directly to the trustee; if no trustee has been appointed, directly to SIPC. The notice and claim form (referred to above) will give instructions.

It is important that customers submit their completed claim forms promptly within the time limits set forth in the notice and in accordance with the instructions to the claim form. Failure to to so may result in the loss of all or a portion of customer's claim for funds and securities.

12. Will a customer get back all of the securities in the accounts?

Usually, yes; but sometimes no. Here's why:

For various reasons, a failed firm may not have all customer securities on hand. The trustee attempts to purchase such missing securities in the market, providing a fair and orderly market for the securities can be found.

When missing securities cannot be replaced by market purchases, the customer receives cash based on the market value of the securities as of the value date (see question 13).

13. How is a customer's claim for securities valued?

Claims are valued as of a date prescribed by the Act ("value date"), generally the day customer protection proceedings commence.

To the extent possible (as indicated above), claims for securities are satisfied by delivering securities to customers. The amount of cash paid instead of securities reflects their worth on the value date and may, of course, differ from the securities' value on the date payment is made.

14. How quickly can a customer expect to receive property in the account?

This will vary from proceeding to proceeding. As a general rule, most customers can expect to receive their property in one to three months. When the records of the firm are accurate, deliveries of some securities and cash to customers may begin shortly after the trustee receives the completed claim forms from customers, or even earlier if the trustee can transfer customer accounts to another broker-dealer. On the other hand, there may be delays of several months where the firm's records are not accurate, or where it appears that the firm or its principals were involved in fraudulent activities. Some delays also may be caused by the need to send stock certificates to transfer agents with specific instructions to issue smaller denominations and issue certificates in other names. This can be a time-consuming operation.

15. How are stock options protected?

All exchange-traded securities option positions will be closed with the exception of covered short positions when the customer's broker has caused the cover to be deposited with either its correspondent broker or the Options Clearing Corporation. The fact that the customer has given his broker the underlying securities does not guarantee the position is covered for purposes of an SIPC liquidation proceeding; accordingly, a customer with a short option position should ascertain whether cover has been so deposited.

16. How is the amount of a customer's claim determined?

The amount of the customer's claim, excluding any securities registered in his name and returned to him, is called his "net equity." The net equity of a customer's account is determined by adding the total value of cash and securities the firm owes the customer and subtracting the total value of cash and securities the customer owes the firm.

17. Must the customer pay what he owed the firm to the trustee?

Usually no, because indebtedness is taken into account in computing a customer's net equity and the customer will receive a pro rata share of the securities in the account valued as of the value date. However, with the trustee's approval and within a time period determined by the trustee but not exceeding 60 days from publication of the notice described in question 10, the customer may pay the debit balance and receive all of the securities in the account subject to the limitations described in question 1.

When the customer owes the firm more than the firm owes the customer, the customer must pay the difference to the trustee.

18. Which customers are ineligible for protection from SIPC funds?

SIPC's funds may not be used to pay claims of any customer who also is: (1) a general partner, officer, or director of the firm; (2) the beneficial owner of 5% or more of any class of equity security of the firm (other than certain nonconvertible preferred stocks); (3) a limited partner with a participation of 5% or more in the net assets or net profits of the firm; (4) someone with the power to exercise a controlling influence over the management or policies of the firm; or (5) a broker or dealer or bank acting for itself rather than for its own customer or customers.

19. Who are members of SIPC?

Broker-dealers registered with the Securities and Exchange Commission (other than banks registered as municipal securities dealers) whose principal business is conducted within the United States, its territories or possessions are automatically members of SIPC with two exceptions:

—Broker-dealers whose business as a broker-dealer is exclusively (1) the distribution of shares of mutual funds, (2) the sale of variable annuities, (3) the business of insurance, or (4) the furnishing of investment advice to investment companies or insurance company separate accounts.

—Broker-dealers whose securities business is limited to United States Government securities and who are registered with the Securities and Exchange Commission under a provision of law which does not confer SIPC membership. Investors interested in whether a particular Government securities dealer is a member of SIPC should make appropriate inquiries.

An SIPC member displays this sign:

20. Who runs SIPC?

SIPC's Board of Directors which consists of seven members. Five are appointed by the President of the United States (subject to Senate confirmation), of whom two are representatives of the general public and three, the securities industry. From the public members, the President designates the Chairman and Vice Chairman. In addition, one member each is designated by the Secretary of the Treasury and the Federal Reserve Board from among their respective officers and employees.

The Securities and Exchange Commission has certain oversight and regulatory functions with respect to SIPC.

21. Where does SIPC get its money?

The money required to protect customers beyond that which is available from the property in the possession of the failed broker-dealer is advanced by SIPC from a fund maintained for that purpose. The sources of money for the SIPC Fund are assessments collected from SIPC members and interest on investments in United States Government securities.

22. Is there emergency financing in the event the SIPC Fund is insufficient?

Yes. In an emergency, SIPC may borrow up to $1 billion from the U.S. Treasury through the Securities and Exchange Commission if the Commission determines such a loan is necessary to protect customers and maintain confidence in United States securities markets. SIPC must present a plan which provides as reasonable an assurance of prompt repayment as may be feasible under the circumstances. If the Commission determines industry assessments would not satisfactorily repay the loan, it may impose a transaction fee on purchasers of equity securities at a rate not exceeding $1/50$ of 1% of the purchase price ($.20 per $1,000). This fee would not apply to transactions of less than $5,000.

23. Who examines the operational and financial conditions of SIPC members?

The securities exchanges and the National Association of Securities Dealers, Inc. (NASD) are the "examining authorities" for their members. SIPC has no authority to examine or inspect its members.

APPENDIX C

The Discount Futures Broker Directory

To my knowledge, this is the first directory of discount futures brokers. It is excerpted from Mercer's *1990 Discount Futures Directory*, which provides more extensive information about the brokers and commissions in this field.

The information provided should be a good starting point for finding a suitable discount futures broker. The descriptions of the firms' highlights and specialties, in most cases, have been provided by the firms themselves in response to a questionnaire mailed by Mercer. Over half of those contacted responded.

However, even more than in the case of discount stockbrokers, it is essential that the individual investor check out each firm—its reputation and financial solidity. As I have indicated in Chapter 16, The Futures Market, there is no SIPC in the futures field which will guarantee the safety of the individual's investment if the firm fails, and Mercer has not conducted any investigation of the firms' credentials.

If the firm is an "introducing broker" then the firm's clearing broker (futures commission merchant) should be reviewed in detail, since it is the clearing firm that will hold title to your investment.

CHAPTER 1

The Futures Brokers

Access Discount Commodities
5485 Harpers Farm Road
Suite 224
Columbia, MD 21043

Telephone Number:

    Local   301/997-5580

Allegiance Financial
141 W. Jackson Boulevard
Suite 2201
Chicago, IL 60604

Telephone Number:

    Toll-Free (nationwide)   800/362-8117

Products/Services: 24-hour worldwide execution services; direct access to salaried trading-desk account specialists; access to highly liquid money market funds; immediate fills on all actively traded contracts; and no-wait, toll-free telephone lines

Amber Trading
2546 W. 46th Street
Chicago, IL 60632

Telephone Number:

    Toll-Free (in-state)   800/888-5895

Anspacher Futures of Wyoming
232 E. Second Street
Suite 203B
Casper, WY 82601

Telephone Number:

    Local   307/235-1305

Products/Services: All future commodities and options

Specialties/Highlights: Specializes in crude oil futures, cattle, T-bonds, grains

Arneday Incorporated
15515 San Fernando
Mission Boulevard, Suite 5
Mission Hills, CA 91345

Telephone Numbers:

    Toll-Free (nationwide)   800/266-2254
    Local   818/365-6421

Products/Services: Discount brokerage futures, options, and stocks

Specialties/Highlights: Hold for fills; free charts and CRB blue sheet to all clients

Beddows Commodities, Inc.
1001 U.S. Highway 1
Suite 601
Jupiter, FL 33477

Telephone Number:

Local   407/744-0900

Bernstein Futures, Inc.
60 Revere Drive
Suite 870
Northbrook, IL 60062

Telephone Number:

Toll-Free (nationwide)   800/446-9999

Boston Financial Group
150 Broadway
Suite 1309
New York, NY 10038

Telephone Number:

Local   212/962-0710

Products/Services: Discount commodity futures and options

Specialties/Highlights: Trades all markets, specializing in financials, currencies and metals

Cary Scarborough
114 McKay Street
Pittsburgh, PA 15218

Telephone Number:

Local   412/247-1773

Delta Futures Group
4607 Dodge Street
Omaha, NE 68132

Telephone Numbers:

    Toll-Free (nationwide)   800/234-8470
    Local   402/553-8470

Products/Services: All commodity and financial futures and options

Specialties/Highlights: Todd Hultman and John Goetzmann provide personalized service

Dreyfuss Group Ltd.
34700 Pacific Coast Highway
San Clemente, CA 92624

Telephone Number:

    Toll-Free (nationwide)   800/747-8723

E. David Commodities Co.
300 Garden City Plaza
Garden City, NY 11530

Telephone Number:

    Local   516/248-6900

Products/Services: Daily update by your personal broker; weekly market letter

First American Discount Corp.
211 W. Quincy
Suite 350
Chicago, IL 60606

Telephone Number:

    Toll-Free (nationwide)   800/621-4415

First Texas Futures, Inc.
2974 L.B.J. Freeway
No. 425
Dallas, TX 75234

Telephone Numbers:

    Toll-Free (nationwide)   800/638-8788
    Local   214/620-1300

Products/Services: Discount and full-service accounts

Specialties/Highlights: Fast, accurate fills

Futures Discount Group
600 W. Jackson Boulevard
Suite 300
Chicago, IL 60606

Telephone Numbers:

    Toll-Free (nationwide)   800/872-6673
    Local   312/444-1155

Products/Services: Boutique Brokerage Firm; managed account at low discount commissions; proprietary "growth" family trading; assistance through broker/assist program; "Commission-Back Offer" on managed accounts

Specialties/Highlights: Fast, accurate fills; fast call backs; exceptional service

G & G Brokerage, Inc.
6399 Wilshire Boulevard
Suite 901
Los Angeles, CA 90048

Telephone Number:

    Toll-Free (nationwide)   800/334-9306

Hedgers, Inc.
4800 Main Street
Suite 201
Kansas City, MO 64112

Telephone Number:

    Toll-Free (nationwide)   800/821-5545

Highlands Trading Co.
231 S. Jefferson Street
Chicago, IL 60606

Telephone Number:

    Toll-Free (nationwide)   800/343-6379

Ira Epstein & Company
626 W. Jackson Boulevard
Chicago, IL 60606

Telephone Numbers:

    Toll-Free (nationwide)   800/284-6000
    Local   312/207-1800

Products/Services: Two times daily hotline; market letters from Ira Epstein and other trading advisers; access to overseas markets; commission rebates on market letters, charts, etc.

Specialties/Highlights: Competitive discount commissions; retail and managed accounts available; INFOline; real-time computerized quotes

Jack Carl/312 Futures
222 W. Adams
Chicago, IL 60606

Telephone Number:

    Toll-Free (nationwide)   800/621-3424

Products/Services: Accurate, real-time quotes; computerized technical trading analysis; one-on-one broker assistance; direct link to world currency and precious metal exchanges, 24 hours a day; rebates for using your own quote machine

Klein & Co. Futures, Inc.
90 West Street
Suite 706
New York, NY 10006

Telephone Number:

 Local 212/233-6111

Products/Services: Member and clearing member of all NY commodity exchanges; does not compete as brokers and traders; professionally staffed order desk; prompt accurate statements, clearing, and break resolution

Specialties/Highlights: Futures Commission Merchant (FCM) clearing member; clearing members for all NY commodities relationships to clear other domestic and EFP markets

Lind-Waldock
30 S. Wacker Drive
Suite 1712
Chicago, IL 60606

Telephone Number:

 Toll-Free (nationwide) 800/621-0762

Products/Services: Liberal Treasury bill policy; 24-hour trading service; clearing memberships at the 7 major futures exchanges; international trading offering access to United States, London, Sydney, and Singapore markets

The Discount Futures Broker Directory

Mendelsohn Enterprises
50 Meadow Lane
Zephyrhills, FL 33544

Telephone Number:

Local   813/973-0496

Products/Services: Brokerage; "Profit Taker 2000-Futures" trading software consultation

Specialties/Highlights: Provides discount brokerage, consultation, and investment software for futures traders

Myers Commodity Corp.
2001 Beach Street
No. 824
Fort Worth, TX 76103

Telephone Numbers:

Toll-Free (nationwide)   800/356-9092
Local   817/654-2488

Products/Services: Small opening account balance; discount round-turn rates on futures and futures options; customer always has access to president of firm

Specialties/Highlights: Discount commodity trading with a personal touch

Norman Kern & Company
175 W. Jackson Boulevard
Chicago, IL 60606

Telephone Number:

Toll-Free (nationwide)   800/962-4501

Robert Barnett Commodities
4767 Park Granada
No. 101
Calabasa, CA 91302

Telephone Number:

    Toll-Free (nationwide)   800/558-6668

SRD Associates
643 West 550 South
Box 277
Orem, UT 84059

Telephone Numbers:

    Toll-Free (nationwide)   800/733-8723
    Local   801/224-9126

Products/Services: Discount commissions; futures hotline trading; free charts and technical analysis; personal "small firm" service; 800-line service; managed accounts; self-directed accounts; "test" monitor hotlines at no charge.

Specialties/Highlights: Specializes in automatic trading; hotlines for daily and intra-day signals; constant research

Touchstone Trading Co.
5840 S. Memorial
Suite 330
Tulsa, OK 74145

Telephone Number:

    Toll-Free (nationwide)   800/777-5620

Products/Services: Offers managed accounts and discount brokerage

The Discount Futures Broker Directory

Specialties/Highlights: Gary Clayton, with his 20 years of professional trading experience, provides a managed account service; with 10 years experience as a floor trader, offers discount service.

Traders Network
304 N. Cleveland Avenue
Loveland, CO 80537

Telephone Number:

    Toll-Free (nationwide)   800/521-0705

Trans-Inter. Commodities, Ltd.
98-901 Ainanui Loop
Aiea, HI 96701

Telephone Number:

    Toll-Free (nationwide)   800/366-3842 (800/FON-ETIC)

Products/Services: Commodity futures & commodity options; discounts; broker-guided; managed accounts

Specialties/Highlights: Small firm providing close client–broker relationship and optimum service; trade advice based primarily on technical orientation; return of commissions if account not profitable at end of first 30 days

Voss & Co., Inc.
6320 Augusta Drive
Suite 1200
Springfield, VA 22150

Telephone Number:

    Toll-Free (nationwide)   800/426-8106

Wolf Commodities Corp.
9609 Kentsdale Drive
Potomac, MD 20854

Telephone Number:

    Local   301/365-6220

World Trading Group, FL
3020 N. Federal Highway
Fort Lauderdale, FL 33306

Telephone Number:

    Toll-Free (nationwide)   800/776-2226

APPENDIX D

The Discount Publications Directory

As a purchaser of this book, you are entitled to discounts on three types of investment-related publications.

BOOKS

Over 50 books on a wide range of investment topics are described in this Appendix. All of them are available to readers at a *20% discount* from list price.

MERCER DISCOUNT SURVEYS

Also available at a *20% discount* to readers of the book is their initial copy of any of the *Mercer Discount Surveys*.

HOW TO ORDER

To order, cite this book and send a check for 80% of the list price of the item(s) plus $3.95 for postage and handling to: Mercer, Inc., 80 Fifth Ave, Suite 800, New York, NY 10011.

Attention: Book Orders; or call 212-807-6800 with a Visa or MasterCard number. Please allow 3–4 weeks for delivery.

NEWSLETTERS

To order a newsletter, contact the publisher directly at the address or phone number listed. The discounts or special terms will vary, and are noted along with the description provided of each newsletter and publisher.

CHAPTER 1

Books

A GUIDE TO ASIAN STOCK MARKETS
Robert Lloyd George

The stock markets of the East are only now opening to smart U.S. investors willing to learn the ropes. *A Guide to Asian Stock Markets* is a guide to investing in this high-profit, but little-known field.

$ 39.95

BOND RISK ANALYSIS: A Guide to Duration and Convexity
Livingston G. Douglas

A seasoned pro explains the basic tenets of bond risk analysis in an easy-to-read work filled with examples. This reference book for bond portfolio managers, traders, and salespeople explains and illustrates how to analyze the risk inherent in any transaction and minimize its impact on any type of bond.

$ 34.95

THE CONSERVATIVE INVESTOR'S GUIDE TO TRADING OPTIONS

LeRoy Gross

Risk-averse investors can now learn how to use options to reduce their exposure, hedge their securities positions, and enhance returns. The author has counseled many clients on the prudent and profitable use of options.

$ 21.95

DIVERSIFY: The Investor's Guide to Asset Allocation Strategies

Gerald W. Perritt and Alan Lavine

This book explains why and how to diversify, how asset allocation works, and how different assets correlate with one another. The authors explore the positive impact of asset allocation as it applies to a wide cross-section of investors, ranging from a young couple with children to people planning for retirement.

$ 22.95

DIVIDENDS DON'T LIE: Finding Value in Blue-Chip Stocks

Geraldine Weiss and Janet Lowe

The authors describe a system that is simple—stick to quality blue-chip stocks with reliable dividend histories.

$ 12.95

DON'T SELL STOCKS ON MONDAY

Yale Hirsch

The author focuses on seasonal and monthly trends which may impact stock prices.

$ 24.95

THE DOW JONES-IRWIN BUSINESS AND INVESTMENT ALMANAC, 1990

Sumner N. Levine

This reference tool includes: major and group stock market averages, price/earning ratios, reviews of the major futures markets, charts for futures-traded commodities, tables showing options premium movements, performance of mutual funds, Sotheby's Art Market Trends, and comparative living.

$ 29.95

DOW THEORY REDUX

Michael Sheimo

The Classic Dow Investment Theory revised and updated by the author for the 1990s.

$ 22.95

THE EUROPEAN BOND MARKETS

The European Bond Commission

Prepared by members of the European Bond Commission, this 600 + -page book offers a definitive reference guide to the bond markets of 13 European countries.

$ 60.00

THE EUROPEAN OPTIONS AND FUTURES MARKETS: An Overview and Analysis for Money Managers and Traders

The European Bond Commission

The European Bond Commission has prepared an overview and analysis of these burgeoning futures/options markets. Experts from the major exchanges, banks, and trading houses around Europe have been assembled by the Commission to present a comprehensive review of these markets.

$ 60.00

FACTS ON FUTURES: Winning in the Futures Markets (paperback)

Jake Bernstein

A popular introduction to futures trading.

$ 19.95

FINANCIAL SERVICES: Insiders' Views on the Future of the Finance Industry

Mark Coler et al.

Responding to the dramatic changes affecting this industry, this book presents a capsule view of its state of flux; emphasizing new financial products, the broadening role of equity securities, and success in marketing. Each chapter is contributed by an expert in the field.

$ 29.95

FUNDAMENTAL ANALYSIS: A Back-to-the-Basic Investment Guide to Selecting Quality Stocks.

John C. Ritchie, Jr.

This comprehensive guidebook shows readers how to gather and interpret past records of assets, earnings, sales, products, management, and markets to assess whether a particular stock is undervalued or overvalued.

$ 24.95

FUTURES TRADING

Robert E. Fink and Robert B. Feduniak

Provides a comprehensive, definitive examination of every facet of the complex arena of futures trading. Includes highly readable charts and graphs, plus case studies and market profiles, making the book useful to professionals and serious students alike, Covers both financial instruments and hard commodities.

$ 49.95

GLOBAL INVESTING: The Templeton Way
Norman Berryessa and Eric Kirzner

Explores the thinking of John Templeton, a successful pioneer of global investing. Also discusses modern developments in investment finance theory and applications and what's available in the global investment market.

$ 27.50

THE GLOBAL INVESTOR: How to Buy Stocks Around the World
Thomas R. Keyes and David Miller

Discusses the types of investments available, including open- and closed-end funds and multinational corporations; the mechanics of currency exchange; how orders are handled; how to choose a global broker; and trading strategies.

$ 29.95

GOLD INVESTMENT
Eugene J. Sherman

Answers questions relating to gold as an investment: its benefit in a large portfolio, its use as a vehicle for diversification, and the risks of owning gold. Examines the relationships between dollar–gold prices and such things as new mine production, aggregate gold supply, and investment demand. Also covered is the Prudent Man Rule and modern portfolio theory regarding gold investment.

$ 39.95

THE HANDBOOK FOR NO-LOAD FUND INVESTORS, 9th Edition
Sheldon Jacobs

This valuable 500+ -page reference book acclaimed as the "best mutual funds investment guide of the year" by Sylvia Porter's magazine, is really three books in one: a complete text on mutual fund investing; performance data going back 10 years, plus special performance charts on 171 of the most popular funds; and a complete directory of no-load and low-load funds including toll-free numbers.

$ 29.95

HANDBOOK FOR RAISING CAPITAL: Financing Alternatives for Emerging and Growing Businesses

Lawrence Chimerine, Robert F. Cushman, and Howard D. Ross

Get the straight facts on every facet of financing, from bank loans to industrial bonds to the new creative credit in instruments. Describes the advantages and disadvantages and a variety of strategies for obtaining financing so you can find the best financing method for your needs.

$ 67.50

THE HANDBOOK OF INTERNATIONAL INVESTING

Carl Beidleman, Editor

This 900-page volume provides a comprehensive introduction to international investing by 38 different authors—acknowledged experts in their fields, scholars, and leading practitioners.

$ 65.00

THE HULBERT GUIDE TO FINANCIAL NEWSLETTERS: Performance Ratings of more than 100 Investment Newsletters, 3rd Edition, (paperback)

Mark Hulbert

Provides investors with clear and objective evaluations of over 100 investment newsletters—from the recognized authority on tracking and rating newsletters.

$ 24.95

INDEX OPTIONS AND FUTURES: The Complete Guide
Donald L. Luskin
An excellent, if somewhat technical, introduction to the subject.

$ 34.95

THE INDIVIDUAL INVESTOR'S GUIDE TO NO-LOAD MUTUAL FUNDS
American Association of Individual Investors
A highly acclaimed guide to over 300 mutual funds.

$ 19.95

INVESTING IN UTILITIES: A Comprehensive, Industry-by-Industry Guide for Investors and Money Managers
Daniel D. Singer
Focusing on electric, telecommunications, and natural gas industries, this exhaustive work gives the reader everything he or she needs to know to understand these industries, to properly evaluate the companies within them, and to make informed investment decisions.

$ 21.95

THE INVESTOR'S GUIDE TO COIN TRADING
Scott Travers

$ 24.95

THE INVESTOR'S GUIDE TO FIDELITY FUNDS
Peter G. Martin and Byron B. McCann
For investors who prefer to stay within the Fidelity family of funds.

$ 17.95

THE JAPANESE BOND MARKETS: An Overview and Analysis

Frank J. Fabozzi, Editor

Editor Frank J. Fabozzi draws upon an elite group of international bond experts to present a detailed and comprehensive picture of all facets of the Japanese fixed-income markets, including the various securities that are issued and traded and the strategies that are used to trade and hedge.

$ 47.50

LOW-RISK / HIGH-PROFIT FUTURES TRADING: Proven Strategies for More Successful Investing

Charles A. Cerami

A guide to low-risk approaches to futures markets for conservative-minded traders and investors.

$ 34.95

MARKET WIZARDS: Interviews with Top Traders

Jack D. Schwager

In this book of interviews with top traders, the author sketches detailed profiles of the extraordinary personalities who turned meager stakes into fortunes, converted financial setbacks into greater-than-ever riches, or used the market as an ally on their road to wealth and power. These traders tell in their own words how they make millions of dollars each year.

$ 19.95

MULTIFUND INVESTING: How to Build a High Performance Portfolio of Mutual Funds

Michael D. Hirsch

The multifund investor gets full-time, professional money management, great diversification, and a portfolio that is easy to manage.

$ 37.50

THE NASDAQ HANDBOOK, Revised Edition
National Association of Securities Dealers

This book, which sold over 20,000 copies in its first edition, is the only complete reference source to the NASDAQ over-the-counter market. It was designed for the everyday use of investors, investment professionals, and financial planners.

$ 29.95

THE 100 BEST STOCKS TO OWN IN AMERICA
Gene Walden

An entertaining and practical investment guide that features the top 100 public companies traded on U.S. stock exchanges. To select these companies, the author conducted extensive research and interviews.

$ 19.95

OPTIONS AS A STRATEGIC INVESTMENT
Lawrence G. McMillan

This reference for options strategies offers market-tested help that lets you maximize the earnings potential of your portfolio while reducing downside risk. Describes the strategic uses of new and established options investments, complete with examples that demonstrate the power of each strategy.

$ 44.95

THE PROFESSIONAL'S GUIDE TO THE U.S. GOVERNMENT SECURITIES MARKETS
George H. Bollenbacher

An opportunity for money managing professionals to understand what really goes on inside the government securities market. It addresses such issues as the characteristics of the securities traded, regulations and the appropriate agencies and SRPs, and the impact of the Federal Reserve Board on money market pricing.

$ 39.50

THE PRUDENT INVESTOR: The Definitive Guide to Professional Investment Management

James P. Owen

With some 10,000 investment advisers to choose from, the task of selecting the right investment manager is formidable. How can the high net-worth individual or the pension fund trustee/sponsor confidently select from among all the alternatives? The author provides a step-by-step guide.

$ 27.50

THE PRUDENT SPECULATOR AL FRANK ON INVESTING

Al Frank

Strategies from one of the more successful and better-known newsletter writers of the decade.

$ 22.95

REUTERS GLOSSARY: International Economic & Financial Terms

Reuters

A useful reference dictionary from this leading news service.

$ 12.95

THE S/B STOCK MARKET RATIO: Profiting from Legal Insider Trading

Edwin A. Buck

Two decades of research by the author shows that insiders are 95% predictive when they buy, and 85% when they sell stock legally in their own companies. In this book, Buck explains his techniques of tracking and analyzing legal insider trades, giving precise directions on how to assemble and use the information for profit.

$ 14.95

THE SPICER AND OPPENHEIM GUIDE TO SECURITIES MARKETS AROUND THE WORLD

The Spicer and Oppenheim Financial Services Group

A leading international accounting and financial services firm provides a useful guide to the world's stock markets.

$ 19.95

STAN WEINSTEIN'S SECRETS FOR PROFITING IN BULL AND BEAR MARKETS

Stan Weinstein

One of the better newsletter writers discusses his successful methods for timing investments to produce consistently profitable results.

$ 24.95

TOTAL FINANCIAL PLANNING

Harold W. Gourgues and David E. Homrich

This thorough, step-by-step guide for serious investors and their advisers stresses the importance of constructing a tailor-made financial plan to meet the specific needs of an individual and provides a multitude of alternatives to apply and adapt to these needs.

$ 64.95

TREASURY SECURITIES: Making Money with Uncle Sam

Donald R. Nichols

A basic introduction to investing in Treasury and U.S. Government agency securities.

$ 24.95

UNDERSTANDING AND USING MARGIN (paperback)

Michael T. Curley

A "self-teaching" seminar on the subject.

$ 19.95

WINNING WITH YOUR STOCKBROKER: In Good Times and Bad

David Koehler and Gene Walden

Useful for the investor who would prefer to deal with a full-service broker. Describes how to select, evaluate, and work most effectively with a full-service broker.

$ 19.95

CHAPTER 2

Mercer Discount Surveys

THE COUNTRY FUND HANDBOOK

Mark Coler, Editor

Describes over 50 publicly traded funds that allow investors to buy funds on U.S. stock exchanges that own diversified stock portfolios of over 30 countries. Frequently, these funds can be purchased at a substantial discount to their underlying net asset value. As the first guide of its kind, *The Country Fund Handbook* provides detailed information about each of these funds to help the investor make the right choice.

$29.95

THE DISCOUNT BROKERAGE COMMISSION SURVEY, 7th EDITION

Mark Coler, Editor

The definitive source of information on discount brokerage commissions since 1983. Analyzes thousands of commission charges by over 150 banks and discount brokers to identify the 30 least expensive discounters for each of 25 benchmark stock, bond, and option trades (75 total). Identifies exact commissions; lists names and addresses.

$74.95

THE DISCOUNT BROKERAGE COMMISSION SURVEY—BONDS, 7th EDITION

Mark Coler, Editor

The definitive source since 1983. Computer analysis of thousands of commission charges by over 150 banks and discount brokers to determine the 30 least expensive discounters for each of 25 benchmark bond trades. Identifies exact commissions; lists names and addresses.

$29.95

THE DISCOUNT BROKERAGE COMMISSION SURVEY—OPTIONS, 7th EDITION

Mark Coler, Editor

The definitive information source on discount brokerage commission rates since 1983. Computer analysis of thousands of commission charges by over 150 banks and discount brokers to determine the 30 least expensive discounters for each of 25 benchmark option trades. Identifies exact commissions; lists names and addresses.

$29.95

THE DISCOUNT BROKERAGE COMMISSION SURVEY—STOCKS, 7th EDITION

Mark Coler, Editor

The definitive information source on discount brokerage commission rates since 1983. Computer analysis of thousands of commission charges by over 150 banks and discount brokers to determine the 30 least expensive discounters for each of

25 benchmark stock trades. Identifies exact commissions; lists names and addresses.

$34.95

THE DISCOUNT FINANCIAL DIRECTORY (INVESTOR EDITION), 7th EDITION

Mark Coler, Editor

The definitive directory on discount brokerage. Profiles over 200 independent discount brokers, bank discounters, and discount futures brokers. Provides names, addresses, products, services, margin rates, and other useful information. Over 200 pages.

$94.95

THE DISCOUNT FUTURES BROKER SURVEY

Mark Coler, Editor

Detailed profiles of over 75 independent discount futures brokers. Provides names, addresses, products, services, and comparative commission charge information.

$29.95

THE DISCOUNT IRA SURVEY

Mark Coler, Editor

Identifies the 100 banks and discount brokers with the lowest start-up costs, annual fees, and commission charges for self-directed IRAs.

$29.95

THE DISCOUNT STOCK BROKER DIRECTORY, 7th EDITION

Mark Coler, Editor

Detailed profiles of over 75 independent discount stock brokers. Provides names, addresses, products, services, margin rates, and other useful information. Over 200 pages.

$29.95

THE INTERNATIONAL FUND HANDBOOK

Mark Coler, Editor

Over 100 closed- and open-end funds permit U.S. investors to participate in the international market. This directory profiles the funds and provides essential information to help the investor make the right choice.

$34.95

THE SHAREHOLDERS DISCOUNT HANDBOOK

Mark Coler, Editor

Many companies offer their shareholders little known, but substantial discounts on products, services, dividend reinvestments, and additional share purchases. This unique handbook identifies over 200 such companies and describes what type of discounts they offer.

$24.95

CHAPTER 3
Newsletters

AgBiotech Stock Letter
P.O. Box 40460
Berkeley, CA 94704

Telephone Number:
  Local   415/843-1842
Editors: Jim McCamant/Martin Brooks
Description: Focuses on the changes Biotech is bringing to America's largest industry—farming.
Annual Subscription Cost: $165
Trial Subscription: $39 for 3 months
Telephone Hotline: No
Issues per Year: 12

The Astute Investor
P.O. Box 988
Paoli, PA 19301

Telephone Number:
  Local   215/296-2411

Editor: Robert Nurock
Description: *The Astute Investor* is a comprehensive stock market advisory letter which carries an ongoing discussion of the fundamental and technical backgrounds which affect investor expectations. It also includes a discussion of the Technical Market Index, which the editor formerly provided to *Wall Street Week*.
Annual Subscription Cost: $247
Trial Subscription: $57 for 2 months
Telephone Hotline: Yes
Issues per Year: 24

Bob Brinker's Marketimer
P.O. Box 7005
Princeton, NJ 08543

Telephone Number:
    Local   201/359-8838
Editor: Robert Brinker
Description: Includes information on market timing; recommends no-load funds, model portfolios, and Federal Reserve monetary policy.
Annual Subscription Cost: $145
Trial Subscription: $45 for 3 months
Telephone Hotline: No
Issues per Year: 12 plus special bulletins.

The Cabot Market Letter
P.O. Box 3044
Salem, MA 01970

Telephone Number:
    Local   508/745-5532
Editor: Carlton Lutts
Description: Published since 1970, *The Cabot Market Letter* advises on buying and selling common stocks using Cabot's Momentum Analysis approach. There are two portfolios: Cabot's Model Portfolio, limited to 12 growth stocks, and

Cabot's Conservative Growth and Income Portfolio, limited to 6 stocks of growing companies that pay regular dividends.
Annual Subscription Cost: $215
Telephone Hotline: Yes
Issues per Year: 24
Special Offer to Readers: $87 for 1 year.

The Chartist
P.O. Box 758
Seal Beach, CA 90740

Telephone Number:
    Local   213/596-2385
Editor: Dan Sullivan
Description: Technically oriented stock recommendations.
Annual Subscription Cost: $150
Trial Subscription: $80 for 6 months
Telephone Hotline: Yes
Issues per Year: 24
Special Offer to Readers: $25 for 6 issues.

The Colony Group Investment Letter
199 State Street
Boston, MA 02109

Telephone Number:
    Local   617/723-8200
Editors: Peter J. Raimondi, III/Robert L. Driscoll, Jr.
Description: Includes Market Comments; Stock Selections, stock choice for the month; Recommended List, recommended stocks; Model Mutual Fund Portfolio, recommended mutual funds; And Other Points of View, excerpts from investment publications.
Annual Subscription Cost: $45
Trial Subscription: $10 for 3 issues
Telephone Hotline: No
Issues per Year: 12

Crawford Perspectives
205 E. 78th Street, Suite 12-R
New York, NY 10021

Telephone Number:
    Local   212/628-1156
Editor: Arch Crawford
Description: A "market timing" newsletter. Methods include astronomic cycles analysis backed up by technical market analysis.
Annual Subscription Cost: $250
Trial Subscription: $85 for 3 issues
Telephone Hotline: No
Issues per Year: 10
Special Offer to Readers: $50 off a 1-year subscription, or a 3-issue trial for $50.

The Dines Letter
P.O. Box 22
Belvedere, CA 94920

Telephone Number:
    Not available
Editor: James Dines
Description: *The Dines Letter* offers comprehensive market analysis; and specific advice on particular stocks, market trends, and the precious metals markets.
Annual Subscription Cost: $195
Trial Subscription: $115 for 6 months
Telephone Hotline: No
Issues per year: 24

Donoghue's Moneyletter
P.O. Box 6640
Holliston, MA 01746

Telephone Number:
    Local   508/429-5930
Editor: Daniel Bates

Description: Describes and recommends no-load and low-load stock, bond, and money market mutual fund strategies designed to maximize after-tax returns. Each issue offers specific buy, hold, and sell recommendations and portfolio allocation advice for four risk categories of investors. Also provides updates on market trends and developments in the financial services industry that affect individual investors.
Annual Subscription Cost: $99
Trial Subscription: $49 for 6 months
Telephone Hotline: Yes
Issues per Year: 24
Special Offer to Readers: 24 issues for $87. Includes a complimentary copy of *Donoghue's Mutual Funds Almanac* (regularly $26).

Dow Theory Forecasts
7412 Calumet Ave
Hammond, IN 46324-2692

Telephone Number:
    Local   219/931-6480
Editors: Richard L. Evans/Charles Carlson
Description: A weekly investment advisory newsletter offering analysis of the primary market trend, according to the interpretation of the Dow Theory principles, and investment advice on individual securities. Investment recommendations each week—investment grade, income, growth, low priced, and speculative. There are industry surveys, turnaround selections, dividend highlights, quarterly utility ratings, stocks in the news, and periodic sell advice. Full-term readers also have consultation privileges.
Annual Subscription Cost: $198
Trial Subscription: $5 per week; free sample upon request
Telephone Hotline: No

The Elliott Wave Theorist
P.O. Box 1618
Gainesville, GA 30503

Telephone Number:
    Local   404/536-0309
Editor: Robert Prechter
Description: A 10-page monthly publication thoroughly analyzing Elliot Waves, Fibonacci relationships, fixed time cycles, momentum, sentiment and supply/demand factors in a comprehensive approach covering stocks, precious metals, interest rates, and the economy.
Annual Subscription Cost: $233
Trial Subscription: $55 for 2 months
Telephone Hotline: No
Issues per Year: 12
Special Offer to Readers: Book, 2-month trial subscription, and special report; this $99 value is $66 for readers.

Fidelity Insight
MFIA
P.O. Box 9135
Wellesley, MA 02181

Telephone Number:
    Local   617/235-4432
Description: Mutual Fund Investors Association (MFIA) is the independent association of Fidelity investors. Its sole purpose is to provide objective, independent analysis; information; and advice on Fidelity funds.
Annual Subscription Cost: $149
Trial Subscription: $34 for 4 months
Telephone Hotline: Yes
Issues per Year: 12
Special Offer to Readers: 4-month introductory membership to MFIA for $34.

Fidelity Monitor
P.O. Box 1294
Rocklin, CA 95677

Telephone Number:
    Local   916/624-0191
Description: Provides information and recommendations on all Fidelity funds. Models include a growth portfolio which aims to outperform the S&P 500, and a select system that projects 30% growth per year.
Annual Subscription Cost: $96
Trial Subscription: $48 for 6 months
Telephone Hotline: Yes
Issues per Year: 12
Special Offer to Readers: A free sample issue upon request.

Fund Exchange
1200 Westlake Ave. N.
Seattle, WA 98109-3530

Telephone Number:
    Toll-Free (nationwide)   800/423-4893
Editor: Paul Merriman
Description: *Fund Exchange* is a monthly newsletter devoted to the selection and market timing of equity, bond, gold, and international funds. Subscribers are offered 10 different portfolios depending on their investment objectives and risk tolerance.
Annual Subscription Cost: $125
Trial Subscription: $49 for 6 months
Telephone Hotline: Yes
Issues per Year: 12
Special Offer to Readers: Available to readers for $99 annually. Includes a free copy of Merriman's book *Market Timing with No-Load Mutual Funds*.

The Garside Forecast
P.O. Box 1812
Santa Ana, CA 92702

Telephone Number:
    Local   714/259-1670
Editor: Ben Garside
Description: A technically oriented service which provides timing from the very short term to long-term. It features the Counter Force Theory developed by Ben Garside in 1965 and the 5-month lead time Market Timing and Trend Projector, developed in 1972.
Annual Subscription Cost: $125
Trial Subscription: $75 for 6 months
Telephone Hotline: Yes
Issues per Year: 24
Special Offer to Readers: One-time 20% subscription discount.

The Global Portfolio
Mercer, Inc.
80 Fifth Avenue
New York, NY 10011

Telephone Number:
    Local   212/807-6800
Editor: Mark Coler
Description: Edited by the author of this book, this new newsletter provides investment ideas from leading experts that individual investors can use to take advantage of the best performing markets of the past two decades: international investments—country funds, global and regional funds, open- and closed-end mutual funds, and international stocks traded on U.S. markets (ADRs); and prospects for foreign markets.
Annual Subscription Cost: $195
Trial Subscription: $45 for 3 months

Issues per Year: 12
Special Offer to Readers: 50% off regular or trial subscription price.

Growth Fund Guide
Growth Fund Research Building
Rapid City, SD 57709

Telephone Number:
  Local   605/341-1971
Editor: Walter Rouleau
Description: Specializes in top performing no-load and money market funds. Analyzes market trends and provides long-term, up-to-date semi-log charts on a monthly basis.
Annual Subscription Cost: $89
Trial Subscription: $49 for 6 months
Telephone Hotline: Yes
Issues per Year: 12

The Hulbert Financial Digest
316 Commerce Street
Alexandria, VA 22314

Telephone Number:
  Local   703/683-5905
Editor: Mark Hulbert
Description: The nation's premier source of objective performance data on the track records of advisory newsletters, tracking the performance of well over 300 separate model portfolios set up in accordance with the advice contained in some 125 separate investment newsletters. *The HFD* also reports on advisory sentiment among these advisers and publishes a list of those stocks and mutual funds that are most and least recommended among these newsletters.
Annual Subscription Cost: $135
Trial Subscription: $38 for 5 issues

Telephone Hotline: Yes
Issues per Year: 12
Special Offer to Readers: Readers may subscribe at half-price, or $67.50 for 1 year.

Indicator Digest
KCI Communications
1101 King Street, Suite 400
Alexandria, VA 22314

Telephone Number:
    Toll-Free (nationwide)   800/832-2330
Editor: Stephen Leeb
Description: Each 8-page issue consists of Dr. Leeb's general trends and projections for the economy and markets; his Model Portfolio which consists of the best combination of stocks at any given moment; the Hot Corner which features low-priced stocks for speculators; and Trading Strategies, which is aimed at shorter-term investors.
Annual Subscription Cost: $175
Trial Subscription: $150 for 6 months
Telephone Hotline: Yes
Issues per Year: 24

The Insiders
Institute for Econometric Research
Ft. Lauderdale, FL 33306

Telephone Number:
    Toll-Free (nationwide)   800/327-6720
Editors: Norman Fosback/Glen King Parker
Description: Comprehensive information based on insider trading in all listed stocks; recommendations.
Annual Subscription Cost: $100
Telephone Hotline: Yes
Issues per Year: 24
Special Offer to Readers: $49 per year or special 1-month trial free.

Intelligence Report
Phillips Publishing, Inc.
Potomac, MD 20854

Telephone Number:
    Toll-Free (nationwide)   800/722-9000
Editor: Richard C. Young
Description: Analyzes market conditions and events to provide specific, straightforward advice on which funds to buy, when to sell, and how to manage your portfolio for maximum gains with minimal risks.
Annual Subscription Cost: $99
Special Offer to Readers: Two years (24 issues) for $179; save $119 off the regular rate.

The International Harry Schultz Letter
FERC P.O. Box 622 CH-1001 Lavsanne Switzerland

No Telephone Number
Editor: Harry Schultz
Description: The 12-page newsletter includes advice on stocks, bonds, commodities, metals, currencies and personal investment protection, and privacy. *HSL* also offers a special Forecast issue each January.
Annual Subscription Cost: $275
Telephone Hotline: No
Issues per Year: 11
Special Offer to Readers: $50 for 2 issues.

Investech Market Analyst
2472 Birch Glen
Whitefish, MT 59937

Telephone Number:
    Local   406/862-7777
Editor: James Stack

Description: Each issue analyzes the Federal Reserve
and stock market and presents specific
recommendations for profiting in stocks
and mutual funds.
Annual Subscription Cost: $235
Telephone Hotline: Yes
Issues per Year: 18
Special Offer to Readers: $160 per year—a $75 savings.

Investment Quality Trends
7440 Girald Avenue, Suite 4
La Jolla, CA 92037

Telephone Number:
    Local   619/459-3818
Editor: Geraldine Weiss
Description: The focus of the newsletter is on quality and
value in the stock market; 350 Blue Chip stocks
are followed. The service identifies undervalued
and overvalued prices through historic measures
of dividend yield.
Annual Subscription Cost: $250
Trial Subscription: $28 for 2 months
Telephone Hotline: No
Issues per Year: 24

The Investment Reporter
Canadian Business Service
Toronto, Ontario

Telephone Number:
    Local   416/869-1177
Description: Canada's oldest stock market newsletter;
published every week. Key Stocks for Profitable
Long-Term Investment, the monthly Investment
Planning Guide, and research on major
Canadian companies as well as others not
covered by stock brokerage research
departments are included.

The Discount Publications Directory 467

Annual Subscription Cost: $235
Trial Subscription: $47 for 3 months
Telephone Hotline: No
Issues per Year: 52

L/G No-Load Fund Analyst
300 Montgomery Street
San Francisco, CA 94104

Telephone Number:
    Local   415/989-8513
Editors: Ken Gregory/Craig Litman
Description: Monthly: Model portfolios.
Quarterly: Statistical Tables covering over 100 top funds.
Annual Subscription Cost: $149
Telephone Hotline: No
Issues per Year: 12

Market Logic
Institute for Econometric Research
Ft. Lauderdale, FL 33306

Telephone Number:
    Toll-Free (nationwide)   800/327-6720
Editors: Norman Fosback/Glen King Parker
Description: This comprehensive service includes forecasts of average market price levels and of the major market trend; current buy and sell recommendations; insider buying and selling; best-situated stocks; option corner; special opportunities in convertibles, warrants, and index futures; monitors 50 sophisticated leading indicators; and glamour stock index. Also summarizes the current advice of the nation's most widely-read advisory services, and a column on tax strategies for investors.
Annual Subscription Cost: $200
Telephone Hotline: Yes
Issues per Year: 24

Special Offer to Readers: $95 per year for readers; special 1-month free trial.

Market Mania
P.O. Box 1234
Pacifica, CA 94044

Telephone Number:
  Local   415/355-9666
Editor: Glenn Cutler
Description: Covers two areas of the market: general market timing with an overview and analysis of technical, sentiment, and momentum indicators to determine market direction and recommended exposure; and recommendations on undervalued and growth stocks.
Annual Subscription Cost: $119
Trial Subscription: $43 for 3 months
Telephone Hotline: Yes
Issues per Year: 12
Special Offer to Readers: Special introductory trial of 3 months plus hotline for $39 (regularly $43 without hotline).

The Marketarian Letter
P.O. Box 1283
Grand Island, NB 68802

Telephone Number:
  Toll-Free (nationwide)   800/658-4325
Editors: Gerald Theisen/Jess Helleberg
Description: A technically oriented 8-page newsletter that uses both common and proprietary indicators in evaluating the stock market. Also included are specific stock recommendations, stock market timing, and mutual fund recommendations.
Annual Subscription Cost: $225
Trial Subscription: $39 for 3 months
Telephone Hotline: Yes
Issues per Year: 18

Medical Technology Stock Letter
P.O. Box 40460
Berkeley, CA 94704

Telephone Number:
   Local   415/843-1857
Editor: Jim McCamant
Description: This 8-page newsletter specializes in medical biotechnology stocks.
Annual Subscription Cost: $260
Trial Subscription: $49 for 6 issues
Telephone Hotline: Yes
Issues per Year: 24

MPT Fund Review
P.O. Box 6349
Incline Village, NV 89450

Telephone Number:
   Local   415/527-5116
Editors: Bruno Terkaly/Treanna Allbaugh
Description: Analyzes and provides recommendations for mutual funds and stocks (concentrating on smaller capitalization stocks), utilizes Modern Portfolio Theory.
Annual Subscription Cost: $125
Trial Subscription: $39 for 2 months
Telephone Hotline: No
Issues per Year: 12
Special Offer to Readers: 1 year for $93 (25% off regular price).

MPT Review
P.O. Box 5695
Incline Village, NV 89450

Telephone Number:
   Local   702/831-7800
Editor: Louis Navellier

Description: A monthly stock advisory service that specializes in Modern Portfolio Theory and quantitative analysis. Each issue features an extensive Buy List of over 200 stocks.
Annual Subscription Cost: $195
Trial Subscription: $49 for 2 issues
Telephone Hotline: Yes
Issues per Year: 12

Mutual Fund Forecaster
Institute for Econometric Research
3471 No. Federal Highway
Ft. Lauderdale, FL 33306

Telephone Number:
 Toll-Free (nationwide) 800/327-6720
Editors: Norman Fosback/Glen King Parker
Description: The profit projections and risk ratings for over 450 funds with comprehensive coverage of all leading stock funds, both loads and no-loads.
Annual Subscription Cost: $100
Telephone Hotline: Yes
Issues per Year: 12
Special Offer to Readers: $49 per year or special 1-month free trial.

Mutual Fund Strategist
P.O. Box 446
Burlington, VT 05402

Telephone Number:
 Local 802/658-3513
Editor: Charlie Hooper
Description: Employs a market timing strategy in combination with top-performing no-load mutual funds with the objective of beating the market over any 5-year period with about 50% of the risk associated with a buy-and-hold approach.
Annual Subscription Cost: $149

Trial Subscription: $94 for 6 months
Telephone Hotline: Yes
Issues per Year: 12

NASDAQ Review Special Situations
37 East 28th Street
New York, NY 10016

Telephone Number:
    Toll-Free (nationwide)   800/237-8400, x 61
Editors: Robert J. Flaherty/Michael Woods
Description: Founded in 1958, *NASDAQ Review* recommends one new *NASDAQ* stock each month and updates prior recommendations.
Annual Subscription Cost: $150
Telephone Hotline: No
Issues per Year: 12

New Issues
Institute for Econometric Research
Ft. Lauderdale, FL 33306

Telephone Number:
    Toll-Free (nationwide)   800/327-6720
Editors: Norman Fosback/Glen King Parker
Description: Analysis of all important new offerings, follows up research reports; low price stock of the month.
Annual Subscription Cost: $200
Telephone Hotline: Yes
Issues per Year: 12
Special Offer to Readers: $95 per year or special 1-month free trial.

No-Load Fund Investor
P.O. Box 283
Hastings-on Hudson, NY 10706

Telephone Number:
    Local   914/693-7420

Editor: Sheldon Jacobs
Description: A complete, no-load fund advisory service, providing investors with all facts, strategies, and timing techniques needed to invest successfully in no-load mutual funds. The service has two complementary publications offered at a combination subscription rate of $100 per year.
Annual Subscription Cost: $89
Trial Subscription: $49 for 6 months
Telephone Hotline: No
Issues per Year: 12
Special Offer to Readers: A free sample issue.

OTC Insight
Insight Capital Management, Inc.
Moraga, CA 94556

Telephone Number:
   Local   415/376-1362
Editor: James Collins
Description: *OTC Insight* uses a quantitative approach to screen thousands of OTC stocks to find 100 top performing companies. Stocks selected for *OTC Insight* are established growing companies.
Annual Subscription Cost: $245
Telephone Hotline: No
Issues per Year: 12
Special Offer to Readers: Save $50 off a 1-year subscription.

The Outlook
Standard & Poor's Corp.
New York, NY 10004

Telephone Number:
   Local   212/208-8786
Editor: Arnold Kaufman
Description: Market analysis and forecast policy; stock appreciation ranking system ranks 800 popular

stocks; supervised master list of recommended issues.
Annual Subscription Cost: $268
Telephone Hotline: No
Issues per Year: 52
Special Offer to Readers: $29.95 for 3 months; new customers receive a 7-part Investor's Kit.

The PAD System Report
P.O. Box 554
Oxford, OH 45056

Telephone Number:
   Local   513/529-2859
Editor: Daniel Alan Seiver
Description: A monthly market letter which applies the long-term approach to investing outlined in the editor's book *Outperforming Wall Street*. Each issue highlights one or two stocks. Three model portfolios of these stocks are reviewed every month. Every issue also includes commentary on, and the outlook for, the stock market and the economy, with specific advice for investors.
Annual Subscription Cost: $195
Telephone Hotline: No
Issues per Year: 12
Special Offer to Readers: $35 for 3 months.

Personal Finance
KCI Communications
1101 King Street, Suite 400
Alexandria, VA 22314

Telephone Number:
   Toll-Free (nationwide)   800/832-2336
Editor: Stephen Leeb
Description: America's most popular full-coverage investment letter. Unlike most other financial adviser services, *Personal Finance* doesn't rely

on a single voice; you get recommendations from the top experts in each investment field.
Annual Subscription Cost: $118
Telephone Hotline: Yes
Issues per Year: 24

The Peter Dag Investment Letter
65 Lakefront Drive
Akron, OH 44319

Telephone Number:
    Local   216/644-2782
Editor: George Dagnino
Description: This investment letter provides timing advice on the stock market, short-term interest rates, bond market, gold, and the commodity index.
Annual Subscription Cost: $250
Trial Subscription: $75 for 3 months
Telephone Hotline: No
Issues per Year: 29
Special Offer to Readers: Free sample issue.

Plain Talk Investor
1500 Skokie Boulevard, Suite 203
Northbrook, IL 60062

Telephone Number:
    Local   708/564-1955
Editor: Fred Gordon
Description: Each issue contains discussions of market conditions from both the fundamental and technical approach, but distilled to readable personalized format; portfolio contains specific sell information and recommended stocks are followed in each issue.
Annual Subscription Cost: $115
Trial Subscription: $55 for 6 months
Telephone Hotline: No
Issues per Year: 12
Special Offer to Readers: $95 for 1 year.

The Discount Publications Directory 475

The Scott Letter
Cole Publications
Box K-132
Richmond, VA 23288

Telephone Number:
    Toll-Free (nationwide)   800/356-3508
Editor: George Cole Scott
Description: A comprehensive monthly newsletter covering the closed-end fund industry which features full-length interviews with leading fund managers and contains a portfolio of recommended funds for investors of differing objectives. The thrust is total return. The report prefers equity funds selling at discounts to net asset values, but covers over 127 bond funds as well.
Annual Subscription Cost: $110
Telephone Hotline: No
Issues per Year: 12
Special Offer to Readers: $50 for 6-month trial; free sample copy.

Sector Investor
P.O. Box 5627
San Mateo, CA 94402

Telephone Number:
    Local   415/344-1845
Editor: Roger Moen
Description: Concentrates exclusively on Fidelity's Select Portfolios—a set of 36 sector funds (which focus on stocks of particular industry segments). Specific buy/sell recommendations based on technical analysis.
Annual Subscription Cost: $99
Trial Subscription: $49 for 5 months
Telephone Hotline: Yes
Issues per Year: 12

Special Offer to Readers: $10 for a sample issue plus a "Getting Started" packet (does not include the hotline).

Switch Fund Timing
P.O. Box 25430
Rochester, NY 14625

Telephone Number:
   Local   716/385-3122
Editor: David G. Davis
Description: Each monthly issue includes: Recommended Position, Mutual Fund Recommendations, Market Timing, Directory of Mutual Funds, Model Stock Portfolio, Stock of The Month, and Flash Bulletins.
Annual Subscription Cost: $89
Trial Subscription: $29 for 3 months
Telephone Hotline: No
Issues per Year: 12

The Sy Harding Investor Forecasts
P.O. Box 342016
Palm Coast, FL 32035-2016

Telephone Number:
   Local   904/446-0823
Editor: Sy Harding
Description: Makes specific buy and "short" recommendations. Seeks out special situations. Utilizes proprietary technical analysis for market direction and specific recommendations.
Annual Subscription Cost: $175
Telephone Hotline: Yes
Issues per Year: 17
Special Offer to Readers: Special price of $125 for 1-year subscription, plus 28-page study and 5 issues of companion

publication, *The Investors' Moneytree Reports;* or 3-issue sampler subscription for $10.

System & Forecasts
150 Great Neck Road
Great Neck, NY 11021

Telephone Number:
    Local   516/829-6444
Editor: Gerald Appel
Description: A technically oriented market timing newsletter which specializes in short- to intermediate-term trading of bonds, mutual funds, stock index options, and stock index futures contracts. Trading is based upon proprietary market timing signals provided to subscribers on a daily basis.
Annual Subscription Cost: $175
Telephone Hotline: Yes
Issues per Year: 12
Special Offer to Readers: $145 for 1 year—a $30 discount.

APPENDIX E

The Mutual Funds Directory

CHAPTER 1
Stock Funds

The Acorn Fund
2 No. LaSalle Street
Chicago, IL 60602

Telephone Numbers:
   Toll-Free (nationwide)   800/922-6769
   Local   312/621-0630
Type of Fund: Small Co. Growth
Adviser: Harris Assoc. LP
Year Organized: 1970
Ticker Symbol: ACRNX
Minimum Investment: Initial, $4000; Subsequent, $1000
Minimum IRA Investment: Initial, $200; Subsequent, $200
Registered for Sale: All states except Alabama, Arkansas, Mississippi, New Hampshire, New Mexico, North Dakota, Utah, Vermont
Fund Size: $854 million as of 2/9/90
Sales Fee (if any):   None

Expense Ratio: 0.80% for year ending 12/31/88
Portfolio Turnover: 1 Year, 36%; 3 Years, 34%
IRA Fees: Annual, $10; Initial, $10; Closing, $10

The Boston Company Capital Appreciation Fund
One Boston Place
Boston, MA 02108

Telephone Numbers:
    Toll-Free (nationwide)   800/225-5267
    Toll-Free (local)   800/343-6324
Type of Fund: Growth
Adviser: The Boston Co. Advisor, Inc.
Year Organized: 1947
Ticker Symbol: BCCAX
Minimum Investment: Initial, $1000; Subsequent, none
Minimum IRA Investment: Initial, $500; Subsequent, none
Registered for Sale: All states
Fund Size: $639 million as of 2/9/90
Sales Fee (if any):   None
Expense Ratio: 1.31% for year ending 5/1/89
Portfolio Turnover: 1 Year, 24%; 3 Years, 37%
IRA Fees: Annual, $10; Initial, $5; Closing, none

David L. Babson Growth Fund
2440 Pershing Road
Kansas City, MO 64108

Telephone Numbers:
    Toll-Free (nationwide)   800/422-2766
    Local   816/471-5200
Type of Fund: Growth
Adviser: David L. Babson & Co.
Year Organized: 1959
Ticker Symbol: BABSX
Minimum Investment: Initial, $500; Subsequent, $50
Minimum IRA Investment: Initial, $250; Subsequent, $50
Registered for Sale: Information not available
Fund Size: $273 million as of 2/23/90

Sales Fee (if any):   None
Expense Ratio: 0.81% for year ending 6/30/88
Portfolio Turnover: 1 Year, 26%; 3 Years, 20%
IRA Fees: Annual, $10; Initial, none; Closing, $10

Dodge & Cox Balanced Fund, Inc.
One Post Street, 35th Floor
San Francisco, CA 94104

Telephone Number:
   Local   415/981-1710
Type of Fund: Balanced
Adviser: Dodge & Cox
Year Organized: 1931
Ticker Symbol: DODBX
Minimum Investment: Initial, $1000; Subsequent, $100
Minimum IRA Investment: Information not available
Registered for Sale: Most states
Fund Size: $48 million as of 2/9/90
Sales Fee (if any):   None
Expense Ratio: 0.77% for year ending 12/31/88
Portfolio Turnover: 1 Year, 9%; 3 Years, 15%
IRA Fees: Annual, $10; Initial, none; Closing, $15

Dodge & Cox Stock Fund
One Post Street, 35th Floor
San Francisco, CA 94104

Telephone Number:
   Local   415/434-0311
Type of Fund: Growth Inc.
Adviser: Dodge & Cox
Year Organized: 1965
Ticker Symbol: DODGX
Minimum Investment: Initial, $1000; Subsequent, $100
Minimum IRA Investment: Information not available
Registered for Sale: California, Connecticut, District of Columbia, Georgia, Hawaii, Massachusetts, Michigan, Nevada,

New York, Oregon, Utah, Washington, Wyoming
Fund Size: $112 million as of 2/9/90
Sales Fee (if any): None
Expense Ratio: 0.69% for year ending 12/31/88
Portfolio Turnover: 1 Year, 10%; 3 Years, 10%
IRA Fees: Annual, $10; Initial, none; Closing, $15

Dreyfus Growth Opportunity Fund, Inc.
666 Old Country Road
Garden City, NY 11530

Telephone Numbers:
    Toll-Free (nationwide)   800/645-6561
    Local   718/895-1206
Type of Fund: Growth
Adviser: The Dreyfus Corporation
Organized: 1972
Ticker Symbol: DREQX
Minimum Investment: Initial, $2500; Subsequent, $100
Minimum IRA Investment: Initial, $750; Subsequent, none
Registered for Sale: All states
Fund Size: $581 million as of 2/23/90
Sales Fee (if any): None
Expense Ratio: 0.91% for year ending 2/28/88
Portfolio Turnover: 1 Year, 129%; 3 Years, 56%
IRA Fees: Annual, $5; Initial, $8; Closing, none

The Evergreen Limited Market Fund, Inc.
2500 Westchester Avenue
Purchase, NY 10577

Telephone Numbers:
    Toll-Free (nationwide)   800/235-0064
    Local   914/694-2020
Type of Fund: Small Co. Growth
Adviser: Saxon Woods Asset Management Corp.
Year Organized: 1983
Ticker Symbol: Information not available

Minimum Investment: Information not available
Minimum IRA Investment: Information not available
Registered for Sale: Information not available
Fund Size: $39 million as of 2/9/90
Sales Fee (if any):   None
Expense Ratio: 1.47% for year ending 5/31/88
Portfolio Turnover: 1 Year, 47%; 3 Years, 56%
IRA Fees: Annual, $10; Initial, none; Closing, none

Fidelity Puritan Fund
82 Devonshire Street
Boston, MA 02109

Telephone Numbers:
   Toll-Free (nationwide)   800/544-6666
   Local   617/523-1919
Type of Fund: Equity Inc.
Adviser: Fidelity Management & Research Co.
Year Organized: 1946
Ticker Symbol: FPURX
Minimum Investment: Initial, $1000; Subsequent, $250
Minimum IRA Investment: Initial, $500; Subsequent, $250
Registered for Sale: All states
Fund Size: $4860 million as of 2/9/90
Sales Fee (if any):   2%
Expense Ratio: 0.72% for year ending 7/31/88
Portfolio Turnover: 1 Year, 88%; 3 Years, 85%
IRA Fees: Annual, $10; Initial, $10; Closing, none

Fidelity Trend Fund
82 Devonshire Street
Boston, MA 02109

Telephone Numbers:
   Toll-Free (nationwide)   800/544-6666
   Local   617/523-1919
Type of Fund: Growth
Adviser: Fidelity Management & Research Co.
Year Organized: 1958

The Mutual Funds Directory 485

Ticker Symbol: FTRNX
Minimum Investment: Initial, $1000; Subsequent, $250
Minimum IRA Investment: Initial, $500; Subsequent, $250
Registered for Sale: All states
Fund Size: $883 million as of 2/27/90
Sales Fee (if any):   None
Expense Ratio: 0.58% for year ending 3/1/90
Portfolio Turnover: 1 Year, 37%; 3 Years, 128%
IRA Fees: Annual $10; Initial, none; Closing, $10

Founders Blue Chip Fund
3033 East First Avenue, Suite 810
Denver, CO 80206

Telephone Numbers:
    Toll-Free (nationwide)   800/525-2440
    Local   303/394-4404
Type of Fund: Growth
Adviser: Founders Asset Management
Year Organized: 1938
Ticker Symbol: FRMUX
Minimum Investment: Initial, $1000; Subsequent, $100
Minimum IRA Investment: Initial, $500; Subsequent, $100
Registered for Sale: All states except New Hampshire
Fund Size: $231 million as of 2/27/90
Sales Fee (if any):   None
Expense Ratio: 0.87% for year ending 12/12/88
Portfolio Turnover: 1 Year, 58%; 3 Years, 42%
IRA Fees: Annual, $10; Initial, none; Closing, none

Founders Growth Fund, Inc.
3033 East First Avenue, Suite 810
Denver, CO 80206

Telephone Numbers:
    Toll-Free (nationwide)   800/525-2440
    Local   303/394-4404
Type of Fund: Growth
Adviser: Founders Asset Management

Year Organized: 1962
Ticker Symbol: FRGRX
Minimum Investment: Initial, $1000; Subsequent, $100
Minimum IRA Investment: Initial, $500; Subsequent, $100
Registered for Sale: All states except New Hampshire
Fund Size: $111 million as of 2/27/90
Sales Fee (if any): None
Expense Ratio: 1.38% for year ending 12/12/88
Portfolio Turnover: 1 Year, 179%; 3 Years, 142%
IRA Fees: Annual, $10; Initial, none; Closing, none

GIT Equity Trust—Special Growth Portfolio
1655 North Fort Myer Drive
Arlington, VA 22209

Telephone Numbers:
    Toll-Free (nationwide)   800/336-3063
    Local   703/528-6500
Type of Fund: Small Co. Growth
Adviser: Bankers Finance Investment Management Corp.
Year Organized: 1983
Ticker Symbol: GISGX
Minimum Investment: Initial, $1000; Subsequent, none
Minimum IRA Investment: Initial, $500; Subsequent, none
Registered for Sale: All states except Alaska, Montana, North
                          Dakota, Oklahoma, South Dakota, Utah
Fund Size: $42.8 million as of 2/9/90
Sales Fee (if any): None
Expense Ratio: 1.5% for year ending 7/31/88
Portfolio Turnover: 1 Year, 27%; 3 Years, 8%
IRA Fees: Annual, $12; Initial, none; Closing, none

Gradison Growth Trust—Established Growth Fund
580 Walnut Street
The 580 Building
Cincinnati, OH 45202

Telephone Numbers:
    Toll-Free (nationwide)   800/543-1818
    Local   513/579-5700

Type of Fund: Small Co. Growth
Adviser: Gradison & Co., Inc.
Year Organized: 1983
Ticker Symbol: GETGX
Minimum Investment: Initial, $1000; Subsequent, $50
Minimum IRA Investment: Initial, $1000; Subsequent, $50
Registered for Sale: Arizona, California, Colorado, Connecticut, Florida, Georgia, Illinois, Indiana, Kentucky, Massachusetts, Maryland, Michigan, New Jersey, New York, Ohio, Pennsylvania, South Carolina, Texas, Virginia, Washington
Fund Size: $24 million as of 2/9/90
Sales Fee (if any): None
Expense Ratio: 1.57% for year ending 4/30/88
Portfolio Turnover: 1 Year, 26%; 3 Years, 80%
IRA Fees: Annual, $5; Initial, $10; Closing, none

IAI Regional Fund, Inc.
1100 Dain Tower
P.O. Box 357
Minneapolis, MN 55440

Telephone Number:
 Local 612/371-2884
Type of Fund: Growth
Adviser: Investment Advisers, Inc.
Year Organized: 1980
Ticker Symbol: IARGX
Minimum Investment: Initial, $5000; Subsequent, $1000
Minimum IRA Investment: Initial, $100; Subsequent, none
Registered for Sale: Arizona, California, Colorado, Illinois, Iowa, Maryland, Michigan, Minnesota, Missouri, Montana, Nevada, New York, North Dakota, Pennsylvania, South Dakota, Tennessee, Texas, Washington, Wisconsin
Fund Size: $120 million as of 2/9/90
Sales Fee (if any): None
Expense Ratio: 1.0% for year ending 5/31/89

Portfolio Turnover: 1 Year, 93%; 3 Years, 132%
IRA Fees: None

IAI Stock Fund, Inc.
1100 Dain Tower
P.O. Box 357
Minneapolis, MN 55440

Telephone Number:
  Local   612/371-2884
Type of Fund: Aggressive Growth
Adviser: Investment Advisers, Inc.
Year Organized: 1971
Ticker Symbol: IASKX
Minimum Investment: Initial, $2500; Subsequent, $1000
Minimum IRA Investment: Initial, $100; Subsequent, none
Registered for Sale: Most states
Fund Size: $73 million as of 2/27/90
Sales Fee (if any):   None
Expense Ratio: 1.0% for year ending 5/31/89
Portfolio Turnover: 1 Year, 48%; 3 Years, 67%
IRA Fees: None

Janus Fund, Inc.
100 Fillmore Street, Suite 300
Denver, CO 80206

Telephone Numbers:
  Toll-Free (nationwide)   800/525-3713
  Local   303/333-3863
Type of Fund: Aggressive Growth
Adviser: Janus Capital Corp.
Year Organized: 1970
Ticker Symbol: JANSX
Minimum Investment: Initial, $1000; Subsequent, $50
Minimum IRA Investment: Initial, $500; Subsequent, $50
Registered for Sale: All states
Fund Size: $705 million as of 2/27/90
Sales Fee (if any):   None

The Mutual Funds Directory   489

Expense Ratio: 0.92% for year ending 1/22/90
Portfolio Turnover: 1 Year, 205%; 3 Years, 214%
IRA Fees: Annual, $10; Initial, none; Closing, none

Lehman Opportunity Fund, Inc.
55 Water Street
New York, NY 10041

Telephone Numbers:
    Toll-Free (nationwide)   800/221-5350
    Local   212/668-8578
Type of Fund: Aggressive Growth
Adviser: Lehman Management Co.
Year Organized: 1978
Ticker Symbol: LOPPX
Minimum Investment: Initial, $1000; Subsequent, $100
Minimum IRA Investment: Initial, $250; Subsequent, $50
Registered for Sale: All states
Fund Size: $120 million as of 3/8/90
Sales Fee (if any):   None
Expense Ratio: 1.19% for year ending 1/1/90
Portfolio Turnover: 1 Year, 14%; 3 Years, 24%
IRA Fees: Annual, $10; Initial, $5; Closing, $10

Lindner Fund, Inc.
200 South Bemiston
P.O. Box 11208
St. Louis, MO 63105

Telephone Number:
    Local   314/727-5305
Type of Fund: Growth
Adviser: Lindner Management Corp.
Year Organized: 1973
Ticker Symbol: LDNRX
Minimum Investment: None
Minimum IRA Investment: None
Registered for Sale: Most states
Fund Size: $593 million as of 2/16/90

Sales Fee (if any):   None
Expense Ratio: 1.07% for year ending 6/30/88
Portfolio Turnover: 1 Year, 21%; 3 Years, 33%
IRA Fees: Annual, $10; Initial, none; Closing, none

Loomis-Sayles Capital Development Fund
P.O. Box 449
Back Bay Annex
Boston, MA 02117

Telephone Numbers:
    Toll-Free (nationwide)   800/345-4048
    Local   617/578-1333
Type of Fund: Growth
Adviser: Loomis, Sayles & Co.
Year Organized: 1960
Ticker Symbol: LOMCX
Minimum Investment: Initial, none; Subsequent, $50
Minimum IRA Investment: Initial, none; Subsequent, $25
Registered for Sale: All states
Fund Size: $215 million as of 2/16/90
Sales Fee (if any):   None
Expense Ratio: 0.92% for year ending 12/31/88
Portfolio Turnover: 1 Year, 301%; 3 Years, 209%
IRA Fees: Annual, $10; Initial, $5; Closing, $5

Loomis-Sayles Mutual Fund
P.O. Box 449
Back Bay Annex
Boston, MA 02117

Telephone Numbers:
    Toll-Free (nationwide)   800/345-4048
    Local   617/578-1333
Type of Fund: Balanced
Adviser: Loomis, Sayles & Co.
Year Organized: 1929
Ticker Symbol: LOMMX
Minimum Investment: Initial, $250; Subsequent, $50

The Mutual Funds Directory 491

Minimum IRA Investment: Initial, $25; Subsequent, $25
Registered for Sale: All states
Fund Size: $323 million as of 2/9/90
Sales Fee (if any):   None
Expense Ratio: 1.01% for year ending 5/1/89
Portfolio Turnover: 1 Year, 218%; 3 Years, 127%
IRA Fees: Annual, $10; Initial, $5; Closing, $5

Mathers Fund, Inc.
100 Corporate North, Suite 201
Bannockburn, IL 60015

Telephone Numbers:
    Toll-Free (nationwide)   800/962-3863
    Local   312/295-7400
Type of Fund: Growth
Adviser: Mathers and Co.
Year Organized: 1965
Ticker Symbol: MATRX
Minimum Investment: Initial, $1000; Subsequent, $200
Minimum IRA Investment: None
Registered for Sale: All states except Maine, Montana, New Hampshire, North Dakota, South Dakota, Vermont
Fund Size: $211 million as of 2/9/90
Sales Fee (if any):   None
Expense Ratio: 1.01% for year ending 5/31/89
Portfolio Turnover: 1 Year, 148%; 3 Years, 174%
IRA Fees: Annual, $10; Initial, none; Closing, none

Mutual Beacon Fund, Inc.
51 John F. Kennedy Parkway
Short Hills, NJ 07078

Telephone Numbers:
    Toll-Free (nationwide)   800/448-3863
    Local   201/912-2100
Type of Fund: Growth Inc.
Adviser: Heine Securities Corp.

Year Organized: 1985
Ticker Symbol: BEGRX
Minimum Investment: Initial, $50,000; Subsequent, $1000
Minimum IRA Investment: Initial, $2000; Subsequent, $1000
Registered for Sale: All states
Fund Size: $455 million as of 5/30/90
Sales Fee (if any): None
Expense Ratio: 0.6% for year ending 12/31/88
Portfolio Turnover: 1 Year, 87%; 3 Years, 113%
IRA Fees: Annual, $10; Initial, $10; Closing, none

Mutual Qualified Fund, Inc.
51 John F. Kennedy Parkway
Short Hills, NJ 07078

Telephone Numbers:
    Toll-Free (nationwide) 800/448-3863
    Local 201/912-2100
Type of Fund: Growth Inc.
Adviser: Heine Securities Corp.
Year Organized: 1980
Ticker Symbol: MQIFX
Minimum Investment: Initial, $1000; Subsequent, $50
Minimum IRA Investment: None
Registered for Sale: All states
Fund Size: $1587 million as of 2/9/90
Sales Fee (if any): None
Expense Ratio: 0.62% for year ending 12/31/88
Portfolio Turnover: 1 Year, 86%; 3 Years, 124%
IRA Fees: Annual, $10; Initial, $10; Closing, none

Mutual Shares Fund
51 John F. Kennedy Parkway
Short Hills, NJ 07078

Telephone Numbers:
    Toll-Free (nationwide) 800/448-3863
    Local 201/912-2100
Type of Fund: Growth Inc.

Adviser: Heine Securities Corp.
Year Organized: 1949
Ticker Symbol: MUTHX
Minimum Investment: Initial, $5000; Subsequent, $100
Minimum IRA Investment: Initial, $2000; Subsequent, $100
Registered for Sale: All states
Fund Size: $3640 million as of 2/9/90
Sales Fee (if any):   None
Expense Ratio: 0.67% for year ending 12/31/88
Portfolio Turnover: 1 Year, 90%; 3 Years, 122%
IRA Fees: Annual, $10; Initial, $10; Closing, none

Neuberger & Berman Manhattan Fund, Inc.
342 Madison Avenue
New York, NY 10173

Telephone Numbers:
    Toll-Free (nationwide)   800/367-0770
    Local   212/850-8300
Type of Fund: Aggressive Growth
Adviser: Neuberger & Berman Management, Inc.
Year Organized: 1966
Ticker Symbol: CNAMX
Minimum Investment: Initial, $1000; Subsequent, $100
Minimum IRA Investment: Initial, $250; Subsequent, $50
Registered for Sale: All states
Fund Size: $429 million as of 2/9/90
Sales Fee (if any):   None
Expense Ratio: 1.2% for year ending 12/31/88
Portfolio Turnover: 1 Year, 70%; 3 Years, 96%
IRA Fees: Annual, $9; Initial, none; Closing, $7

Neuburger & Berman Partners Fund, Inc.
342 Madison Avenue
New York, NY 10173

Telephone Numbers:
    Toll-Free (nationwide)   800/367-0770
    Local   212/850-8300

Type of Fund: Growth
Adviser: Robert C. Vitale (1988); Dietrich Weismann (1984)
Year Organized: 1968
Ticker Symbol: PARTX
Minimum Investment: Initial, $1000; Subsequent, $100
Minimum IRA Investment: Initial, $250; Subsequent, $50
Registered for Sale: All states
Fund Size: $786 million as of 2/9/90
Sales Fee (if any):   None
Expense Ratio: 0.95% for year ending 6/30/88
Portfolio Turnover: 1 Year, 210%; 3 Years, 181%
IRA Fees: Annual, $9; Initial, none; Closing, $7

Nicholas II, Inc.
700 N. Water Street
Milwaukee, WI 53202

Telephone Number:
    Local   414/272-6133
Type of Fund: Small Co. Growth
Adviser: Nicholas Co, Inc.
Year Organized: 1983
Ticker Symbol: NCTWX
Minimum Investment: Initial, $1000; Subsequent, $100
Minimum IRA Investment: None
Registered for Sale: All states
Fund Size: $422 million as of 2/9/90
Sales Fee (if any):   None
Expense Ratio: 0.74% for year ending 7/4/90
Portfolio Turnover: 1 Year, 88%; 3 Years, 25%
IRA Fees: Annual, $10; Initial, none; Closing, $15

Primecap Fund
P.O. Box 2600
Valley Forge, PA 19482

Telephone Numbers:
    Toll-Free (nationwide)   800/662-7447
    Local   215/648-6000
Type of Fund: Growth

Adviser: Primecap Management Co.
Year Organized: 1984
Ticker Symbol: VPMCX
Minimum Investment: Initial, $10,000; Subsequent, $1000
Minimum IRA Investment: Initial, $500; Subsequent, $100
Registered for Sale: All states
Fund Size: $313 million as of 6/1/90
Sales Fee (if any):   None
Expense Ratio: 0.83% for year ending 12/31/88
Portfolio Turnover: 1 Year, 26%; 3 Years, 15%
IRA Fees: Annual, $10; Initial, $10; Closing, none

Reich & Tang Equity Fund, Inc.
100 Park Avenue
New York, NY 10017

Telephone Numbers:
    Toll-Free (nationwide)   800/221-3079
    Local   212/370-1240
Type of Fund: Growth
Adviser: Reich & Tang, Inc.
Year Organized: 1985
Ticker Symbol: RCHTX
Minimum Investment: Initial, $5000; Subsequent, none
Minimum IRA Investment: Initial, $250; Subsequent, none
Registered for Sale: Most states
Fund Size: $112 million as of 3/1/90
Sales Fee (if any):   None
Expense Ratio: 1.11% for year ending 12/31/88
Portfolio Turnover: 1 Year, 27%; 3 Years, 35%
IRA Fees: Annual, $10; Initial, $10; Closing, $10

Safeco Equity Fund, Inc.
Safeco Plaza
Seattle, WA 98185

Telephone Numbers:
    Toll-Free (nationwide)   800/426-6730
    Local   206/545-5530
Type of Fund: Growth Inc.

Adviser: Safeco Asset Management Co.
Year Organized: 1932
Ticker Symbol: SAFQX
Minimum Investment: Initial, $1000; Subsequent, $100
Minimum IRA Investment: Initial, $250; Subsequent, $100
Registered for Sale: Most states
Fund Size: $60 million as of 3/1/90
Sales Fee (if any):   None
Expense Ratio: 0.96% for year ending 1/22/90
Portfolio Turnover: 1 Year, 63%; 3 Years, 85%
IRA Fees: Annual, $5; Initial, none; Closing, none

Scudder Capital Growth Fund, Inc.
160 Federal Street
Boston, MA 02110

Telephone Numbers:
    Toll-Free (nationwide)   800/225-2470
    Local   617/439-4640
Type of Fund: Growth
Adviser: Scudder, Stevens & Clark
Year Organized: 1956
Ticker Symbol: SCDUX
Minimum Investment: Initial, $1000; Subsequent, none
Minimum IRA Investment: Initial, $240; Subsequent, none
Registered for Sale: All states
Fund Size: $1009 million as of 6/1/90
Sales Fee (if any):   None
Expense Ratio: 0.88% for year ending 2/1/90
Portfolio Turnover: 1 Year, 55%; 3 Years, 58%
IRA Fees: None

Scudder International Fund, Inc.
160 Federal Street
Boston, MA 02110

Telephone Numbers:
    Toll-Free (nationwide)   800/225-2470
    Local   617/439-4640

The Mutual Funds Directory   497

Type of Fund: International
Adviser: Scudder, Stevens & Clark
Year Organized: 1953
Ticker Symbol: SCINX
Minimum Investment: Initial, $1000; Subsequent, none
Minimum IRA Investment: Initial, $240; Subsequent, none
Registered for Sale: All states
Fund Size: $879 million as of 6/4/90
Sales Fee (if any):   None
Expense Ratio: 1.22% for year ending 8/1/89
Portfolio Turnover: 1 Year, 48%; 3 Years, 66%
IRA Fees: None

Selected American Shares, Inc.
1331 Euclid Avenue
Cleveland, OH 44115

Telephone Number:
    Toll-Free (nationwide)   800/553-5533
Type of Fund: Growth Inc.
Adviser: Selected Financial Services, Inc.
Year Organized: 1933
Ticker Symbol: SLSAX
Minimum Investment: Initial, $1000; Subsequent, $100
Minimum IRA Investment: None
Registered for Sale: All states
Fund Size: $370 million as of 3/2/90
Sales Fee (if any):   None
Expense Ratio: 1.11% for year ending 10/6/89
Portfolio Turnover: 1 Year, 35%; 3 Years, 40%
IRA Fees: Annual, $10; Initial, $5; Closing, $5

SIT "New Beginning" Growth Fund, Inc.
1714 First Bank Place West
Minneapolis, MN 55402

Telephone Numbers:
    Toll-Free (nationwide)   800/332-5580
    Local   612/332-3223

Type of Fund: Small Co. Growth
Adviser: Sit Investment Management Co.
Year Organized: 1981
Ticker Symbol: NBNGX
Minimum Investment: Initial, $2000; Subsequent, $100
Minimum IRA Investment: None
Registered for Sale: Most states
Fund Size: $58 million as of 3/1/90
Sales Fee (if any): None
Expense Ratio: 1.19% for year ending 12/31/89
Portfolio Turnover: 1 Year, 88%; 3 Years, 81%
IRA Fees: None

Steinroe Special Fund, Inc.
P.O. Box 1143
Chicago, IL 60690

Telephone Numbers:
    Toll-Free (nationwide)   800/338-2550
    Local   312/368-7826
Type of Fund: Growth
Adviser: Stein Roe & Farnham
Organized: 1968
Ticker Symbol: SRSPX
Minimum Investment: Initial, $1000; Subsequent, $100
Minimum IRA Investment: Initial, $500; Subsequent, $50
Registered for Sale: All states
Fund Size: $320 million as of 3/1/90
Sales Fee (if any): None
Expense Ratio: 0.99% for year ending 9/30/88
Portfolio Turnover: 1 Year, 42%; 3 Years, 116%
IRA Fees: Annual, $10; Initial, none; Closing, $5

Strong Total Return Fund, Inc.
P.O. Box 2936
Milwaukee, WI 53201

Telephone Numbers:
    Toll-Free (nationwide)   800/368-3863
    Local   414/359-1400

Type of Fund: Growth Inc.
Adviser: Strong/Corneliuson Capital Management, Inc.
Year Organized: 1981
Ticker Symbol: STRFX
Minimum Investment: Initial, $250; Subsequent, $200
Minimum IRA Investment: Initial, $250; Subsequent, none
Registered for Sale: All states
Fund Size: $1065 million as of 3/2/90
Sales Fee (if any):   None
Expense Ratio: 1.2% for year ending 12/31/89
Portfolio Turnover: 1 Year, 305%; 3 Years, 224%
IRA Fees: Annual, $10; Initial, none; Closing, $15

Twentieth Century Giftrust Investors
605 West 47th Street
P.O. Box 419200
Kansas City, MO 64141

Telephone Numbers:
    Toll-Free (nationwide)   800/345-2021
    Local   816/531-5575
Type of Fund: Aggressive Growth
Adviser: Investors Research Corp.
Year Organized: 1983
Ticker Symbol: TWGTX
Minimum Investment: Initial, $100; Subsequent, none
Minimum IRA Investment: None
Registered for Sale: All states
Fund Size: $24 million as of 3/2/90
Sales Fee (if any):   None
Expense Ratio: 1% for year ending 12/31/88
Portfolio Turnover: 1 Year, 157%; 3 Years, 123%
IRA Fees: None

The Value Line Fund, Inc.
711 Third Avenue
New York, NY 10017

Telephone Numbers:
    Toll-Free (nationwide)   800/223-0818
    Local   212/687-3965

Type of Fund: Growth Inc.
Adviser: Value Line, Inc.
Year Organized: 1949
Ticker Symbol: VLIFX
Minimum Investment: Initial, $1000; Subsequent, $100
Minimum IRA Investment: None
Registered for Sale: All states
Fund Size: $194 million as of 3/1/90
Sales Fee (if any): None
Expense Ratio: 0.71% for year ending 12/31/88
Portfolio Turnover: 1 Year, 108%; 3 Years, 145%
IRA Fees: Annual, $10; Initial, none; Closing, none

Vanguard Index Trust 500 Portfolio
P.O. Box 2600
Valley Forge, PA 19482

Telephone Numbers:
    Toll-Free (nationwide)   800/662-2739
    Local   215/648-6000
Type of Fund: Growth Inc.
Adviser: The Vanguard Group, Inc.
Year Organized: 1976
Ticker Symbol: VFINX
Minimum Investment: Initial, $3000; Subsequent, $100
Minimum IRA Investment: Initial, $500; Subsequent, $100
Registered for Sale: All states
Fund Size: $2315 million as of 6/4/90
Sales Fee (if any): None
Expense Ratio: 0.22% for year ending 12/31/88
Portfolio Turnover: 1 Year, 10%; 3 Years, 29%
IRA Fees: Annual, $10; Initial, $10; Closing, none

Vanguard W.L. Morgan Growth Fund
P.O. Box 2600
Valley Forge, PA 19482

Telephone Numbers:
    Toll-Free (nationwide)   800/662-2739
    Local   215/648-6000

Type of Fund: Growth
Adviser: Wellington Management Co.
Year Organized: 1968
Ticker Symbol: VMRGX
Minimum Investment: Initial, $3000; Subsequent, $100
Minimum IRA Investment: Initial, $500; Subsequent, $100
Registered for Sale: All states
Fund Size: $732 million as of 3/1/90
Sales Fee (if any):   None
Expense Ratio: 0.55% for year ending 12/31/88
Portfolio Turnover: 1 Year, 32%; 3 Years, 31%
IRA Fees: Annual, $10; Initial, $10; Closing, none

Vanguard Wellesley Income Fund
P.O. Box 2600
Valley Forge, PA 19482

Telephone Numbers:
    Toll-Free (nationwide)   800/662-7447
    Local   215/648-6000
Type of Fund: Balanced
Adviser: Wellington Management Corp.
Year Organized: 1970
Ticker Symbol: VWINX
Minimum Investment: Initial, $3000; Subsequent, $100
Minimum IRA Investment: Initial, $500; Subsequent, $100
Registered for Sale: All states
Fund Size: $787 million as of 3/2/90
Sales Fee (if any):   None
Expense Ratio: 0.51% for year ending 12/31/88
Portfolio Turnover: 1 Year, 45%; 3 Years, 18%
IRA Fees: Annual, $10; Initial, $10; Closing, none

Vanguard Wellington Fund
P.O. Box 2600
Valley Forge, PA 19482

Telephone Numbers:
    Toll-Free (nationwide)   800/662-7447
    Local   215/648-6000

Type of Fund: Balanced
Adviser: Wellington Management Corp.
Year Organized: 1928
Ticker Symbol: VWELX
Minimum Investment: Initial, $3000; Subsequent, $100
Minimum IRA Investment: Initial, $500; Subsequent, $100
Registered for Sale: All states
Fund Size: $2340 million as of 6/4/90
Sales Fee (if any):   None
Expense Ratio: 0.47% for year ending 11/30/88
Portfolio Turnover: 1 Year, 55%; 3 Years, 25%
IRA Fees: Annual, $10; Initial, $10; Closing, none

CHAPTER 2
Bond Funds

Columbia Fixed Income Securities Fund, Inc.
1301 S.W. 5th Avenue
P.O. Box 1350
Portland, OR 97207

Telephone Numbers:
    Toll-Free (nationwide)   800/547-1037
    Local   503/222-3600
Type of Bond Portfolio: Corporate; Maturity: long (10 years+)
Adviser: Columbia Funds Management Company
Year Organized: 1983
Minimum Investment: Initial, $1000; Subsequent, $100
Minimum IRA Investment: None
Fund Size: $105 million as of 2/23/90
Sales Fee (if any):   None
Expense Ratio: 0.74% for year ending 2/16/90
Portfolio Turnover: 1 Year, 114%; 3 Years, 114%
IRA Fees: Annual, $25; Initial, none; Closing, none

Dreyfus Intermediate Tax Exempt Bond Fund, Inc.
666 Old Country Road
Garden City, NY 11530

Telephone Numbers:
 Toll-Free (nationwide)   800/645-6561
 Local   718/895-1206
Type of Bond Portfolio: Municipal; Maturity: intermediate (3–10 years)
Adviser: The Dreyfus Corporation
Year Organized: 1983
Minimum Investment: Initial, $2500; Subsequent, $100
Minimum IRA Investment: None
Fund Size: $1116 million as of 6/4/90
Sales Fee (if any):   None
Expense Ratio: 0.69% for year ending 12/31/88
Portfolio Turnover: 1 Year, 36%; 3 Years, 67%
IRA Fees: None

Dreyfus New York Insured Tax Exempt Bond Fund, Inc.
666 Old Country Road
Garden City, NY 11530

Telephone Numbers:
 Toll-Free (nationwide)   800/645-6561
 Local   718/895-1206
Type of Bond Portfolio: Municipal; Maturity: long (10 years +)
Adviser: The Dreyfus Corporation
Year Organized: 1986
Minimum Investment: Initial, $2500; Subsequent, $100
Minimum IRA Investment: None
Fund Size: $80 million as of 6/4/90
Sales Fee (if any):   None
Expense Ratio: 0.23% for year ending 12/31/88
Portfolio Turnover: 1 Year, 32%; 3 Years, not available
IRA Fees: None

Dreyfus New York Intermediate Tax Exempt Bond Fund, Inc.
666 Old Country Road
Garden City, NY 11530

Telephone Numbers:
    Toll-Free (nationwide)   800/645-6561
    Local   718/895-1206
Type of Bond Portfolio: Municipal; Maturity: intermediate
                          (3–10 years)
Adviser: The Dreyfus Corporation
Year Organized: 1986
Minimum Investment: Initial, $2500; Subsequent, $100
Minimum IRA Investment: None
Fund Size: $94 million as of 6/4/90
Sales Fee (if any):   None
Expense Ratio: 0% for year ending 12/31/88 (fee waived)
Portfolio Turnover: 1 Year, 1%; 3 Years, not available
IRA Fees: None

Dreyfus New York Tax Exempt Bond Fund, Inc.
666 Old Country Road
Garden City, NY 11530

Telephone Numbers:
    Toll-Free (nationwide)   800/645-6561
    Local   718/895-1206
Type of Bond Portfolio: Municipal; Maturity: long
                          (10 years +)
Adviser: The Dreyfus Corporation
Year Organized: 1983
Minimum Investment: Initial, $2500; Subsequent, $100
Minimum IRA Investment: None
Fund Size: $1687 million as of 6/4/90
Sales Fee (if any):   None
Expense Ratio: 0.72% for year ending 5/31/88
Portfolio Turnover: 1 Year, 57%; 3 Years, 15%
IRA Fees: None

Dreyfus Short Intermediate Government Fund
666 Old Country Road
Garden City, NY 11530

Telephone Numbers:
    Toll-Free (nationwide)   800/645-6561
    Local   718/895-1206
Type of Bond Portfolio: Corporate; Maturity:
                                   intermediate/short (under 10 years)
Adviser: The Dreyfus Corporation
Year Organized: 1986
Minimum Investment: Initial, $2500; Subsequent, $100
Minimum IRA Investment: None
Fund Size: $31 million as of 2/23/90
Sales Fee (if any):   None
Expense Ratio: 0% for year ending 11/30/89 (fee waived)
Portfolio Turnover: 1 Year, 89%; 3 Years, not available
IRA Fees: Annual, $5; Initial, $8; Closing, none

Dreyfus Short Intermediate Tax Exempt Bond Fund
666 Old Country Road
Garden City, NY 11530

Telephone Numbers:
    Toll-Free (nationwide)   800/645-6561
    Local   718/895-1206
Type of Bond Portfolio: Municipal; Maturity:
                                   intermediate/short (under 10 years)
Adviser: The Dreyfus Corporation
Year Organized: 1986
Minimum Investment: Initial, $2500; Subsequent, $100
Minimum IRA Investment: None
Fund Size: $66 million as of 6/4/90
Sales Fee (if any):   None
Expense Ratio: 0.35% for year ending 12/31/88
Portfolio Turnover: 1 Year, 2%; 3 Years, not available
IRA Fees: None

Dreyfus Tax Exempt Bond Fund, Inc.
666 Old Country Road
Garden City, NY 11530

Telephone Numbers:
    Toll-Free (nationwide)   800/645-6561
    Local   718/895-1206
Type of Bond Portfolio: Municipal; Maturity: long
                              (10 years +)
Adviser: The Dreyfus Corporation
Year Organized: 1976
Minimum Investment: Initial, $2500; Subsequent, $100
Minimum IRA Investment: None
Fund Size: $3725 million as of 6/4/90
Sales Fee (if any):   None
Expense Ratio: 0.71% for year ending 8/31/88
Portfolio Turnover: 1 Year, 51%; 3 Years, 53%
IRA Fees: None

Dreyfus U.S. Government Intermediate Securities, L.P.
666 Old Country Road
Garden City, NY 11530

Telephone Numbers:
    Toll-Free (nationwide)   800/645-6561
    Local   718/895-1206
Type of Bond Portfolio: Government; Maturity: intermediate
                              (3–10 years)
Adviser: The Dreyfus Corporation
Year Organized: 1987
Minimum Investment: Initial, $2500; Subsequent, $100
Minimum IRA Investment: Initial, $750; Subsequent, none
Fund Size: $62 million as of 6/4/90
Sales Fee (if any):   None
Expense Ratio: 0.47% for year ending 12/31/88
Portfolio Turnover: 1 Year, 21%; 3 Years, not available
IRA Fees: Annual $5; Initial, $8; Closing, none

Fidelity Global Bond Fund
82 Devonshire Street
Boston, MA 02109

Telephone Numbers:
    Toll-Free (nationwide)   800/544-6666
    Local   617/523-1919
Type of Bond Portfolio: Corporate; Maturity: intermediate (3–10 years)
Adviser: Fidelity Management & Research Co.
Year Organized: 1987
Minimum Investment: Initial, $2500; Subsequent, $250
Minimum IRA Investment: Initial, $500; Subsequent, $250
Fund Size: $45 million as of 2/26/90
Sales Fee (if any):   None
Expense Ratio: 1.14% for year ending 10/31/88
Portfolio Turnover: 1 Year, 227%; 3 Years, not available
IRA Fees: Annual, $10; Initial, none; Closing, $10

Fidelity Insured Tax Free Portfolio of Fidelity Municipal Bond Fund
82 Devonshire Street
Boston, MA 02109

Telephone Numbers:
    Toll-Free (nationwide)   800/544-6666
    Local   617/523-1919
Type of Bond Portfolio: Municipal; Maturity: long (10 years +)
Adviser: Fidelity Management & Research Co.
Year Organized: 1985
Minimum Investment: Initial, $2500; Subsequent, $250
Minimum IRA Investment: None
Fund Size: $183 million as of 6/4/90
Sales Fee (if any):   None
Expense Ratio: 0.70% for year ending 3/1/90
Portfolio Turnover: 1 Year; 51%; 3 Years, 57%
IRA Fees: None

Fidelity Intermediate Bond Fund
82 Devonshire Street
Boston, MA 02109

Telephone Numbers:
  Toll-Free (nationwide)   800/544-6666
  Local   617/523-1919
Type of Bond Portfolio: Municipal; Maturity: intermediate
                          (3–10 years)
Adviser: Fidelity Management & Research Co.
Year Organized: 1975
Minimum Investment: Initial, $1000; Subsequent, $250
Minimum IRA Investment: Initial, $500; Subsequent, $250
Fund Size: $604 million as of 2/27/90
Sales Fee (if any):   None
Expense Ratio: 0.87% for year ending 12/31/88
Portfolio Turnover: 1 Year, 59%; 3 Years, 101%
IRA Fees: Annual, $10; Initial, none; Closing, $10

Fidelity Municipal Bond Portfolio
82 Devonshire Street
Boston, MA 02109

Telephone Numbers:
  Toll-Free (nationwide)   800/544-6666
  Local   617/523-1919
Type of Bond Portfolio: Municipal; Maturity: long
                          (10 years +)
Adviser: Fidelity Management & Research Co.
Year Organized: 1976
Minimum Investment: Initial, $2500; Subsequent, $250
Minimum IRA Investment: None
Fund Size: $1066 million as of 6/4/90
Sales Fee (if any):   None
Expense Ratio: 0.50% for year ending 3/1/90
Portfolio Turnover: 1 Year, 64%; 3 Years, 72%
IRA Fees: None

Fidelity New York Tax Free Fund High Yield Portfolio
82 Devonshire Street
Boston, MA 02109

Telephone Numbers:
    Toll-Free (nationwide)   800/544-6666
    Local   617/523-1919
Type of Bond Portfolio: Municipal; Maturity: long
                                (10 years +)
Adviser: Fidelity Management & Research Co.
Year Organized: 1984
Minimum Investment: Initial, $2500; Subsequent, $250
Minimum IRA Investment: None
Fund Size: $384 million as of 6/4/90
Sales Fee (if any):   None
Expense Ratio: 0.63% for year ending 6/29/89
Portfolio Turnover: 1 Year, 49%; 3 Years, 51%
IRA Fees: None

Fidelity New York Tax Free Fund Insured Portfolio
82 Devonshire Street
Boston, MA 02109

Telephone Numbers:
    Toll-Free (nationwide)   800/544-6666
    Local   617/523-1919
Type of Bond Portfolio: Municipal; Maturity: long
                                (10 years +)
Adviser: Fidelity Management & Research Co.
Year Organized: 1984
Minimum Investment: Initial, $2500; Subsequent, $250
Minimum IRA Investment: None
Fund Size: $214 million as of 6/4/90
Sales Fee (if any):   None
Expense Ratio: 0.67% for year ending 4/30/88
Portfolio Turnover: 1 Year, 29%; 3 Years, not available
IRA Fees: None

Fidelity Ohio Tax Free Portfolio
82 Devonshire Street
Boston, MA 02109

Telephone Numbers:
    Toll-Free (nationwide)   800/544-6666
    Local   617/523-1919
Type of Bond Portfolio: Municipal; Maturity: long
                                        (10 years +)
Adviser: Fidelity Management & Research Co.
Year Organized: 1985
Minimum Investment: Initial, $2500; Subsequent, $250
Minimum IRA Investment: None
Fund Size: $215 million as of 6/4/90
Sales Fee (if any):   None
Expense Ratio: 0.73% for year ending 12/31/88
Portfolio Turnover: 1 Year, 23%; 3 Years, 32%
IRA Fees: None

Fidelity Spartan Government Fund
82 Devonshire Street
Boston, MA 02109

Telephone Numbers:
    Toll-Free (nationwide)   800/544-6666
    Local   617/523-1919
Type of Bond Portfolio: Government; Maturity: long
                                        (10 years +)
Adviser: Fidelity Management & Research Co.
Year Organized: 1989
Minimum Investment: Initial, $10,000; Subsequent, $1000
Minimum IRA Investment: None
Fund Size: $322 million as of 6/4/90
Sales Fee (if any):   None
Expense Ratio: 0.65% for year ending 4/30/89
Portfolio Turnover: 1 Year, 277%; 3 Years, not available
IRA Fees: Annual, $10; Initial, none; Closing, $10

Neuberger & Berman Limited Maturity Bond Fund, Inc.
342 Madison Avenue
New York, NY 10173

Telephone Numbers:
    Toll-Free (nationwide)   800/367-0770
    Local   212/850-8300
Type of Bond Portfolio: Corporate; Maturity: short
                                    (under 3 years)
Adviser: Neuberger & Berman Management, Inc.
Year Organized: 1986
Minimum Investment: Initial, $5000; Subsequent, $200
Minimum IRA Investment: None
Fund Size: $115 million as of 6/4/90
Sales Fee (if any):   None
Expense Ratio: 0.5% for year ending 2/29/88
Portfolio Turnover: 1 Year, 158%; 3 Years, not available
IRA Fees: Annual, $9; Initial, none; Closing, $7

Northeast Investors Trust
50 Congress Street, Suite 1000
Boston, MA 02109

Telephone Numbers:
    Toll-Free (nationwide)   800/225-6704
    Local   617/523-3588
Type of Bond Portfolio: Taxable; Maturity: intermediate
                                    (3–10 years)
Adviser: Northeast Investors Trust
Year Organized: 1950
Minimum Investment: Initial, $1000; Subsequent, none
Minimum IRA Investment: Initial, $500; Subsequent, none
Fund Size: $385 million as of 3/1/90
Sales Fee (if any):   None
Expense Ratio: 0.61% for year ending 2/1/90
Portfolio Turnover: 1 Year, 33%; 3 Years, 52%
IRA Fees: Annual, $5; Initial, $5; Closing, $10

T. Rowe Price Tax-Free Income Fund, Inc.
100 E. Pratt Street
Baltimore, MD 21202

Telephone Numbers:
    Toll-Free (nationwide)   800/638-5660
    Local   301/547-2308
Type of Bond Portfolio: Municipal; Maturity: long (10 years +)
Adviser: T. Rowe Price Associates, Inc.
Year Organized: 1976
Minimum Investment: Initial, $2000; Subsequent, $100
Minimum IRA Investment: None
Fund Size: $1127 million as of 6/4/90
Sales Fee (if any):   None
Expense Ratio: 0.65% for year ending 2/29/88
Portfolio Turnover: 1 Year, 181%; 3 Years, 188%
IRA Fees: None

T. Rowe Price Tax-Free Short Intermediate Fund, Inc.
100 E. Pratt Street
Baltimore, MD 21202

Telephone Numbers:
    Toll-Free (nationwide)   800/638-5660
    Local   301/547-2308
Type of Bond Portfolio: Municipal; Maturity: short (under 3 years)
Adviser: T. Rowe Price Associates, Inc.
Year Organized: 1983
Minimum Investment: Initial, $2000; Subsequent, $100
Minimum IRA Investment: None
Fund Size: $221 million as of 6/4/90
Sales Fee (if any):   None
Expense Ratio: 0.74% for year ending 2/29/88
Portfolio Turnover: 1 Year, 225%; 3 Years, 129%
IRA Fees: None

Scudder Managed Municipal Bonds
160 Federal Street
Boston, MA 02110

Telephone Numbers:
    Toll-Free (nationwide)   800/225-2470
    Local   617/439-4640
Type of Bond Portfolio: Municipal; Maturity: long (10 years +)
Adviser: Scudder, Steven & Clark
Year Organized: 1976
Minimum Investment: Initial, $1000; Subsequent, none
Minimum IRA Investment: None
Fund Size: $691 million as of 6/4/90
Sales Fee (if any): None
Expense Ratio: 0.61% for year ending 12/31/88
Portfolio Turnover: 1 Year, 76%; 3 Years, 78%
IRA Fees: None

Steinroe Intermediate Bond Fund
P.O. Box 1143
Chicago, IL 60690

Telephone Numbers:
    Toll-Free (nationwide)   800/338-2550
    Local   312/368-7826
Type of Bond Portfolio: Government/Corporate; Maturity: intermediate (3–10 years)
Adviser: Stein Roe & Farnham
Year Organized: 1978
Minimum Investment: Initial, $1000; Subsequent, $100
Minimum IRA Investment: Initial, $500; Subsequent, $50
Fund Size: $164 million as of 3/1/90
Sales Fee (if any): None
Expense Ratio: 0.73% for year ending 11/1/89
Portfolio Turnover: 1 Year, 33%; 3 Years, 241%
IRA Fees: Annual, $10; Initial, none, Closing, $5

Vanguard Bond Market Fund
P.O. Box 2600
Valley Forge, PA 19482

Telephone Numbers:
    Toll-Free (nationwide)   800/662-2739
    Local   215/648-6000
Type of Bond Portfolio: Corporate; Maturity: intermediate/long (3 years +)
Adviser: Vanguard Group, Inc.
Year Organized: 1986
Minimum Investment: Initial, $3000; Subsequent, $100
Minimum IRA Investment: Initial, $500; Subsequent, $50
Fund Size: $117 million as of 3/2/90
Sales Fee (if any):   None
Expense Ratio: 0.3% for year ending 12/31/88
Portfolio Turnover: 1 Year, 21%; 3 Years, not available
IRA Fees: Annual, $10; Initial, $10; Closing, none

Vanguard Fixed Income Securities Fund GNMA Portfolio
P.O. Box 2600
Valley Forge, PA 19482

Telephone Numbers:
    Toll-Free (nationwide)   800/662-2739
    Local   215/648-6000
Type of Bond Portfolio: Government; Maturity: intermediate/long (3 years +)
Adviser: Wellington Management Co.
Year Organized: 1980
Minimum Investment: Initial, $3000; Subsequent, $100
Minimum IRA Investment: Initial, $500; Subsequent, $100
Fund Size: $2292 million as of 6/4/90
Sales Fee (if any):   None
Expense Ratio: 0.33% for year ending 1/31/88
Portfolio Turnover: 1 Year, 22%; 3 Years, 32%
IRA Fees: Annual, $10; Initial, $10; Closing, none

Vanguard Fixed Income Securities Fund-Investment Grade Bond Portfolio
P.O. Box 2600
Valley Forge, PA 19482

Telephone Numbers:
    Toll-Free (nationwide)   800/662-2739
    Local   215/648-6000
Type of Bond Portfolio: Corporate; Maturity: long (10 years +)
Adviser: Wellington Management Co.
Year Organized: 1973
Minimum Investment: Initial, $3000; Subsequent, $100
Minimum IRA Investment: Initial, $500; Subsequent, $100
Fund Size: $897 million as of 3/2/90
Sales Fee (if any):   None
Expense Ratio: 0.37% for year ending 1/31/88
Portfolio Turnover: 1 Year, 63%; 3 Years, 56%
IRA Fees: Annual, $10; Initial, $10; Closing, none

Vanguard Fixed Income Securities Fund-Short Term Bond Portfolio
P.O. Box 2600
Valley Forge, PA 19482

Telephone Numbers:
    Toll-Free (nationwide)   800/662-2739
    Local   215/648-6000
Type of Bond Portfolio: Corporate; Maturity: short (under 3 years)
Adviser: Vanguard Group
Year Organized: 1982
Minimum Investment: Initial, $3000; Subsequent, $100
Minimum IRA Investment: Initial, $500; Subsequent, $100
Fund Size: $553 million as of 3/2/90
Sales Fee (if any):   None
Expense Ratio: 0.33% for year ending 1/31/88
Portfolio Turnover: 1 Year, 258%; 3 Years, 460%
IRA Fees: Annual, $10; Initial, $10; Closing, none

The Mutual Funds Directory 517

Vanguard Fixed Income Securities Fund-Short Term Government Bond Portfolio
P.O. Box 2600
Valley Forge, PA 19482

Telephone Numbers:
   Toll-Free (nationwide)   800/662-2739
   Local   215/648-6000
Type of Bond Portfolio: Government; Maturity: short (under 3 years)
Adviser: Vanguard Group, Inc.
Year Organized: 1987
Minimum Investment: Initial, $3000; Subsequent, $100
Minimum IRA Investment: Initial, $500; Subsequent, $100
Fund Size: $188 million as of 3/2/90
Sales Fee (if any):   None
Expense Ratio: Information not available
Portfolio Turnover: Information not available
IRA Fees: Annual, $10; Initial, $10; Closing, none

Vanguard Fixed Income Securities Fund-U.S. Treasury Bond Portfolio
P.O. Box 2600
Valley Forge, PA 19482

Telephone Numbers:
   Toll-Free (nationwide)   800/662-2739
   Local   215/648-6000
Type of Bond Portfolio: Government; Maturity: long (10 years +)
Adviser: Vanguard Group, Inc.
Year Organized: 1982
Minimum Investment: Initial, $3000; Subsequent, $100
Minimum IRA Investment: Initial, $500; Subsequent, $100
Fund Size: $516 million as of 6/4/90
Sales Fee (if any):   None
Expense Ratio: 0.32% for year ending 1/31/88
Portfolio Turnover: 1 Year, 182%; 3 Years, not available
IRA Fees: Annual, $10; Initial, $10; Closing, none

Vanguard Municipal Bond Fund-Insured Long-Term Portfolio
**P.O. Box 2600
Valley Forge, PA 19482**

Telephone Numbers:
    Toll-Free (nationwide)   800/662-2739
    Local   215/648-6000
Type of Bond Portfolio: Municipal; Maturity: long
                                 (10 years +)
Adviser: The Vanguard Group
Year Organized: 1984
Minimum Investment: Initial, $3000; Subsequent, $100
Minimum IRA Investment: None
Fund Size: $1096 million as of 6/4/90
Sales Fee (if any):   None
Expense Ratio: 0.29% for year ending 8/31/88
Portfolio Turnover: 1 Year; 28%; 3 Years, 20%
IRA Fees: None

Vanguard Municipal Bond Fund-Intermediate-Term Portfolio
**P.O. Box 2600
Valley Forge, PA 19482**

Telephone Numbers:
    Toll-Free (nationwide)   800/662-2739
    Local   215/648-6000
Type of Bond Portfolio: Municipal; Maturity: intermediate
                                 (3–10 years)
Adviser: The Vanguard Group
Year Organized: 1977
Minimum Investment: Initial, $3000; Subsequent, $100
Minimum IRA Investment: Information not available
Fund Size: $1201 million as of 6/4/90
Sales Fee (if any):   None
Expense Ratio: 0.29% for year ending 8/31/88
Portfolio Turnover: 1 Year, 89%; 3 Years, 13%
IRA Fees: None

The Mutual Funds Directory 519

Vanguard Municipal Bond Fund-Limited-Term Portfolio
P.O. Box 2600
Valley Forge, PA 19482

Telephone Numbers:
    Toll-Free (nationwide)   800/662-2739
    Local   215/648-6000
Type of Bond Portfolio: Municipal; Maturity: short (under 3 years)
Adviser: The Vanguard Group
Year Organized: 1987
Minimum Investment: Initial, $3000; Subsequent, $100
Minimum IRA Investment: None
Fund Size: $219 million as of 6/4/90
Sales Fee (if any):   None
Expense Ratio: 0.29% for year ending 8/31/88
Portfolio Turnover: 1 Year, 122%; 3 Years, not available
IRA Fees: None

Vanguard Municipal Bond Fund-Long-Term Portfolio
P.O. Box 2600
Valley Forge, PA 19482

Telephone Numbers:
    Toll-Free (nationwide)   800/662-2739
    Local   215/648-6000
Type of Bond Portfolio: Municipal; Maturity: long (10 years +)
Adviser: The Vanguard Group
Year Organized: 1977
Minimum Investment: Initial, $3000; Subsequent, $100
Minimum IRA Investment: None
Fund Size: $690 million as of 6/4/90
Sales Fee (if any):   None
Expense Ratio: 0.29% for year ending 8/31/88
Portfolio Turnover: 1 Year, 34%; 3 Years, 32%
IRA Fees: None

CHAPTER 3

Money Market Funds

Dreyfus Money Market Instruments, Inc. Government Securities Series
666 Old Country Road
Garden City, NY 11530

Telephone Numbers:
   Toll-Free (nationwide)   800/645-6561
   Local   718/895-1206
Type of Money Fund: Nontaxable; U.S. Government securities funds
Adviser: The Dreyfus Corporation
Year Organized: 1979
Minimum Investment: Initial, $2500; Subsequent, $100
Minimum IRA Investment: Initial, $750; Subsequent, none
Fund Size: $349 million as of 6/12/90
Sales Fee (if any):   None
Expense Ratio: 0.72% for year ending 12/31/88
IRA Fees: Annual, $5; Initial, $8; Closing, none

Dreyfus Worldwide Dollar Money Market Fund, Inc.
666 Old Country Road
Garden City, NY 11530

Telephone Numbers:
    Toll-Free (nationwide)   800/645-6561
    Local   718/895-1206
Type of Money Fund: Taxable; Internationally based money funds
Adviser: The Dreyfus Corporation
Year Organized: 1989
Minimum Investment: Initial, $2500; Subsequent, $100
Minimum IRA Investment: Initial, $750; Subsequent, none
Fund Size: Over $7357 million as of 5/28/90
Sales Fee (if any):   None
Expense Ratio: 0.17% for year ending 12/31/89
IRA Fees: Annual, $5; Initial, $7.50; Closing, none

Fidelity Cash Reserves
82 Devonshire Street
Boston, MA 02109

Telephone Numbers:
    Toll-Free (nationwide)   800/544-6666
    Local   617/523-1919
Type of Money Fund: Taxable; Internationally based money funds
Adviser: Fidelity Management & Research Co.
Year Organized: 1979
Minimum Investment: Initial, $1000; Subsequent, $250
Minimum IRA Investment: Initial, $500; Subsequent, $250
Fund Size: $10,494 million as of 6/12/90
Sales Fee (if any):   None
Expense Ratio: 0.65% for year ending 11/30/88
IRA Fees: Annual, $10; Initial, none; Closing, $10

Fidelity Daily Income Trust
82 Devonshire Street
Boston, MA 02109

Telephone Numbers:
    Toll-Free (nationwide)   800/544-6666
    Local   617/523-1919
Type of Money Fund: Taxable
Adviser: Fidelity Management & Research Co.
Year Organized: 1974
Minimum Investment: Initial, $5000; Subsequent, $500
Minimum IRA Investment: None
Fund Size: $2894 million as of 6/1/90
Sales Fee (if any):   None
Expense Ratio: 0.69% for year ending 3/1/90
IRA Fees: None

Fidelity Spartan Money Market Fund
82 Devonshire Street
Boston, MA 02109

Telephone Numbers:
    Toll-Free (nationwide)   800/544-6666
    Local   617/523-1919
Type of Money Fund: Taxable
Adviser: Fidelity Management & Research Co.
Year Organized: 1989
Minimum Investment: Initial, $10,000; Subsequent, $1000
Minimum IRA Investment: None
Fund Size: $8307 million as of 6/12/90
Sales Fee (if any):   None
Expense Ratio: 0.15% for year ending 6/29/89
IRA Fees: Annual, $10; Initial, $10; Closing, none

Fidelity U.S. Treasury Money Market Fund, L.P.
82 Devonshire Street
Boston, MA 02109

Telephone Numbers:
    Toll-Free (nationwide)   800/544-6666
    Local   617/523-1919

Type of Money Fund: U.S. Government securities funds
Adviser: Fidelity Management & Research Co.
Year Organized: 1988
Minimum Investment: Initial, $2500; Subsequent, $250
Minimum IRA Investment: None
Fund Size: $224 million as of 6/12/90
Sales Fee (if any):   None
Expense Ratio: 0.65% for year ending 12/89
IRA Fees: None

Harbor Money Market Fund
One Sea Gate
Toledo, OH 43666

Telephone Numbers:
   Toll-Free (nationwide)   800/422-1050
   Local   419/274-2477
Type of Money Fund: Taxable
Adviser: Harbor Capital Advisors, Inc.
Year Organized: 1987
Minimum Investment: Initial, $2000; Subsequent, $500
Minimum IRA Investment: None
Fund Size: $47 million as of 6/12/90
Sales Fee (if any):   None
Expense Ratio: 0.70% for year ending 2/28/90
IRA Fees: Annual, $10; Initial, $5; Closing, none

Kemper Money Market Fund, Inc.
120 S. LaSalle Street
Chicago, IL 60603

Telephone Numbers:
   Toll-Free (nationwide)   800/621-1048
   Local   312/781-1121
Type of Money Fund: Taxable
Adviser: Kemper Financial Services
Year Organized: 1974
Minimum Investment: Initial, $1000; Subsequent, $100
Minimum IRA Investment: Initial, $250; Subsequent, $50
Fund Size: $7440 million as of 6/12/90

Sales Fee (if any): None
Expense Ratio: 0.5% for year ending 7/31/88
IRA Fees: Annual, $12; Initial, none; Closing, none

Merrill Lynch Ready Assets Trust
P.O. Box 9011
800 Scudders Mill Road
Princeton, NJ 08543

Telephone Numbers:
    Toll-Free (nationwide)   800/211-7210
    Local   609/282-2800
Type of Money Fund: Taxable
Adviser: Merrill Lynch Asset Management, Inc.
Year Organized: 1975
Minimum Investment: Initial, $5000; Subsequent, $1000
Minimum IRA Investment: Initial, $250; Subsequent, none
Fund Size: $10,398 million as of 6/12/90
Sales Fee (if any): None
Expense Ratio: 0.62% for year ending 12/31/88
IRA Fees: None

Neuberger & Berman Municipal Money Fund, Inc.
342 Madison Avenue
New York, NY 10173

Telephone Numbers:
    Toll-Free (nationwide)   800/367-0700
    Local   212/850-8300
Type of Money Fund: Nontaxable
Adviser: Neuberger & Berman Management, Inc.
Year Organized: 1984
Minimum Investment: Initial, $2000; Subsequent, $200
Minimum IRA Investment: None
Fund Size: $180 million as of 6/12/90
Sales Fee (if any): None
Expense Ratio: 0.69% for year ending 10/31/88
IRA Fees: None

The Mutual Funds Directory

Newton Money Fund
330 E. Kibourn Avenue
2 Plaza East, Suite 1150
Milwaukee, WI 53202

Telephone Numbers:
    Toll-Free (nationwide)   800/242-7229
    Local   414/271-0440
Type of Money Fund: Taxable
Adviser: M&I Investment Management Corp.
Year Organized: 1981
Minimum Investment: Initial, $1000; Subsequent, $250
Minimum IRA Investment: Initial, $500; Subsequent, $250
Fund Size: $175 million as of 6/12/90
Sales Fee (if any):   None
Expense Ratio: 0.4% for year ending 11/30/89
IRA Fees: Annual, $10; Initial, none; Closing, $10

Paine Webber Cashfund, Inc.
1285 Avenue of the Americas
New York, NY 10019

Telephone Number:
    Local   212/713-2000
Type of Money Fund: Taxable
Adviser: Paine Webber
Year Organized: 1978
Minimum Investment: Initial, $5000; Subsequent, $500
Minimum IRA Investment: Initial, $1000; Subsequent, $500
Fund Size: $5033 million as of 5/28/89
Sales Fee (if any):   None
Expense Ratio: 0.58% for year ending 3/31/88
IRA Fees: Annual, $25; Initial, $25; Closing, $50

T. Rowe Price Tax-Exempt Money Fund, Inc.
100 E. Pratt Street
Baltimore, MD 21202

Telephone Numbers:
    Toll-Free (nationwide)   800/638-5660
    Local   301/547-2308
Type of Money Fund: Nontaxable
Adviser: T. Rowe Price Associates, Inc.
Year Organized: 1980
Minimum Investment: Initial, $2000; Subsequent, $100
Minimum IRA Investment: None
Fund Size: $993 million as of 6/12/90
Sales Fee (if any):   None
Expense Ratio: 0.6% for year ending 2/29/88
IRA Fees: None

Scudder Cash Investment Trust
160 Federal Street
Boston, MA 02110

Telephone Numbers:
    Toll-Free (nationwide)   800/225-2470
    Local   617/439-4640
Type of Money Fund: Taxable
Adviser: Scudder, Stevens & Clark
Year Organized: 1975
Minimum Investment: Initial, $1000; Subsequent, none
Minimum IRA Investment: Initial, $240; Subsequent, none
Fund Size: $1626 million as of 6/12/90
Sales Fee (if any):   None
Expense Ratio: 0.66% for year ending 11/1/89
IRA Fees: None

Selected Daily Government Fund
1331 Euclid Avenue
Cleveland, OH 44115

Telephone Number:
    Toll-Free (nationwide)   800/553-5533

Type of Money Fund: Taxable
Adviser: Selected Financial Services, Inc.
Year Organized: 1988
Minimum Investment: Initial, $1000; Subsequent, $250
Minimum IRA Investment: Initial, $1000; Subsequent, $100
Fund Size: $128 million as of 6/12/90
Sales Fee (if any):   None
Expense Ratio: 0.7% for year ending 12/31/88
IRA Fees: Annual, $10; Initial, $5; Closing, $5

Selected Daily Income Fund
1331 Euclid Avenue
Cleveland, OH 44115

Telephone Number:
    Toll-Free (nationwide)   800/553-5533
Type of Money Fund: Taxable
Adviser: Selected Financial Services, Inc.
Year Organized: 1988
Minimum Investment: Initial, $1000; Subsequent, $250
Minimum IRA Investment: Initial, $1000; Subsequent, $100
Fund Size: $581 million as of 6/12/90
Sales Fee (if any):   None
Expense Ratio: 0.7% for year ending 12/31/88
IRA Fees: Annual, $10; Initial, $5; Closing, $5

Selected Daily Tax-Exempt Fund
1331 Euclid Avenue
Cleveland, OH 44115

Telephone Number:
    Toll-Free (nationwide)   800/553-5533
Type of Money Fund: Nontaxable
Adviser: Selected Financial Services, Inc
Year Organized: 1988
Minimum Investment: Initial, $1000; Subsequent, $250
Minimum IRA Investment: None
Fund Size: $110 million as of 6/12/90
Sales Fee (if any):   None

Expense Ratio: 0.7% for year ending 12/31/88
IRA Fees: None

The Value Line Cash Fund, Inc.
711 Third Avenue
New York, NY 10017

Telephone Numbers:
    Toll-Free (nationwide) 800/223-0818
    Local 212/687-3965
Type of Money Fund: Taxable
Adviser: Value Line, Inc.
Year Organized: 1979
Minimum Investment: Initial, $1000; Subsequent, $100
Minimum IRA Investment: None
Fund Size: $526 million as of 6/12/90
Sales Fee (if any): None
Expense Ratio: 0.65% for year ending 12/31/88
IRA Fees: Annual, $10; Initial, none; Closing, none

The Value Line U.S. Government Securities Fund, Inc.
711 Third Avenue
New York, NY 10017

Telephone Numbers:
    Toll-Free (nationwide) 800/223-0818
    Local 212/687-3965
Type of Money Fund: U.S. Government securities funds
Adviser: Value Line, Inc.
Year Organized: 1981
Minimum Investment: Initial, $1000; Subsequent, $250
Minimum IRA Investment: None
Fund Size: $244.5 million as of 3/1/90
Sales Fee (if any): None
Expense Ratio: 0.67% for year ending 8/31/88
IRA Fees: Annual, $10; Initial, none; Closing, none

Vanguard Money Market Reserves—Federal Portfolio
P.O. Box 2600
Valley Forge, PA 19482

Telephone Numbers:
    Toll-Free (nationwide)   800/662-2739
    Local   215/648-6000
Type of Money Fund: U.S. Government securities funds
Adviser: Vanguard Group
Year Organized: 1981
Minimum Investment: Initial, $3000; Subsequent, $100
Minimum IRA Investment: Initial, $500; Subsequent, $100
Fund Size: $173 million as of 6/12/90
Sales Fee (if any):   None
Expense Ratio: 0.33% for year ending 11/30/88
IRA Fees: Annual, $10; Initial, $10; Closing, none

Vanguard Money Market Reserves—Prime Portfolio
P.O. Box 2600
Valley Forge, PA 19482

Telephone Numbers:
    Toll-Free (nationwide)   800/662-2739
    Local   215/648-6000
Type of Money Fund: Taxable
Adviser: Vanguard Group
Year Organized: 1975
Minimum Investment: Initial, $3000; Subsequent, $100
Minimum IRA Investment: Initial, $500; Subsequent, $100
Fund Size: $12,482 million as of 6/12/90
Sales Fee (if any):   None
Expense Ratio: 0.33% for year ending 11/30/88
IRA Fees: Annual, $10; Initial, $10; Closing, none

Vanguard Money Market Reserves—U.S. Treasury Portfolio
P.O. Box 2600
Valley Forge, PA 19482

Telephone Numbers:
    Toll-Free (nationwide)   800/662-2739
    Local   215/648-6000
Type of Money Fund: U.S. Government securities funds
Adviser: Vanguard Group
Year Organized: 1983
Minimum Investment: Initial, $3000; Subsequent, $100
Minimum IRA Investment: Initial, $500; Subsequent, $100
Fund Size: $803 million as of 6/12/90
Sales Fee (if any):   None
Expense Ratio: 0.70% for year ending 11/30/88
IRA Fees: Annual, $10; Initial, $10; Closing, none

Vanguard Municipal Bond Fund Money Market Portfolio
P.O. Box 2600
Valley Forge, PA 19482

Telephone Numbers:
    Toll-Free (nationwide)   800/662-2739
    Local   215/648-6000
Type of Money Fund: Nontaxable
Adviser: The Vanguard Group
Year Organized: 1980
Minimum Investment: Initial, $3000; Subsequent, $100
Minimum IRA Investment: None
Fund Size: $2403 million as of 6/12/90
Sales Fee (if any):   None
Expense Ratio: 0.29% for year ending 8/31/88
IRA Fees: None

Vantage Money Market Funds—Cash Portfolio
1345 Avenue of the Americas
New York, NY 10105

Telephone Numbers:
    Toll-Free (nationwide)   800/522-9300 or 800/221-3434
    Local   212/356-2900
Type of Money Fund: Taxable
Adviser: Smith Barney, Harris, Upham & Co.
Year Organized: 1982
Minimum Investment: Initial, $20,000; Subsequent, $1000
Minimum IRA Investment: None
Fund Size: $1195 million as of 6/12/90
Sales Fee (if any):   None
Expense Ratio: 0.6% for year ending 8/31/88
IRA Fees: None

Vantage Money Market Funds—Government Portfolio
1345 Avenue of the Americas
New York, NY 10105

Telephone Numbers:
    Toll-Free (nationwide)   800/522-9300
    Local   212/356-2900
Type of Money Fund: U.S. Government securities funds
Adviser: Smith Barney, Harris, Upham & Co.
Year Organized: 1982
Minimum Investment: Initial, $20,000; Subsequent, $1000
Minimum IRA Investment: None
Fund Size: $129 million as of 3/6/90
Sales Fee (if any):   None
Expense Ratio: 0.59% for year ending 8/31/88
IRA Fees: None

CHAPTER 4
International Funds

OPEN-END FUNDS

Clipper Fund, Inc.
9601 Wilshire Boulevard, Suite 828
Beverly Hills, CA 90210

Telephone Number:
    Local   213/278-5033
Type of Fund: International fund
Adviser: Pacific Financial Research
Year Organized: 1984
Ticker Symbol: CFIMX
Minimum Investment: Initial, $25,000; Subsequent, $1000
Minimum IRA Investment: Initial, $1000; Subsequent, $100
Registered for Sale: Most states
Fund Size: $128 million as of 2/23/90
Sales Fee (if any):   None
Expense Ratio: 1.24% for year ending 12/31/88

Portfolio Turnover: 1 Year, 33%; 3 Years, 40%
IRA Fees: Annual, $10; Initial, none; Closing, $10

Fidelity Europe Fund
82 Devonshire Street
Boston, MA 02109

Telephone Numbers:
    Toll-Free (nationwide)   800/544-6666
    Local   617/523-1919
Type of Fund: International fund
Adviser: Fidelity Management & Research Co.
Year Organized: 1986
Ticker Symbol: FIEUX
Minimum Investment: Initial, $2500; Subsequent, $250
Minimum IRA Investment: Initial, $500; Subsequent, $250
Registered for Sale: All states
Fund Size: $222 million as of 2/26/90
Sales Fee (if any):   None
Expense Ratio: 1.89% for year ending 12/30/89
Portfolio Turnover: 1 Year, 160%; 3 Years, 241%
IRA Fees: Annual, $10; Initial, none; Closing, $10

Fidelity Overseas Fund
82 Devonshire Street
Boston, MA 02109

Telephone Numbers:
    Toll-Free (nationwide)   800/544-6666
    Local   617/523-1919
Type of Fund: International fund
Adviser: Fidelity Management & Research Co.
Year Organized: 1984
Ticker Symbol: FOSFX
Minimum Investment: Initial, $2500; Subsequent, $250
Minimum IRA Investment: Initial, $500; Subsequent, $250
Registered for Sale: All states
Fund Size: $1010 million as of 2/27/90
Sales Fee (if any):   None

Expense Ratio: 1.06% for year ending 12/30/89
Portfolio Turnover: 1 Year, 100%; 3 Years, 122%
IRA Fees: Annual, $10; Initial, none; Closing, $10

Japan Fund, Inc.
160 Federal Street
Boston, MA 02110

Telephone Numbers:
    Toll-Free (nationwide)   800/535-2726
    Local   617/439-4640
Type of Fund: International fund specializing in 1 country
Adviser: Asia Management, Inc.
Year Organized: 1961
Ticker Symbol: SJTNX
Minimum Investment: Initial, $1000; Subsequent, none
Minimum IRA Investment: Initial, $240; Subsequent, none
Registered for Sale: All states
Fund Size: $418 million as of 2/9/90
Sales Fee (if any):   None
Expense Ratio: 0.75% for year ending 12/31/88
Portfolio Turnover: 1 Year, 39%; 3 Years, 38%
IRA Fees: Annual, $12; Initial, none; Closing, none

Nomura Pacific Basin Fund, Inc.
180 Maiden Lane
New York, NY 10038

Telephone Numbers:
    Toll-Free (nationwide)   800/833-0018
    Local   212/208-9366
Type of Fund: International fund investing in 1 region
Adviser: Nomura Investment Management Co., Ltd.
Year Organized: 1985
Ticker Symbol: NPBFX
Minimum Investment: Initial, $10,000; Subsequent, $5000
Minimum IRA Investment: None
Registered for Sale: Most states
Fund Size: $70 million as of 3/1/90

The Mutual Funds Directory   535

Sales Fee (if any):   None
Expense Ratio: 1.22% for year ending 3/30/88
Portfolio Turnover: 1 Year, 61%; 3 Years, not available
IRA Fees: Annual, $30; Initial, $30; Closing, none

T. Rowe Price International Trust: International Bond Fund
100 E. Pratt Street
Baltimore, MD 21202

Telephone Numbers:
    Toll-Free (nationwide)   800/638-5660
    Local   301/547-2308
Type of Bond Portfolio: International fund
Adviser: T. Rowe Price
Year Organized: 1986
Minimum Investment: Initial, $2000; Subsequent, $100
Minimum IRA Investment: Initial, $2000; Subsequent, $50
Fund Size: $268 million as of 3/2/90
Sales Fee (if any):   None
Expense Ratio: 1.2% for year ending 12/31/88
Portfolio Turnover: 1 Year, 368%; 3 Years, not available
IRA Fees: Annual, $10; Initial, none; Closing, none

T. Rowe Price International Trust: International Stock Fund
100 E. Pratt Street
Baltimore, MD 21202

Telephone Numbers:
    Toll-Free (nationwide)   800/638-5660
    Local   301/547-2308
Type of Fund: International fund
Adviser: Rowe Price-Fleming International, Inc.
Year Organized: 1980
Ticker Symbol: PRITX
Minimum Investment: Initial, $1000; Subsequent, $100
Minimum IRA Investment: Initial, $500; Subsequent, $50
Registered for Sale: All states
Fund Size: $857 million as of 2/9/90
Sales Fee (if any):   None

Expense Ratio: 1.16% for year ending 12/31/88
Portfolio Turnover: 1 Year, 42%; 3 Years, 56%
IRA Fees: Annual, $10; Initial, none; Closing, none

Trustees' Commingled Fund International Equity Portfolio
P.O. Box 2600
Valley Forge, PA 19482

Telephone Numbers:
    Toll-Free (nationwide)   800/662-7447
    Local   215/648-6000
Type of Fund: International fund
Adviser: Batterymarch Financial Management
Year Organized: 1983
Ticker Symbol: VTRIX
Minimum Investment: Initial, $10,000; Subsequent, $1000
Minimum IRA Investment: Initial, $500; Subsequent, $100
Registered for Sale: All states
Fund Size: $645 million as of 3/2/90
Sales Fee (if any): None
Expense Ratio: 0.51% for year ending 12/31/88
Portfolio Turnover: 1 Year, 14%; 3 Years, 29%
IRA Fees: Annual, $10; Initial, $10; Closing, none

Vanguard World Fund International Growth Portfolio
P.O. Box 2600
Valley Forge, PA 19482

Telephone Numbers:
    Toll-Free (nationwide)   800/662-2739
    Local   215/648-6000
Type of Fund: International fund
Adviser: Schroder Capital Management, Inc.
Year Organized: 1961
Ticker Symbol: VWIGX
Minimum Investment: Initial, $3000; Subsequent, $100
Minimum IRA Investment: Initial, $500; Subsequent, $100
Registered for Sale: All states
Fund Size: $685 million as of 3/2/90
Sales Fee (if any): None

Expense Ratio: 0.67% for year ending 8/31/88
Portfolio Turnover: 1 Year, 71%; 3 Years, 39%
IRA Fees: Annual, $10; Initial, $10; Closing, none

CLOSED-END FUNDS

Asia Pacific Fund
One Seaport Plaza
New York, NY 10292

Telephone Number:
    Local   212/214-3334
Adviser: Barring International Investment (Far East) Limited
Year Organized: 1987
Ticker Symbol: APB
Fund Orientation: Stock/Regional

Brazil Fund, Inc.
345 Park Avenue
New York, NY 10154

Telephone Numbers:
    Toll-Free (nationwide)   800/225-2470
    Local   212/326-6200
Adviser: Scudder, Stevens & Clark Inc.
Year Organized: 1988
Ticker Symbol: BZF
Fund Orientation: Stock/Country

Clemente Global Growth Fund, Inc.
767 Third Avenue
New York, NY 10017

Telephone Number:
    Local   212/759-3339
Adviser: Clemente Capital Inc.
Year Organized: 1987
Ticker Symbol: CLM
Fund Orientation: Stock/Global

First Australia Fund, Inc.
One Seaport Plaza
New York, NY 10292

Telephone Number:
    Local   212/214-3334
Adviser: EquitiLink Australia Limited
Year Organized: 1985
Ticker Symbol: IAF
Fund Orientation: Stock/Country

First Australia Prime Income Fund
One Seaport Plaza
New York, NY 10292

Telephone Number:
    Local   212/214-3334
Adviser: EquitiLink Australia Limited
Year Organized: 1986
Ticker Symbol: FAX
Fund Orientation: Bond/Country

First Iberian Fund, Inc.
One Seaport Plaza
New York, NY 10292

Telephone Number:
    Local   212/214-3334
Adviser: Iberiancorp Gestion B.V.
Year Organized: 1987
Ticker Symbol: IBF
Fund Orientation: Stock/Country

Future Germany Fund, Inc.
31 West 52nd Street
New York, NY 10019

Telephone Number:
    Local   212/474-7000

Adviser: Deutschebank Capital
Year Organized: 1990
Ticker Symbol: FGF
Portfolio Holdings: Bond
Fund Orientation: Country

Germany Fund, Inc.
31 West 52nd Street
New York, NY 10019

Telephone Number:
 Toll-Free (nationwide) 800/642-0144
Adviser: Capital Management International GmbH of Deutsche Bank
Year Organized: 1986
Ticker Symbol: GER
Fund Orientation: Stock/Country

Global Government Plus Fund, Inc.
One Seaport Plaza
New York, NY 10292

Telephone Number:
 Local 212/214-3334
Adviser: The Prudential Investment Corporation
Year Organized: 1987
Ticker Symbol: GOV
Fund Orientation: Bond/Global

Global Income Plus Fund
1285 Avenue of the Americas
New York, NY 10019

Telephone Number:
 Local 212/703-4000
Adviser: Mitchell Hutcins Asset Management, Inc.
Year Organized: 1988
Ticker Symbol: GLI
Fund Orientation: Bond/Global

Global Yield Fund, Inc.
One Seaport Plaza
New York, NY 10292

Telephone Number:
  Local 212/214-3334
Adviser: The Prudential Investment Corporation
Year Organized: 1986
Ticker Symbol: PGY
Fund Orientation: Money/Global

Helvetia Fund, Inc.
521 Fifth Avenue
New York, NY 10175

Telephone Number:
  Local 212/867-7660
Adviser: Helvetia Capital Corp.
Year Organized: 1987
Ticker Symbol: SWZ
Fund Orientation: Stock/Country

India Growth Fund
1 Boston Place
Boston, MA 02108

Telephone Number:
  Toll-Free (nationwide) 800/331-1710
Adviser: Unit Trust of India Investment Advisory Services
    Limited
Year Organized: 1988
Ticker Symbol: IGF
Fund Orientation: Stock/Country

Italy Fund, Inc.
31 West 52 Street
New York, NY 10019

Telephone Number:
  Local 212/767-3034

Adviser: Shearson Lehman Global Asset Management S.A.
Year Organized: 1986
Ticker Symbol: ITA
Fund Orientation: Stock/Country

Kleinwort Benson Australian Income Fund, Inc.
200 Park Avenue, 24th Floor
New York, NY 10166

Telephone Number:
　　Local　212/687-2515
Adviser: Erica Investment Management (Overseas) Limited
Year Organized: 1986
Ticker Symbol: KBA
Fund Orientation: Bond/Country

Korea Fund, Inc.
345 Park Avenue
New York, NY 10154

Telephone Number:
　　Local　212/326-6200
Adviser: Scudder, Stevens & Clark, Inc.
Year Organized: 1984
Ticker Symbol: KF
Fund Orientation: Stock/Country

Malaysia Fund, Inc.
1221 Avenue of the Americas
New York, NY 10020

Telephone Number:
　　Local　212/703-4000
Adviser: Morgan Stanley Asset Management, Inc.
Year Organized: 1987
Ticker Symbol: MF
Fund Orientation: Stock/Country

Mexico Fund, Inc.
77 Aristoteles Street, 3rd Floor
Mexico DF 11560

Contact:
OBSA International, Inc.
342 Madison Avenue, Suite 909
New York, NY 10173
Telephone Number:
    Local   212/492-6485
Adviser: Impulsora del fondo Mexico, S.A. de C.V.
Year Organized: 1981
Ticker Symbol: MXF
Portfolio Holdings: Stock
Fund Orientation: Country

New Germany Fund, Inc.
31 West 52nd Street
New York, NY 10019

Telephone Number:
    Local   212/474-7000
Adviser: Deutschebank Capital
Year Organized: 1990
Ticker Symbol: GF
Portfolio Holdings: Bond
Fund Orientation: Country

Scudder New Asia Fund, Inc.
345 Park Avenue
New York, NY 10154

Telephone Number:
    Local   212/326-6200
Adviser: Scudder, Stevens & Clark Ltd.
Year Organized: 1987
Ticker Symbol: SAF
Fund Orientation: Stock/Regional

Spain Fund, Inc.
1345 Avenue of the Americas
New York, NY 10105

Telephone Number:
    Toll-Free (nationwide)   800/227-4618
Adviser: Alliance Capital Management L.P.
Year Organized: 1988
Ticker Symbol: SNF
Fund Orientation: Stock/Country

Taiwan Fund
111 Devonshire Street
Boston, MA 02109

Telephone Number:
    Toll-Free (nationwide)   800/334-9393
Adviser: China Securities Investment Trust Corporation
Year Organized: 1986
Ticker Symbol: TWN
Fund Orientation: Stock/Country

Templeton Emerging Markets Fund, Inc.
700 Central Avenue
St. Petersburg, FL 33701

Telephone Number:
    Local   813/823-8712
Adviser: Templeton, Galbraith & Hansberger Ltd.
Year Organized: 1987
Ticker Symbol: EMF
Fund Orientation: Stock

Templeton Global Governments Income Trust
700 Central Avenue
St. Petersburg, FL 33701

Telephone Number:
    Local   813/823-8712

Adviser: Templeton, Galbraith & Hansberger Ltd.
Year Organized: 1988
Ticker Symbol: TGG
Fund Orientation: Bond/Global

Templeton Global Income Fund, Inc.
700 Central Avenue
St. Petersburg, FL 33701

Telephone Number:
 Local 813/823-8712
Adviser: Templeton, Galbraith & Hansberger Ltd.
Year Organized: 1988
Ticker Symbol: GIM
Fund Orientation: Bond/Global

Templeton Value Fund, Inc.
700 Central Avenue
St. Petersburg, FL 33701

Telephone Number:
 Local 813/823-8712
Adviser: Templeton, Galbraith & Hansberger Ltd.
Year Organized: 1988
Ticker Symbol: TVF
Fund Orientation: Stock/Global

Thai Fund, Inc.
Vanguard Funds
Ctr P.O. Box 1102
Valley Forge, PA 19482

Telephone Number:
 Local 215/703-4000
Adviser: Morgan Stanley Asset Management, Inc.
Year Organized: 1988
Ticker Symbol: TTF
Fund Orientation: Stock/Country

United Kingdom Fund, Inc.
245 Park Avenue, 14th Floor
New York, NY 10167

Telephone Number:
  Local   212/272-6404
Adviser: Warburg Investment Management International Ltd.
Year Organized: 1987
Ticker Symbol: UKM
Fund Orientation: Stock/Country

Worldwide Value Fund, Inc.
111 South Calvert Street
Baltimore, MD 21202

Telephone Number:
  Local   301/539-3400
Adviser: Lombard Odier International Portfolio Management Limited
Year Organized: 1986
Ticker Symbol: VLU
Fund Orientation: Stock/Global

CHAPTER 5

Other Closed-End Funds

ACM Government Opportunity Fund, Inc.
1345 Avenue of the Americas
New York, NY 10105

Telephone Number:
    Toll-Free (nationwide)   800/227-4618
Adviser: Alliance Capital Management, L.P.
Year Organized: 1988
Ticker Symbol: AOF
Portfolio Holdings: Bond
Fund Orientation: Bond

ACM Managed Income Fund, Inc.
1345 Avenue of the Americas
New York, NY 10105

Telephone Number:
    Toll-Free (nationwide)   800/227-4618

Adviser: Alliance Capital Management
Year Organized: 1988
Ticker Symbol: AMF
Portfolio Holdings: Bond
Fund Orientation: Bond

Allstate Municipal Income Trust II
Two World Trade Center, 72nd Floor
New York, NY 10048

Telephone Number:
     Local   212/392-2550
Adviser: Allstate Investment Management Company
Year Organized: 1988
Ticker Symbol: ALT
Fund Orientation: Municipal bond

American Capital Bond Fund, Inc.
2800 Post Oak Blvd
Houston, TX 77056

Telephone Number:
     Local   713/993-0500
Adviser: American Capital Asset Management, Inc.
Year Organized: 1970
Ticker Symbol: ACB
Fund Orientation: Bond

American Capital Income Trust
2800 Post Oak Blvd
Houston, TX 77056

Telephone Number:
     Local   713/421-9696
Adviser: American Capital Asset Management, Inc.
Year Organized: 1988
Ticker Symbol: ACD
Portfolio Holdings: Bond
Fund Orientation: Bond

Bunker Hill Income Securities, Inc.
P.O. Box 70220
Pasadena, CA 91117-7220

Telephone Number:
    Local   213/229-1290
Adviser: Security Pacific Investment Managers, Inc.
Year Organized: 1973
Ticker Symbol: BHL
Fund Orientation: Bond

Circle Income Shares, Inc.
P.O. Box 44027
Indianapolis, IN 46244

Telephone Number:
    Local   317/639-8180
Adviser: Bank One, Indianapolis, NA
Year Organized: 1973
Ticker Symbol: CINS
Fund Orientation: Bond

CNA Income Shares, Inc.
CNA Plaza
Chicago, IL 60685

Telephone Numbers:
    Toll-Free (nationwide)   800/343-5601
    Local   312/822-4181
Adviser: Continental Assurance Company
Year Organized: 1973
Ticker Symbol: CNN
Fund Orientation: Bond

Colonial Intermediate High Income Fund
One Financial Center
Boston, MA 02111

Telephone Number:
    Local   617/426-3750

Adviser: Colonial Management Associates, Inc.
Year Organized: 1988
Ticker Symbol: CIF
Fund Orientation: Bond

Comstock Partners Strategy Fund, Inc.
45 Broadway
New York, NY 10006

Telephone Number:
  Toll-Free (nationwide) 800/543-6217
Adviser: Comstock Partners, Inc
Year Organized: 1988
Ticker Symbol: CPF
Fund Orientation: Bond

Dean Witter Government Income Trust
Two World Trade Center, 72nd Floor
New York, NY 10048

Telephone Number:
  Local 212/392-2550
Adviser: InterCapital Division of Dean Witter Reynolds, Inc.
Year Organized: 1988
Ticker Symbol: GVT
Fund Orientation: Bond

Dreyfus Municipal Income, Inc.
666 Old Country Road
Garden City, NY 11530

Telephone Number:
  Toll-Free (nationwide) 800/633-6122
Adviser: The Dreyfus Corporation
Year Organized: 1988
Ticker Symbol: DMF
Fund Orientation: Municipal bond

Dreyfus Strategic Governments Income, Inc.
666 Old Country Road
Garden City, NY 11530

Telephone Number:
 Toll-Free (nationwide) 800/334-6899
Adviser: The Dreyfus Corporation
Year Organized: 1988
Ticker Symbol: DSI
Fund Orientation: Bond

First Boston Income Fund, Inc.
12 East 49th Street
New York, NY 10017

Telephone Number:
 Local 212/648-6069
Adviser: First Boston Asset Management Corporation
Year Organized: 1987
Ticker Symbol: FBF
Fund Orientation: Bond

First Boston Strategic Income Fund, Inc.
12 East 49th Street
New York, NY 10017

Telephone Number:
 Local 212/648-6069
Adviser: First Boston Asset Management Corp.
Year Organized: 1988
Ticker Symbol: FBI
Fund Orientation: Bond

First Financial Fund, Inc.
One Seaport Plaza
New York, NY 10292

Telephone Number:
 Toll-Free (nationwide) 800/451-6788
 Local 212/214-3334
Adviser: Wellington Management

Year Organized: 1987
Ticker Symbol: FF
Portfolio Holdings: Stock
Fund Orientation: Financial

First Iberian Fund, Inc.
One Seaport Plaza
New York, NY 10292

Telephone Number:
    Local   212/214-3334
Adviser: Iberiancorp Gestion B.V.
Year Organized: 1987
Ticker Symbol: IBF
Portfolio Holdings: Stock
Fund Orientation: Country

Germany Fund, Inc.
31 West 52nd Street
New York, NY 10019

Telephone Number:
    Toll-Free (nationwide)   800/642-0144
Adviser: Capital Management International GmbH of
            Deutsche Bank
Year Organized: 1986
Ticker Symbol: GER
Portfolio Holdings: Stock
Fund Orientation: Country

High Income Advantage Trust
Two World Trade Center, 72nd Floor
New York, NY 10048

Telephone Number:
    Local   212/392-2550
Adviser: InterCapital Division of Dean Witter Reynolds, Inc.
Year Organized: 1987
Ticker Symbol: YLD
Fund Orientation: Bond

Intercapital Income Securities, Inc.
Two World Trade Center, 72nd Floor
New York, NY 10048

Telephone Number:
    Local   212/392-2550
Adviser: InterCapital Division of Dean Witter Reynolds, Inc.
Year Organized: 1973
Ticker Symbol: ICB
Fund Orientation: Bond

John Hancock Income Securities Trust
101 Huntington Avenue
Boston, MA 02199

Telephone Number:
    Local   617/375-1500
Adviser: John Hancock Advisers, Inc.
Year Organized: 1973
Ticker Symbol: JHS
Fund Orientation: Bond

Kemper High Income Trust
120 South LaSalle Street
Chicago, IL 60603

Telephone Number:
    Toll-Free (nationwide)   800/643-2211
Adviser: Kemper Financial Services, Inc.
Year Organized: 1988
Ticker Symbol: KHI
Fund Orientation: Bond

Kemper Intermediate Government Trust
120 South LaSalle Street
Chicago, IL 60603

Telephone Number:
    Toll-Free (nationwide)   800/643-2211

Adviser: Kemper Financial Services, Inc.
Year Organized: 1988
Ticker Symbol: KGT
Fund Orientation: Bond

Kleinwort Benson Australian Income Fund, Inc.
200 Park Avenue, 24th Floor
New York, NY 10166

Telephone Number:
 Local 212/687-2515
Adviser: Erica Investment Management (Overseas) Limited
Year Organized: 1986
Ticker Symbol: KBA
Portfolio Holdings: Bond
Fund Orientation: Country

Lomas Mortgage Securities
2001 Bryan Tower, Suite 3600
Dallas, TX 75201

Telephone Number:
 Toll-Free (nationwide) 800/543-6217
Adviser: Lomas Securities Advisers, Inc.
Year Organized: 1988
Ticker Symbol: LSF
Fund Orientation: Bond

MFS Intermediate Income Trust
500 Boylston Street
Boston, MA 02116

Telephone Number:
 Local 617/954-5000
Adviser: Massachusetts Financial Services Company
Year Organized: 1988
Ticker Symbol: MIN
Fund Orientation: Bond

Montgomery Street Income Securities, Inc.
101 California Street, Suite 4100
San Francisco, CA 94111

Telephone Numbers:
    Toll-Free (nationwide)   800/225-2470
    Local   415/981-8191
Adviser: Scudder, Stevens & Clark, Inc.
Year Organized: 1973
Ticker Symbol: MTS
Fund Orientation: Bond

Mutual of Omaha Interest Shares, Inc.
10235 Regency Circle
Omaha, NB 68114

Telephone Number:
    Local   402/397-8555
Adviser: Mutual of Omaha Fund Management Company
Year Organized: 1972
Ticker Symbol: MUO
Fund Orientation: Bond

Pacific American Income Shares, Inc.
P.O. Box 983
Pasadena, CA 91102

Telephone Number:
    Local   818/584-4300
Adviser: Western Asset Management Company
Year Organized: 1973
Ticker Symbol: PAI
Fund Orientation: Bond

Prudential Intermediate Income Fund, Inc.
One Seaport Plaza
New York, NY 10292

Telephone Number:
    Local   212/214-3334

Adviser: The Prudential Investment Corporation
Year Organized: 1988
Ticker Symbol: PIF
Fund Orientation: Bond

Prudential Strategic Income Fund, Inc.
One Seaport Plaza
New York, NY 10292

Telephone Number:
 Local 212/214-3334
Adviser: The Prudential Investment Corporation
Year Organized: 1988
Ticker Symbol: PSF
Fund Orientation: Bond

Putnam High Yield Municipal Trust
One Post Office Square
Boston, MA 02109

Telephone Number:
 Local 617/292-1000
Adviser: Putnam
Year Organized: 1989
Ticker Symbol: PYM
Fund Orientation: Municipal bond

Putnam Intermediate Government Income Trust
One Post Office Square
Boston, MA 02109

Telephone Number:
 Local 617/292-1000
Adviser: The Putnam Management Company, Inc.
Year Organized: 1988
Ticker Symbol: PGT
Fund Orientation: Bond

Putnam Master Income Trust
One Post Office Square
Boston, MA 02109

Telephone Number:
  Local   617/292-1000
Adviser: The Putnam Management Company, Inc.
Year Organized: 1987
Ticker Symbol: PMT
Fund Orientation: Bond

Putnam Master Intermediate Income Trust
One Post Office Square
Boston, MA 02109

Telephone Number:
  Local   617/292-1000
Adviser: The Putnam Management Company, Inc.
Year Organized: 1988
Ticker Symbol: PIM
Fund Orientation: Bond

Putnam Premier Income Trust
One Post Office Square
Boston, MA 02109

Telephone Number:
  Local   617/292-1000
Adviser: The Putnam Management Company, Inc.
Year Organized: 1988
Ticker Symbol: PPT
Fund Orientation: Bond

State Mutual Securities Trust
440 Lincoln Street
Worcester, MA 01605

Telephone Number:
  Local   508/852-1000

Adviser: State Mutual Life Assurance Company of America
Year Organized: 1972
Ticker Symbol: SMS
Fund Orientation: Bond

Transamerica Income Shares, Inc.
1150 S. Olive Street
Los Angeles, CA 90015

Telephone Number:
 Local 213/742-4141
Adviser: Transamerica Investment Services, Inc.
Year Organized: 1972
Ticker Symbol: TAI
Fund Orientation: Bond

Vestaur Securities, Inc.
Centre Sq. West, 11th Floor
P.O. Box 7558
Philadelphia, PA 19101

Telephone Number:
 Local 215/567-3969
Adviser: First Pennsylvania Bank N.A.
Year Organized: 1972
Ticker Symbol: VES
Fund Orientation: Bond

World Income Fund
800 Scudders Mill Road
Plainsboro, NJ 08536

Telephone Number:
 Local 609/282-2800
Adviser: Fund Asset Management, Inc.
Year Organized: 1988
Ticker Symbol: WOI
Portfolio Holdings: Bond
Fund Orientation: Bond

Index

A

AAII Journal, 26
Access Discount Commodities, 426
Account executives, 389–94
ACM Government Opportunity Fund, Inc., 546
ACM Managed Income Fund, Inc., 546–47
Acorn Fund, 480–81
Active traders, and discounters, 32, 35
  and self-directed IRAs, 125, 127
"Adam Smith's Money World," 27
ADRs, 109–10
Advice, investment, 22, 23–28, 398
Allegiance Financial, 426–27
Allstate Municipal Income Trust II, 547
Amber Trading, 427
American Association of Individual Investors, 26
American Capital Bond Fund, Inc., 547
American Capital Income Trust, 547
American Depository Receipts (ADRs), 109–10
American Security Bank, 273
American Stock exchange, and DOT, 18
American Trust & Savings Bank, 273
Ameritrust Co., 273–74
Amoskeag Bank, 274
AmSouth, 274
Andrew Peck Associates, Inc., 180
Anspacher Futures of Wyoming, 427
Arbour Securities, 181
Arizona Bank, 275
Arneday Incorporated, 427
Arnold Securities, 182
Asia Pacific Fund, 537
Associations, 26
Atlantic Bank of New York, 275

Atlantic Discount Brokerage
    Services Corp., 183

B

Baker & Co., Inc., 185
Ball, George, 92
Bank of America, and Charles
    Schwab purchase, 36, 37
Bank of Baltimore, 276
Bank of Boston, 276–77
Bank brokers, 37–39
    listed, 271–341
Bank of Delaware, 277
Bank IV, 275–76
Bank of Hawaii, 277–78
Bank of New England, 278
Bank of New York, 278
Bank of Oklahoma, 278–79
Bank One, 279
Bank One Milwaukee, N.A., 279
Bankers Trust Company, 280
Banks, and discount services, 14
Bankwest N.A., 280
Barclays Bank, 280–81
Barnett Bank, 281
Barron's, 26, 103, 116
Barry W. Murphy & Co., Inc., 186
BayBanks, Inc., 281–82
Beddows Commodities, 428
Benham, Jim, 102
Berlind Securities, Inc., 187
Bernstein Futures, Inc., 428
Bidwell & Company, 188
"Big three" discounters, 35–37, 87
Blue Chip (Major Market Index),
    151–52
Boatmen's National Bank of St.
    Louis, 282
Bollinger, John, 27
Bond funds, 71, 91–99
    closed-end, 113–17
    corporate bond funds, 98–99
    government bond funds, 97–98
    high-yield (junk bond) funds,
        95–96, 99

listed, 503–19
municipal bond funds, 94–95
one state funds, 94–95
selecting, 91–94
Unit Investment Trusts, 96–97
Bonds, discounter savings on, 51–52
Boone County National Bank, 282
Boston Company Capital
    Appreciation Fund, 481
Boston Financial Group, 428
Bowery, 283
Brazil Fund, Inc., 537
Broadway National Bank, 283
Broker, choosing a, 29–39
    bank brokers, 37–39, 271–342
    (check #s)
    big three discounters, 35–37
    deep discounters, 34–35
    full service or discounter, 29–32
    regional discounters, 39
Broker's call rates, 53
Brokers Exchange, Inc., 189
Brown & Company, 190
Brown Forman, 171
Browning Ferris, 85
Bruno, Stolze & Company, Inc., 191
Bull & Bear Securities, Inc., 192
Bull market of 1980s, 14
Bunker Hill Income Securities, Inc.,
    548
Burke Christensen & Lewis
    Securities, Inc., 193
"Business Day," 27
"Business Report," 27
Business Week, 26, 103

C

"Calls," 93
Calvert funds, 102
Calvert Securities Corporation,
    195
Capital Bank, 283–84
Cary Scarborough, 428
Casco Northern Bank, N.A., 284
Centerre Bank, 284

Index

Central Bank of The South, N.A., 285
Central Carolina Bank, 285
Changing Times, 26, 103
Charles Schwab, 36, 37, 242
Charleston National Bank, 285–86
Chase Lincoln First, 286
Chase Manhattan Bank, 286
Chemical Bank, 287
Circle Income Shares, Inc., 548
Citibank, 287
Citizens and Southern Bank, 288
Clemente Global Growth Fund, Inc., 537
Clipper Fund, Inc., 532–37
Closed-end bond funds, 113–17
  avoiding new funds, 114
  discount concerns, 115–17
  listed, 537–45
Closed-end funds, listed, 546–57
Closed-end mutual funds, 68–69
  international, 110–11
CNA Income Shares, Inc., 548
Coins, discount, 165–66, 167–68
Collectibles, 167
Colonial Intermediate High Income Fund, 548–49
Colorado National Bank of Denver, 288
Columbia Fixed Income Securities Fund, Inc., 503
Comerica Bank, 288–89
Commerce Bank of St. Louis, 289
Commerce National Bank, 289–90
Commercial paper, 103, 105, 130
Commissions, 15, 33, 39
  comparisons, 43–47
  of discount futures brokers, 144–45
Commission structure explained, 58–59
Commodity discounters, 21
Common Message Switch, 371
Complimentary pairing, 47
Comstock Partners Strategy Fund, Inc., 549

Connecticut Bank and Trust Company, 290
Connecticut National Bank, 290
Continental Bank, 290–91
Continental Bank and Trust, 291
Continental Illinois National Bank, 291–92
CoreStates Securities Corp., 196
Corporate bond funds, 98–99
Country funds, 115, 116
  listed, 537–45
Crestar Bank, 292
Custodial service, of discounters, 409–10

D

David L. Babson Growth Fund, 481–82
Dean Witter Government Income Trust, 549
Deep discounters, 34–35
  designation in directory explained, 60–61
  mutual funds and, 87
Delaware Trust Company, 292–93
Delta Futures Group, 429
Deposit Guaranty National Bank, 293
Designated Order System, 18–19, 369, 372
Dime Savings Bank of New York, 293
Discount Brokerage Directory, 180–270
  deep discounter designation explained, 60–61
  features of, 56–60
  no-load mutual funds explained, 83–84
  summary of, 55–61
Discount brokerages, 3–11, 177–79, 357–61
  "big three," 35–37
  choosing among, 29–39
  dealing with, 381–88

Discount brokerages *(Continued)*
  differences among, 21–22
  emergence of, 355–57
  features and services of, 374–80, 389–401
  frills of, 402–12
  and full service, choosing between, 345–49
  futures brokers, 144–46, 425–36
  history of, 13–14
  listed, 180–270
  low costs explained, 14–15
  of no-load mutual funds, 76–79
  orders, quotes, and information from, 18, 383–85
  safety and regulation of, 15–18
  savings with, 41–54
  services of, 19–21
Discount futures brokers, 144–46
  listed, 425–36
Discount investing, questions and answers, 3–11
Dividend reinvestment plans, 171
Dodge & Cox Balanced Fund, Inc., 482
Dodge & Cox Stock Fund, 482–83
Dominion Bank, 293–94
DOT, 18–19, 369, 372
Downstate Discount Brokerage, Inc., 198
Drexel Burnham Lambert, 148
Dreyfus Group Ltd., 429
Dreyfus Growth Opportunity Fund, Inc., 483
Dreyfus Intermediate Tax Exempt Bond Fund, Inc., 504
Dreyfus Money Market Instruments, Inc. Government Securities Series, 520
Dreyfus Municipal Income, Inc., 549
Dreyfus New York Insured Tax Exempt Bond Fund, Inc., 504
Dreyfus New York Intermediate Tax Exempt Bond Fund, Inc., 505
Dreyfus New York Tax Exempt Bond Fund, Inc., 505
Dreyfus Short Intermediate Government Fund, 506
Dreyfus Short Intermediate Tax Exempt Bond Fund, 506
Dreyfus Strategic Governments Income, Inc., 550
Dreyfus Tax Exempt Bond Fund, Inc., 507
Dreyfus U.S. Government Intermediate Securities, L.P., 507
Dreyfus Worldwide Dollar Fund, 104
Dreyfus Worldwide Dollar Money Market Fund, Inc., 521

E–F

E. David Commodities Co., 429
Equity mutual funds. *See* Stock funds
European American Bank, 294
Evergreen Limited Market Fund, Inc., 483–84
Exchange Services, Inc., 199
Federal Reserve Offices, listed, 137–41
Fidelity Bank, 294
Fidelity Brokerage Services, Inc., 36–37, 38, 200
Fidelity Cash Reserves, 521
Fidelity Daily Income Trust, 522
Fidelity Europe Fund, 533
Fidelity Global Bond Fund, 508
Fidelity Insured Tax Free Portfolio of Fidelity Municipal Bond Fund, 508
Fidelity Intermediate Bond Fund, 509
Fidelity Magellan fund, 65
Fidelity Municipal Bond Portfolio, 509
Fidelity New York Tax Free Fund High Yield Portfolio, 510

Index

Fidelity New York Tax Free Fund Insured Portfolio, 510
Fidelity Ohio Tax Free Portfolio, 511
Fidelity Overseas Fund, 533–34
Fidelity Puritan Fund, 484
Fidelity Spartan Government Fund, 104, 511
Fidelity Spartan Money Market Fund, 522
Fidelity Trend Fund, 484–85
Fidelity U.S. Treasury Money Market Fund, L.P., 522–23
Fifth Third Securities, Inc., 295
Financial World, 26
First Alabama Bank, 295
First of America Bank, 306
First American Bank of Georgia, N.A., 296
First American Discount Corp., 429
First Australia Fund, Inc., 538
First Australia Prime Income Fund, 538
First Bank Minneapolis, 296
First Bank of North Dakota, 296–97
First Boston Income Fund, Inc., 550
First Boston Strategic Income Fund, Inc., 550
First Capital Bank, 297
First Citizens Bank, 297
First City National Bank of Houston, 298
First Commercial Trust, 298
First Eastern Bank, 299
First Fidelity Bank, 299
First Financial Fund, Inc., 550
First Iberian Fund, Inc., 538, 551
Firstier Bank, 300
First Institutional Securities Corp. 201
First Interstate Bancorp of California, 300
First Interstate Bank of Billings, 301
First Interstate Bank of Des Moines, 301
First Interstate Bank of Great Falls, 302
First Interstate Bank of Idaho, 302
First Interstate Bank of Nevada, 302–03
First National Bank, 303
First National Bank in Albuquerque, 303
First National Bank in Wichita, 304
First National Bank of Chicago, 304
First National Bank of Commerce, 305
First National Bank of Maryland, 305
First National Bank of Omaha, 306
First National Brokerage Services, 202–03
First Pennsylvania Bank, 306–07
First Rule of Transfer, 369–70
First Security Bank, 307
First Security National Bank & Trust Co., 307–08
First Tennessee Bank, 308
First Texas Futures, Inc., 430
First Union Brokerage Services, 204–05
First Union National Bank, 308
First Valley Bank (Lehigh Securities), 309
First Wachovia Bank and Trust, 309
First Wisconsin National Bank, 309–10
Fleet Bank, 310
Florida National Bank, 310
Forbes, 26
Foreign currency funds, 111–12
Foreign money funds, 106. *See also* International funds
Founders Blue Chip Fund, 485
Founders Growth Fund, Inc., 485–86
Freeman Welwood & Co., Inc., 206–07

Frills, of discount brokerages, 402–12
    custodial service, 409–10
    interest, 407–9
    margin, 402–7
    reporting, 410–11
Full service and discounter compared
    bond purchase costs, 51–52
    choosing between, 29–32
    option purchase costs, 49–51
    stock purchase costs, 43–44, 48, 50
Future Germany Fund, 116, 538–39
Futures Discount Group, 430
Futures market, 143–52
    discount futures brokers, 144–46, 425–36
    investment precautions, 147–48
    protecting capital, 150–51

G

General Mills, 171
German stocks, 116
Germany Fund, 116, 539, 551
G & G Brokerage, Inc., 430
GIT Equity Trust—Special Growth Portfolio, 486
Glass-Steagall Act, 37
Global funds, 108
Global Government Plus Fund, Inc., 539
Global Income Plus Fund, 539
Global portfolio, 112
Global Portfolio, 25n, 112, 117
Global Yield Fund, Inc., 540
Government bond funds, 97–98, 135
Government notes and bonds, 133–34, 135
Gradison Growth Trust—Established Growth Fund, 486–87

H

Harbor Money Market Fund, 523
Harper-Scherwin/Securities Research, Inc., 208
Hedgers, Inc., 431
Helvetia Fund, Inc., 540
Heritage Investment Securities, Inc., 209
Harris Bank, 311
Hart, Ed, 27
Hibernia National Bank, 311
High Income Advantage Trust, 551
Highlands Trading Co., 431
High-yield (junk bond) funds, 95–96, 99
Howard Savings Bank, 311–12
Hulbert Financial Digest, 25, 91
Hulbert, Mike, 25
Huntington National Bank, 312

I

IAI Regional Fund, Inc., 487–88
IAI Stock Fund, Inc., 488
Icahn & Co., Inc., 210
Idaho First National Bank, 312
Illinois Company Investments, Inc., 211
Index funds, 84–85
India Growth Fund, 540
Individual retirement accounts. *See* Self-directed IRAs
Insurance of discount accounts, 17, 57, 394–98, 413–23
Integrated Resources, 105
Intercapital Income Securities, 552
International funds, 107–12
    closed-end funds, 110–11
    foreign currency funds, 111–12
    global portfolio, 112
    listed, 532–45
Investment advice, 22, 23–28
    books, 23–24, 439–450
    newsletters, 24–25, 455–478
Investments, selecting your own, 363–68

Index

Investing at a Discount, the Newsletter, 25
Investor's Daily, 26
Ira Epstein & Company, 431
IRAs. *See* Self-directed IRAs
Irving Bank Corporation, 313
Italy Fund, Inc., 540–41

J

Jack Carl/312 Futures, 431–432
Jackson County Bank, 313
Jack White & Company, Inc., 212
Janus Fund, Inc., 488–89
Japan Fund, Inc., 534
J.D. Seibert & Company, Inc., 246
John Finn & Company, Inc., 213
John Hancock Income Securities Trust, 552
John Howard Discount Brokerage, Inc., 214
Junk bond funds, 95–96, 99

K

Kangas, Paul, 148
Kashner Davidson Securities Corp., 215
K. Aufhauser & Company, Inc., 184
Kemper High Income Trust, 552
Kemper Intermediate Government Trust, 552–553
Kemper Money Market Fund, Inc., 523–24
Kennedy, Cabot & Co., 216
Key Bank, 313–14
Key Bank of Idaho, 314
Klein & Co. Futures, Inc., 432
Kleinwort Benson Australian Income Fund, Inc., 541, 553
Korea Fund, Inc., 541

L

LaSalle National Bank, 314
Lehigh Securities, 315

Lehman Opportunity Fund, Inc., 489
Liberty National Bank, 315
Limited partnerships, 153–63
  choosing, 156–58
  discounts, 160–63
  management fees and overhead, 157–58
  secondary market, 158–60
  track records of, 158
  upfront costs, 157
Lindner Fund, Inc., 489–90
Lind-Waldock, 432
Liquidations, 17
Load funds, 75
Lomas Mortgage Securities, 553
Loomis-Sayles Capital Development Fund, 490–91
Lynch, Peter, 65, 92

M

Malaysia Fund, Inc., 541
Manufacturers Hanover, 316
Margin call, 53–54
Margin lending, 52–54, 402–7
Marine Midland Bank, 316–17
Marquette de Bary Co., Inc., 218
Marriott Hotels, 170
Marsh Block & Co., 219
Mathers Fund, Inc., 491
Max Ule with Meyers, Pollock, Robbins, Inc., 220
Mbank, 315
Mellon Bank, 317
Mendelsohn Enterprises, 433
Mercer Discount Surveys, 33, 451–54
Mercer Discount Financial Directory, 55
  deep discounter designation, 60–61
  excerpt from, 180–270
  features of, 56–60
Mercer 1989 Discount Brokerage Commission Survey, 34

Mercer 1989 Discount Futures Broker Survey, 145
Mercer 1989 Discount IRA Survey, 121–22
Mercer 1989 Options Commissions Survey,
Mercer 1989 Stock Commission Survey, 41, 42, 124
Merchants National Bank & Trust Co., 317–18
Merchants Trust Company, 318
Meridian Bank, 318
Merrill Lynch Ready Assets Trust, 524
Mexico Fund, Inc., 542
MFS Intermediate Income Trust, 553
Midlantic Securities Corp., 319
Money, 26, 103
Money funds, 71–72
Money market funds, 101–6
　listed, 520–31
　and treasury bills compared, 106
　yield comparisons, 104
Money market mutual funds. *See* Money market funds
"Money Talk," 27
Montgomery Street Income Securities, Inc., 554
Mortgage and Realty Trust, 105
M&T Bank, 316
Municipal bond funds, 94–95
Muriel Siebert & Co., Inc., 221
Mutual Beacon Fund, Inc., 491–92
Mutual fund prospectus, sample fee table from, 78
Mutual funds
　accountability of, 25
　basic types of, 11, 67–70
　discounters of industry, 75–79
　international funds, 107–12
　investments in, 70–72
　merits of, 66–67
　money market funds, 101–6
　quality of, 74–75
　rules for investing in, 73
　stock funds, 70–71, 81–89
　tax advantages of, 88
　turnover costs, 86–87
Mutual of Omaha Interest Shares, Inc., 554
Mutual Qualified Fund, Inc., 492
Mutual Shares Fund, 492–93
Myers Commodity Corp., 433

N

NASDAQ, 110
National Association of Securities Dealers Automated Quotations, 110
National Bank of Alaska, 319
National Bank of Commerce, 319–20
National Bank of Detroit, 320
National Bank of Georgia, 320
National Bank of Washington, 321
National City Bank, 321
National City Bank of Minneapolis, 322
National Westminster Bank USA, 322
NEIE Discount Brokerage Services, 222
Neuberger & Berman Limited Maturity Bond Fund, Inc., 512
Neuberger & Berman Manhattan Fund, Inc., 493
Neuberger & Berman Municipal Money Fund, Inc., 524
Neuberger & Berman Partners Fund, Inc., 493–94
New Germany Fund, 116, 542
Newton Money Fund, 525
New York Stock Exchange (NYSE), 13
　and DOT, 18
New York Times, 26, 103, 116
Nicholas II, Inc., 494
No-load mutual funds, 76–79

Nomura Pacific Basin Fund, Inc., 534–35
Norman Kern & Company, 433
Norstar Bank of Commerce, 322–23
Northeastern Bank of Pennsylvania, 323
Northeast Investors Trust, 512
Northern Trust Company, 323
Northwest Bank Des Moines, N.A., 324

O

Olde Discount Stockbrokers, 223
Old Kent Bank & Trust Company, 324
One state funds, 94–95
One Valley Bank, N.A., 325
Open-end mutual funds, 67–68
 listed, 532–37
Options, discounter savings on, 49–51
Order execution, and discounters, 18–19, 21
Order handling, 57–58
Orders, types of, 398–99
Oregon First Bank, 325
Over-the-counter market, 13
 in ADRs, 110
Overhead, 15
OvestMarine Brokerage Service, 224

P

Pace Securities, Inc., 225–26
Pacific American Income Shares, Inc., 554
Pacific Brokerage Services, Inc., 227
Paine Webber Cashfund, Inc., 525
Parsons Securities, Inc., 228
Peoples Bank, 326
Peremel & Co., Inc., 229
Periodicals, 26
Pfizer, 171

Piedmont Trust, 326
"Pink sheets," 110
Pittsburgh National Bank, 326–27
Planters Bank, 327
Precious coins, 167–68
Precious metals, 167–68
Price wars, in money market funds, 103, 104
Primecap Fund, 494–95
Prime Motor Inns, 170
Prime rate loans, 53
"Profit Motive," 27
Provident Bank, 327
Prudential Intermediate Income Fund, Inc., 554–55
Prudential Strategic Income Fund, Inc., 555
Pulaski Bank and Trust Company, 328
Putnam High Yield Municipal Trust, 555
Putnam Intermediate Government Income Trust, 555
Putnam Master Income Trust, 556
Putnam Master Intermediate Income Trust, 556
Putnam Premier Income Trust, 556

Q-R

Quick, Leslie, 36
Quick & Reilly, Inc., 36, 230
Quotation lines, 399–400
Ralston Purina, 170
"Random walk," 154
Recom Securities, Inc., 231
Reference rate loans, 53
Regulation of discounters, 15–18
Reich & Tang Equity Fund,Inc., 495
REPOs, 17
Repurchase agreements, 17
Research advice, 15
Reserve fund, 101
Richard Blackman & Co, Inc., 232
Robert Barnett Commodities, 434
Robert Thomas Securities, Inc., 233

Robinson Securities, 234–35
Rodecker & Company Investment Brokers, Inc., 236
Rogers, Jim, 27
Roland Francis & Co., Inc., 237
Royal/Grimm & Davis, Inc., 239
Rukeyser, Louis, 27
Russo Securities, Inc., 240

S

Safeco Equity Fund, Inc., 495–96
Safety, of discounters, 15–18
St. Louis Discount Securities, Inc., 241
Sales rep's commissions, 15
Savings bonds, 135–36
Savings, with discount brokers, 41–54
    bonds, 51–52
    commissions compared, 47, 48
    margin lending, 52–54
    options, 49–51
    stocks, 41–46
Schwab, Charles, 36
S.C. Costa Company Inc., 197
Scottsdale Securities, Inc., 243
Scudder Capital Growth Fund, Inc., 496
Scudder Cash Investment Trust, 526
Scudder International Fund, Inc., 496–97
Scudder Managed Municipal Bonds, 514
Scudder New Asia Fund, Inc., 542
Seaport Securities Corporation, 244–45
SEC, 14
Secondary market limited partnerships, 158–60
Securities and Exchange Commission, 14, 357–62
    and SIPC insurance, 395
Securities Industries Automation Corporation, 371

Securities Investor Protection Act of 1970, 394
Securities Investor Protection Corporation, 16–17, 57, 394–97, 413–23
    basic protection, 414–18
    customer protection proceedings, 418–23
Security Pacific Bancorporation Northwest, 328
Security Pacific National Bank, 328–29
Selected American Shares, Inc., 497
Selected Daily Government Fund, 526
Selected Daily Income Fund, 527
Selected Daily Tax-Exempt Fund, 527–28
Self-directed IRAs, 121–27
    investment variety of, 122
    maximizing savings with, 123–24
    taxes and, 124
Sentinel Securities, Inc., 247–48
70% Off: The Investor's Guide to Discount Brokerage, 48
Sharebroker discounters, 47
Shareholder discounts and privileges, 169–71
Shawmut Bank, 329
Shearman Ralston, Inc., 249
Shochet Securities, Inc., 250
Signet Bank, 329
Silby, Wayne, 101–2
SIPC, 16–17, 57, 394–97, 414–23
    basic protection, 414–18
    customer protection proceedings, 418–27
SIT "New Beginning" Growth Fund, Inc., 497–98
South Carolina National Bank, 330
Southeast Bank, N.A., 330–31
South Shore Bank, 330
SouthTrust Bank, 331
Sovran Bank, 331
Spain Fund, Inc., 543

Index   569

Spear Securities, Inc., 251
Squibb, 171
SRD Associates, 434
Standard & Poor's 500 Index, 151
State First National Bank, 332
State Mutual Securities Trust, 556–57
Steinroe Intermediate Bond Fund, 514
Steinroe Special Fund, Inc., 498
StockCross, Inc., 252
Stock funds, 70–71, 81–89
   Dow Jones Industrial compared, 81–82
   index fund, 84–85
   listed, 480–502
   turnover costs, 86–87
Stock Mart, 253–54
Stocks, discounter savings on, 41–46
   average costs, 42–44, 45
   specific transactions, 44–46
Strong Total Return Fund, Inc., 498–99
Summit Bank, 332
Sunburst Bank, 332–33
SunTrust Bank, 333
SunWest Bank, 333–34
Sussex Bank, 334

T

Taiwan Fund, 543
Tandy, 171
Tax advantages, mutual funds, 88
Television, and investment shows, 27–28
Templeton Emerging Markets Fund, Inc., 543
Templeton Global Governments Income Trust, 543–44
Templeton Global Income Fund, Inc., 544
Templeton Value Fund, Inc., 544
Texas Securities, Inc., 255
Thai Fund, Inc., 544

Thomas F. White & Co., Inc., 256–57
Touchstone Trading Co., 434–35
Traders Network, 435
Tradex Brokerage Service, Inc., 258–59
Transamerica Income Shares, Inc., 557
Trans-Inter. Commodities, Ltd., 435
Treasury bills and bonds, 129–136
   bills and money funds compared, 106, 130–31
   reinvestment option, 133
   tax advantages of, 130
   yield, 130–31
Treasury Direct system, 129, 131–33, 134
   Federal Reserve offices listed, 137–41
T. Rowe Price Discount Brokerage, 238
T. Rowe Price International Trust: International Bond Fund, 535
T. Rowe Price International Trust: International Stock Fund, 535
T. Rowe Price Tax-Exempt Money Fund, Inc., 526
T. Rowe Price Tax-Free Income Fund, Inc., 513
T. Rowe Price Tax-Free Short Intermediate Fund, Inc., 513
Trust Company Bank, 334
Trustees' Commingled Fund International Equity Portfolio, 536
Tuttle Securities, 260
Twentieth Century Giftrust Investors, 499

U

Union Bank, 334–35
Union Bank and Trust Co., 335

Union National Bank of Little Rock, 335
Union Planter's National Bank of Memphis, 336
United Bank of Arizona, 336
United Jersey Banks, 336–37
United Kingdom Fund, Inc., 545
United Missouri Banks, 337
Unit Investment Trusts, 69–70, 96–97
U.S. National Bank of Oregon, 337
U.S. Savings bonds, 135–36
U.S. Treasury bills. *See* Treasury bills and bonds

V

Valley Bancorporation, 338
Valuebroker discounters, 47
Value Line Cash Fund, Inc., 528
Value Line Fund, Inc., 499–500
Value Line U.S. Government Securities Fund, Inc., 528
Vanguard Bond Market Fund, 515
Vanguard Fixed Income Securities Fund GNMA Portfolio, 515
Vanguard Fixed Income Securities Fund-Investment Grade Bond Portfolio, 516
Vanguard Fixed Income Securities Fund-Short Term Bond portfolio, 516
Vanguard Fixed Income Securities Fund-Short Term Government Bond Portfolio, 517
Vanguard Fixed Income Securities Fund-U.S. Treasury Bond Portfolio, 517
Vanguard Index Trust 500 Portfolio, 500
Vanguard Money Market Funds—Cash Portfolio, 531
Vanguard Money Market Reserves—Federal Portfolio, 529
Vanguard Money Market Reserves—Prime Portfolio, 529
Vanguard Money Market Reserves—U.S. Treasury Portfolio, 530
Vanguard Municipal Bond Fund-Insured Long-Term Portfolio, 518
Vanguard Municipal Bond Fund-Intermediate-Term Portfolio, 518
Vanguard Municipal Bond Fund-Limited-Term Portfolio, 519
Vanguard Municipal Bond Fund-Long-Term Portfolio, 519
Vanguard Municipal Bond Fund Money Market Portfolio, 530
Vanguard W.L. Morgan Growth Fund, 500–01
Vanguard Wellesley Income Fund, 501
Vanguard Wellington Fund, 501–02
Vanguard World Fund International Growth Portfolio, 536–37
Vantage Money Market Funds—Government Portfolio, 531
Varney, Stuart, 27
Vermont National Bank, 338
Vestaur Securities, Inc., 557
VNB Investment Services, Inc., 338–39
Voss & Co., Inc., 261–62, 435

W–Z

Wall Street Discount Corporation, 263–64
Wall Street Journal, 26, 103, 116
"Wall $treet Week," 27
Walt Disney, 171
Washington Trust Bank, 339

Index

Waterhouse Securities, Inc., 265–66
Wells Fargo Bank, 339
Whitehall Securities, Inc., 267
Wilmington Trust, 340
Wisconsin Discount Securities Corporation, 268
Wolf Commodities Corp., 436
World Income Fund, 557
World Trading Group, FL, 436
Worldwide Value Fund, Inc., 545
Worthen Bank and Trust Company, N.A., 340
York Securities, 269
Young, Stovall and Company, 270
Zions First National Bank, 340–41